THE WORKS
AND CORRESPONDENCE OF
DAVID RICARDO

VOLUME V

PLAN OF THE EDITION

THE WORKS
AND CORRESPONDENCE OF

David Ricardo

Edited by Piero Sraffa
with the Collaboration of M. H. Dobb

VOLUME V

Speeches and Evidence
1815–1823

LIBERTY FUND
INDIANAPOLIS

This book is published by Liberty Fund, Inc., a foundation established to encourage study of the ideal of a society of free and responsible individuals.

𒀎𒀮 𒅗𒄿

The cuneiform inscription that serves as our logo and as the design motif for our endpapers is the earliest-known written appearance of the word "freedom" (*amagi*), or "liberty." It is taken from a clay document written about 2300 B.C. in the Sumerian city-state of Lagash.

First published by Cambridge University Press in 1951.

This edition of *The Works and Correspondence of David Ricardo* is published by Liberty Fund, Inc., under license from the Royal Economic Society.

10 09 08 07 06 05 04 P 5 4 3 2 1

Library of Congress Cataloging-in-Publication Data

Ricardo, David, 1772–1823.
[Works. 2004]
The works and correspondence of David Ricardo / edited by Piero Sraffa; with the collaboration of M. H. Dobb.
p.   cm.
Originally published: Cambridge: At the University Press for the Royal Economic Society, 1951–1973.
Includes bibliographical references and index.
Contents: v. 1. On the principles of political economy and taxation—
ISBN 0-86597-965-0 (pbk.: alk. paper)
1. Economics.   2. Taxation.   I. Sraffa, Piero.
II. Dobb, M. H.   III. Title.

HB161.R4812 2004
330.15'13'092—dc21   2002016222
ISBN 0-86597-969-3 (vol. 5: pbk.: alk. paper)
ISBN 0-86597-976-6 (set: pbk.: alk. paper)

Liberty Fund, Inc.
8335 Allison Pointe Trail, Suite 300
Indianapolis, IN 46250-1684

Text and cover design by Erin Kirk New, Watkinsville, Georgia
Typography by Impressions Book and Journal Services, Inc., Madison, Wisconsin
Printed and bound by Edwards Brothers, Inc., Ann Arbor, Michigan

CONTENTS OF VOLUME V

LIST OF SPEECHES

SPEECHES ON VARIOUS OCCASIONS

PREFATORY NOTE

THIS volume of Ricardo's Works is devoted to the spoken word: it contains his speeches in the House of Commons, his evidence before Parliamentary Committees and other speeches and addresses on various occasions. These have never before been collected, or indeed reprinted from the contemporary records. Yet McCulloch, who had experience of Ricardo's 'easy, fluent and agreeable' style of speaking and conversing, held that in clearness and facility 'his speeches were greatly superior to his publications.'

The volume, apart from the introduction to the Speeches, was to a large extent prepared before the war. Its making-up into page proof was interrupted by war-time restrictions in 1943, and was completed after the end of the war in 1946. The editorial introductions and notes, from the nature of the material, are rather more extensive than in other volumes. More frequent quotation has been made from the unpublished diaries of John Lewis Mallet, and special acknowledgement for permission to do so must be made to the late Sir Bernard Mallet. It has also seemed appropriate to include Lord Brougham's sketch of Ricardo in Parliament, a first-hand though not unprejudiced view.

In the preparation of this volume much valuable assistance was given by Mrs Barbara Lowe.

P.S.

TRINITY COLLEGE
CAMBRIDGE
August 1951

INTRODUCTION TO THE SPEECHES
IN PARLIAMENT

I. *Entering Parliament*

Ricardo entered Parliament in the early part of 1819 after he had retired from the Stock Exchange and had written his main works on Political Economy. He remained a member of the House of Commons until his death in September 1823, after five years of active parliamentary life marked by constant attendance and frequent speeches.

The first suggestion that Ricardo should enter Parliament is in a letter from James Mill in the autumn of 1814, urging him to place himself 'in that situation in which his tongue, as well as his pen might be of use.'[1] This was at the time when Ricardo had just acquired Gatcomb Park with the intention of giving up business activity in the City. This intention could not be immediately carried out because of 'the immense concerns in business'[2] which entirely occupied him in the spring and early summer of 1815. In August of that year Mill writes again: 'You now can have no excuse for not going into parliament, and doing what you can to improve that most imperfect instrument of government.' He adds, 'in a short time you would be a very instructive, and a very impressive speaker.'[3] Ricardo's reply was characteristic: 'Your parliamentary scheme is above all others unfit for me,—my inclination does not in the least point that way. Speak indeed! I could not, I am sure, utter three sentences coherently'.[4]

In October 1816 Mill reverted to the subject, when, in connec-

---

[1] Letter of 30 Sept. 1814, below, VI, 138.
[2] Below, VI, 240.
[3] *ib.* 252.
[4] *ib.* 263.

tion with the absence of Francis Horner from Parliament, which
he deplored, he wrote: 'You ought indeed to be in parliament,
and you must at any rate make arrangements for it at the general
election.'[1] At the end of November of that year Ricardo declined
'an earnest invitation to become a candidate for the representation
of Worcester', where a vacancy had occurred. Confronted with
the need to answer by return of post, and with the danger of being
'hurried into all the horrors of a contested election', his 'decision
was as prompt as the occasion required'[2] and Mill in reply
expressed full agreement with the decision to decline the offer.
'If I were in your situation (Mill wrote), the rottenest Borough
I could find would be my market, with nothing to do but part
with a sum of money.'[3]

A year later, in December 1817, Edward Wakefield, a friend of
Mill who acted as land agent to Ricardo, was negotiating for the
borough of Portarlington: the seat for which Ricardo was
eventually returned in 1819. This was a typical pocket borough in
Ireland, in the patronage of the Earl of Portarlington.[4] Ten years
earlier, on 28 April 1807, when a General Election was imminent,
we find Wellington, then, as Sir Arthur Wellesley, Chief Secretary
for Ireland, writing from Dublin Castle: 'Lord Portarlington is
in England, and the agent who settled for that borough upon the
last general election was Mr Parnell.[5] We have no chance with
him, and it would be best to arrange the matter with Lord
Portarlington. I heard here that he had sold the return for six
years at the last election, and if that should be true, of course we
shall not get it now.'[6] In fact, at the General Election on 23 May
1807 William Lamb (afterwards Lord Melbourne) was returned
for Portarlington as an opposition member; but appears to have

[1] Below, VII, 85–6.
[2] *ib.* 101–2.
[3] *ib.* 110. The sale of seats had been
subjected to heavy penalties by an
Act of 1809; this however remained
a dead letter till the Reform Act of
1832. (See Erskine May's *Constitutional History of England,* 3rd ed.,
1912, vol. I, p. 233.)
[4] Wakefield in a book on Ireland
which he had written some years

earlier had noted: 'Portarlington
borough has twelve self-elected
burgesses. Lord Portarlington is
the patron.' (*An Account of Ireland,
Statistical and Political,* London,
Longman, 1812, vol. II, p. 308.)
[5] Afterwards Sir Henry Parnell.
[6] Letter to C. Long, in Wellington's *Civil Correspondence and
Memoranda* (*Ireland, 1807–1809*),
London, 1860, p. 17.

'lost his seat in 1812 for his support of catholic emancipation'.[1] At the General Election of 1816, however, another oppositionist, Richard Sharp, a close friend of Ricardo, was returned for the seat and still held it at the time of Wakefield's negotiations.

The approach to Wakefield had been made by an agent of the Earl of Portarlington with the object of raising a loan on the security of the Portarlington estates including the borough.[2] The Earl had already borrowed large sums on annuities,[3] and his estates had been assigned to trustees, one of whom was Sir Henry Parnell, his brother-in-law and an opposition member of Parliament. It was intended to use the proposed loan to pay off the annuities encumbering the estates. The amount required was 'from 10 to £20,000'.[4] Wakefield offered to lend the money on condition that he could nominate the member for the borough at 'the market price of the day', this price to be determined by 'some distinguished and honourable member of the house …—say such a person as Mr. Grenfell'.[5] He thereupon wrote to Ricardo that, if these terms were accepted, the seat would be placed at his service.[6]

The Earl's agent, however, proceeded to enquire whether Ricardo, if elected, would vote with the Ministers; and on receiving Wakefield's reply that 'politics must not be named—but perfect freedom', the negotiations came to an end, on the

[1] *Dictionary of National Biography.*
[2] See Wakefield's letters to Ricardo of 7 Dec. 1817, 24 Dec. 1817 and 4 Dec. 1818, below, VII, 216, 232 and 346.
[3] This was the 2nd Earl of Portarlington (1781–1846). As a Colonel in the Light Dragoons, he had been present at the Battle of Waterloo, where his horse had been shot under him. 'He did not join his regiment in the field of Waterloo till 7 p.m., though it had been engaged all day, and this, though proceeding apparently from negligence or "severe illness" rather than from cowardice, caused his retirement from the Army.' He afterwards ruined himself by gaming, racing and 'other

dissipations still more censurable'; and 'the opulent fortune inherited from a long line of honoured ancestry was nearly exhausted.' (*Complete Peerage*, vol. XII, ed. 1945, and *Gentleman's Magazine*, Feb. 1846, p. 202.)
[4] At first £50,000 had been asked for. (See below, VII, 347.)
[5] Below, VII, 216. Cp. Warburton's letter of 8 July 1818: 'I understand that in spite of the insecure tenure by which a seat would be held owing to the King's advanced age, that the usual price, £5000, has been given for being returned during the continuance of the Parliament.' (*ib.* 276 and cp. 252.)
[6] *ib.* 217.

ground that 'Lord Portarlington found there was nothing to be
got by returning an opposition man'.[1] The fact, noted by
Wakefield, that the Earl's agent (N. Kirkland) was cousin of
Charles Arbuthnot, Patronage Secretary in the Government,
suggests that it was he, even more than Lord Portarlington, who
was anxious to secure the return of a ministerialist.

A number of other seats were also considered about this time.[2]
Nothing resulted, however, from these negotiations, and by the
time of the General Election Ricardo had become reconciled to
having no seat. He writes to Malthus on 24 June 1818: 'I believe
it is now finally settled that I am not to be in Parliament, and truly
glad I am that the question is at any rate settled, for the certainty
of a seat could hardly compensate me for the disagreeables
attending the negociation for it';[3] and to Trower on 27 June: 'My
own endeavors to get a seat in the House have not been attended
with success, but I believe that amongst all those who are
disappointed, in a similar manner, there is not one more resigned
than I am. I could meet with nothing where I should not have
had a contest, which I was exceedingly unwilling to encounter'.[4]
At the General Election, on 11 July 1818, the sitting member,
Richard Sharp, was again returned for Portarlington.

Soon after the General Election independent negotiations were
started by Brougham; and although these were again for the
Portarlington seat, they do not seem to have been connected with
the previous negotiations of Wakefield.[5] The first that Ricardo
heard of it was at the end of August 1818, when after a visit of
Mill to Gatcomb they went to Gloucester together, where Mill
received a letter from Brougham containing a definite offer in

---

[1] Below, VII, 347.
[2] These included a borough 260
miles from London, with 76 voters
'who are discontented with their
present patron and have deputed a
confidential person to London to
find one' (Wakefield to Ricardo,
28 Feb. 1818, *ib.* 254); also Wootton
Bassett (Whishaw to Ricardo, 27
May 1818, *ib.* 264) and a Cornish
borough, and two other seats, 'the
one is a close one, the other with

very little doubt of success and
without any expense to a Candidate
unless he succeeds' (letters from
Thomas Crosse, the solicitor, to
Ricardo, 10 and 11 June 1818; MS
in Ricardo Papers).
[3] Below, VII, 269.
[4] *ib.* 272.
[5] Cp. the opening of Wakefield's
letter of 4 Dec. 1818, below, VII,
346.

connection with the seat. To this Ricardo promptly consented, on 'the terms proposed', subject only to his solicitor seeing that 'all is right and secure'.[1] On receipt of Ricardo's answer Brougham wrote: 'I have arranged all about Ricardo'. He had seen Sir Henry Parnell and 'we settled everything as he (R) could wish—The titles will take some little time—but all is sure.'[2] The terms were that Ricardo should make a loan of between £20,000 and £36,000 against a mortgage on the Portarlington estates,[2] and should pay £4,000 for the seat 'secured for four years' (implying the right of re-election in the event of an early dissolution)[3] and in addition 'a chance of sitting 7 years' (in case of there being no dissolution and Parliament lasting its full term).[4] There seems to have been some misunderstanding as to whether Ricardo was to receive the maximum rate of interest fixed by Irish law (6 per cent) or by English law (5 per cent).[5] In the event, the loan was of £25,000 and the interest 6 per cent.[6]

While Ricardo was not actually seated until February 1819, the delay was not due to the disagreement about terms or to the long drawn-out difficulties over the security for the loan. As Brougham had promised Mill, Ricardo was seated 'the very first day that the forms of Parliament will admit',[7] or very nearly so. For a new writ could not be issued until the new Parliament had met and the fourteen days allowed for presenting election petitions had expired. Parliament was opened by the Regent on 21 January 1819, and the first writs for new elections in vacant seats were

---

[1] Letter to Mill, 8 Sept. 1818, *ib.* 293 and cp. 359.

[2] Quoted in Mill's letter of 23 Sept. 1818, *ib.* 300.

[3] *ib.* 355.

[4] Below, VIII, 330.

[5] See below, VII, 355, 359, 363.

[6] This appears from Statements of Account of Ricardo's solicitors, Bleasdale, Lowless & Crosse, which give the principal of the loan to Lord Portarlington as £25,000 and the half-yearly interest, payable on 1 May and 1 November at Pugert & Co., as £750. (MS in Ricardo Papers.) See also Ricardo's reference to £250 as the equivalent of 1 per cent. on the loan, below, VII, 359.

A somewhat exaggerated version of this transaction was given by Daniel O'Connell in a speech on Parliamentary Reform on 8 March 1831: 'Lord Portarlington wanted to borrow 40,000*l.* or 50,000*l.* at an interest beyond that which was allowed by the Law of the Land. The sum was lent to him by the late Mr. Ricardo, and Mr. Ricardo accordingly came into that House as the hon. member for Portarlington.' (*Hansard*, 3rd Series, III, 201.)

[7] Below, VII, 355.

issued on 5 February. The writ for the return of a member for Portarlington, in the room of Richard Sharp who had accepted the Chiltern Hundreds, was issued on 8 February. Ricardo was returned to Parliament on 20 February 1819, and took his seat on the 26th.[1]

The arrangements for the loan to Lord Portarlington took a long time to complete. When at last all the legal documents seemed to be in order, difficulties arose on account of the encumbrances which had to be removed to give priority to Ricardo's mortgage: some of the annuitants refusing to be paid off or to assign their annuities. It was not until the autumn of 1820 that these difficulties were finally overcome, and the £25,000 paid over.[2]

Within a year of this Lord Portarlington was applying to Ricardo for a further loan of £6,000. This was in order to buy another estate, or more precisely, as Ricardo's solicitor Crosse put it, 'to replace a sum given by the Honble Mrs. Damer to his Lordship to purchase the estate but which he diverted to another purpose.' Ricardo seems to have regarded the estates which were already mortgaged to him as adequate security for the additional loan, but Parnell urged that he should take a security on the new estate, 'as otherwise it will enable his Lordship to Mortgage it and procure a further loan from some other person.'[3]

At the time of the General Election of 1820, which followed the death of George III, there were reports that Ricardo was to contest the County of Gloucester; but these he denied, saying that he would never have consented to 'embark on so perilous an undertaking' as that of contesting a county with 'an old and powerful family' (namely, that of the Duke of Beaufort).[4] As he

---

[1] See Sharp's letter to Ricardo, 25 Feb. 1819, in which he instructs him as to the procedure for taking his seat, below, VIII, 17–18.

[2] A series of letters to Ricardo from his solicitors, Bleasdale, Lowless & Crosse, dated between 2 Sept. 1818 and 9 Dec. 1820, contain references to these transactions; Statements of Account record the payments. (MS in Ricardo Papers.)

[3] Quotations from Crosse's letter to Ricardo of 6 July 1821; Ricardo's view on the mortgage is given in a letter to Crosse, dated Wotton-underedge, 28 June 1821. (MS copies in Ricardo Papers.) There is no evidence that this additional loan was actually made.

[4] Below, VIII, 156 and 162–3.

wrote to Trower: 'My late constituents at Portarlington appear to be a very good tempered set of gentlemen, and will I am sure elect me without hesitation to the next Parliament.'[1] He was, in fact, returned again for Portarlington on 27 March 1820.[2]

II. *Ricardo in Parliament*

'If I could, without much trouble, get into the New Parliament I would', Ricardo had written to Trower in 1818. 'I should neither be Whig nor Tory but should be anxiously desirous of promoting every measure which should give us a chance of good government. This I think will never be obtained without a reform in Parliament.'[3]

His attitude in the House on political questions was summed up after his death by the *Globe and Traveller* newspaper[4] as follows: 'Mr Ricardo was generally regarded as a moderate oppositionist. He was, however, the most decided and thorough Reformer within the walls of Parliament. With respect to government he had embraced the principles of Bentham. He was invariably found at his post on the Opposition benches, and, on every division, he voted on the side of the people.' On these subjects his speeches were few, the principal ones being that on Lord John Russell's motion for a Reform of Parliament on 24 April 1823 and his last speech for Free Discussion of Religious Opinions on 1 July 1823.

It was to economic subjects that most of his speeches were devoted. He entered on his parliamentary career with a considerable reputation as the originator of the currency plan embodied in Peel's Bill of 1819;[5] and on the occasion of his first important speech, which was on the Resumption of Cash Pay-

---

[1] *ib.* 162. For a proposal made to Ricardo in December 1820 to extend the tenure of his seat, see *ib.* 327 and 330.

[2] In 1822, when there was the prospect of a vacancy at Liverpool (represented at the time by Canning), Ricardo was invited to become a candidate for that constituency. This, however, he declined, declaring himself 'unfit both for the

contest, and for the dignity you would confer on me.' (See below, IX, 182.)

[3] Letter of 22 March 1818, below, VII, 260.

[4] 16 Sept. 1823.

[5] This was passed a short time *after* Ricardo came into Parliament (not before, as is said in Brougham's *Sketch,* below, p. xxxii).

ments, 'he did not rise until he was loudly called upon from all sides of the House.'[1] However, following his proposal of a tax on capital to pay off the national debt, which was regarded as a 'wild sort of notion' even by his own friends,[2] the attitude of the House towards him underwent some change, and he came to be looked upon as a theorist. As he wrote to McCulloch in the summer of 1820: 'I am treated as an ultra reformer and a visionary on commercial subjects by both Agriculturists and Manufacturers. Do you not observe that even Mr. Baring, the professed but I think lukewarm friend of free trade, did not nominate me on his committee.'[3]

With the growing severity of the depression in agriculture his speeches became increasingly concerned with the relation of Peel's Bill (and of the monetary policy that had followed it) to agricultural distress. Here he frequently found himself on the same side as the Government in his speeches, in repelling the attacks of the country gentlemen who attributed the depression to the effects of that measure and to the burden of taxation. At the same time, he opposed the Ministers when they found a remedy for the situation in protection. In the later years of Ricardo's parliamentary career there was a gradual transition of the Tory Government towards a more liberal commercial policy, under the auspices of Wallace, Huskisson and Robinson,[4] and with it the removal of a number of restrictions on trade; as a result at this stage Ricardo is found speaking more frequently in support of government measures.

It may be noted that shortly before his death Ricardo had promised his friend Joseph Hume that he would assist him in his proposed motion against the laws restricting the emigration of artizans, the exportation of machinery and the combination of workmen. And when Hume introduced the motion on 12 February

---

[1] McCulloch's *Life and Writings of Mr Ricardo*, prefixed to his edition of Ricardo's *Works*, 1846, p. xxviii. Cp. below, p. 9, n. 1.
[2] See for Brougham, below, p. 56; Grenfell, below, p. 270; Mallet, below, VIII, 147, n.

[3] Letter of 13 June 1820, below, VIII, 197.
[4] See his speeches in praise of these three Ministers, respectively, below, p. 246, 305, and 248.

1824, he opened his speech with a commemorative passage on Ricardo, with which Huskisson associated himself; this is quoted on p. 332 below.

The record of Ricardo's votes is necessarily incomplete. At that time (and until 1836) only the numbers in divisions were recorded officially, while the names were ignored. On questions of special interest, however, it was usual for members of the opposition to give their list to the reporters, thus securing publication of their own names in the newspapers and in *Hansard*.[1] During Ricardo's period in Parliament (from 26 Feb. 1819 to the end of the Session of 1823) *Hansard* records 224 such opposition lists, and Ricardo appears in 167 of them.[2] In a contemporary analysis of the lists of the minorities on 36 questions (selected as being of particular importance) divided upon in the Sessions of 1821 and 1822, Ricardo appears in 28—only six members appearing more frequently.[3]

These figures probably understate Ricardo's regularity in attendance, since there were occasions, however rare, when he refrained from voting with the Opposition.[4] Of 9 questions on which, exceptionally, both majority and minority lists were recorded in 1821 and 1822[5] Ricardo appears in all of them on the side of the Opposition, with the exception of one (the vote on the Roman Catholic claims, discussed below) in which he is not included in either list.[6]

His votes at the end of the debates in which he took part (when known) are as a rule recorded in this volume at the end of each speech. Some of his votes on other occasions are also of interest. His first recorded vote in the House (on 2 March 1819) was in support of Mackintosh's motion for reducing the number of offences subject to capital punishment; and he voted again for similar motions on 23 May and 4 June 1821 and 21 May 1823.

---

[1] Erskine May's *Constitutional History of England*, 3rd ed., 1912, vol. 1, p. 345–6.
[2] The total comprises 6 majority lists (when the Government was defeated) and Ricardo is in all these. The figures are based on the tables of contents in *Hansard*.

[3] *The Pamphleteer*, Vol. xxi (No. xlii, 1823), p. 313 ff. Hume heads the list with 34 divisions.
[4] See, *e.g.*, below, p. 123.
[5] Analysed in *The Pamphleteer, ib.* p. 301 ff.
[6] On this last question the Ministers were divided.

He also voted for Bennet's motions for the abolition of punishment by flogging (30 April and 7 July 1823). Throughout the special session called after Peterloo in 1819 he voted against the measures known as the 'Six Acts', in addition to speaking against one of them; and later (on 8 May 1821) he voted for the repeal of another, the Blasphemous and Seditious Libels Act. He supported Sir Francis Burdett's motion, on 16 May 1821, for an investigation into the Peterloo massacre. He voted against the Irish Insurrection Bill on 7 and 8 February 1822 and against its continuance on 8 July of the same year and on 12 May 1823; and he seconded Hume's motion for abolishing the office of Lord-Lieutenant of Ireland on 25 June 1823. On foreign affairs he voted for Mackintosh's motion (21 February 1821) on the action of the Powers of the Holy Alliance with respect to the revolution in Naples; for Lord W. Bentinck's motion (21 June 1821) concerning the affairs of Sicily; and for Hume's motion (14 May 1822) on the state of the Ionian islands where martial law had been proclaimed. He voted against the Foreign Enlistment Bill (on 3 and 10 June 1819) and against the renewal of the Alien Bill (on 7 July 1820 and again on 1 July 1821).

The fact that Ricardo does not appear in the list of members who voted on Plunket's motion for the Roman Catholic claims which was adopted on 28 February 1821 (either in the majority or in the minority which in this case are both given) is curious:[1] the more so since we know from a letter to Trower that he was present at the debate and that he was unreservedly in favour of the motion.[2] Professor Cannan, in his essay on 'Ricardo in Parliament', has conjectured that he remained neutral, and asks: 'Can it have been due to some compact with the power which gave him his seat for Portarlington?'[3] It is true that some members for Irish constituencies, in fear of offending their

---

[1] It was noticed at the time by the radical *Electors' Remembrancer* (London, Sherwood, 1822) which gives a record of each member's votes and has this entry on Ricardo (p. 73): 'Voted for the Queen; one of the patriotic phalanx that supported Mr. Hume. A most excellent member. We do not find his name in the Catholic Emancipation division.'

[2] Letter of 2 March 1821, below, VIII, 350–1.

[3] *Economic Journal*, 1894, p. 254; reprinted in his *The Economic Outlook*, 1912, p. 96–7.

Protestant patrons, refrained from voting for the Catholic claims, or if they voted felt that they did so 'at the imminent hazard of their seats';[1] and it was in fact the seat of Portarlington which, as we have seen above (p. xv), William Lamb lost in 1812 for supporting Catholic emancipation. All this lends plausibility to Cannan's suggestion. On the other hand it is clear from what we know of the negotiations by which Ricardo acquired his seat that there were no political conditions attached. The financial situation of Lord Portarlington had disastrously deteriorated since 1812, and Ricardo had been able to negotiate from the strong position of the lender of a large sum. But the decisive consideration is that during the period 1819–1823 *Hansard* did in fact give on a second occasion the list of those voting for the claims of the Roman Catholics, and Ricardo's name appears in this list (namely that on Brougham's motion of 26 June 1823 in support of a petition 'from the Roman Catholics of Ireland complaining of the Inequality in the Administration of the Law').[2]

A more probable explanation is that the omission of Ricardo's name in the case of Plunket's motion was due to a mistake in the division list. We have seen above that these lists were entirely unofficial; they were also often inaccurate, and on the occasion in question there were said to have been several omissions.[3]

III. *Committees on which Ricardo Served*

While he was in Parliament, Ricardo was a member of several Select Committees, which are listed below. He was appointed to the first of these within a few days of taking his seat, but after that

[1] Letter of C. W. Wynn, 5 Nov. 1821, in the Duke of Buckingham's *Memoirs of the Court of George IV,* 1859, vol. I, p. 218.
[2] This division was overlooked by Cannan, possibly because the debate is described in *Hansard* by the inadequate title of 'Administration of the Law in Ireland'. Cannan notices another division list on the Roman Catholic question given in *Hansard:* on this occasion however (30 April 1822) only the names of those voting against the Catholic claims are recorded, and as one would expect Ricardo is not among them.
[3] The *Electors' Remembrancer* of 1822, which has been mentioned above, refers to another member (H. Baring) as having 'voted for Catholic Emancipation, we believe, though his name is not on the division' (p. 16); and for three other similar cases of omission, on both sides in the same division, see pp. 11, 25 and 45. Cp. also below, p. 273, n.

for nearly two years he was not on any other committee. (As we have seen above, Baring refrained from nominating Ricardo for his Foreign Trade Committee in 1820; and although nominated for the Agricultural Committee of 1820, he was not in fact appointed to it.[1]) In his last session, however, we find him so busy with committees every morning that these, together with his regular attendance in the House, (as he wrote to Trower in July 1823)[2] 'fully occupied' his time.

POOR LAW COMMITTEE. The Select Committee on the Poor Law was appointed on 9 February 1819. Ricardo was added on 1 March. Chairman, Sturges Bourne. It heard evidence between 19 March and 28 June from 3 witnesses. Reported on 30 June 1819. The immediate recommendations of the report were limited to the removal of impediments to 'the free circulation of labour' and emigration; it also recommended, however, that ultimately parishes should be freed from 'the impracticable obligation of finding employment' for all who need it, and that relief should be confined to those unable to work.

AGRICULTURAL COMMITTEE 1821. The Select Committee on Petitions complaining of the Depressed State of Agriculture was appointed on 7 March 1821.[3] Chairman, T. S. Gooch. Sat for 14 weeks and heard 42 witnesses. Reported on 18 June 1821. The examination of the agricultural witnesses 'was throughout conducted with great ability by Mr Ricardo, Mr Huskisson, and others', according to the *Scotsman* (2 June 1821). Ricardo's letters contain many references to this. He 'worked very hard' in the Committee[4] 'against a host of adversaries, in the shape of witnesses, as well as members'.[5] Regarding one witness, Thomas Attwood, he says, 'his claims to infallibility have been sifted by Huskisson and myself';[6] and of another, William Jacob, 'I ... persevered in my questions to him, till I believe he thought me rude'.[7] He himself called two merchants as witnesses, Thomas Tooke and Edward Solly.[8] The report was drafted by Huskisson[9] but considerably

[1] See below, p. 56, n.
[2] Below, IX, 311.
[3] See below, p. 86–7.
[4] Below, VIII, 369.
[5] *ib.* 358.
[6] *ib.* 370.
[7] Below, IX, 87.
[8] Below, VIII, 373–4.

[9] It was believed in some quarters at the time that Ricardo was a joint author of the report (see Trower's letter of 22 July 1821, below, IX, 28; also *Glasgow Herald*, 25 June 1821, quoted by Smart, *Economic Annals, 1821–1830*, p. 16). For Ricardo's denial see his reply to Trower, below, IX, 37.

altered in Committee in a protectionist direction. Ricardo's opinion of it will be found below, pp. 151–2, and is summed up in a letter to McCulloch with the words: 'considering the composition of the committee it is better than could be expected'.[1] The report was not debated in the House but referred to the Agricultural Committee of the following year.

A glimpse of what went on inside the Committee is given by two entries in J. L. Mallet's MS Diary:

'7 May 1821. *Ricardo in the Agricultural Committee.* I dined yesterday at Ricardo's. There was a good deal of conversation upon the agricultural Committee. Ricardo says that they look upon him as a mere Theorist, but that they are very civil and allow him to take his own course with a view of establishing his principles by evidence. As to opinion the Committee is a perfect *Babel.* There are not two men agreed.

'10 May 1821. *Agriculture Committee.* Ricardo is left very much to himself in the Agricultural Committee. Baring who promised to assist him has not taken any share in the proceedings. Huskisson has been of service; and the Government are evidently on his side and wish to resist these greedy and unreasonable *Lords of the Soil,* as Cobbet calls them; but it is a dangerous task. Lord Londonderry[2] spoke yesterday for an hour in the Committee, and Ricardo says that he would have defied any man to have made a tolerable grasp of the real opinion of His Lordship. This is a most happy faculty in Lord Londonderry.'

AGRICULTURAL COMMITTEE 1822. The Select Committee on the Allegations of the several Petitions presented to the House in the last and present Sessions of Parliament complaining of the Distressed State of Agriculture was appointed on 18 February 1822, largely with the same membership as the Committee of 1821:[3] Huskisson although a member did not attend. Chairman, Lord Londonderry. The Committee took no evidence and reported on 1 April 1822. The report which was strongly protectionist gave rise to a prolonged debate in the House which ended in the passing of the new Corn Law (see below, p. 148 ff.). Ricardo discusses this report and contrasts it with that of the Committee of the previous year in *Protection to Agriculture,* above, IV, 244 ff.

COMMITTEE ON PUBLIC ACCOUNTS. The Select Committee on the Public Accounts of the United Kingdom annually laid before

---

[1] Below, VIII, 390; cp. IX, 7–8, 37.   [3] See below, pp. 129 and 138.
[2] *i.e.* Castlereagh.

Parliament was appointed on 18 April 1822. Chairman, Lord Palmerston. The Committee took no evidence. Reported on 31 July 1822. The report recommended that the accounts should be simplified so as to present as in a balance sheet the income and expenditure of each year. (An attempt had already been made by the Government in this direction at Ricardo's suggestion; see below, p. 145.)

COMMITTEE ON STATIONERY. The Select Committee on the Printing and Stationery supplied to the House of Commons and to the Public Departments was appointed on 14 May 1822. Chairman, Lord Binning. It heard evidence from 54 witnesses. Reported on 30 July 1822. The Committee considered complaints of corrupt practices in the Stationery and Printing Departments and recommended, *inter alia,* the stamping of all paper used in public offices with 'a peculiar mark' to prevent theft.

COMMITTEE ON SEWERS. The Select Committee on the powers vested in and exercised by the Commissioners of Sewers in the Metropolis was appointed on 25 February 1823. Chairman, Peter Moore. It heard evidence from 4 witnesses between 5 March and 19 June. Reported on 10 July 1823, reporting only the evidence, without offering any opinion.

COMMITTEE ON LAW MERCHANT. The Select Committee on the state of the Law relating to Goods, Wares, and Merchandise intrusted to Merchants, Agents, or Factors was appointed on 15 May 1823. Chairman, John Smith. It heard evidence from 52 witnesses. Reported on 13 June 1823. The Committee's main recommendation was: 'That a person possessing a bill of lading, or other apparent symbol of property, not importing that such property belongs to others, shall be considered as the true owner, so far as respects any person who may deal with him, in relation to such property, under an ignorance of his real character.' (This corresponded with Ricardo's opinion as expressed in a speech on 12 May 1823, below, p. 293.)

COMMITTEE ON THE LABOURING POOR IN IRELAND. The Select Committee on the condition of the Labouring Poor in Ireland, with a view to facilitating the application of the Funds of Private Individuals and Associations for their Employment in Useful and Productive Labour was appointed on 20 June 1823. Ricardo was added to the Committee on 23 June. Chairman, Spring Rice. It heard evidence from 18 witnesses between 23 June and 4 July. Reported on 16 July 1823. The appointment of the Committee arose from a petition from Ireland, presented on 18 June 1823, praying the House to consider how far 'Mr. Owen's plan for the employment of the poor ... could be applied to the employment of the peasantry of Ireland'. The report, while admitting that Owen's plan might be suitable for private experiment, regarded it as not a 'fit subject of legislative assistance'. Ricardo comments on the subject of the enquiry in a letter to Trower, below, IX, 313–14.

IV. *How the Speeches were Reported*

Parliamentary reporting in Ricardo's time was something very different from the official shorthand reporting of the present day. The whole business was a private venture of the newspapers, and their reporters had only recently gained even a bare toleration in the House. One cannot form an estimate of the authenticity of Ricardo's speeches as they have come down to us without some idea as to how they were recorded.

The pioneer in the reporting of debates was the *Morning Chronicle*, which was founded in 1769 and conducted by William Woodfall. At a time when the taking of notes by strangers in the House was strictly prohibited, Woodfall was enabled by an extraordinary memory to write up a whole debate after listening to it from the Strangers' Gallery. When in 1789 James Perry took over the editorship from him, he introduced the system of 'division of labour': this consisted in employing a team of reporters, each of whom sat in on the debate for a 'turn' of three-quarters of an hour and then, on being relieved in the Gallery by a colleague, left to write up his report at the office.[1] From that time onwards, even though the system came to be universally adopted, the *Morning Chronicle* 'was distinguished by its superior excellence in reporting the proceedings of Parliament.'[2]

---

[1] See the chapters on Parliamentary Reporting in James Grant's *The Great Metropolis,* 1838, 2nd series, vol. II, p. 200–1 and *The Newspaper Press,* 1871, vol. II, p. 169–70; and M. Macdonagh, *The Reporters' Gallery,* 1913, pp. 268 and 282.

[2] 'The Periodical Press', in *Edinburgh Review,* May 1823, p. 363;

Cobbett took the same view, since he wrote of another paper (the *New Times*) that, 'after the *Morning Chronicle*', it contained 'by far the best report of the speeches in Parliament.' (*Cobbett's Weekly Political Register,* 16 Feb. 1822, p. 388–9.)

Towards the close of the eighteenth century, when 'the use of notebooks and pencils by "strangers" was still an unholy sight in the eyes of the Speaker', the reporters established the practice of taking seats in the back row of the Strangers' Gallery where, 'sitting remotely in the shadows', they could take notes 'without being observed from the Chair';[1] and a few years later the Speaker acknowledged their right to the exclusive occupation of the back row.[2] This position, however, 'not only did not facilitate their hearing what was said by the members when addressing the House, but exposed them to great annoyance from the talking of the strangers on the five or six rows of seats before them.'[3] As late as 1819, 'they were still forbidden to take notes anywhere save on the back row';[4] and in that year one of the reporters of the *Morning Chronicle,* Peter Finnerty, was brought to the Bar of the House and reprimanded for having persisted in taking notes while sitting in the front row of the Strangers' Gallery.[5]

Apart from these handicaps, there was among the reporters themselves a general prejudice against verbatim reporting. This was based on the idea that shorthand writers are incompetent to report a good speech, because 'they attend to words without entering into the thoughts of the speaker.'[6] At the same time it was held that the reporter taking down a speech in long-hand was obliged to 'clothe the idea in his own phraseology' and to endeavour to 'make the style as correct and elegant as possible.'[7] As it has been tersely put, he 'gave eloquence to the stammerer and concentration to the diffuse'.[8]

This type of reporting, however, required that 'the reporter must thoroughly understand the subject discussed, and be qualified to follow the reasoning ... of the speaker.'[9] Ricardo's matter did not easily lend itself to writing-up by reporters, and as he says in a letter to Trower, 'It is a great disadvantage to

[1] Macdonagh, *op. cit.* p. 28
[2] *ib.* p. 309.
[3] *The Newspaper Press,* vol. II, p. 181.
[4] Macdonagh, *op. cit.* p. 326.
[5] 18 June 1819, *Hansard,* XL, 1182–8.

[6] Autobiography of Lord Campbell (himself a former reporter), in his *Life,* ed. by Mrs Hardcastle, 1881, vol. I, p. 106.
[7] *The Great Metropolis,* 2nd series, vol. II, p. 209.
[8] Macdonagh, *op. cit.* p. 445.
[9] Lord Campbell, *ib.* p. 106.

me that the reporters not understanding the subject cannot readily follow me—they often represent me as uttering perfect nonsense.'[1]

The Parliamentary Debates, printed by, and 'published under the superintendence of' T. C. Hansard, was also a private concern, and while it had by this time gained a definite ascendancy, short-lived rivals still appeared from time to time.[2] Hansard had no reporters of his own, and his publication was compiled by collation of various newspaper reports or from copies supplied by the speakers or published by them in pamphlet form.[3] By advertisements in the press and in his own publication he invited the 'communication' of speeches for his work.

Hansard however was far from being a complete record: some speeches and even whole debates were not reported in it at all, even though they had appeared in the newspapers. Omissions were no doubt in many cases caused by the inadequacy of newspaper reports and the difficulty of securing better ones, but in others they were probably due merely to the need to limit the size of the volumes.

Two or three volumes of *Hansard* were devoted to each session, and these appeared after considerable delay: thus the volume containing the debates of the first three months of 1821 was not advertised as 'ready for delivery' until nearly a year later; and it was announced that the volume covering the following period, up to the close of the session on 11 July 1821, would be published in October 1822.[4]

The editor of the *Parliamentary Debates* since its foundation in 1803 was John Wright. The method by which he proceeded in his work can be seen from a letter which he wrote to Ricardo to obtain a report of his speech of 11 June 1823:

[1] Letter of 5 March 1822, below, IX, 175; cp. VIII, 357.
[2] Two of these have been collated. *Dolby's Parliamentary Register* (86 numbers, at 2d. each, covering the Session 1819) and *Cobbett's Parliamentary Register* (one vol. for the Session 1820). Only the latter has yielded any additions, which are given in footnotes to the speeches.
[3] See the evidence of T. C. Hansard, jun. in 'Report from the Select Committee on Parliamentary Reporting', 1878, Q. 159–162.
[4] Advt. of *Hansard,* N.S. vols. IV and V, in *Scotsman,* 2 March 1822.

WRIGHT TO RICARDO[1]

112 Regent Street.
August 20. 1823.

Sir,

As I am very desirous that a correct report of your Speech on
Mr Western's motion should be preserved in *The Parliamentary
Debates* I beg leave to say that I shall be very glad if you could
find leisure to furnish me with such report in the course of *ten days*.
I enclose the Newspaper reports which you will find very scanty—
so much so, that I think it would be less trouble to write out
the whole, than to attempt to correct what is printed. I shall be
glad to be favoured with a line on the subject, and am, Sir,

Your faithful humble Sert.
J. WRIGHT

David Ricardo Esq.

Ricardo complied with this request, as appears from the note
attached to the speech in *Hansard* (see below, p. 309).

The way in which Ricardo on a similar occasion used the newspaper cuttings which were sent to him is graphically shown by
the facsimile of the original report, which he prepared for
Hansard, of his famous speech of 24 May 1819 on the Resumption
of Cash Payments (below, facing p. 332).[2]

So much care in securing a full record from the speakers was
apparently used by Wright only for major speeches, and the
quality of the rendering in their case is markedly superior to that
of the lesser ones. In other cases he probably contented himself
with making a compilation from the newspaper reports.

Thus, from the picture that we have of parliamentary reporting

[1] Addressed: 'David Ricardo, Esq.
M.P./Gatcombe Park/Gloucester-
shire'.—MS in Ricardo Papers. This
is the only extant letter from Wright
to Ricardo.
[2] This manuscript is part of a
volume of autographs entitled
*Twenty two Speeches in Parliament
in the handwriting of the Peers and
Commoners by whom they were
delivered. 1810–1821,* which was
prepared by J. Wright in 1838 for
a collector (Dawson Turner) from
'copy' used by the printer of
Hansard. (Puttick and Simpson's
sale of the MS Library of the late
D. Turner, 6 June 1859, lot 366;
Clumber Library sale at Sotheby's,
16 Feb. 1938, lot 1396.) Ricardo's
manuscript is signed 'R' at the end,
and compositor's marks and the
editor's additions can be noticed
in various places. The cuttings are
from the *Morning Chronicle.*

at that time, it seems clear that we cannot read Ricardo's speeches with the same confidence in their authenticity as we can his writings, or even his evidence.[1]

There is, however, one speech of which we are now able to read Ricardo's own report, undoubtedly written within a day after the debate; that is the speech on Mr Western's Motion of 10 July 1822.[2] The original transcript, hitherto unpublished, was found in the Mill-Ricardo papers and is given in the present volume instead of *Hansard's* version, of which it is four times as extensive. This report, having been written by Ricardo himself so soon after delivering it, has an authority unequalled by any others, even by those of which we know, or can guess from their quality, that they were revised by him, since this revision would normally be carried out months later, owing to the delays in the preparation of *Hansard.* One can therefore take the report of the speech of 10 July 1822 as a standard by which to judge the quality of the others.

V. *The Speeches in the Present Edition*

In the present edition Ricardo's speeches have been reprinted from *The Parliamentary Debates* (referred to throughout as *Hansard*).[3] However, in every case in which *Hansard's* report seemed doubtful for one reason or another, it has been collated with the reports in the newspapers; and whenever one of the latter seemed more plausible, this has been given as an alternative in a footnote. Extensive, though not systematic, collation of a general kind with newspaper reports has also been carried out; and in many cases this has made it possible to add in footnotes passages from the newspapers where these are fuller. Moreover, a dozen of Ricardo's parliamentary speeches, which have been found in the newspapers but are not reproduced in *Hansard,* have been included, and the fact noted.[4]

---

[1] The minutes of evidence before Committees were taken by short-hand writers appointed by the two Houses of Parliament from 1813 onwards (see Macdonagh, *op. cit.* p. 439).

[2] See below, p. 231.

[3] The volumes concerned are XXXIX–XLI and New Series, I–IX (with the exception of III which is entirely devoted to the Queen's Trial in the House of Lords).

[4] On the other hand, some speeches which are reported in *Hansard* so

The titles of the speeches are those given by *Hansard* to the respective debates. Each of Ricardo's speeches is introduced by summaries or brief quotations from previous speakers, which indicate the subject of the debate or are referred to by Ricardo. At the end of each speech is given the result of the division, if any, on the question under consideration; and occasionally extracts from subsequent speakers who replied to Ricardo. This and other editorial matter is throughout distinguished by smaller type.

LORD BROUGHAM'S SKETCH OF RICARDO IN PARLIAMENT

[From *Historical Sketches of Statesmen who flourished in the Time of George III, Second Series,* by Henry Lord Brougham, London, Charles Knight, 1839, pp. 188–191]

The Bill which usually goes by Mr. Peel's name had been passed for restoring the currency a short time before Mr. Ricardo came into Parliament; but the Committee (commonly called the Second Bullion Committee), out of whose Report the measure arose, had fully adopted the principle and had clearly followed the plan laid down by Mr. Ricardo. When he took his place in the House of Commons, after the high reputation which had preceded him, he necessarily appeared to some disadvantage under the weight of the great expectations formed of him. But, as far as these were reasonable, however ample, they were fully answered. His speaking, his conduct, his manner, were all unexceptionable, and all suited to the man, his high station among philosophers, his known opinions on political affairs, his kindly nature, and his genuine modesty. There was something about him, chiefly a want of all affectation as well as pretension in everything he said or did, that won the respect of every party. His matter was ever of high

meagrely (mostly in two or three lines) as to seem trivial have been omitted. The references to these in *Hansard* are as follows: New Series, I, 1131–2; V, 508, 1207; VI, 794, 1015; VII, 1091, 1504, 1522; IX, 151, 439, 738, 974, 992, 1429, 1438.

value. Whether you agreed or differed with him, you were well pleased to have it brought out and made to bear upon the question, if indeed the pursuit of right and truth was your object. His views were often, indeed, abundantly theoretical, sometimes too refined for his audience, occasionally extravagant from his propensity to follow a right principle into all its consequences, without duly taking into account in practice the condition of things to which he was applying it, as if a mechanician were to construct an engine without taking into consideration the resistance of the air in which it was to work, or the strength and the weight and the friction of the parts of which it was to be made. When he propounded, as the best way of extricating us from our financial embarrassments, that the capital of the country should be taxed 700 or 800 millions, and the debt at once paid off, and defended this scheme upon the twofold ground, that what a debtor owes is always to be deducted from his property and regarded as belonging to his creditors, and that the expense of managing the debt and raising the revenue to pay the interest would be a large saving to the nation, he assumed as true two undeniable facts, but he drew a practical inference not more startling at its first statement than inadmissible when closely examined upon the clearest grounds of both expediency and justice. It may even be doubted whether the only feasible portion of the plan, the diminution of interest from time to time effected by threats of repaying the principal, or rather redeeming the annuities (the only thing to which the public creditor is entitled), be not a step too far in this direction both as to justice and policy. In like manner he always greatly undervalued the amount of the depreciation in the currency upon prices generally, estimating it solely by the difference between the Mint price and the Market price of gold; and so confidently did he believe in this speculative estimate, that his practical plan for restoring the currency was grounded upon it. But while such were his errors, and those of a kind to excite very strong feelings in certain large and important classes in the House of Commons, he was uniformly and universally respected for the sterling qualities of his capacity and his character, which were acknowledged by all.

His speaking was of an admirable description; clear, simple, correct in diction, copious in argument, pregnant with information, but never thrown away. He reserved the share which he took in debate for questions to which his attention had been particularly directed, with which he was familiar, and to which he attached great importance. Hence, even his extreme opinions upon questions connected with the reform of the constitution in Church and State gave no offence; for he appeared not to court the opportunity of delivering them, but as if compelled by a sense of duty to declare his mind, careless or indisposed otherwise to make a speech. Few men have, accordingly, had more weight in Parliament; certainly none who, finding but a very small body of his fellow-members to agree with his leading opinions, might be said generally to speak against the sense of his audience, ever commanded a more patient or even favourable hearing; and, as this was effected without any of the more ordinary powers of oratory or of entertainment possessed by others, it might be regarded as the triumph of reason, intelligence, and integrity over untoward circumstances and alien natures. The regret felt for his loss was in proportion to the high estimation in which he had been held during the three years that he sat in Parliament; and the country, as well as its representatives, justly sorrowed over a great light extinguished prematurely, which had already proved so useful, and which might have been expected to render so much greater and longer service in illuminating the world.

David Ricardo 1822

from a bust made at Florence.

Emery Walker Ltd ph sc.

SPEECHES IN
THE HOUSE OF COMMONS

SESSION 1819

POOR RATES MISAPPLICATION BILL

25 March 1819

Mr. STURGES BOURNE moved for leave to bring in a bill, which, 25 March 1819 he declared, was intended to prevent the payment of the wages of labour out of the poor rates; no relief should in future be given to able-bodied labourers in employment, but their children should be provided for and set to work.

Mr. RICARDO thought, that the two great evils for which it was desirable to provide a remedy, were, the tendency towards a redundant population, and the inadequacy of the wages to the support of the labouring classes; and he apprehended, that the measure now proposed would not afford any security against the continuance of these evils. On the contrary, he thought that, if a provision were made for all the children of the poor, it would only increase the evil; for if parents felt assured that an asylum would be provided for their children, in which they would be treated with humanity and tenderness, there would then be no check to that increase of population which was so apt to take place among the labouring classes. With regard to the other evil, the inadequacy of the wages, it ought to be remembered, that if this measure should have the effect of raising them, they would still be no more than the wages of a single man, and would never rise so high as to afford a provision for a man with a family.

[On the second reading see below, p. 6.]

FIRST REPORT FROM THE
BANK OF ENGLAND COMMITTEE—
CASH PAYMENTS BILL

5 *April* 1819

Mr. PEEL, the chairman of the secret committee, presented their first report, which recommended that cash payments, which had been partially resumed, should be suspended until the final report of the committee had been received and a legislative measure passed thereupon; he moved for leave to bring in a bill to that effect. Mr. TIERNEY, a member of the committee, opposing the motion, said that the only effect of the bill would be to save a little expense to the Bank whereas 'any sacrifice ought to be made rather than that good faith should not be preserved.'

Mr. RICARDO began by requesting the indulgence of the House, which he hoped he should experience, especially as he was about to dispute the opinions of the right hon. gentleman[1] who had just spoken with so much eloquence. It appeared to him very extraordinary, indeed, that the Bank should be called upon as the right hon. gentleman argued, to issue gold at 3*l*. 17*s*. while they were obliged to pay 4*l*. 1*s*. for that very gold. Those who obtained the gold upon such terms must, of course, profit by the difference, and they could only derive that profit by acting contrary to law—that was either by clandestinely exporting the gold, or by melting it down. Would parliament consent to allow such a class of persons to obtain profit at the expense of the Bank? Such a class was, indeed, he apprehended, the very last to which parliament would consent to grant any peculiar favour or protection. That the resumption of cash payments by the Bank must be preceded by a reduction of its paper issues, was quite obvious. But then that reduction ought to be gradual,

---

[1] Mr. Tierney.

and in order to enable the Bank to resume its cash payments, 5 April 1819 such a measure as that now proposed appeared to him essentially necessary. He approved of the views of the right hon. gentleman as to the provision of an adequate guard against the repetition of the dangers, hitherto resulting from the improvident conduct of the Bank. He also agreed, that before the Bank could pay in gold, it must take measures to replenish its coffers, and that to replenish its coffers by pro-viding an adequate supply of gold, it must reduce its issue of notes. But, with a view to enable the Bank to resume its payments in cash, he was decidedly of opinion that the pro-posed measure was essentially necessary, and was sorry that it had not before now been adopted.

Leave was given to bring in the bill, which was then passed.

MR. LYTTELTON'S MOTION
RESPECTING STATE LOTTERIES

4 *May* 1819

Mr. LYTTELTON moved a series of resolutions for the abolition 4 May 1819 of State Lotteries.

Mr. RICARDO supported the motion, and pointed out the evils which arose from the drawings of the lottery so often in the year. He quoted the resolutions of a society to which many of the ministers belonged, deprecating the lottery; and observed, that they were thus condemning, as individuals, the law which they came to support by their votes.[1]

The House divided: for the motion, 84; against it, 133. Ricardo voted for the motion.

---

[1] *The New Times* reports: 'Mr. RICARDO arose amidst loud cries of *Question!* and partly from that circumstance, as well as from the very low tone of voice in which he spoke was almost entirely

SINKING FUND

13 *May* 1819

Mr. GRENFELL moved for a committee on the sinking fund. The present system was for the commissioners for the redemption of the national debt to go four times a week into the city to purchase stock, which in effect 'they bought with borrowed money—the money borrowed from the loan-contractors.' 'This was creating a new debt for no other purpose than to destroy an old one: selling new stock cheap in order to buy old stock dear.' His object was to convince the House of the expediency of applying the sinking fund to diminish the loan which was to be raised for the service of the year. The saving to the public which might have been effected if this method had been applied from 1793 to 1813 amounted to 20,000,000*l.* and on the loan of 1815 the saving might have been upwards of 2,000,000*l.* Amongst those who differed from him in this opinion some were under a bias from self-interest. 'Loan-contractors were not in his judgment exactly that description of persons by whose advice in these matters a chancellor of the exchequer ought to be governed. In 1814, the right hon. gentleman had stated in his place, that, having conferred with a number of gentlemen contracting for the loan with regard to the propriety of acting on his (Mr. Grenfell's) suggestion, they all, with one exception only, signified their disapprobation of it, and recommended a loan of 24,000,000*l.* instead of 12,000,000*l.* The exception to which he alluded was that of his honourable friend (Mr. Ricardo),[1] who, greatly to his credit, observed to the chancellor of the exchequer, that if he considered his own interest merely, he must agree with his brother contractors; but if he were to consult the advantage of the

inaudible in the gallery during the few observations which he made. We understood the Hon. Member to say, that by the operation of the Lottery System, vices were thrown in the way of the people as a lure. The morality of the people was sacrificed for the sake of the tax raised from the Lottery, which was a consideration of far less importance than that which was sacrificed for it. The Hon. Member proceeded to trace the frequency of suicide in England to the operation of this tax, but his voice here became quite drowned amidst loud calls of *Question!* and coughing.'

[1] That Ricardo was the individual alluded to had already been stated by Grenfell in the preface to his pamphlet of 1817, mentioned below, p. 22, n. 1.

country, he should advise the application of the sinking fund, and a loan of 12,000,000*l.* only.'

The CHANCELLOR OF THE EXCHEQUER objected to the motion, on the ground that it would fetter the discretion of government. As to the case of the loan in 1815 'it was true that a great profit had been made upon the loan alluded to, but it was contracted for previous to the battle of Waterloo, and the profit was derived from conquest, and the successful termination of hostilities.' With regard to the supposed saving of 20,000,000*l.* upon all the loans contracted for during the war, if the system of applying to the sinking fund had been adopted, the sum mentioned did not exceed two per cent of the amount borrowed in that period. 'Instead of a profit, however, a loss had been sometimes incurred, which would probably have balanced the amount of the saving. The contractors, too, would have objected, and offered less favourable terms.' 'One great advantage attending the present system was, that it produced a general steadiness of prices....Were it not for the regular purchases made by the commissioners, there would be few real buyers, and persons under the necessity of selling would be at the mercy of stock-jobbers.'

Mr. RICARDO said, that he understood the hon. mover to have argued, not that the commissioners, if subscribers for the loans, would have procured for the public the profit which arose from the events of war or peace; but that they would have retained for the public that regular premium which the contractors obtained independently of the events of peace or war—which they were entitled to for undertaking the risk of such extensive undertakings, but which of course, under the present plan, was lost to the public. In that opinion he heartily concurred, as he could not conceive the advantage which could arise from giving the commissioners sums to lay out in the purchase of stock, while sellers were sent by the government to supply them with the stock which they were to buy. The contractors for the loan brought their stock to market just in the same degrees as the commissioners purchased it: they did not dispose of it in the mass, but brought it weekly and daily to market to provide for their instalments.

Any gentleman who supposed that if that process did not go on, it would be in the power of the jobbers to make hard terms with the sellers of stock, must have been perfectly ignorant of the stock market [Hear! hear!], for competition was no where carried to such an extent, and no where operated with more benefit to the public. His hon. friend had alluded to the opinion which he (Mr. Ricardo) had given before the chancellor of the exchequer in 1814. He had certainly then given the opinion which he had long entertained. He should have shrunk into the earth before those who had long known his sentiments if he had given any other; but he knew that those gentlemen who gave a contrary opinion, had given it just as conscientiously; for great and sincere differences of judgment on this subject existed in the city. To him it certainly appeared, that if the process of the sinking fund had an effect on the stock market, a similar process must produce an effect on all other markets in the country, and that, for instance, it must be contended that the chancellor of the exchequer could produce an effect on the corn-market, by sending a commissioner to buy a quarter of wheat, while he sent a contractor to sell the same quantity.

The House divided on the motion: Ayes, 39; Noes, 117. Ricardo voted for the motion.

POOR RATES MISAPPLICATION BILL

17 *May* 1819

On this bill [cp. above, p. 1] being brought in for the second reading,

Mr. RICARDO opposed the bill, principally on the ground that it tended to increase the population. If at present there existed a difficulty in supporting the poor, in what situation would the country be placed in twenty years hence, when these children so educated grew up to manhood? The bill was only the plan of Mr. Owen, in a worse shape, and carried to a greater extent.

The bill was then read a second time. On 11 June 1819 it was read a third time and passed.

BANK OF ENGLAND— RESUMPTION OF CASH PAYMENTS

24 *May* 1819

The reports of the secret committee on the resumption of cash payments were taken into consideration and Mr. PEEL, the chairman of the secret committee, moved a series of resolutions embodying their recommendations. The resolutions were as follows:

1.—THAT it is expedient to continue the Restriction on payments in Cash by the Bank of England, beyond the time to which it is at present limited by law.

2.—THAT it is expedient that a definite period should be fixed for the termination of the Restriction on Cash Payments; and that preparatory measures should be taken, with a view to facilitate and ensure, on the arrival of that period, the payment of the Promissory Notes of the Bank of England in the legal Coin of the Realm.

3.—THAT in order to give to the Bank a greater control over the issues of their Notes than they at present possess, provision ought to be made, for the gradual repayment to the Bank of the sum of Ten Millions; being part of the sum due to the Bank, on account of Advances made by them for the public service, and on account of the purchase of Exchequer Bills under the authority of acts of the Legislature.

4.—THAT it is expedient to provide, by law, that from the 1st February 1820, the Bank shall be liable to deliver, on demand, Gold of standard fineness, having been assayed and stamped at His Majesty's mint, a quantity of not less than sixty ounces being required in exchange for such an amount of Notes of the Bank as shall be equal to the value of the Gold so required, at the rate of Four pounds one shilling per ounce.

5.—THAT from the 1st October 1820, the Bank shall be liable to deliver, on demand, Gold of standard fineness, assayed and stamped as before mentioned, a quantity of not less than sixty ounces being required in exchange for such an amount of Notes as shall be equal to the value of the Gold so required, at the rate of £.3. 19. 6. per ounce.

6.—THAT from the 1st May 1821, the Bank shall be liable to deliver, on demand, Gold of standard fineness, assayed and stamped as before mentioned, a quantity of not less than sixty ounces being required in exchange for such an amount of Notes as shall be equal in value to the Gold so required, at the rate of £.3. 17. $10\frac{1}{2}$. per ounce.

7.—THAT the Bank may at any period between the 1st February 1820 and the 1st May 1821 undertake to deliver Gold of standard fineness assayed and stamped as before mentioned, at any rate between the sums of Four pounds one shilling per ounce, and £.3. 17. $10\frac{1}{2}$. per ounce; but that such intermediate rate having been once fixed by the Bank, that rate shall not be subsequently increased.

8.—THAT from the 1st May 1823, the Bank shall pay its Notes, on demand, in the legal Coin of the Realm.

9.—THAT it is expedient to repeal the Laws, prohibiting the melting and the exportation of the Coin of the Realm.

The first three resolutions were agreed to. To the fourth resolution Mr. ELLICE proposed an amendment, namely, 'That the Bank have it in its option to pay, after the 1st of May, 1821, either in legal coin, or in gold, at 3*l.* 17*s.* $10\frac{1}{2}$ per oz.' The amendment was supported by Mr. TIERNEY and opposed by the CHANCELLOR OF THE EXCHEQUER.[1] Mr. MANNING (a Bank director) objected to the fourth and subsequent resolutions because they 'would have the effect of fettering the Bank so as to cause an inconvenient reduction of the currency.'

[1] Although the Resolutions were passed on 26 May in their original form, Ellice's amendment was accepted on the third reading of the bill on 14 June; the Lords on 23 June changed the date from May 1821 to May 1822 and this was finally agreed to by the Commons on 25 June 1819.

[*The transcript of this speech prepared for* Hansard *by Ricardo   partly with cuttings from the* Morning Chronicle's *report, is reproduced in the plate facing p. 332 below. In the text* Hansard's *capitalization and spelling are retained, but other deviations from the MS are corrected.*]   24 May 1819

Mr. RICARDO[1] said, he was fully persuaded of the truth of the declaration of the hon. director, that the Bank wished to resume cash payments, but he was just as fully persuaded that they did not know how to set about it. When called before the committee, the directors individually admitted that the price of bullion and the rate of exchanges were affected by the amount of their issues; but when collected in their own court they resolved that "they conceive it to be their duty to declare, that they are unable to discover any solid foundation for such a sentiment."[2] And now, in the Remonstrance which they have made to the chancellor of the exchequer, they again admit that the exchanges are affected by their issues, for they condemn the measure recommended by the committee for restoring the exchange to par, on the ground of its being calculated to force them to contract the amount of their circulation, which they represent as fatal to the public interest.[3] When they avowed such inconsistent opinions, and after the experience which the House had had of their conduct, it would be the highest indiscretion in parliament not to take out of their hands the preparations for the resumption of cash payments. He did not think this a question only between the Bank and ministers, as it had been

[1] *The Times's* report opens: 'Mr. RICARDO rose, amidst loud invitations.'
[2] Resolution of the Court of Directors of the Bank of England, 25 March 1819, printed in the 'Second Report from the [Commons'] Secret Committee on the Expediency of the Bank resuming Cash Payments', 1819, p. 263.
[3] 'Representation, agreed upon the 20th day of May 1819, by The Directors of The Bank of England, and laid before The Chancellor of The Exchequer', in *Parliamentary Papers,* 1819, vol. III.

argued by his right hon. friend (Mr. Tierney), but rather one
between ministers and the Bank on one side, and the country
on the other. He was therefore disposed to concur with his
right hon. friend in any measure which might be devised to
keep the ministers also under control. One principle was
clear, and was of the utmost importance in the consideration
of this subject,—it was this, that those who had the power
of regulating the quantity of the circulating medium of the
country, had the power of regulating the rate of the exchanges, and the price of every commodity. This power
clearly resided in the hands of the directors of the Bank, and
it was a most formidable one. It quite astonished him that
Mr. Harman could imagine that it was in the power of an
individual to influence the exchanges against the wish of the
Bank;[1] which was just as reasonable as to suppose that an
individual could regulate the price of corn or any other
commodity of general consumption. This question was one
of immense importance in principle, but in the manner of
bringing it about was trivial, and not deserving half an hour's
consideration of the House. The difficulty was only that of
raising the currency 3 per cent in value[2] [Hear, hear!]. And
who could doubt that even in those states in which the
currency was entirely metallic, it often suffered a variation
equal to this, without inconvenience to the public [Hear!]. In
this country we had nothing but paper in circulation, and
therefore every variation in the value of our currency was
shown by the price of gold, but where metal alone circulated,
it could not be doubted that gold might, from various cir-

[1] See the evidence of Jeremiah
Harman, late Governor of the
Bank, to the Commons' Committee on the Resumption of
Cash Payments, appended to
'Second Report', 1819, pp. 41–2.
[2] On 4 March, to the Commons'
Committee, Ricardo had given
the figure as 5 or 6 per cent; on
24 March, to the Lords' Committee, as 4 per cent, and now, on
24 May, 3 per cent. The variation
in these figures reflected the
falling market price of gold.

cumstances, become more or less valuable, and thus affect all contracts, though from there being no other standard to measure it by, its variations were less palpable. His particular reason for supporting the measure under consideration was this. By withdrawing paper, so as to restore the note to its bullion value (an alteration, by the bye, only of 3 per cent.), the House would have done all that was required [Hear, hear!]. But if the House adopted the proposition of the hon. gentleman (Mr. Ellice), another variation in the value of the currency would take place, which it was his (Mr. R.'s) wish to guard against. If that amendment were agreed to, an extraordinary demand would take place for gold, for the purpose of coinage which would enhance the value of the currency 3 or 4 per cent in addition to the first enhancement [Hear, hear!].—As to the plan under the consideration of the House, it was that which the Bank directors, if they were wise, should wish for [hear!]. They should wish to fill the circulation with paper, and so long as they had the privilege of giving gold bullion for their notes, there would be no coin in circulation—they would have the monopoly. They had no real interest in the depreciation of the currency; it would be rather their interest to raise it, even to double the value. They were in the situation of creditors, not of debtors; their whole capital being in money or other securities representing money [Hear, hear!]. As to the resolution which bore that the government should repay the Bank a certain sum, he could not agree with it. The House having taken a security that the currency should be of a certain value, they had done enough, and should not farther interfere with the proceedings of the directors, who should answer to their proprietors only for the management of their concerns. The Bank might, if this resolution were agreed to, feel some difficulty in putting forth the amount of currency which was required. For though what the directors thought a check, namely, the rate of interest on money, was no check at all as to the amount of issues, as Adam Smith, Mr. Hume, and others had satisfactorily proved; yet as the Bank directors were governed by certain traditional limits, or something like limits, in discounting to individual merchants, they might have difficulty in keeping up the requisite amount of currency.[1] A director, in his evidence before the committee, had said, that the Bank did not confine themselves to this limit where the individual's credit was undoubted; but it should be recollected that the Bank was a cautious and timid body, and if they had no other means of supplying the requisite amount of circulation but by discounting bills, he feared the public might suffer from a scarcity of currency. He was certainly for leaving them to conduct all such transactions according to their own discretion and pleasure, provided only that such a check was established as should guard against a redundancy. The proposed mode of resuming cash payments appeared to him the easiest that could be imagined. The Bank would be placed under no restraint at first, nor any sudden necessity of reducing its issues. An opportunity would be afforded of effecting the

---

[1] Cp. for this sentence *The Times's* report: 'Their [the Bank directors'] error was, in supposing that the rate of interest would always point out a proper limit to their issues; but the rate of interest had been proved both by Hume and Adam Smith to depend, not on the quantity of money, but on the profits on stock; even though they did not advance anything to government, it was in their power, by an excess of discounts, to make the circulation redundant. The Bank directors were, in the management of their discounts, he had some reason to believe, governed by old habits. One of their rules was, he understood, to fix a particular limit, beyond which they would not extend their accommodation to any individual.' The references are to the evidence of Samuel Thornton, a Bank Director, to the Commons' Committee, 'Second Report', 1819, p. 146; to Hume's essay *Of Interest;* and to the *Wealth of Nations,* Bk. II, ch. iv; Cannan's ed., vol. 1, p. 335 ff.

object in the most gradual manner; and even when bullion payments should be made at the Mint price, the inconvenience would be but inconsiderable. Till October 1820, the Bank need make no reduction, and then a slight one [hear!]; and he had no doubt that if they were cautious they might arrive at cash payments without giving out one guinea in gold. The Bank should reduce their issues cautiously; he only feared they would do it too rapidly [hear!]. If he might give them advice, he should recommend to them not to buy bullion, but even though they had but a few millions, if he had the management of their concerns, he should boldly sell. Every sale would improve the exchanges, and till gold fell to 3*l.* 17*s.* 6*d.* there would be no necessity for the Bank to make any purchases. He was only sorry that the Bank was not to be obliged by the resolutions to buy all the bullion offered to them at 3*l.* 17*s.* 6*d.* lest through excessive caution they might starve the circulation. The Mint, it was true, was to remain open to the public, who might coin the bullion which they obtained from the Bank. Mr. Mushett, whose evidence respecting the coinage was worthy of attention, from its accuracy and general ability, had stated, that with a capital of 300,000*l.* the Mint could supply the public with 12,000,000*l.* a year.[1] Yet a year was a long time to wait for twelve millions, and it might easily happen, that in the interim between the reduction of the Bank issues and the supply afforded from the Mint, the country might seriously feel the deficiency. It was on that account that he should have wished a resolution inserted, to compel the Bank to give its notes for bullion (at 3*l.* 17*s.* 6*d.*) on demand. With the exception of this omission, the plan was, in his opinion, perfectly safe and gentle.— With regard to what had fallen from his right hon. friend

---

[1] See his evidence to the Lords' Committee on the Resumption of Cash Payments appended to their 'Reports', 1819, p. 207.

(Mr. Tierney) respecting the graduated scale of payments not having been submitted to the directors, he referred him to the examination of Mr. Thornton before the Lords' committee where he would see that that gentleman's evidence was wholly in favour of the plan.[1] He was quite astonished that such an alarm prevailed at a reduction of perhaps one million in four years, and could only ascribe it to the indiscreet language of the Bank[2] [Hear, hear!]. The hon. director[3] had that night told them not to withdraw confidence from the Bank. The House did not withdraw its confidence from the Bank from any doubt of its wealth, or integrity, but from a conviction of its total ignorance of the principles of political economy [hear, and a laugh]. The Bank had had ample time to reduce their issues, so as to lower the price of gold; yet, in spite of the times repeatedly fixed for the resumption of cash payments, they had never done so. It was not the business of the directors to consider the interest of the public. That was the business of his majesty's ministers; and when the hon. director told them that the directors had lost so much on the purchase of gold, and so much on the issue of tokens, his question was, why had they done so? Their business was with the interest of the proprietors, for whom they were trustees, not with the interests of the public. The directors were answerable to the proprietors for these misapplications of their funds. He (Mr. R.) had been astonished that the undivided profits of the Bank had been so small, which he should have imagined, must have at least amounted to ten millions;[4] but now, by the confession of the hon. gentleman, the matter

---

[1] 'Reports', 1819, pp. 222–4.

[2] *The Times's* report adds 'and to the remonstrance which they had addressed to government, and in which they actually sounded the alarm'.

[3] Mr. Manning.

[4] The surplus, according to the Commons' Committee, was £5,202,320 ('Second Report', p. 4). Ricardo had estimated it at more than thirteen millions in 1816 (see above, IV, 135).

was explained. The directors had scattered a million here and a million there according to their views of the wants of the ministry or the country, without any regard to the interest of the proprietors [Hear, hear!]. The hon. director had advised them not to cramp the currency, and had referred to their experience of 1797. But that was not a parallel case. It was a season of alarm and panic, when every man had wished to have gold in his house in fear of an invasion. His right hon. friend (Mr. Tierney) had asked, what, under the plan proposed was the holder of 10*l.* to do, for he could not get bullion at the Bank. According to the amendment, the right hon. gentleman was in no great hurry to give this poor man either bullion or specie. But were they doing nothing by the plan for the holders of notes of 10*l.?* The holder of a 10*l.* note would be improved in his condition; for by restoring the currency to its proper value, and by making 1,000*l.* worth what it purported to be, instead of what it now really was, worth only 970*l.*, his note of 10*l.* would be proportionally increased in value. Although he could not go to the Bank for gold, he might resort to any goldsmith who would let him have the proportion of gold to which his note was entitled; and the difference to him would be so trifling, as not to be worthy of consideration in the decision of a great question.—It had been said, on the part of the Bank, that they were ready to pay, if repaid the advances which they had made to the government.[1] But how came they to make those advances to government, if not assured of repayment at a certain time? The Bank had not been forced to make those advances, but the directors had such an extraordinary disposition to act as ministers [a laugh, and hear, hear!]. It would however, be better if those directors would rather

---

[1] See the joint evidence of four Bank Directors to the Commons'   Committee, 'Second Report', 1819, p. 148.

attend to their own interests, and those of their constituents.—
A most fearful and destructive depreciation had at one time
taken place; but from that we had recovered, and he was
happy to reflect that we had so far retraced our steps. We had
nearly got home, and he hoped his right hon. friend would
lend them his assistance to enable them to reach it in safety.
He would venture to state that in a very few weeks all alarm
would be forgotten, and at the end of the year, we should all
be surprised to reflect that any alarm had ever prevailed at a
prospect of a variation of 3 per cent in the value of the circulating medium. His own general opinion was, that an unfavourable state of exchange must always proceed from a
redundant currency. If corn were imported and paid for in
bullion it was a proof that bullion was the cheapest commodity. Suppose all the Bank-notes now in circulation to be
withdrawn, and their place filled by gold coin, would not
gold become infinitely cheaper? If our paper had been of
any intrinsic value, it would, having become cheap from
excess, have been exported also. He thought it right here to
pay the tribute of his approbation to the late excellent regulations of the Mint.[1] He entirely approved of making gold the
standard, and of keeping silver as a token currency. It
appeared to him to be a solid improvement in the system of
our coinage. Nothing could be clearer than that government
had the power, by limiting the quantity, to regulate the value
of the silver; it was on that principle that the committee and
all other persons recommended the reduction of paper
currency. The hon. gentleman (Mr. J. P. Grant) indeed had
observed, that the silver coin might be imitated abroad; supposing this to be the fact, the value of the silver coin might
be lessened, but that of the gold would not therefore be

[1] The Proclamations of Feb. 1817 for any amount and silver coin
which made gold coin legal tender only up to forty shillings.

raised. The silver was not a legal tender above 40*s.*, and gold might always be demanded. It was true that 105*l.* might be offered in silver instead of 100*l.* in gold; but this could have no effect in altering the relation between gold and all other commodities. He should be happy to argue this question with the hon. member or with the noble "Old Merchant,"[1] [a laugh!] on some occasion when it would be less irrelevant to the subject under consideration.—The hon. member sat down amidst loud and general cheering from all sides of the House.[2]

Mr. Alderman HEYGATE then addressed the chair, but the impatience of the House produced a temporary confusion, in the midst of which, after one or two observations, the worthy alderman sat down.

Lord CASTLEREAGH then suggested that the debate be adjourned till the following day and the House rose at two o'clock.

---

[1] Lord Lauderdale, who had published a few days before as a pamphlet *Three Letters on the Causes of the Present State of the Exchanges, and Price of Gold Bullion*, as printed in '*The Times*' under the signature of '*An Old Merchant*', with an Introductory Address by the Earl of Lauderdale, London, Budd and Calkin, 1819.

[2] Mallet, who was present at this debate, writes in his diary: 'The phenomena of that night was Ricardo; who notwithstanding his slender footing in the House, his jewish name and his shrill voice, obtained the greatest attention, and was cheered throughout his speech: which altho' very good and containing much sound argument yet had chiefly the character of broken and detached observations on the preceding speeches; with several traits of pleasantry, which were all successful.—A few days afterwards, the Duke of Wellington having met Ricardo at a large party at Lady Lansdowne's, came up to him, congratulated him on his speech, and on the success of the measure, and remained in conversation with him for 20 minutes.' (J. L. Mallet's MS Diary, entry headed 'Session 1819'.)

25 *May* 1819

　　Mr. PEARSE (a Bank director) 'denied the assertion of an hon. gentleman opposite, that they were not competent to the conduct of their own affairs'; and also denied 'most solemnly' the assertion which had been made 'that the Bank Directors had no serious wish to return to cash payments.'

Mr. RICARDO, in explanation, denied his having said that the Bank were insincere in their declarations. He meant no personal hostility to them as individuals, or as a public body; but he was of opinion, that they had taken wrong steps, and that they did not understand the subject of the currency.

On 26 May the resolutions were agreed to; and a bill or bills were ordered to be brought in by Mr. Peel and the Chancellor of the Exchequer.

EXCHEQUER BILLS

2 *June* 1819

　　On the CHANCELLOR OF THE EXCHEQUER's motion for a grant to pay off certain Exchequer Bills, Mr. GRENFELL suggested that 'as government were now on the eve of raising a large sum of money by loan', the sinking fund should be taken in diminution of the loan. 'This led him to another observation. A rumour was very prevalent to day, which he conceived was nothing but a calumny on the right hon. gentleman, and should continue so to conceive it, unless he had the right hon. gentleman's own authority for believing it. It was a rumour, however, which every body had heard, namely, that the right hon. gentleman had communicated to certain loan-contractors, and to them alone, the amount of the loan which it was his intention to negociate. It must be perfectly unnecessary for him to observe, that if this rumour was true, the right hon. gentleman had given to those persons an undue advantage. It was most unquestionably the right hon. gentleman's duty, when he made such a communication, to make it to the stock exchange, to the public—to make it general.'

The CHANCELLOR OF THE EXCHEQUER replied that 'in the conversations which he had held with a number of persons on the

nature of the financial measures which it might be most expedient
to adopt, he had of course spoken on a great many points connected with those measures; but he denied having made any
secret or private communication of his intentions, of which any
unfair advantage could be taken.'

Mr. RICARDO had heard a statement which set forth,
whether correctly or not he could not say, all the particulars
of the intended loan, the sum to be borrowed, and the days
on which the several payments were to be made. These he
understood had been made known to others by the chancellor
of the exchequer, but not to him or to any one with whom he
was connected.[1] The usual course had been for the chancellor
of the exchequer to give notice to the parties likely to subscribe to the loan, that on such a day he would expect them,
and then when they attended him, to unfold his plan to them.
To communicate his intentions to one party alone, was to
give that party a great and manifest advantage over all the
others. Whether such a communication had been made he
did not know; but the rumour was so general, that he could
not doubt the fact of some communication from the right
hon. gentleman having been made.

The CHANCELLOR OF THE EXCHEQUER again denied that he
had made any other communications except such 'as he should be
very happy to make to the hon. gentleman who had just spoken,
and to receive his advice with respect to them.'

---

[1] Ricardo was preparing to make a bid for the loan.

THE BUDGET

9 *June* 1819

The CHANCELLOR OF THE EXCHEQUER introduced the Budget and announced that a loan of 12 millions had been contracted that morning by competition on very advantageous terms and that, besides, 12 millions would be borrowed from the sinking fund for the service of the year; he also proposed that 3 millions should be raised by additional duties on malt, tobacco, tea, etc., and applied to meet the charges of the new loans. Mr. GRENFELL, who opened the debate for the opposition, devoted most of his speech to an attack upon the Bank. Mr. MELLISH (a Bank director) replied defending the Bank and concluded: 'The hon. member for Portarlington (Mr. Ricardo), found fault with the Bank directors for not having attended sufficiently to the interests of the proprietors; the hon. member for Marlow (Mr. Grenfell), on the contrary, said, that the Bank had too many bonusses, and that the public ought to share in the profits. How were the directors to act so as to meet the wishes of both gentlemen?'

Mr. RICARDO said, he had already opposed the grant of 3 millions towards a sinking fund, because he did not wish to place such a fund at the mercy of ministers, who would take it whenever they thought that urgent necessity required it. He did not mean to say that it would be better with one set of ministers than another; for he looked upon it that all ministers would be anxious, on cases of what they conceived emergency, to appropriate it to the public use. He thought the whole thing a delusion upon the public, and on that account he would never support a tax to maintain it. He would admit that some means should be resorted to for liquidating the public debt, and in this he agreed with the hon. member for Leicester[1] that a great sacrifice should be made; but he could not go with him in thinking, that that ought to be a property tax. That would be attended with the

---

[1] Mr. Mansfield.

same bad effects as the other plan. He would, however, be satisfied to make a sacrifice; the sacrifice would be a temporary one, and with that view he would be willing to give up as large a share of his property as any other individual.[1] [Hear.] By such means ought the evil of the national debt to be met. It was an evil which almost any sacrifice would not be too great to get rid of. It destroyed the equilibrium of prices, occasioned many persons to emigrate to other countries, in order to avoid the burthen of taxation which it entailed, and hung like a mill-stone round the exertion and industry of the country. He therefore never would give a vote in support of any tax which went to continue a sinking fund; for if that fund were to amount to 8 millions, ministers would on any emergency give the same account of it as they did at present. The delusion of it had been seen long ago by all those who were acquainted with the subject; and it would have been but fair and sound policy to have exposed it. On the subject of the loan he had nothing to object. He gave credit to and thanked the chancellor of the exchequer, for his good management within the last two or three days. [a laugh]. It was, he conceived creditable to him to have effected the loan on such good terms, when it was considered that only a few days back the funds were at 65.[2] But though he gave credit to the right hon. gentleman for his plan in one respect, it was but fair to his hon. friend (Mr. Grenfell) near him, to say that this was the advice which he

---

[1] This is Ricardo's first allusion in Parliament to his plan for a tax on capital; cp. below, p. 34.

[2] On 4 June, when it was announced that only 12 millions were to be borrowed from the public, Consols rose from 66 to 70. The loan was taken by Rothschild on 9 June on terms which involved the unusually low bonus of less than $1\frac{1}{4}$ per cent for the contractor. This was generally regarded as too low (Ricardo's bid, which was the next highest, would have involved a bonus of over $2\frac{1}{2}$ per cent), and on the same day the new Omnium fell to $1\frac{1}{2}$ per cent discount.

had given long ago.[1] An hon. Bank director had said that he (Mr. R.) was inconsistent with his hon. friend. He was not bound to agree in every opinion which his hon. friend might hold; but he did not think he was so inconsistent as was said. He would admit, that he had complained of the Bank not having divided their profits. The Bank had made profits no doubt. It was the duty of the directors to do the best for the proprietors; and it was also the duty of government to make as good a bargain for the country as they could. He could not approve of the Bank making presents to government,[2] though he could not blame those to whom they were given, for making the most of their contracts with them.[3]

After further debate,

Mr. RICARDO wished to ask, whether it was to be understood that in the next year, as there would be 11 millions to be raised for the service of the year, and five millions to be paid to the Bank, there would be taken, as in the present year, 12 millions from the sinking fund, leaving the rest to be raised by way of loan?

The CHANCELLOR OF THE EXCHEQUER declined to pledge himself.

---

[1] See *Substance of a Speech addressed to the House of Commons, on the 28th April, 1814, by Pascoe Grenfell, Esq. on the subject of applying The Sinking Fund towards Any Loans Raised for the Public Service*, London, Bagster, 1817.

[2] Should be 'government making presents to the Bank'. Cp. next footnote.

[3] *The Times* reports in addition: 'It was therefore not inconsistent in him to wish that the Bank should share with the proprietors the profits they had made, and to say that the government might have made better bargains with them.'

BANK ADVANCES BILL

16 June 1819

Mr. PEEL moved for leave to bring in a bill to prohibit the Bank of England from making any advances to government unless distinctly authorised by parliament.

Mr. RICARDO thought the Bank ought not to be in any way shackled in the management of their own affairs. Great inconveniencies, in the diminution of the circulating medium, might result from establishing too strict a limit on this subject.[1]

The CHANCELLOR OF THE EXCHEQUER said, 'it was not his opinion that any diminution of the circulating medium was necessary, nor did he believe that any such would take place.'
Leave was then given. On 25 June the bill was passed.

EXCISE DUTIES BILL

18 June 1819

The CHANCELLOR OF THE EXCHEQUER moved that the House should go into a committee on this bill [to raise three millions to be applied to the sinking fund by new taxes on malt, tobacco, tea, etc.; cp. above, p. 20]. The Marquis of TAVISTOCK moved as an amendment, that consideration be postponed six months: it was shameful, he said, that the House of Commons, having relieved their own pockets by repealing the property tax, should now proceed to tax the poor; the only remedy for such practices was a reform of Parliament. The CHANCELLOR OF THE EXCHEQUER 'denied that the new taxes would fall exclusively on the lower classes.' Mr. GRENFELL supported the amendment, 'not because

---

[1] *The Times* reports in addition: 'With respect to Exchequer bills it appeared that the Bank was to be prohibited from purchasing them in the market. (*no, no, from the Chancellor of the Exchequer.*) If he misunderstood that part of the measure, he should be glad to be better informed.'

he thought the state of the representation corrupt, but because this was not, in his opinion, the proper moment to resort to a system of taxation.' After several other members had spoken,

Mr. RICARDO could not agree with the hon. gentleman (Mr. Lamb) that it was desirable to follow the precedent of 1784, at the conclusion of the American war, and to re-establish what he called a sinking fund. It appeared to him that that was the very period to which those who objected to the sinking fund would direct their attention in support of their arguments. What had become of that sinking fund? Had it realized the expectations which had been held out? Were we now less in debt in consequence of its establishment? No—the contrary was the fact; the sinking fund had been converted into facilities, which enabled the minister to contract new debt. It was true we had purchased with it 200 or 300 millions of stock in the market, but had we diminished the debt by those purchases? No, because we had, at the same time, borrowed a still larger sum to enable us to make the purchases. Because, in fact, the moment our expenditure exceeded our income we had a sinking fund in name only; and that part of the taxes which had been paid to the commissioners, and called a sinking fund for the extinction[1] of debt, had been absorbed in providing for a new debt. A sinking fund was only useful—was only what it pretended to be—when a surplus of income was strictly applied to the purposes for which it was established—the extinction of debt. No appropriation of money under the name of sinking fund ever had, and, in his opinion, ever would be constantly applied to this purpose; it would always be considered by ministers as a resource of which they might avail themselves when they were under any difficulty, in raising money by new taxes. In this way had they got rid of the last sinking

---

[1] Misprinted 'estimation' in *Hansard*.

fund, and the same fate would await that which they now seemed solicitous to establish. The language of the noble lord (Castlereagh)[1] confirmed him in his opinion of the use which would eventually be made of it; for he had told it to the House; he had told them that, by creating a sinking fund we should show other countries, we would not suffer ourselves to be insulted. If the sinking fund were applied to frighten other nations by being applied to the purposes of war, it could not be applied to the payment of debt, if money was to be raised to provide for the interest of money hereafter to be borrowed for a new war, there was no utility in making the people pay taxes now, to furnish the means of a war hereafter. It would be much better to let the money remain in their pockets, where it would not fail to accumulate, and not to impose new taxes until new necessities required them. He had a jealous distrust of raising money beyond immediate necessity, and placing it in the hands of ministers; not the present ministers only, but any ministers responsible to a House of Commons constituted like ours. He allowed that so long as we had, in time of war, a sum under the name of sinking fund which would exceed the peace expenditure, we had what would be a real sinking fund when the peace came. So long, for instance, as we had 10 millions called a sinking fund in time of war, while we borrowed near 20 millions merely for the temporary purpose of carrying on the war, we might in a restricted sense be said to have a sinking fund of 10 millions; for on the return of peace it would, if so applied, operate to the reduction of debt. But this was not the case in the last war; the amount of the sinking fund, instead of being really applied to the reduction of debt, had been applied to pay the interest of new debt. And, after all, the meaning was only this; that if when peace

[1] In his speech on 7 June 1819 (*Hansard*, XL, 944–5).

returned we could reduce our expenditure 10 millions annually below our income, we should be able annually to discharge 10 millions of debt; this surely might be done without the mysterious jargon about a fund which answered no purpose but that of delusion. As to the particular taxes, it was unnecessary for him to state his sentiments, seeing he was an enemy to taxation altogether. He could not, however, agree, that they fell on the labourer, because imposed on the objects he consumed. If, indeed, they were imposed on the luxuries of the labourer, they might in some measure diminish his comforts; but the more the articles taxed approached the nature of necessaries, the more completely would they fall on those who employed labourers. It had been said, that these taxes would fall upon the poor-rates; but that amounted to the same thing; for the poor-rates formed, in reality, a fund destined to support labour, however inconvenient it might be to pay it in that way. He perfectly concurred with the noble lord who moved the amendment, in his expressions as to the state of the representation in that House: he could not help expressing his opinion, that the people were not sufficiently represented in it. This might be some satisfaction to the hon. member for Middlesex (Mr. Mellish), who appeared to be pleased the other evening[1] when he discovered a difference of opinion between him and his hon. friend (Mr. Grenfell), as the opinion which his hon. friend was fond of declaring on the subject of parliamentary reform, was diametrically opposite to that which he (Mr. R.) had immediately expressed.

The House having gone into the committee, Mr. Lyttelton objected to the tax on malt, 'that it was imposed on the only remaining luxury, if indeed it was not a necessary, of the poorer classes of this country. He then, adverting to the argument

---

[1] See above, p. 20.

which had fallen from one of the highest authority on questions of political economy in this kingdom (Mr. Ricardo), namely, that a tax upon the necessaries of life did not fall heaviest on the poor; observed, that although he might be disposed to admit the truth of that principle, yet in this case, as being upon an article, the very last, as it might be said, before those necessaries, the duty did fall heaviest upon that class.'

Mr. RICARDO explained. He said, that he hoped the House and his hon. friend would understand that he was not contending that the taxing of necessaries was not injurious to labourers, but that it was no more injurious to them than any other mode of taxation. In fact, all taxation had a tendency to injure the labouring classes, because it either diminished the fund employed in the maintenance of labour, or checked its accumulation. In the argument which he had used, he had supposed that it was necessary to raise a certain sum by taxes, and then the question was whether by taxing necessaries, the burthen would be particularly borne by the labouring classes. He thought not—he was of opinion that they would ultimately fall on the employers of labour, and would be only prejudicial to the labourers in the same way as most other taxes would be, inasmuch as they would diminish the fund employed in the support of labour.

On 28 June the bill was passed.

[The session closed on 13 July 1819.]

SESSION 1819–1820

SEDITIOUS MEETINGS PREVENTION BILL

6 *December* 1819

Parliament was called together in order to consider a series of measures (the Six Acts) for counteracting and suppressing 'the seditious practices so long prevalent in the manufacturing districts of the country' (speech of the PRINCE REGENT on the opening of the session, 23 November 1819). Lord CASTLEREAGH introduced the first of these measures, the Seditious Meetings Prevention Bill, on 29 November. It was read a second time on 2 December (when Ricardo voted No, with the minority). On 6 December the bill was again considered.

Mr. RICARDO said, he was anxious very briefly to express his opinion on this subject. He thought that, in the course of this discussion, sufficient attention had not been given to the importance of the right to be curtailed. If the people's right of meeting and petitioning consisted only in the right of meeting to petition for the removal of grievances, it was not of so much importance, and the curtailment of it was not of such serious interest. But the right was, a right of meeting in such numbers, and showing such a front to ministers as would afford a hope that bad measures would be abandoned, and that public opinion would be respected. It might be compared, in this view, with the right of that House to address the Crown. If the right of that House consisted in passing resolutions only, and if they could not follow up their resolutions by refusing the supplies, and by calling up a spirit of resistance in the country, the Crown could despise their interference. It was the same with the right of the people to petition. If they could not meet in such numbers as to make them be respected, their petitions would have no effect. At the same time, he admitted, that those meetings were attended with very great inconvenience. It could not be denied that circumstances might arise when the government should be fairly administered, and yet distress might arise from causes which the government could not control, and wicked and designing men might produce a great degree of mischief; it did not appear to him that such meetings were the sort of check which ought to exist in a well-administered government; but it was necessary to have some check, because if they left men to govern without any control in the people, the consequence would be despotism. The check which he would give, could be established only by a reform of parliament. Then, instead of petitioning, and from the worst part of the people perhaps, being the check, that House would become the best check which any government could have, and with that check the people would be perfectly satisfied. He had read with surprise the abhorrence of radical reform expressed by several members of that House. He believed there were among the advocates of that measure, designing and wicked men. But he also knew that there was a great number of very honest men who believed universal suffrage and annual parliaments were the only means of protecting the rights of the people, and establishing an adequate check upon government. He had the same object as they professed to have in view; but he thought that suffrage far from universal would effect that object, and form a sufficient check. He therefore thought it would be madness to attempt a reform to that extent, when a less extensive reform would be sufficient.

On 13 December the bill was read a third time and passed; in the division (for, 313; against, 95) Ricardo voted against the bill.

SIR W. DE CRESPIGNY'S MOTION
RESPECTING MR. OWEN'S PLAN[1]

16 *December* 1819

16 Dec. 1819   Sir W. DE CRESPIGNY moved that a select committee be appointed to inquire into the plan of Robert Owen, Esq. for ameliorating the condition of the lower classes. The CHANCELLOR OF THE EXCHEQUER, opposing the motion, read an extract from Mr. Owen's speech of 21 Aug. 1817[2] and declared that, 'as an official individual, he could not agree to a grant of the public money for the establishment of a plan that had been introduced to the public by a speech, in which all religions were pronounced false, and all systems of government bad.' Mr. BROUGHAM supported the motion, although he rejected the principle upon which the plan was founded, 'that of the increase of population being a benefit to the country.'

Mr. RICARDO observed, that he was completely at war with the system of Mr. Owen, which was built upon a theory inconsistent with the principles of political economy, and in his opinion was calculated to produce infinite mischief to the community. Something had fallen from an hon. member on a former night, on the subject of the employment of machinery.[3] It could not be denied, on the whole view of the subject, that machinery did not lessen the demand for labour; while, on the other hand, it did not consume the produce of the soil, nor employ any of our manufacturers[4]. It might also be mis-applied by occasioning the production of too much cotton, or too much cloth; but the moment those articles ceased in consequence to pay the manufacturer, he

---

[1] Cp. Ricardo's speech on Owen's plan, at a meeting held in the Freemasons' Hall on 26 June 1819, below, p. 467.
[2] See below, VII, 177, n. 2.
[3] On 9 December, in a debate on the State of the Manufacturing Districts, Mr. John Smith 'alluded to the rapid inroad which machinery had made upon manual labour within only a few years. He did not mean to contend that this was not a great improvement upon the old system, but it was an undoubted fact that it had thrown a great many hands out of employment.'
[4] Misprinted 'manufactures' in *Hansard*.

would devote his time and capital to some other purpose.[1]
Mr. Owen's plan proceeded upon this—he who was such an
enemy to machinery, only proposed machinery of a different
kind: he would bring into operation a most active portion of
machinery, namely, human arms. He would dispense with
ploughs and horses in the increase of the productions of the
country, although the expense as to them must be much less
when compared with the support of men. He confessed he
did not agree in the general principles of the plan under consideration, but he was disposed to accede to the proposition
of a committee. Spade husbandry Mr. Owen recommended
as more beneficial to production. He was not informed
enough on the interests of agriculture to give an opinion, but
that was a reason for sending the subject to a committee. For
what did the country want at the present moment? A demand for labour. If the facts stated of spade husbandry were
true, it was a beneficial course, as affording that demand. And
though government or the legislature would not be wisely
employed in engaging in any commercial experiment, it
would be advantageous that it should, under present circumstances, circulate useful information and correct prejudices.
They should separate such considerations from a division
of the country into parallelograms, or the establishment
of a community of goods, and similar visionary schemes.[2]

---

[1] The last two sentences are reported in the *British Press* as follows: 'He never could think that
machinery could do mischief to
any country, either in its immediate or its permanent effect.
Machinery, indeed, in one way
might be carried too far, that is,
where it is employed in the manufacture of a particular commodity, as for instance, in the
manufacture of cotton, but where
the individual extended it too far
it would not repay him, and he
would be soon obliged to reduce it, or employ it in another
channel.'

[2] *The Times* reports in addition:
'He was for ascertaining the fact;
and as soon as the farmer knew
that it was his interest to pursue
a different system, he would
adopt it as a matter of course.'

Before he sat down, he trusted the House would excuse his offering a few observations on what he considered the cause of the distresses of the country. He fully concurred in what had fallen from his hon. and learned friend[1] on the subject of population. The proportion of the capital to population regulated the amount of wages, and, to augment them, it was important to increase the capital of the country. But when he heard honourable members talk of employing capital in the formation of roads and canals, they appeared to overlook the fact, that the capital thus employed must be withdrawn from some other quarter. The causes of the insufficiency of capital, and the consequent disproportion between wages and population, were to be attributed to many circumstances, for some of which government were not to blame. Supposing a country with a numerous population, large capital, and a limited soil, the profits of that capital will be smaller there, than in a country populous, with lesser portion of capital, and with a great extent of soil. This country was one of large capital, but of increasing population and of an extent of soil necessarily limited; of course profits would be lower in it than in countries which had not the same limitation: still, though the profits were smaller, the capital continued in this kingdom, not only because persons felt a solicitude to keep their property under their own eye, but because the same confidence was not reposed in the security of others: the moment, however, other kingdoms, by their laws and institutions, inspired greater confidence, the capitalist would be induced to remove his property from Great Britain to a situation where his profits would be more considerable: this arose from no fault in the government; but the effect of it was to produce a deficiency of employment and consequent distress. Then came the question, had we

[1] Mr. Brougham.

taken the proper steps to prevent the profits upon capital
from being lower here than in other countries? On the contrary had we not done everything to augment and aggravate
the evil? Had we not added to the natural artificial causes for
the abduction of capital? We had passed corn laws, that
made the price of that necessary of life, grain, higher than in
other and neighbouring countries, and thus interfered with
the article which was considered the chief regulator of wages.
Where grain was dear, wages must be high, and the effect of
high wages was necessarily to make the profits on capital
low. A second cause arose out of the fetters upon trade, the
prohibitions against the import of foreign commodities,
when, in fact, better and cheaper than our own. This was
done in a spirit of retaliation; but he contended, that whatever line of policy other nations pursued, the interest of this
nation was different: wherever we could obtain the articles
we wanted at the cheapest rate, there we ought to go for
them; and wherever they were cheapest, the manufacture
would be the most extensive, and the amount of it[1], and invitation to capital, the greatest. Another cause of the existing
disposition to send capital out of the country was to be found
in the national debt. Instead of paying our expences from
year to year, Great Britain had constantly pursued a system
of borrowing, and taxes were accumulated not only to pay
the simple interest, but sometimes even the compound interest of the debt; and the amount was now so enormous,
that it became a matter of calculation, whether it was worth
a capitalist's while to continue in a country where he not
only obtained small profits, but where he was subjected to a
great additional burthen. Every pecuniary motive impelled
him rather to quit than to remain. For a great many of the
various causes of the evil, some of the principal of which he

---

[1] 'of it' is possibly a misprint for 'of profit'.

had touched upon, there might not exist any immediate remedy. We had, however, a beneficial precedent in the proceedings of the last session. He alluded to the measures taken for a return to payments in specie; and he saw no inconvenience in keeping stedfastly to that system. Parliament had wisely extended the operations of that system over a number of years. They should follow the same course as to the corn laws. After the quantity of capital employed under the faith of legislative enactments in agriculture, it would be a great injustice to proceed to an immediate repeal of those laws. But that House should look to the ultimate good, and give notice, that after a certain number of years, such an injurious system of legislation must terminate. The same observation applied to our prohibitory commercial code. From the variety of interests now in operation under that system, it would not only be necessary to look, but to look stedfastly, to a distant but certain period for its repeal. With respect to the national debt, he felt that he entertained opinions on that point which by many would be considered extravagant. He was one of those who thought that it could be paid off, and that the country was at this moment perfectly competent to pay it off. He did not mean that it should be redeemed at par; the public creditor possessed no such claim—were he paid at the market price, the public faith would be fulfilled. If every man would pay his part of the debt, it could be effected by the sacrifice of so much capital—[1] With respect to the objection, that the effect of that sacrifice would be to bring so much land into the market, that purchasers could not be found for such a glut, the answer was, that the stockholder would be eager to employ his money, as

---

[1] For the first allusion to this plan see above, p. 21; and on its hostile reception by 'the most opposite parties' see Ricardo's letter to Trower, 28 Dec. 1819, below, VIII, 147.

he received it, either in the purchase of land, or in loans to the farmer or landowner, by which the latter might be enabled to become the purchaser, particularly when the government was no longer in the market as a borrower. He was persuaded that the difficulty of paying off the national debt was not so great as was generally imagined; and he was also convinced that the country had not yet nearly reached the limits of its prosperity and greatness. It was only by a comparative reference to the state of other countries that the opposite opinion could be entertained, and such opinion would gain ground as long as so many unnatural temptations, by our policy at home, were held out to withdraw capital from the country. He repeated his conviction that Mr. Owen's plan was in many parts visionary, but yet he would not oppose the appointment of a committee, if it were only for the purpose of seeing whether it was probable that the advantages which that gentleman expected from the use of spade husbandry could be realized.

The House divided: Ayes, 16; Noes, 141. Ricardo voted for the motion.

MOTION FOR PAPERS RESPECTING THE BANK OF ENGLAND AND EXCHEQUER BILLS

22 *December* 1819

Mr. MABERLY moved for 'an account, showing how the sum of five millions voted for the purpose of paying off debt owing to the Bank of England on the 5th July 1819 had been applied.' The CHANCELLOR OF THE EXCHEQUER opposed the motion.

Mr. RICARDO said, it appeared to him that the House would act very unwisely by interfering as to the arrangements entered into by government for the repayment of the

5,000,000*l.* of advances to the Bank. At the same time he was at a loss to conceive what danger could arise from giving any information upon the subject. It had been objected, that the production of that information would lead to extensive stock-jobbing. He thought it would have just the contrary effect; for stock-jobbing was always best assisted by secrecy —by the circumstance of some individuals possessing certain information, which the other parties, with whom they transacted their bargains, were ignorant of. Now, supposing the statement required were made known, no jobbing could take place; because every one would then know all that had occurred, as to the repayments. With regard to what had fallen from the chancellor of the exchequer, that the state of the exchanges afforded a means of knowing what capital was going out of the country, he thought very differently. Supposing he wished to invest a sum of 50,000*l.* in France, or any other country; might he not order his correspondent to invest the produce of the goods he had sent out (50,000*l.* for instance) in the public funds, or in other goods, or in lands? No alteration could take place in the exchanges, unless there was a bill negociated. The official accounts annually laid before the House, relative to our exports and imports, were such, that it was impossible to draw any correct or practical inference from them. He remembered to have heard it stated, that at the time of the union with Ireland, each of the two countries gave a relative and comparative statement of her exports and imports; when Ireland made out that she had exported the larger quantity of commodities to England, and England appeared to have exported the larger quantity to Ireland. No correct information, therefore, could be derived from such returns. He should vote for the motion of his hon. friend.

The motion was negatived.

PETITION OF THE MERCHANTS OF LONDON RESPECTING COMMERCIAL DISTRESS

24 *December* 1819

Mr. IRVING presented a petition from the merchants and traders of London for an inquiry into the causes of the commercial distress. Mr. GRENFELL and Mr. J. SMITH spoke next.

Mr. RICARDO was happy to hear it stated by all the hon. gentlemen who had spoken, that the laws enacted last year[1] concerning the currency of the country, ought not to be disturbed. The country was, unquestionably, in a state of great distress, but he differed in opinion from his hon. friend who presented the petition as to the cause of that distress. His hon. friend thought that this country was in a state of forced currency, and that the evils both at home and abroad arose from the regulations which that House had made relative to the currency. That cause, however, he was convinced, was totally inadequate to produce such an effect, and therefore the evil must be traced to other sources. He might here remark, that his hon. friend had brought an unexpected accusation against him, namely, that he had proposed a plan for the payment of the public debt[2], but that he had not the merit of originality.[3] Now, he did not think that he had ever claimed that merit, for he was aware that many persons before his time had taken a similar view of the subject, and he

---

[1] Peel's Bill, adopted in the previous session.

[2] *Hansard* (following *The Times*) reports 'plan for the regulation of the currency'; what seems to be the correct version is adopted above from the *Morning Chronicle*.

[3] Mr. Irving had said that he could not agree with Ricardo's 'proposed plan for paying off the national debt. There was, he conceived, nothing new in this plan; and if the archives of the Exchequer were searched, similar plans might be found which had been offered very many times within the last 100 years' (*The Times's* report).

hoped that whatever might be the merit of the application which he had made of principles known to others, he had stated his opinions with becoming modesty. He conceived that the distress was chiefly to be ascribed to the inadequacy of the capital of the nation to carry on the operations of trade, manufacture, and commerce. But why was the capital more inadequate now than formerly? If the profits on capital were higher, and labour more productive in other countries, it could not be doubted that capital would be transferred to those countries: no proposition in Euclid was clearer than this. Now, he thought they had greatly aggravated this evil by bad legislation, and he had formerly mentioned instances.[1] He had referred to the corn-laws as one example; and however unpopular the doctrine might be with some gentlemen, he would state his opinion freely, that he believed the corn-laws to have materially increased the evil. These laws had tended to raise the price of sustenance, and that had raised the price of labour, which of course diminished the profit on capital. But of all this evil, the national debt, and the consequent amount of taxation, was the great cause. Hence the main object of the legislature should be to provide for the payment of that debt, and that provision should commence its operation as soon as possible. For as this debt was chargeable upon all the capital of the country, it was obvious that any capital which went out of the country was exonerated from that charge, while the capital which remained was of course compelled to pay a greater proportion of debt and taxes. To guard against this evil, which was productive at once of individual injustice and national injury, the whole capital of the country ought to be assessed for the discharge of the public debt, so that no more capital should be allowed to go out of the country without paying its fair proportion of

[1] Above, p. 33.

that debt. The execution of this plan might be attended with difficulty, but then the importance of the object was worthy of an experiment to overcome every possible difficulty. The whole of the plan through which he proposed the payment of the public debt, might in his view be carried into effect within four or five years. For the discharge of the public debt, he proposed that checks should be issued upon the government to each purchaser, which checks should be kept distinct from the ordinary circulating medium of the country, but should be received by the government in payment of taxes. Thus the debt might be gradually liquidated while the government continued gradually receiving the assessments upon capital to provide for that liquidation. He would not, however, dwell farther upon this chimerical project, as he understood it was considered by every one except himself, but proceed to the consideration of the petition. His hon. friend proposed, as particularly worthy of attention, that a committee of that House should inquire into certain restrictions upon commerce, with a view to their removal. But his hon. friend should reflect, that no immediate effect could be reasonably expected from the labour of such a committee for such a purpose, as the restrictions alluded to, however burthensome, could not be suddenly removed. This removal must, indeed, take place by slow degrees, entwined as they were with the general system of the trade of the country. But still great good might be expected from the investigations of such a committee, who would, he hoped, enter particularly into the consideration of the corn laws. His hon. friend had suggested that a certain modification should take place in the arrangements made towards the removal of the restrictions upon the Bank, namely, that the Bank should not be called upon to pay in bullion until the period arrived for such payment at the lowest rate. Now he, on the contrary, thought that it would be much more for the advantage of the Bank itself, to make the payments in the order already settled; because such payments being made gradually would serve to break the fall, and prepare the Bank for the complete resumption of metallic payments. The only modification, indeed, which he deemed desirable on this subject was, that the Bank should be called upon permanently to pay its notes in bullion, instead of coin; for he could not conceive the policy of incurring the expense of coining gold merely for the purpose of the currency, which could be answered as well, if not more conveniently, by paper. The only object to be provided for in this case was, that the real value of the paper should be equal to its denominative value, according to a settled and universal standard of value, or according to its nominal amount in coin.[1] His hon. friend had recommended the establishment of two standards of value, namely, silver and gold; but this was a project, in his opinion, peculiarly objectionable, because, if there were two standards, there would be greater chance of variation, and the establishment of the least variable standard of value was the object to be desired, with a view to maintain the character of our currency.

Mr. BROUGHAM agreed with Ricardo on several points: 'There was however one point on which he had wished so great an oracle,[2] as he must ever consider him on such subjects, had not pronounced the decided opinion he had. He alluded to the possibility, or, if possible, the adviseableness of paying off the national debt. The proposition was not a new one—it had years ago been suggested by Mr. Hutcheson, indeed, he believed

---

[1] The *Morning Chronicle* reports in addition: 'Care being taken to make this provision, he could see no reason why that arrangement as to payments in bullion, which was now settled for only three years, should not be rendered permanent.'

[2] This phrase was taken up by Cobbett, who thereafter always dubbed Ricardo 'the Oracle'. In the *Register* of 20 May 1820 he writes: 'This gentleman was, last session, called an ORACLE by Mr. Brougham, and, by Mr. Wilberforce, he was described as

every chancellor of the exchequer had a similar proposition made
to him every year. It had in more recent times been brought
before the public by Dr. Watson, bishop of Landaff.[1]... The
effect of such a measure would be to place the property for five
years at the mercy of all the solicitors, conveyancers, and money-
hunters, in the country.'

[Parliament was adjourned on 29 Dec. 1819 and, following the
death of George III, it was dissolved on 28 Feb. 1820.]

a political economist, worthy of the *esteem and admiration* of his contemporaries.' After a long quotation from the above speech he goes on: 'That great ass, Perry, observed, the other day, that, the Inquisition being at an end in Spain, *science* would take a spread in the country; for that a Spaniard might now have "*a Blackstone* or a RICARDO in his library!" A *Ricardo,* indeed!... But this Perry is, at once, the most conceited coxcomb and the greatest fool in this whole kingdom... "*A Ricardo!*" The empty, pompous fool, when it has taken but a few months to shew that "*a Ricardo*" is a heap of senseless, Change-Alley jargon, put upon paper and bound up into book; that the measure, founded upon it, must be abandoned, or will cause millions to be starved, and that it has since been proposed, even by the author himself to supplant it by a plan for paying off the Debt! "*A Ricardo,*" indeed!' (*Cobbett's Weekly Political Register,* 20 May 1820, pp. 700 and 708.)

[1] See *A Proposal for Payment of the Publick Debts* (1714) in *A Collection of Treatises relating to the National Debts and Funds,* by Archibald Hutcheson, London, 1721; and *An Address to the People of Great Britain,* by Richard Watson, London, 1798.

SESSION 1820

The new Parliament assembled on 21 April 1820; the King's speech was delivered on 27 April.

COMMERCIAL RESTRICTIONS—PETITION OF THE MERCHANTS OF LONDON[1]

8 *May* 1820

Mr. BARING presented a petition from the merchants of London, the object of which, he said, 'was a renewal, under certain limitations, of the freedom of trade by the abolition of all injurious restrictions.' It was not his intention to recommend any immediate disturbance of the corn laws. But some alterations were possible at once, including the removal of the duty on the importation of wool, of the restrictions on the importation of timber, and of all prohibitions; the throwing open of the trade in the Indian seas and the repeal of the Navigation laws. Mr. ROBINSON (President of the Board of Trade) said, 'that the restrictive system of commerce in this country was founded in error, and calculated to defeat the object for which it was adopted'; yet it was 'impossible all at once to alter our commercial system'. Lord MILTON concurred in all the principles of the petition. The restrictive system was one of the causes of the distress; another cause was the change lately effected in the currency. This change was necessary, but hon. members had not fully anticipated the embarrassments it would occasion. 'He believed even his hon. friend near him (Mr. Ricardo) had formed too low an estimate of the pressure which a change in our currency would create.'

---

[1] This is the famous Merchants' Petition for Free Trade. It was drawn up by Thomas Tooke, who gives an account of its origin and presentation, as well as its text in full, in Tooke and Newmarch's *History of Prices*, vol. VI, 1857, pp. 331–344 (cp. an anonymous pamphlet attributed to Tooke: *Free Trade—Some Account of the Free Trade Movement as it originated with the Petition of the Merchants of London presented to the House of Commons on 8 May 1820*, London, privately printed, 1853).

Mr. RICARDO begged the noble lord to recollect, that at the time when he spoke on the bullion question last session the price of gold was at 4*l.* 3*s.* per oz. and that now it was at 3*l.* 17*s.* 10½*d.;* there could not, therefore, be such a pressure arising from this measure as the noble lord had described. At the time when that discussion took place,[1] he certainly would rather have been inclined to have altered the standard than to have recurred to the old standard. But while the committee was sitting, a reduction took place in the price of gold, which fell to 4*l.* 2*s.* and it then became a question whether we should sacrifice a great principle in establishing a new standard, or incur a small degree of embarrassment and difficulty in recurring to the old. With regard to the petition before the House, he had heard it with great pleasure; and he was particularly pleased with the liberal sentiments delivered by the right hon. gentleman opposite. It was to him a great source of satisfaction that sound as well as liberal principles were put forward by so important a body as the merchants of London; the only thing that astonished him was, that it was only now that these principles were put forward—that they should have taken so much time in their progress, since they were first promulgated by Adam Smith. However desirable the system now suggested, it could not be denied but that some difficulties lay in the way of its completion. The difficulties were of two kinds; the first difficulty resolved itself into a question of revenue. To increase the sources of revenue was doubtless the object of every wise government; and where taxes of a particular kind pressed heavily upon the people, it did not appear to him a very difficult thing to substitute other taxes. Another difficulty, and a greater, was, respecting the vested interests. Many persons vested

---

[1] This is no doubt misreported; it should read 'In the first instance,' as reported in *Cobbett's Parliamentary Register.*

their capital on the faith of the continuation of the restrictive system, and therefore, however injurious that system might be, nothing could be more unjust than, by the immediate abolition of that system, to occasion the absolute ruin of those who vested large capital on the faith of laws so long established as the restrictive laws. But from this no argument could be surely drawn to continue the system in future times. No argument appeared to him more mischievous— more calculated to promote commotion and rebellion, than this—that if they once did wrong they should never do right, but that they should go on in error and make every mischievous system perpetual. He thought the House ought now to do what was suggested by the bullion committee.[1] There were difficulties of a very formidable kind connected with the system embraced by the committee, at least with its immediate execution. And what was done on that occasion? Why, that which ought to be done on the present—to spread the return to cash payments over a great space of time. So now might they return, gradually return, to a better system of commercial regulation, allowing full time to those who had their property invested, to turn it into other channels. After they had done so, they might say to the capitalists, "The present system will continue only so long as you can accommodate yourselves without any sacrifice of your interests, to the new one which we propose." Some restrictions might thus be removed immediately, without any inconvenience; others might be gradually relaxed, and others might be left till our situation had so greatly improved as to render their removal no inconvenience. He was surprised that the right hon. gentleman[2] who had expressed such liberal principles of political economy, and had so freely declared himself against the policy of our commercial restrictions, had

[1] The Committee of 1819 on the Resumption of Cash Payments.

[2] Mr. Robinson.

yet made a reservation in favour of the corn laws. They were
necessary, he said, to protect the agricultural interests; and
he (Mr Ricardo) would admit the validity of the argument,
provided it could be made to appear that the agriculturists
suffered more burthens than other classes of the community.
But what were their peculiar burthens? They did not suffer
more from the malt-tax, or from the leather tax, or from any
other tax with which he was acquainted, than any other class
of men. These taxes were common to all, and all felt their
pressure alike. But the poor-rates, it was said, operated on
them as a peculiar burthen. Well; if the poor-rates were really
more oppressive to them than to other classes, and tended to
raise the price of grain, he would recommend a countervailing duty on the importation of foreign corn, to the amount of
the operation of that cause. He allowed that the poor-rates
actually raised the price of corn, because they fell upon the
land, and operated as a burthen solely upon agriculturists.
But if, while this burthen was felt by them, other classes of
the community felt equal burthens, they were put to no disadvantage, and ought to receive no protection. He was fully
prepared to admit, that the necessity for supporting the poor
constituted the only or the best apology for the corn-laws.
Tithes likewise were another burthen to the landed interest,
and tended, he would allow, to a certain extent, to raise the
price of grain, and for these he would have no objection to
allow a countervailing duty. There was this difference between poor-rates and tithes—that while we must support the
poor, whatever was the produce, the church could only claim
a tenth of what was raised; for, whatever was the deficiency
of produce, the clergy must conform to their proportion,
and find it sufficient for their support.

Mr. BARING said, 'that there was one point of importance on
which he had the misfortune totally to differ with his hon. friend
(Mr. Ricardo); on that point, as on every other, he would differ

with him with reluctance and with diffidence.' Mr. Baring conceived that on an average during the war as compared with the present time the difference in the currency was at least 25 per cent. 'All the difficulty of the country was in its having a large debt;' creditors had to be paid a higher value than had been received from them. 'To add facilities to the circulation he should probably propose, if events did not alter his opinion, in the first place to make perpetual the plan of his hon. friend for payment in metallic bars instead of coin, for which the country was infinitely indebted to his hon. friend, and in the next place to give the Bank the option of paying, either in gold or in silver, not in depreciated or debased coin, but in weight.'

Mr. RICARDO, in explanation, stated that he had never imagined that the currency had never been depreciated more than 4 per cent. He had merely contended, that at the time when the subject was taken up by parliament in the last year, there was only that depreciation; which was too small to warrant an alteration of the ancient standard. He was well aware that during some of the latter years of the war, the depreciation had been as great as 25 per cent.

The petition was ordered to lie on the table. A similar petition being presented from the chamber of commerce of Edinburgh,

Mr. RICARDO said, he would take that opportunity of making an observation as to the two standards of gold and silver. He fully agreed with his hon. friend,[1] that a payment in both would facilitate the payment of the public creditor; but then there was a question whether two standards would not be more liable to fluctuation than one invariable standard. If payment were made in one metal, it would be liable to less fluctuation than if made in two, and in two it would be less than if made in three; therefore he considered the payment in one metal as preferable, being liable to less fluctuation.

Mr. BARING replied, that he 'considered the difference in this respect as more theoretical than it would be found in practice.'

[1] Mr. Baring.

AGRICULTURAL DISTRESS

12 May 1820

Earl TEMPLE presented six petitions from Buckinghamshire for an inquiry into the depression of agriculture.

Mr. RICARDO was not disposed to refuse inquiry to the petitioners, though he thought, under the present state of the country, such a question ought not to be moved but under the soundest discretion. The labouring classes throughout the kingdom were reduced to the greatest distress. That was not the period, therefore, when measures should be taken to increase the price of corn. The agricultural interest had its depression, but still it was to be considered as one class, whose prosperity ought not to be forced at the sacrifice of the general good. There was not a more important question than that of the corn laws. Nothing, in his mind, was better calculated to afford general relief than the lowering of the price of corn. It was the first step to that great remedy, the making labour productive.

25 May 1820

Lord MILTON presented a petition from the agriculturists of Yorkshire praying for protection against foreign competition.

Mr. RICARDO said, that the object of the petitioners seemed to him to be nothing else than to get a monopoly of the English market. The consequence would be, that the price of corn would be raised, and laid generally on all the other classes. The idea which the petitioners had of protecting duties was a most erroneous one, and would, if acted upon, be destructive of all commerce. If they meant that the countervailing duties should be equal in amount to the difference between the price at which corn could be sold here and that at which it was sold in a foreign market, they went upon a most erroneous principle, and one which, he hoped, would never be introduced. Suppose corn sold here at 80*s.,* and that in Poland it could be procured for 40*s.* or 50*s.;* if, under such circumstances, it were intended to put on a countervailing duty of 30*s.,* there would be an end of all importation, and of every principle of commerce.[1] In that case, the importer would be at a certain loss by the amount of freight, and of course no one would import; the consequence would be, that the price of corn at home would be raised to an exorbitant height. Viewing the question in this light, he hoped that the motion for a committee, whenever it came before the House, would be negatived.

AGRICULTURAL DISTRESS

30 *May* 1820

Mr. HOLME SUMNER moved that the petitions upon the subject of agricultural distresses be referred to a select committee. He contended that the corn law of 1815 was inadequate and that new measures were required. Mr. ROBINSON (President of the Board of Trade) declared that he would oppose the motion unless the enquiries of the committee were confined to abuses which might exist in the execution of the law. Mr. BARING also opposed the motion.

---

[1] This passage is more plausibly reported in *Cobbett's Parliamentary Register:* 'The agriculturists seemed to have an extraordinary notion of a countervailing duty; they called for a duty which should amount to the difference of the cost at which foreigners and that at which we could grow corn. If such a principle were acted upon, all foreign commerce would be put an end to. If, for instance, corn could be grown at 50 shillings in Poland, and at 80 shillings here, they would demand a duty of 30 shillings' etc.

Mr. RICARDO[1] said, that there was one sentiment delivered
by an hon. gentleman in the early part of the debate, in which
he cordially concurred, namely, that in legislative enactments, the interest of one body of men ought not to be consulted at the expense of others, but that each should receive
corresponding consideration in proportion to its importance.
He (Mr. Ricardo) would wish to act up to this maxim, and,
because he consulted the interests of the whole community,
he would oppose the corn-laws. In many of the observations
which he intended to make he had been anticipated by his
hon. friend the member for Taunton.[2] The agriculturists had
contended that they had a right to be protected in a remunerating price for their produce, but they forget that no remunerating price could be fixed. It was in vain to talk of
fixing a remunerating price, which must necessarily change
with circumstances.[3] If by preventing importation the
farmer was compelled, for the national supply, to expend his
capital on poor or unprofitable soils, the remunerating price
at which he could keep this land in cultivation must be very
high, as compared with the price of grain in other countries,
where the soil was better, and less labour was required.
Open the ports, admit foreign grain, and you drive this land
out of cultivation; a less remunerating price would then do
for the more productive lands. You might thus have fifty
remunerating prices according as your capital was employed
on productive or unproductive lands. It became the legisla-

---

[1] This speech was 'in many respects imperfectly reported' by
the newspapers (Ricardo to M^c-
Culloch, below, VIII, 196). *Hansard's* report is mostly made up
of passages alternately taken from
The Times and the *Morning
Chronicle.*
[2] Mr. Baring.

[3] Although the context is taken
by *Hansard* from *The Times,*
this sentence is from the *Morning
Chronicle* which continues: 'They
might fix it at 70 if they pleased,
but the moment the ports were
opened, they would have the
remunerating price of other countries.'

ture, however, not to look at the partial losses which would be endured by a few, who could not cultivate their land profitably, at a diminished remunerative price, but to the general interests of the nation; and, connected with this, he would look to the profits of capital. In his opinion a re-munerating price might have been so fixed, that 50*s.* per quarter would have answered the purpose, but at all events he conceived that if the farmers in the country could raise a sufficient supply for the demand, 70*s.* might be considered as a protecting price.[1]—He would rather have a great quantity of produce at a low rate than a small quantity at a high. By making food cheap, the people would be enabled to purchase a greater quantity of it, and apply a part of their earnings to the purchase of luxuries. The high price of subsistence diminished the profits of capital in the following manner:— the price of manufactured articles—of a piece of cloth for instance—was made up of the wages of the manufacturer, the charges of management, and the interest of capital. The wages of the labourer were principally made up of what was necessary for subsistence; if grain was high, therefore, the price of labour, which might be before at 50 per cent on the manufactured article, might rise to 60, and being sold to the consumer at the same rate, the 10 per cent (difference) would necessarily be a deduction[2] from the profits of stock. If food was high here, and cheap abroad, stock would thus have a tendency to leave the country, and to settle where higher profits could be realized. The right hon. president of the board of trade appeared inconsistent when he denied a com-mittee to inquire into the more important question, and yet agreed to one for discussing such trifling matters as striking

---

[1] This sentence, obviously mis-reported, is taken by *Hansard* from *The New Times;* what pre-cedes and what follows is from *The Times.*

[2] Misprinted 'reduction' in *Hansard.*

the average. This was not what the petitioners wanted; they declared that they could grow as much as the home market required, and they demanded a monopoly of it. He would admit their statement to its full extent. He would even admit that our land was susceptible of a great increase of population, and that we could grow what would be sufficient to support that increase. But then, see what the inference of the petitioners was—they required that importation, therefore, should not be allowed. The answer to the whole of their system was plain. "You can grow those articles, it is true, but then we can get them cheaper from other countries." They could grow them, but was it expedient that they should under those circumstances? All general principles were against it. They might as well urge that as in France, they could grow beet-root for the purpose of producing sugar, as grow grain sufficient for home consumption merely because it could be done. The right hon. gentleman opposite[1] had ridiculed that absurd scheme of Buonaparte in the most pointed language, but all his ridicule applied equally to the growing of corn in this country when we could get it cheaper elsewhere. Another of their arguments was, that as ship-owners and merchants were protected by the navigation laws, and other enactments, so they ought to be protected by prohibitions in return. But he denied that these protections were of any use to the country. The navigation laws were of no use. Nay, he would allow them to take any trade they pleased, and surround it with protections; the measure might be beneficial to the particular trade, but it must be injurious to the rest of the country. There was no principle more clear than this. The argument of the agriculturist was, that the legislature having enabled the ship-owner and cotton manufacturer to injure the community, they should give him

[1] Mr. Robinson.

a privilege to do the same. Again they talked of the tax on malt, as if the tax on malt was not a general burthen, which fell upon every class of the community. Another of their statements was, that they paid 30 per cent[1] on the whole produce of the country. He contended that the land-owner did not pay 30 per cent on the whole produce of the country. The produce of the country was calculated at the value of two hundred millions a year; 30 per cent would be 60,000,000*l.*, and besides that there were the assessed taxes, the customs, and various other sources of revenue, which showed that the calculation of 30 per cent was wrong. They spoke also of the encouragement given to foreign labour, but, he would ask, what article could they import which was not the produce of foreign labour? for which, it was to be observed, that English labour was given in exchange. The error committed in 1816[2] was that of making the corn law a permanent law. It ought to have been a temporary measure, and to have ceased its operation as soon as the existing leases had expired, and the farmer was enabled to make new terms with his landlord. There were many measures that might be adopted with propriety, even in opposition to general principles, for a time, and under the exigencies of the moment, but parliament should always provide for a return to the good system. They should go back to that system as soon and as well as they could, but at all events they should go back. Nothing was more likely to occasion a convulsion than to persevere in a wrong measure merely because it had

---

[1] The *Morning Chronicle* (whose report *Hansard* has adopted in the main for the preceding argument) goes on: 'on the whole raw produce of the country, a statement which, if correct, would make the revenue considerably exceed the amount at which it had ever been estimated.' *Hansard* takes the two sentences which follow in the text from *The Times,* and then reverts to the *Morning Chronicle.*

[2] Should be '1815'.

once for a temporary purpose been adopted. Adverting to the subject of countervailing duties, of which he had formerly spoken,[1] he contended that it was not necessary to constitute a countervailing duty, that it should make up the difference between the price at which a foreigner could sell grain and that at which we could raise it. A countervailing duty, in his opinion, was one which balanced the particular tax laid upon any particular class of the community. Countervailing duties of a different description would entirely destroy all commercial intercourse. He agreed that the interests of the agriculturists, and of the other classes of the community, might be identified, provided we were restrained from inter- course with other nations; but this might not be the case in reference to foreign commerce. It might be the interest of the farmer to confine the manufacturer to the supply which he could afford him at a high price, while the manufacturer might procure the article cheaper from abroad. The price of grain might be raised by two causes—either by a change in the currency, which would affect grain like other articles; or by legislative restrictions, which might alter its relation to other articles. A rise in the price of corn from the latter cause tended to injure all who were not interested in the cultivation of the land, by lowering the profits of stock. It had been said, that the national debt, and the pressure of taxation, were the sources out of which the difficulty had arisen. It was no such thing. If all the taxes and the debt had been got rid of together, the same question would still arise —for while the population of foreign countries was not able to consume the produce of the land, and the population of this country was more than sufficient, there would be a dis- position to import.—Some gentlemen seemed to think that taxation made a difference in the state of the question, as to

[1] See above, p. 48.

our intercourse with foreign nations. It would no doubt be the case, if we taxed one article more than another, that we should cease to supply foreign countries with that commodity; but, if all articles were taxed alike, commerce in general would not be affected. If, for instance, this country produced corn and cloth, and that the production of each commodity was equally taxed, the amount of taxation would not make any difference in the relative advantage which one species of production had over the other, nor consequently in the choice of the commodity which we might supply to other nations, or be supplied with by them. It would be said, however, that taxation would make all things dearer; he admitted that—but though we might thus for a time cease to sell to other countries, we should not cease to buy of them, till the reduction of the quantity of money we possessed reduced prices also, and brought us to a level with them. It was one of the evils of the national debt, that it stood in the way of a reduction of the taxes in the same ratio as the currency was reduced. If, for instance, a tax was imposed of two shillings per yard on cloth worth twenty-two shillings, the country calculated on paying one-eleventh of the value; but when, in the progress of the alteration of the distribution of money, the cloth was reduced to 20*s.* a yard, the tax continuing the same, the country paid 1-10th of the value. There was another argument, which was the most important, because the most plausible argument in favour of the Corn law, viz. the plea that by importing corn, we became dependent on foreign countries. On the ground of economy not a word was to be said by any one who had paid attention to the subject, but in the argument that it was desirable that in war this country should not be dependent on another for subsistence, there was a certain degree of plausibility. In answer to this, it was to be said that if we imported corn in time of peace from any one country to a considerable extent, that country must be in the habit of growing corn specially for our consumption. In the event of a war with us, such a country would suffer extreme distress. We knew the effect of an excess, however small, of the supply of corn over the demand in the reduction of the price of this commodity, the consumption of which could not rapidly be increased, and the overplus of which consequently possessed no exchangeable value. All the agricultural distress we complained of would be not one-tenth of what such a country would suffer. But this went on the supposition that all our supply was to be derived from one country, whereas the fact was, that the supply would be derived from a great variety of countries; and was it probable that we should at once be at war with all of them? He therefore thought that this argument was hardly better founded than the other. This would be the happiest country in the world, and its progress in prosperity would be beyond the power of imagination to conceive, if we got rid of two great evils—the national debt and the corn laws. When he spoke of getting rid of the national debt, he did not mean by wiping it away with a sponge, but by honestly discharging it. His ideas on the subject were known[1] and he had heard no argument to show that the measure he would recommend was not the best policy. If this evil were removed, the course of trade and the prices of articles would become natural and right; and if corn were exported or imported, as in other countries, without restraint, this country, possessing the greatest skill, the greatest industry, the best machinery, and every other advantage in the highest degree, its prosperity and happiness would be incomparably, and almost inconceivably, great. Other topics he would allude to but for the lateness of the hour. Gentlemen had favoured

[1] Cp. above, p. 21.

him more than he had expected. He should oppose the motion because he was persuaded that a committee would be productive of mischief, and not good.

Mr. BROUGHAM, in the course of a speech in support of the motion, said: 'His hon. friend, the member for Portarlington, had argued as if he had dropped from another planet; as if this were a land of the most perfect liberty of trade—as if there were no taxes—no drawback—no bounties—no searchers—on any other branch of trade but agriculture; as if, in this Utopian world, of his hon. friend's creation the first measure of restriction ever thought on was that on the importation of corn; as if all classes of the community were alike—as if all trades were on an equal footing; and that, in this new state, we were called upon to decide the abstract question, whether or not there should be a protecting price for corn? But we were not in this condition—we were in a state of society in which we had manufactures of almost every description, protected in every way, even to criminal enactments, to prevent the raw material from going out of the country, in order thereby to assist the native manufacturer.'

The motion was carried by 150 votes to 101, the Government being left in a minority, and the House adjourned. The following day however a motion of the President of the Board of Trade restricting the terms of reference of the committee was carried by 251 votes to 108.[1]

---

[1] On 31 May, when the committee was being appointed, Mr. Maxwell suggested 'the propriety of adding the names of Baring and Ricardo, the hon. members for Taunton and Portarlington, to the list, as men whose views would never change or influence the truth, whatever way the investigation might present it.' Neither of them however was appointed to serve on the Agricultural committee of this year.

IRISH PROTECTING DUTIES[1]

2 *June* 1820

Mr. CURWEN presented a petition from the woollen cloth manufacturers of Keswick against continuing the protecting duties upon Irish linen.

Mr. RICARDO observed, that it seemed to be admitted on all sides, that these protecting duties ought to be repealed. They had existed for 20 years, which surely was a period quite long enough to give the Irish manufacturers an opportunity of preparing for their repeal, if any such opportunity were necessary; and he really could see no reason for their further continuance.

8 *June* 1820

The CHANCELLOR OF THE EXCHEQUER moved that the duties on several articles produced in Great Britain and Ireland, imported from one country into the other, should be continued till 1825, and thereafter at reduced rates till 1840, when they would finally cease.

Mr. RICARDO said, he was glad to see even that the time was to come when the country would rouse to those right principles, from which there never should have been any deviation; and hoped, that when the question of bounties with respect to linen, was brought forward, a proposition

[1] On 25 May Mr. S. WORTLEY presented a Petition from certain Linen Manufacturers in the county of Forfar, praying that they might be put on the same footing with regard to the bounties on exportation, as the Linen Manufacturers of Ireland. 'Mr. RICARDO considered the practice of giving bounties on exportation as no-thing less than bribing the consumers of our goods to take them off our hands. It was giving a part of the bounty to foreign consumers. At this time of day the system was most absurd, and he was astonished to see it acted upon.' (The *Star,* 26 May 1820. The matter is not mentioned in *Hansard.*)

would be adopted to limit the existence of those bounties also to a certain period, as they were quite as objectionable, upon principle, as the duties referred to in the resolutions before the committee.

Mr. J. FOSTER observed, that the duties alluded to were protecting duties for England as well as for Ireland.[1]

Mr. RICARDO considered those duties injurious to Ireland as well as to England, especially in the intercourse between the two countries.

The resolutions were agreed to.[2]

LOAN—WAYS AND MEANS

9 *June* 1820

The CHANCELLOR OF THE EXCHEQUER stated the terms of the loan of five millions which had been contracted for on this day: 'the contractors had taken the loan at nearly 2 per cent above the current price of stock.'[3]

Mr. RICARDO observed, that the present loan was made on very satisfactory terms. It was impossible, he thought, that it could be obtained at a more favourable rate. He however traced those favourable terms to the recommendation of an hon. friend (Mr. Grenfell) who, some years ago, had advised that the commissioners of the national debt should be allowed to subscribe for the loan to the amount of the balances in their hands.[4] This advice was followed on the

---

[1] This paragraph is from the *Star's* report.

[2] On 30 June, in a debate on Linen bounties, 'Mr. RICARDO considered bounties given to Ireland in this way, as in the nature of a Tax on the people of this country, and therefore he was generally opposed to such measures.'

[3] The contractors were Reid, Irving & Co.; among the unsuccessful lists were those of F. & R. Ricardo, and of N. M. Rothschild.

[4] See above, p. 21–2.

present occasion; but if the old course had been adopted, and the loan had been for 17,000,000*l.*, the result would have been very different. Another cause which tended to procure terms so favourable was the smallness of the loan. It was within the power of a great number of persons to bid for a loan of 5,000,000*l.* and therefore the competition for the present loan was much more extensive than usual, and far greater than if it had been for 17,000,000*l.* In consequence of these circumstances, the right hon. gentleman had certainly obtained such terms as must be highly satisfactory to the country. He conceived that no fairer mode could be devised in forming contracts for the public than by open competition. That system, he hoped, would be generally acted on. An hon. gentleman had, on a former night,[1] asked some questions relative to a large amount of exchequer bills, which had been issued by government at par, when they were at a discount in the market. From the explanation of the right hon. gentleman it seemed that they were given in consequence of a contract for a quantity of silver. Now, it was quite evident that the 7*s.* or 8*s.* received by government from the persons with whom the contract was made would be reimbursed by a profit in the price of the silver; they would undoubtedly raise the price to the amount which they were likely to lose. He thought, in this instance too, that the system of competition should have been acted on, and that they should have been purchased in that way. He wished for some explanation with respect to the quantity of exchequer bills relative to which information had been demanded a few evenings ago.[2] A statement had then been made, which his hon. friend, and other gentlemen, declared they did not understand. It appeared to him to be a very mysterious

---

[1] Mr. Baring, on 11 May (*Hansard*, N.S., I, 303–4). .

[2] By Mr. Grenfell, on 31 May (*ib.* 695 ff.).

transaction, and he could not make it out. It seemed that a provision had been made for appropriating the growing amount of the consolidated fund. His hon. friend had noticed this, and had observed that the growing amount might be made productive and useful to the public. In consequence of his representation a bill had been brought in some time ago, to enable the public to make use of its growing amount, by which it was provided, however, that they should not borrow more than 6,000,000*l.* from it. But it so happened that this growing consolidated fund was not equal to the discharge of the advances that had been made on it in the preceding quarter. He would thus explain himself:—Supposing this was the beginning of the quarter, that the public accounts were made up, and that there was a deficiency of 3,000,000*l.;* the Bank, in the first instance, made this good; and out of the amount of the consolidated fund in the commencing quarter the Bank was repaid those 3,000,000*l.* Supposing, over and above this sum of 3,000,000*l.,* an equal sum accrued, the public, under the act, would, he understood, have the advantage of those 3,000,000*l.,* since, by its provisions, a sum of 6,000,000*l.* might be borrowed for the public service. This was the system; but how, he asked, was it possible that the public could have the advantage of any part of this growing fund, when in fact it was in debt? It was exceedingly difficult for him to comprehend this. In April, 1819, there was a sum of 2,027,000*l.* so issued for the use of the public; and it was stated that from that period to April 1820, the public had the benefit of that money. But how could they have the use or benefit of it out of a growing consolidated fund, on which there was no surplus whatever, but which, on the contrary, was in debt, and that debt amounting to more than the 6,000,000*l.* which they were by the act of parliament empowered to borrow? As he could not understand this, he would be obliged to the right hon. gentleman to inform the House whether the public had really derived advantage from this 2,027,000*l.* from April, 1819, to April, 1820.

The CHANCELLOR OF THE EXCHEQUER explained.

Mr. RICARDO observed, that on the 5th of July, 1819, there was a deficiency of 8,400,000*l.* "But," said the right hon. gentleman, "you have, without interest, 2,600,000*l.*, for which exchequer bills have been deposited." This he denied; and he would contend that the public had not the advantage of that sum.

Later in the debate, Mr. Alderman HEYGATE opposed the present loan and the issuing of bills to repay the Bank, because those measures would produce a reduction in the circulating medium, which must be attended with increased distress in the country: 'such a reduction was at present unnecessary, for the price of gold being the same as the mint price, the Bank note was at par.'

Mr. RICARDO thought it quite unnecessary for the Bank of England to reduce its circulating medium any further than it was at present reduced. The worthy alderman had said, that gold was now at the Mint-price; perhaps he might have said that it was a little under it; for he knew that many persons took gold to the Mint at the Mint-price, in order to have it coined; and this they could not do if gold was not, in fact, a little under that price, because some space of time must elapse before they could receive the benefit of the coinage. But the worthy alderman appeared to labour under a mistake in supposing that a reduction of the circulating medium would be a consequence of this loan, or repaying the Bank. The reduction of bank-notes within the last year did not exceed 2,000,000*l.*; that reduction of 2,000,000*l.* was all that was necessary to bring about that state of the currency which all had united with the finance committee in desiring to see obtained. Indeed, if the Bank was desirous to follow their own interest, it was a clear and obvious one: if they were to effect a very great reduction in their paper, which he should most sincerely lament, the consequence would be such a rise in paper, and such a fall in gold, that individuals would carry their gold to the Mint, and endeavour to fill up the circulation with it. As to the alarm felt by his hon. friend[1] it was quite groundless, for there could be no fear but that the Bank would keep up a sufficient quantity of notes, as their own advantage depended upon the issue. As to the sinking fund, the argument of himself and his hon. friend[2] had been, "Take away all which tends to delude the country—take away so much of that sinking fund as is not in reality an excess of income over expenditure." Therefore he entirely concurred in the opinions of the worthy alderman, that they should immediately get rid of so much of the fund as, being nominal, was merely a delusion.

BANK OF ENGLAND ACCOUNTS

13 *June* 1820

Mr. GRENFELL moved for a number of accounts relating to the Bank and said that, the principles which he had so strenuously contended for having been adopted, 'he trusted the warfare between the Bank of England and himself was over.' He referred again to the large profits which the Bank had made from the public balances in their hands; they had now been reduced, but a further saving of 100,000*l.* might be effected on the charge for the management of the public debt by the Bank. Mr. PEARSE, a Bank director, defended the Bank.

Mr. RICARDO conceived, that if it were true, as had been stated, that the Bank had made no larger profits in conse-

---

[1] Mr. Alderman Heygate.   [2] Mr. Grenfell.

quence of its connexion with government, and its retaining these balances than any private concern which might have held them would have made, it must have managed its own affairs very badly. The hon. director had mentioned, as one of the great advantages which had accrued to the public from the acts of the Bank, the lending of a sum of money, without interest, to the government. But the thing was differently represented by the court of directors at the time. The Bank was then in this situation:—it had been allowed to increase the amount of its capital, instead of dividing a larger amount of profits among the proprietors—that is, instead of making a larger dividend it had been permitted to add to its capital: and the understanding was, that the loan of 3,000,000*l.*, upon which no interest was to become due, was a boon to the public in return for that permission. At some former periods, the remuneration to the Bank must have been enormous, or it was now very considerably underpaid. But his own opinion upon the charge of management was, that the balances in question were now so small, that it was hardly necessary to have brought the subject before the House.

The papers were ordered to be printed.

THE BUDGET

19 *June* 1820

The CHANCELLOR OF THE EXCHEQUER introduced the budget. In the course of his speech he remarked that, as 12 millions were to be borrowed from the sinking fund, 5 millions would remain to be applied by the commissioners for the purchase of stock; these purchases had the effect of regulating the market during the whole year and of preventing sudden fluctuations from forced sales or from combinations of speculators.

Speeches

Mr. RICARDO[1] said, he could not clearly understand the alleged benefit which the money-market was to receive from the right hon. gentleman's arrangement. It was certainly a subject of lamentation that, after five years of peace, we should still find our expenses increasing. According to the right hon. gentleman we had had effectually a sinking fund of but 1,000,000*l.* during the last year; but if this were correct, and the right hon. gentleman were to follow out the statements contained in the report of the finance committee, he would perceive from the expenditure that there had been an actual deficiency. He would here observe, that he found an item of 1,125,000*l.* perfectly unexplained. There was no account by which he could trace the manner in which it was proposed to provide for this item of 1,125,000*l.* The surplus of 1,000,000*l.*, which had been mentioned by the right hon. gentleman, he had already taken into account; but he must contend that this sum of 1,125,000*l.* still appeared as against the accounts given in by the chancellor of the exchequer, whether he looked at this or at that paper[2]. This sum of 1,125,000*l.* ought to appear, therefore, among other outstanding demands. He had a right to presume that the right hon. gentleman was bound to provide for this particular one,

[1] The Budget debate is very imperfectly reported, owing to the excitement prevailing in the House after the announcement which had just been made of the failure of the negotiations between the King and the Queen. According to *Cobbett's Parliamentary Register* during the opening part of the Chancellor's speech 'the noise in every part of the House was so excessive' that it was found necessary to defer the business; and after Ricardo's speech the Chancellor's reply was 'perfectly inaudible'.

[2] *Cobbett's Parliamentary Register* has here in addition '; at the vote which included the interest of other outstanding sums, or at the amount actually paid in the liquidation of similar items; at the actual expenses detailed in those accounts, or at the sums which remained actually unfunded'.

among the others. Next year it was anticipated by that right hon. gentleman that we were to have a sinking fund of between three and four millions. During the present year, he said, that he calculated, after deducting 9,000,000*l*. of unfunded debt to be paid off from 11,000,000*l*., that there would be a sinking fund of about 2,000,000*l*. But the right hon. gentleman seemed to forget, that this imaginary improvement of his was made to appear twice in the same statement. He first of all said, that we should have a sinking fund of such and such an amount; but, when he came to speak of the deficiencies upon the consolidated fund, and of the fund out of which they were to be supplied, he must have forgotten, when he was expatiating upon the sinking fund, that he was alluding to that out of which those very deficiencies were to be so supplied. And, throughout all these accounts, he had clearly forgotten that there was, in the quarter ending in January 1819, a deficiency of 8,000,000*l*. upon exchequer bills. He quite agreed in every word that had fallen from his hon. friend, the member for Penrhyn,[1] respecting the alarming deficiency upon the consolidated fund. He quite concurred with him in saying, that that which was the growing produce of the consolidated fund used to be sufficient to pay all the demands upon it for the current quarter; whereas, instead of this, it was now found insufficient to pay even the arrears of the preceding quarter. During the last year, he considered the finance committee to have pursued a very good plan in letting them know what was the real state of the finances of the country.[2] The committee had allowed them to see, in that, whether their amount was greater or less than it had been at that time twelve months. Now, he had

---

[1] Mr. Grenfell.
[2] See the 'First Report from the Select Committee on Finance, 1819',
reprinted in *Hansard*, Appendix to vol. XL.

endeavoured to apply the very same plan to the accounts of this year; and he found it to apply to them in a most remarkable manner. The committee last year estimated the unfunded debt at 53,133,000*l*. They took the amount of exchequer-bills in circulation, of Irish treasury bills, deficiency bills, &c.; and the result of their estimate was 53,133,000*l*. By the papers before the House, it appeared, that at the period to which they were made out, the unfunded debt was actually diminished in the sum of 2,000,000*l*. only, although the right hon. gentleman calculated that diminution at upwards of 10,000,000*l*. If, however, the papers before them were correct, he must contend, that the amount of actual diminution upon the unfunded debt, between the 5th of January 1819, and the 5th of January 1820, was only 2,000,000*l*. It was now necessary to see in what ratio the funded debt had increased; and by the returns that had been made to the House, they would find that the sum actually received by loan (which loans last year amounted to 24,000,000*l*.) was 18,736,000*l*. Deducting the sinking fund from this, the balance must necessarily be the actual amount to which the funded debt had been increased during the present year; and that increase was to the exact extent to which the unfunded debt had been this year paid off, namely, 2,000,000*l*.: so that, after all the complicated accounts that had been submitted to the House, the general result was this —that they had decreased the unfunded debt 2,000,000*l*. and had increased the funded debt 2,000,000*l*. It had been said that, in point of fact, there was no sinking fund whatever, for that the deficiencies upon the interest of exchequer-bills would amount to a sum about equal to that fund. And indeed it appeared to him, that these deficiencies had increased 1,370,000*l*. more than they amounted to last year. He had one observation more to make about the funding of

7,000,000*l.* of exchequer bills. The hon. member for Pen-
ryhn had paid some compliments to the chancellor of the
exchequer, for having upon this occasion funded in the 5 per
cents, rather than in any other stock. But, in order to contend that that was a judicious measure, he ought first to have
shown that there was a sufficiency of capital to fund in the
5 per cents rather than in the three per cents. If they possessed
a very large sinking fund and that sinking fund was likely to
be operative, then undoubtedly it was proper to fund in a
new stock and create one of 5 per cent in preference to funding in the 3 per cents; and, in that view of the question, he
should have been disposed to have approved of the former of
these measures. But, seeing that they possessed little or no
sinking fund, he was very much disposed to doubt, whether
the terms of such a loan would be of that advantageous
character which his hon. friend seemed disposed to attribute
to them.

COMMITTEE OF SUPPLY[1]

21 *June* 1820

A debate arose on methods of keeping the public accounts.

Mr. RICARDO took the opportunity of objecting to the
manner in which the Chancellor of the Exchequer stated the
budget. He ought to insert, with reference to the former
year, a column of expenditure as well as of receipt. He should
say, "I have received so much from the ways and means—
so much has been expended—and so much remains to be
received on the last year's budget." He did not believe that

---

[1] This debate is not mentioned
in *Hansard*. Ricardo's speech is
here reprinted from the report in
The Times.

the ways and means stated by the right hon. gent. the other evening would be equal to the payments that were chargeable on them. In his opinion, there would be a deficiency of 2,000,000*l.*

The CHANCELLOR OF THE EXCHEQUER observed that in future years more detailed accounts might be produced.

COTTON WEAVERS

28 *June* 1820

29 June 1820   Mr. MAXWELL moved for a select committee to inquire into the means of relieving the distress of the cotton weavers. Amongst the plans to be considered he mentioned: the taxing of 'a machine called "a power-loom"' which competed with the simple loom of the individual weaver ('the capital of the poor man, which consisted in the labour of his two hands, must bear the burden of taxation, since those articles, without which he could not exist, were taxed; while the large capital of the wealthy manufacturer, which he invested in a machine, was suffered to escape any contribution to the revenue'); and the application of public money to provide lands for those who could obtain no employment at their looms. Mr. ROBINSON opposed the motion.

Mr. RICARDO said, that he conceived the duty of government to be, to give the greatest possible development to industry. This they could do only by removing the obstacles which had been created. He complained therefore of government on very different grounds from the hon. mover, for his complaint was against the restrictions on trade, and other obstacles of that description, which opposed the development of industry. The recommendations of the hon. mover were inconsistent with the contrast between one class and another. If government interfered, they would do mischief and no good. They had already interfered, and done mischief by the poor laws. The principles of the hon. mover would likewise violate the sacredness of property, which constituted the great security of society.

The motion was withdrawn.

THE CORONATION

3 *July* 1820

On the order of the day for going into a committee of supply on the expenses of his majesty's coronation,

Mr. RICARDO thought that if the various articles likely to be consumed at the coronation could be bought cheaper in the foreign than the home market, there could be no objection to their not being home manufacture, seeing that they must be purchased by the produce of our own industry.

[The remainder of the session was mainly taken up by the proceedings against the Queen, which were initiated in the House of Lords on 5 July by the introduction of a bill of pains and penalties and brought to a close on 10 November, when the bill was withdrawn. The session closed on 23 Nov. 1820.]

SESSION 1821

The King's speech on the opening of the session was delivered on 23 Jan. 1821.

SUPPLY—BANK OF IRELAND

2 *February* 1821

Mr. GRENFELL asked the Chancellor of the Exchequer whether he was prepared to give any information as to the refusal of the Bank of Ireland to receive the coin of the realm as deposits. The CHANCELLOR OF THE EXCHEQUER was unable to give any information.

Mr. RICARDO observed, that paper in Ireland having become at a premium above the price of gold coin, persons had been under the necessity of incurring the expense of conveying gold coin to Ireland, to remedy an evil arising out of the deficiency of circulation from the failures in the south.[1] If the Bank of Ireland had filled the void so occasioned, as it was their duty to have done, the evil would have been avoided. He was still of opinion, that the system established with regard to the Bank of England,[2] two or three years ago, ought to be perpetuated. If the Bank contemplated paying in gold coin in 1823, as they were now by law required, they must purchase a quantity of gold for that purpose; and to this cause was to be attributed the present disproportion between the price of gold and silver. He hoped, that his right hon. friend would be of opinion, that the system now existing ought to be permanent, and that he would take an early opportunity of bringing forward a measure for that purpose.

[See further p. 98 below.]

[1] In 1820 eleven banks had failed in the South of Ireland.

[2] *i.e.* the system of payments in bullion.

TRADE OF BIRMINGHAM—
PETITION OF THE MERCHANTS

8 February 1821

Mr. DUGDALE presented a petition from the merchants and manufacturers of Birmingham for an inquiry into the causes of the national distress. Mr. BARING said that 'a very considerable part of the distress ... arose from the nature of the currency'; and he suggested 'the expediency of giving to the Bank the option of paying either in gold or silver, that the value of the two precious metals might be rendered more equal, and the present pound sterling, which was somewhat too high, relaxed. He wished to relax a cord which was at present stretched somewhat too tightly.' He did not mean however to 'trench upon the system of the member for Portarlington'. 8 Feb. 1821

Mr. RICARDO said, that if the House would indulge him for a few minutes, he should be desirous to make one or two allusions to what had fallen from his hon. friend below.[1] The great point to which his hon. friend had addressed himself was the origin of the prevailing distress. By some persons this was ascribed to taxation, by others to restrictions on trade, and by his hon. friend to an alteration in the currency, which he seemed indeed to consider as almost the exclusive cause. With this view his hon. friend had entered into a comparison of the prices of corn at various periods, and he stated the fall to be from about 80 to 60*s.*, inferring that other articles had undergone an equal depression. He seemed to think that with a quarter of corn he could now purchase the same quantity of other commodities which he could have obtained with it when corn was at 80*s.* and that the reduction of prices was therefore general and equal. Now, this representation he apprehended was erroneous. He could not agree that prices had fallen generally in the same pro-

---

[1] Mr. Baring.

portion.[1] He believed that the fall in corn had been severe beyond measure, whilst there had been no fall with regard to many other articles, or at any rate no fall in the least degree similar. If the prices of bullion were referred to at former periods, it would be seen that the price of corn had altered to the amount of 25 per cent. He was surprised to find his hon. friend making a statement from which, if correct, it must be inferred, that the distresses began at the moment when the last change in the currency took place. Now, if he looked back to the price of bullion in the flourishing year 1818, and compared it with the present price, it would be seen that the difference did not exceed 6 or 7 per cent. To this extent other prices might have since been affected, and he had no doubt that there had been a considerable reduction of prices in other countries. Wine had fallen here, and so had cotton

---

[1] The argument that follows in the text may be integrated by comparison with the *Courier's* report: 'The fall in the price of corn had been peculiarly severe, produced by causes wholly distinct from any reference to the recent alteration in the currency. He should call the attention of his Honourable Friend to the price of bullion since that alteration and at the present time, and then he would ask him to show how any such fluctuation in the price of bullion could have operated to produce a diminution in the price of corn to the amount of 25 per cent.? The difference between the price of bullion now and at the period at which it was stated our agricultural and commercial prosperity was at its height, was not more than from 6 to 7 per cent. How then could it be maintained that the alteration in our currency, which only affected the price of bullion at the rate of from 6 to 7 per cent., could be the cause of those distresses in those very rare branches to the amount of 25 per cent.? He was not engaged in any commercial transactions, but he had heard that there had been a great fall in other articles; in wine, for instance, he had heard there had been a reduction of price to the amount of 25 per cent.; in cotton also, he understood there was a diminution; but he also was informed, that a fall in the value of those articles had taken place in other countries. He would state the prices of bullion for the four years previously to the year in which the alteration in the currency began to get into operation. In 1816 the price of bullion was £4. 1s.,' etc.

goods; but he believed that fall was not more than equal to that which had occurred in most parts of Europe. In 1816 the price of gold was at 4*l.* an ounce. In the following year it was 4*l.* and 6*d.* In 1818 bullion still did not rise above 4*l.* 2*s.* and 4*l.* 3*s.*, and in 1819, when the plan which he had the honour to recommend was adopted by the House, it was at 4*l.* 1*s.* The question, then,[1] before the House was, whether it was advisable to return to the old standard, or to take the existing market rate, which was then about 4 per cent above that standard as the measure of value in future. But his hon. friend had argued on this subject as if bullion had been at that time, as it formerly was, at 5*l.* or 5*l.* 10*s.*, an ounce. If, instead of being at 4*l.* 1*s.* bullion had been much higher, he should not have proposed a recurrence to the mint standard. What he was anxious about, was not to restore the old, but to establish a fixed standard; for, however desirable it might be to a body of merchants or bankers to possess the power of raising or lowering a fourth or fifth the value of the currency, and to make 3*l.* 17*s.* 10$\frac{1}{2}$*d.* at one time, equivalent to 5*l.* at another, it was a power destructive of every engagement, and finally ruinous to every interest. He was not anxious to restore the old standard; but the market price of bullion being then only 4*l.* 1*s.*, he did not think it necessary to deviate from the ancient standard. What increased his surprise at the view which his hon. friend had taken in tracing all our distress to a variation in the currency was, that when a few years back we had so much greater variations, we had no such distress. With regard to the depression of agriculture, he believed it was a good deal owing to the laws[2] which were enacted for the purpose of protecting it. It was certainly desirable that those engaged in the production of corn should have a vent when an excess of supply existed. When two or

---

[1] 'at that time' (*Courier*).   [2] 'to those very laws' (*Courier*).

three good harvests followed in succession, we might, if prices were at all on a level with those on the continent, export it after a fall of three or four shillings a quarter; but at present there must be a destructive fall before it could be sent abroad. The hon. member for Cumberland,[1] as well as the hon. member for Staffordshire,[2] had talked of the extreme pressure of taxes on agriculture; as if they were found, in that respect, to be peculiarly burdensome. The stockholder was described as being comparatively free from these effects; but it would not be difficult to show, that all taxes fell upon the consumers of those commodities to which they were annexed; and if this were not the case, he did not see what right the landowner had to ask for protection. He could demonstrate, if it were necessary, that taxes always raised the price of that commodity on which they were laid, and therefore fell on the consumer. Was it not impossible that farmers could continue to grow corn for a series of years unless they obtained remunerating prices?—[3] He would now offer a very

[1] Mr. Curwen.
[2] Mr. Littleton.
[3] A clearer report of what follows is given by the *Courier:* 'With respect to what had fallen from his Honourable friend (Mr. Baring) as to the option of paying in the two metals, he must own he had heard such a proposition from him with pain. He regretted also to perceive, that the suggestion of the Member for Cumberland (Mr. Curwen,) as to any reduction of the interest of the fundholder, was received with cheers by many Members of that House. Combining that suggestion with what had fallen from his Honourable Friend as to the alteration relative to the payment in two metals, he should only say, that if ever it should be necessary to interfere with the dividend of the fundholder, let it be done openly, and not by stratagem. His objection to the proposition of his Honourable Friend was, that it partook of the character of a delusion. It applied a standard different from that which the law contemplated when it enacted the payment in one metal. Were that option given to the Bank, the person who applied at present for sixty ounces of gold bullion would be told by the Bank, that they would not pay him in gold, but in silver, which in its relative value to gold was lower. All contracts would be disturbed as often, as from various causes the relative value between

few remarks on what had been thrown out as to the restoration of two metals as a standard. It gave him pain, however,
to hear any allusions made to the subject of not paying the
public creditor, and to find that they met with the reception
which they did in some quarters. If, indeed, the dividend was
to be reduced, he trusted that it would be done openly, and
that no stratagem or delusion would be practised. With
regard to the plan of his hon. friend, he was sorry that he
could not approve of it, recommending, as it did, a different
standard from that fixed in 1819; at least, he could not help
thinking that the plan amounted to this when he heard his
hon. friend say, that the string was too tight, and that it was
desirable to empower the Bank to pay either in gold or silver.
This appeared to him to be a complete departure from the
true and sound principles of currency. No currency could be
of the same value perpetually, any more than other articles
could always retain the same price. Gold bullion, however,
was the commodity which varied the least; and if a contract
was made to pay 100*l.* at a future period, the contract would
be most faithfully performed by the payment of that sum in
gold. But it might suit the purpose of the debtor to pay it in
silver, whilst, by so doing, the creditor would sustain a loss.
The two metals seldom maintained the same proportion to
each other long. The price of the one might rise, while that of
the other fell. So the Bank being now under an obligation to
pay 60 ounces of gold, would enable a person who received
it, to propose more, or a greater nominal amount of commodities than he would if he paid in silver. The relative

these two metals fluctuated. But even if the proposition of his Honourable Friend was acted upon, he could not obtain the object he had in view, he could not procure the very relaxation to which he had alluded. What was it that at that moment produced the variation between the metals, to the higher price of gold? Was it not the operations of the Bank? That corporation were so timid,' etc.

value of the two metals had varied since the act of parliament; but what was the cause of that variation? It was this: the Bank being a timid body, seldom clinging to the true principles of circulation, had taken alarm, and had made great and unnecessary purchases of gold, although they found, by experience, that no person applied to them for any. He almost doubted whether a single bar had been demanded from them since the commencement of the new plan.[1] If the Bank were enabled, according to his hon. friend's proposition, to pay in silver instead of gold, they would now realize a profit equal to the difference between 4s. $11\frac{1}{2}d$. and 5s. 2d. As soon as this profit should cease, the two metals would have recovered their relative value, and then it would be difficult to discover the value of his hon. friend's proposition. He had proved last session that the two metals might vary to the extent of three per cent; but his hon. friend then remarked, that this might be true in theory, but in France, where the experiment had been tried, the difference did not exceed one per mill. Still it was something to find that the possibility of the variation was admitted. He entirely agreed in all that had been said with regard to the retrenchment in our expenditure being the principal, if not the only source of relief. The committee would, he doubted not, without preconceived or particular views, inquire whether the present system of restrictions on trade was advantageous to the country. He should only add, with respect to the rents of land, that no interests could be more distinct than those of the owners and occupiers; yet it did happen that the latter were persuaded to petition that House for regulations which might be beneficial to one class, but most injurious to themselves.[2]

[1] See below, p. 368–9.
[2] Instead of the last two sentences

the *Courier* reports: 'He did not expect   much   benefit   from   the

8 Feb. 1821

Mr. BARING expressed once more his conviction that 'from the operation of the plan lately adopted by the legislature with regard to the resumption of cash-payments,...the value of the pound sterling, with reference to the price of commodities, had advanced one-third, or at least one-fourth, above that which it bore during the latter years of the war.' He again urged the policy of allowing a double tender, of silver as well as of gold. As a practical man he could see no purpose in having a single standard: 'although the establishment of such a standard might be more agreeable to the views of the Royal Society, or other abstract philosophers, who would regulate weights and measures by the vibrations of the pendulum.'

Mr. RICARDO remarked, that the difference between his hon. friend's opinion and his own was this, that he maintained the advance of the pound sterling with reference to the price of commodities to be only about 4 or 5 per cent, which was equal to the difference between the price of gold at $4l$. $1s$. and $3l$. $17s$. $10\frac{1}{2}d$. an ounce, while his hon. friend maintained that advance to be equal to 25 per cent. But how came it, he would ask, that although Russia, Austria, and France had adopted the same system as this country in the issue of paper, there should be such a difference in this country alone as his hon. friend had stated? He, however, differed from the views of his hon. friend, the principle of whose animadversions would in a great measure operate against any metallic currency whatever. With respect to his hon. friend's recommendation of a double tender, it was obvious, that if that recommendation were adopted, the Bank, although it seldom saw its own interest, would be

proposed Committees on Trade and Agriculture. He should vote for the latter, upon the understanding that the question should be fully discussed, and to consider if, in place of additional restrictions, the wiser course would not be to repeal those that already existed. The petitions of the Agriculturists had been signed by landholders and occupiers, the latter being persuaded by the owners to petition for that which, though beneficial to them, must in the same proportion be injurious to the occupier.'

likely to realise a considerable sum by the purchase of silver at its present reduced price of 4*s.* 11*d.* an ounce. But as this purchase would serve to raise silver to the Mint price of 5*s.* 2*d.* and comparatively to advance the price of gold, the consequence of which would be to drive gold out of the country, this was, among other reasons, an argument with him for resisting his hon. friend's doctrine.

The petition was ordered to be printed.

CORN AVERAGES

26 *February* 1821

Mr. ROBINSON (President of the Board of Trade) introduced a resolution for simplifying the methods by which the average prices of corn were ascertained for the purposes of the corn law; he also proposed to include the Isle of Man in the returns in order to prevent frauds. Mr. CURWEN said, 'he was sure that, within a very limited period, the country had lost at least a million by the frauds which had been committed. Large quantities of corn were imported from Denmark into the Isle of Man, and from thence shipped off to England. The greatest injury resulted to the English farmer from the introduction of foreign grain.'

Mr. RICARDO conceived that the effect of the measure would be to raise the importation price. An hon. member[1] had spoken of the injury which an accumulation of foreign corn occasioned in the English market. That might be so; but the only remedy for this evil was, for this country to lower the prices of corn nearly to the standard of the prices of the continent. The only way to keep out foreign corn, was by putting high duties upon the importation of it. Now, suppose a year of scarcity had arrived, and that a high duty had been placed on the importation of foreign corn, would any

---

[1] Mr. Curwen.

minister at such a time of distress, attempt to enforce that duty—and shut out relief from a starving people? Impossible; and, therefore, the ports would be left open and free, and the immense importation which the hon. gentleman looked upon as so great a misfortune, would take place. Much had been said as to a remedy for the distress of the agriculturist: he was of opinion, that the only remedy for that distress was the total repeal of the corn laws and, sooner or later, a measure of that sort would be adopted.

The resolution was agreed to.

STATE OF THE REVENUE—REPEAL OF THE HOUSE AND WINDOW DUTIES

6 March 1821

Mr. MABERLY proposed a series of resolutions for the retrench- ment of public expenditure and for a reduction of 50 per cent upon all duties on inhabited houses and windows. The motion was opposed by the CHANCELLOR OF THE EXCHEQUER and by Mr. HUSKISSON, who contended 'that we were not at liberty to take off taxes, unless we preserved the Sinking Fund.'

Mr. RICARDO reminded the right hon. gentleman,[1] that the proposal of this night was not to reduce the Sinking Fund two millions, but to reduce the taxes to that amount; not by taking from the Sinking Fund, but by increased economy. The object was, to relieve the country from a part of the burdens under which it at present laboured. If, however, the motion had been to reduce the Sinking Fund, it should have met with no opposition from him. He considered it a delusion which was encouraged and made to amount to a certain sum, that ministers might be enabled finally to lay their

[1] Mr. Huskisson.

hands upon it and devote it to purposes of unnecessary expenditure. Though the loan of last year amounted to
24,000,000*l.* there were 9,000,000*l.* of exchequer bills and
17,000,000*l.* of Sinking Fund, so that there was in fact a
surplus of 2,000,000*l.* On the other side, it was asked whether
it was intended to diminish the Consolidated Fund, which
was the security to the public creditor? Yet ministers had
been doing so year after year, until the deficiency amounted
to 8,000,000*l.* Now, however, they were greatly alarmed at
such a proposal, when in truth the object of the hon. mover
was merely to reduce the expenditure. For the year ending
the 5th of January, 1821, the Sinking Fund was estimated at
2,500,000*l.* He hoped it would turn out so; but his opinion
undoubtedly was, that it would be considerably below that
amount. It appeared to him that the diminution of the unfunded debt, between 5th January 1820, and 5th January
1821, amounted to very nearly 8,000,000*l.* while the Sinking
Fund for the present year was 17,000,000*l.* making together
25,000,000*l.* This was in diminution of the debt; but, on the
other hand, what had been added to it? The chancellor of the
exchequer took a loan of 17,000,000*l.* and funded exchequer
bills to the amount of 7,000,000*l.* so that an amount of stock
equal to 24,000,000*l.* was added to the debt. Besides this
there was a deficiency of the Consolidated Fund to the
amount of 400,000*l.* Deducting therefore 24,400,000*l.* debt,
incurred from the 25,000,000*l.* debt reduced, 600,000*l.* was
the only real decrease; and he could call nothing a Sinking
Fund, but what operated a reduction of the national debt.

The House divided: For the motion, 83; Against it, 109.
Ricardo voted for the motion.

MR. GOOCH'S MOTION FOR A
COMMITTEE ON AGRICULTURAL
DISTRESS

7 *March* 1821

Mr. GOOCH moved for the appointment of a committee to 7 March 1821 inquire into the distress of the agricultural interest. He trusted 'that the gentlemen who usually opposed the agricultural interest—and especially that individual amongst them who was so highly distinguished for his knowledge of political economy (Mr. Ricardo), would permit the committee to see what good they could effect by their deliberations. Trade and agriculture were so interwoven with each other, that they appeared to him as but one interest; and he had always deemed it wicked to consider them as jarring with each other.' He considered the agricultural interest as the basis of all the others, and therefore he asked the House to give to it 'that protection which its value to the state demanded.' Sir E. KNATCHBULL seconded the motion. Mr. ROBINSON (President of the Board of Trade) said that although the grounds on which he had objected to a similar motion the year before were applicable to all times, yet as a matter of feeling rather than one of expediency he would now consent to the inquiry. After some further debate,

Mr. RICARDO[1] rose to defend his conduct and opinions, which had been repeatedly attacked in the course of the discussion. When he heard that all the interests of the country were equally consulted, he could not help saying, because he felt it, that the interests of landlords were chiefly considered. He had been represented as a mercantile man, having a particular interest which he consulted. He denied that he was

---

[1] Writing to McCulloch on 23 March 1821 Ricardo says that the newspapers have misrepresented him, but 'in many parts of my speech I have been best reported by the British Press' (below, VIII, 357); in the same letter he gives his own account of this speech. Accordingly, by exception, the *British Press'* report is reproduced in the text above, whilst *Hansard's* report (which is derived mainly from the *Courier* and for the rest from the *Morning Chronicle*) is given below, p. 87 ff.

interested either as a mercantile man or as a fundholder. He was a landed proprietor, and his interests were bound up with that of the House. He agreed with the Member for Essex,[1] that high or low price in corn was nothing in itself. But he maintained the principle of a free trade in corn; not altogether a free trade in practice, but the general right should be allowed to every man, and every class of men, to apply their labour and resources in the most profitable way for themselves, which would be also the most profitable for the country. The effects of a free trade would be to get corn at the most advantageous rate. He wanted a countervailing duty to the home grower, to recompence all the additional charges which he had to pay in taxes above the charges borne by the foreign grower; but the protecting duty should not exceed the difference of those charges.[2] The attention of the House had been called to the terrible effects which would be produced upon native agriculture, by allowing a free importation of cheap corn from the Continent. He would endeavour to shew what would be the real effect. The prices of corn would be reduced immediately, and agriculture might be distressed more than at present. But the labour of this country would be immediately applied to the production of other and more profitable commodities, which might be exchanged for cheap foreign corn if the lands were thrown out of cultivation, through too great a reduction of prices to compensate the production of grain at home. He had a

---

[1] Mr. Western, who had said, that 'it was not by the money price of bread that the labouring classes were affected...; and he firmly believed that, taking a view of the prices throughout Europe, in those countries where bread was the cheapest, the labourer had the least share of it.'

[2] As Ricardo writes to McCulloch (below, VIII, 356) his principle of a countervailing duty 'has been misrepresented in all the papers'. For his own statement, see *Protection to Agriculture*, above, IV, 243.

great objection to a permanent duty on importations of corn; he still more strongly objected to a graduated duty, to rise in proportion as corn fell, and to fall as corn rose. Suppose the case of a bad crop; the grower would naturally look for the remedy for the loss of quantity in the superior price, from which he would be cut off by the adoption of a graduated protecting price. The Honourable Member for Oxford[1] had asked for the solution of what might be called a riddle, uttered by him (Mr. Ricardo), that the immediate opening of the ports to importations of foreign corn, would be so far from disabling the country to pay the present nominal amount of taxes, that the country would be enabled from that very circumstance to pay a larger nominal amount of taxes. The Hon. Member should immediately have a solution. Suppose the country, instead of the present system of agriculture, could find out one which with far more ease of execution and with much less expense, would produce the same or a greater quantity of corn than was at present grown by the existing system, a great deal of labour would be thrown out of employment in agriculture; but let the House keep their eyes on the effects of the capital which would be liberated. Would not this capital be employed in the production of other commodities? and would all the commodities so produced be an addition of capital and gain to the whole country? Hon. Gentlemen asked how there could be any gain to the country when the price of corn would fall to one-half? His answer was, that the new commodities produced would contain a positive value, besides the value which would exist on the corn. In like manner would free importation of corn lead to a release of capital, which would be

---

[1] Mr. Lockhart, probably in the debate on Corn Averages, 26 February; his speech is only briefly reported in *Hansard* (IV, 945).

employed in producing commodities, bringing so much additional gain; for though the commodities as well as the grain would be at a lower rate of prices, they would contain a value sufficient, from their quantity, not only to remunerate their production, but to pay all the charges required by Government. He agreed with an observation of a Noble Person in another place,[1] that part of the distress was owing to too much corn being produced, and agriculture must lessen its produce so as to suit the demand. He knew that taxation was an evil; but it could not be truly said that the taxation on agriculture prevented corn from remunerating the expense of its production. If the charges for growing or producing any thing were great, the price demanded for the article would correspond. If his hat or any thing else were taxed, he had, as the consumer, to pay an additional price for it; and where taxation went too far, it would diminish the consumption of the commodity so taxed. In other words, taxation tended to reduce the demand for the taxed commodity, but it did not prevent the remuneration of all the expenses of production for so much of the commodity as was in demand. It was wrong to say that corn could not be produced on account of the taxes on agriculture. The Member for Wareham[2] had given a most convincing instance of the truth of this position, by explaining the duty on salt, which he stated to amount to 3,000*l.* upon the value of every 190*l.* Three thousand pounds duty were paid on salt, and yet salt yielded a sufficient profit to the producer. He did not mean to say that there was no hardship suffered by the consumer; but this proved that taxation alone did not prevent

[1] Lord Liverpool's assertion in the House of Lords that 'one great cause of the public distress was an excess of production'; (23 Jan. and 21 Feb. 1821, *Hansard*, N.S., IV, 14 and 829).

[2] Mr. Calcraft, in the debate on the House and Window Duties, on 6 March.

an adequate remuneration to the corn-grower. It had been said that importation would throw the whole of the lands out of cultivation. But this was assuming that the remunerating price was for every grower the same; whereas, corn was raised in some lands at 40s. and in others at not less than 70s. He had been asked how the cheap corn, when imported, could be paid for? By selling commodities? If that were not practicable, it must be because it would be more advantageous to grow corn than to part with commodities for it. A great deal had been said about the warehousing system. He had been asked, who would speculate in corn with the prospect of large quantities being let out upon the market at a very diminished price? He would, if he were inclined to speculate, do it in corn. Having the market to himself while corn was under 80s. he would deal, and when it was 79s. without any dread or jealousy of a commodity which was not allowed to enter the market.[1] The Member for Cumberland[2] had put a question to him categorically. Could we grow corn at the same rate as on the Continent?—No; and for that reason he would have it imported: that was precisely the argument he went upon. The Member for Winchelsea,[3] not then in his place, had asked, "Where has the Honourable Member (Mr. Ricardo) been? Has he just descended from some other planet? Does he know that a great deal of capital is engaged in agriculture, which would be then (in case of a free trade) thrown out of

---

[1] The last four sentences are more intelligibly reported in the *Morning Chronicle:* 'The warehousing system had been much alluded to in the debate, and it was asked, who would speculate when there was corn in the warehouses ready for market when the price rose to 80s.? He would, for one, because till the price came up to 79s. he should feel that he had nothing to fear.'

[2] Mr. Curwen.

[3] Mr. Brougham; cp. his speech of 30 May 1820, above, p. 56. See also Ricardo's note in ed. 3 of *Principles,* above, I, 269.

that employment?" This was considering the means without reference to the end sought. The end proposed in the employment of all capital was to obtain abundant production. He would say that if he could get corn so much cheaper than it could be grown, he deemed the capital employed in growing corn, to the exclusion of corn more cheaply to be acquired, a nuisance. Better such capital were altogether annihilated. But it would not be annihilated. The greater part of it would be turned into profitable channels. Something had been said about the national debt, and he had been represented as holding the landed property pledged to the payment of the debt. In his opinion not only landed, but funded, and every other kind of property, was pledged to the payment. It was unfair to leave the whole expense of the war on the shoulders of some of their fellow-citizens. After some further arguments to shew the advantages of a free trade, and after expressing his hopes that the country would recover from the unnatural depression under which it laboured, he stated that he had some fears lest the Committee, when appointed, should attempt to raise the protecting prices, from a vague hope of deriving relief therefrom for the present difficulties of agriculture. He concluded by saying, that he had a great objection to a permanent duty, but he had still greater to a graduated one. He hoped that if any were adopted, it would be the lowest countervailing duty which could be calculated to repay the additional charges of taxation suffered by the home-grower.

The motion was agreed to, and the committee was appointed. Among the members were: Mr. Gooch (Chairman), Lord Castlereagh, Mr. F. Robinson, Mr. Huskisson, Mr. Brougham, Mr. Wodehouse, Mr. Baring, Sir E. Knatchbull, Mr. H. Sumner, Mr. Western, Mr. S. Wortley, Lord Althorp, Sir H. Parnell, Mr. Sturges Bourne.

Mr. DICKINSON moved, that Mr. Ricardo should be added to the committee.

Mr. GOOCH had no objection.

Mr. Ricardo, Mr. Curwen, and Mr. Denis Browne, were added to the committee.[1]

[*The following is* Hansard's *report. Cp. above, p.* 81, *footnote.*]

Mr. RICARDO disclaimed any intention of imputing unworthy motives to any of the various parties whose interests were concerned in the question; but he would say, as he had said before, that the interest of the landholders must necessarily be opposed to that of the consumers in the present case. Some hon. gentlemen had been pleased to address him as a mercantile man, as if he had a particular interest to serve. He would answer, that he was not a mercantile man—that he was not a man of funded property, but that he was a landed proprietor, and, as such, had the same interest in the question with many of those who had opposed him. He did not look to the interest of any one party in the state, but to that of the whole country. He agreed in one opinion which had fallen from the hon. member for Essex, that it was not the money price of corn they were discussing, but the labour price; and it was on that very ground that he contended for the policy of a free trade. And what did a free trade mean?—that they should devote the capital which they possessed to the more extensive production of any commodity; corn, for instance. It would result, that the greater the capital which they could so devote, the more of the article would they be able to procure. While he said this, he begged that he might not be understood as advocating an unlimited free trade in corn; for there were circumstances attending that question which rendered it imperative upon the legislature to impose some shackles upon a trade, which, more than any other, being once without restraint, speedily required them. And this led him to consider what had been urged by many gentlemen upon the subject of countervailing duties. If the agriculturists would show that they had any particular taxes to cope with, which other producers had not, then, undoubtedly, they ought to have a countervailing duty to that amount: and not only so, but there ought to be a drawback allowed upon exportation to that amount. The great principle upon which they should go was this—to make the price of their corn approximate, as nearly as possible, to the price it bore in other countries. He was more sanguine, undoubtedly, than many; but he was not such an enthusiast as to suppose that, under present circumstances, they could reach at one step this great and true principle of all

---

[1] On the report of this Committee see below, pp. 114 and 129.

corn trade. Much had been said, affirming and denying the direct interest of landholders in monopolizing the market. He would say, without hesitation, that gentlemen of landed property had an interest in getting the monopoly of the market for their own corn. In the mode in which they had gone about it, however, they had not been very dexterous or successful. The hon. member for Cumberland [Mr. Curwen] had said, with great propriety and truth, that for many years past a glut of corn had always come into the country whenever the price had risen above 80s. This fact confirmed the objections which had been raised to protecting duties upon that commodity. Although a duty on the importation of corn would not be so wise a measure as the approach to that system which he had suggested as constituting the true principle of a corn trade; yet he did think that a permanent duty upon importation would be a much wiser measure than that which had been proposed and advocated. Let them rather have a certain moderate duty which should have a tendency to produce a price of corn that should not be very variable. The last desideratum was of the very highest importance, as much of the evil arose from the fluctuation of prices. The system which had been proposed by the hon. member for Bridgenorth [Mr. Whitmore], of duties that should rise as the price of corn fell, and fall as the price of corn rose, he could not consider a very wise one. What would be the situation of the grower, if such a system were put in practice? Supposing he had to contend with the deficiencies of a short crop in one season, he naturally expected to make up for them in the next season. But the adoption of these duties would leave him no such remedy for his misfortunes. The hon. member for Oxford had the other evening appeared surprised at one or two positions which he had ventured to advance. The hon. gentleman had called upon him to solve this riddle, as he called it, namely, "if you open your ports, and import the immense quantities of corn which then will inundate the country, how can it be said the country will be better able to sustain a money taxation? —so far from it, the means she now possesses, now applicable to that purpose, will be withdrawn from her." But it was not difficult to give the required solution. Suppose the case of a country which was cultivating its own lands, and received no supply from abroad;—a country that had a much better mode and practice of agriculture than others; and which, in consequence of that circumstance, could, with less trouble and expense than they could do, grow all that was necessary for her purpose. It was clear that, under such circumstances, the price of corn would be much lowered there. But, let gentlemen keep their eyes upon the capital that would be thus liberated from the land. Would that be idle? Would that be employed in no way? Would it not be employed for the purchase and obtaining of other commodities? Would not those commodities be of value in the country, and by their value afford to pay that additional taxation which he had alluded to, in the position that had so much startled the hon. member for Oxford? "But," said that hon. gentleman again, "do you mean to say, that if the price of corn be lessened one half, the country can afford to pay the same money taxation?" He answered confidently, "Yes," these commodities of which he had spoken would enable her to pay it. An opinion had been given in another place, which he thought had been treated with too much levity. It did appear to him, that that opinion was well founded; for he also was one who thought that the low price of corn, under which we were at present labouring, was occasioned by too great a supply. He did not think it to be the consequence of taxation. Whether that abundance was the effect of too great an importation, or arose from a diminution of the demand, still the depression was in every case, if the price did not repay the producer, to be attributed to no other cause but the too great supply. Taxation, undoubtedly, was a very great evil; no man was more ready to deprecate the present system and extent of the taxation than he was; but how did it operate? Take the commonest article of trade; a hat, for instance. If the hat were taxed, the price of the hat rose of course. Enemy as he was to all taxation, he must say that it was not to taxation only that he attributed the distresses of the farmer; and they who did so, attributed the evil, he thought, to a wrong cause. The hon. member for Wareham had said a great deal, to show that those distresses were principally to be imputed to the heavy duties upon salt. Every person who used salt was injured to a certain degree by that tax: no doubt it was a very grievous burthen, but it was certainly not an adequate reason to be assigned for the present distressed state of agriculture. It had been said that such large quantities of corn had been imported, and at so low a rate, that all the poor lands would go out of cultivation. This he took to be a fallacy: and to proceed from hon. members erroneously supposing that all corn was grown at the same remunerating price. But nothing was more clear than that price was as 30*s*. in some instances, and 40*s*., 50*s*., 60*s*., and 70*s*. in others. The hon. member for Essex had told the House what small quantities of corn, after all, had been imported within the last ten or twelve years, from foreign countries. Another hon. gentleman, however, was for prohibiting the importation of foreign corn altogether, and asked them how they were to pay for it? Why, as for that matter, they ought not to contract the debt, if they could not pay for it; and if the fact was that they could not pay for foreign corn, that was pretty good security, he should conceive, that they would grow it themselves. Then there was the warehousing system. It had been said, "who will speculate in corn, when he knows what a tremendous quantity of it is hanging over him?" He would for one; for, if he had bought his corn at 79*s.*, and it was now selling for 70*s.* he would keep it on hand; and take care not to sell it till it had got above 79*s.* Then if it rose only to 80*s.*, he evidently had the market in his own hands. The hon. member for Cumberland had asked, "Can we grow corn in England on the same terms as the foreign grower." To this he would answer "No:" and for that very reason he would import it. But, what was the proposed end of all capital, if it was not this—that the possessor should procure a great abundance of produce with it? Now if he could prove that by getting rid of all that capital which is employed in land, he could make more profitable use of it, then he contended, that that was in effect so much capital gained by him. But here again an erroneous idea prevailed. The House was told of the capital which was employed in land, and told in a manner as if it was absolutely and entirely vested in it. Let them just consider, however, the wages of labour, the price of improvements, the charges of manure, and they would find that the total cost of all these items would be a capital saved. The hon. member for Kent [Sir E. Knatchbull] had spoken in a very disparaging manner of thrashing machines. Now, in his opinion, every thing which tended to lessen human labour was an advantage to mankind. Something also had been said on the subject of the national debt. He had no particular individual interest in it, because he derived no revenue from it; but he would say, that the landed interest, the agricultural interest, the trading and every other public interest, were pledged to the public debt. What could be more dishonourable than for a state to carry on the expenses of war by the money advanced upon her good credit by her own subjects, and then to turn round upon those from whom she had borrowed it, and say—"We are insolvent, and we will not pay you." It was totally unworthy of an enlightened and honourable assembly to entertain a proposition so monstrous. The hon. member for Cumberland appeared to entertain a very strange idea of the nature of countervailing duties. He had said, that the countervailing duties should amount to all the difference between the price for which the foreigner could grow corn, and that for which we could afford to grow it. But the fact was by no means so. The House might remember the large capital employed in France during the continental system of exclusion, in obtaining a species of sugar from beet. Now, the question was, when that exclusion was abolished, and sugars could be imported, what were they to do with the capital employed in the beet process? The hon. member, on his proposition, would have required a countervailing duty to the amount of the difference between the price at which sugar could be so imported, and that at which it could be extracted from beet. Another argument was, that rent and capital would be annihilated if the land was thrown out of cultivation. He did not mean to deny that the House ought to deal tenderly with all the interests concerned; but though opening the ports would throw a good many labourers out of employment in land, it would open other sources of labour. The hon. member for Bridgenorth [Mr. Whitmore] had taken an unfavourable view of the state of the country. For his own part, he had better hopes. He could not help feeling that the difficulties of the country were nearly at an end, and that the present unnatural state of depression must soon cease to be felt. He thought we were now reviving; and nothing could so much contribute to that revival as the relief of the people from taxation by every possible means. He had great apprehension from the appointment of this committee, because he feared that it would look for relief to restrictions upon importation. If restrictions were to be imposed, he would rather have a fixed duty than a graduated one, as being most likely to produce permanent benefit to the country.

BANK CASH PAYMENTS BILL

19 *March* 1821

The CHANCELLOR OF THE EXCHEQUER reminded the House that by the Act of 1819, the Bank of England were entitled, at their option, to issue gold coin on the 1st of May 1822, and were bound to resume cash payments on the 1st of May 1823. He would now propose that this optional power should be brought into practical operation on the 1st of May 1821. Two circumstances justified the anticipation: first, the rapid accumulation of treasure in the Bank, which by restricting the circulation of other countries produced an unfavourable effect on commerce; secondly, the widespread forgery of Bank-notes, which could only be diminished by the progressive substitution of coin for Bank-notes. Mr. BARING moved that the principle of the Act of 1819 be reconsidered. He thought the distress of the country was due to the rise in the value of the currency and the increased burden of debt, which had followed the return to cash payments. 'He was not himself bold enough to recommend a departure from the standard,' but he would propose two remedies for the evils of the present system. 'The first was to render permanent the plan of paying Bank-notes in bullion, or to continue what he hoped he might, without disrespect, call the Ricardo system; for, in his opinion, the permanent establishment of that plan was peculiarly calculated to relieve the tension which was at present felt in the currency of the country.' As to the danger of forgery, it could not require much ingenuity to invent a Bank-note more difficult to imitate than the present clumsy one; or, instead of the small notes, he would propose a gold token. 'The second remedy which he had to propose was, the establishment of a double standard, namely, gold and silver.'

Mr. RICARDO[1] began by observing, that his hon. friend[2] had set out with contending for the propriety of establishing two standards: whereas a great part of his argument had gone to put the gold standard out of the question altogether. He had truly said, that in 1797, permission was given to the Bank of England, by act of parliament, to increase or diminish the amount of its circulation as it might think proper. Now, though he agreed that such a power could not have been lodged in hands less inclined to abuse that permission, he did consider it a power most dangerous to have been entrusted to any men, under any circumstances. It was undoubtedly true that the Bank had had it in its power to have kept the currency at a standard as if it had been composed entirely of gold and silver. He maintained that it had then the full power of doing so. The Bank of England, however, neglected that duty; and, in 1819, when the war had terminated, it became absolutely necessary that the House should adopt the steps it had adopted towards payment in bullion.

[1] Ricardo wrote to McCulloch that the newspaper reports of this speech were so unlike what he had said that he could scarcely recognise it (below, VIII, 358–9). *Hansard's* report only slightly improves on that of *The Times*.
[2] Mr. Baring.

The question with the House, then, was—"Shall we take the standard of our currency at its present depreciation? or shall we take it as it existed previously to the year 1797?" His noble friend, the member for Salisbury (lord Folkestone), had, with a great deal of good sense and judgment, proposed to fix the standard at the price at which gold then was. On that point he had differed from his noble friend, thinking that gold was not then sufficiently depreciated, had it been more depreciated, he should have preferred that plan to the adoption of a more variable standard. His hon. friend[1] who had called him a theorist[2], seemed himself to have undergone a great change of sentiment. His own opinion always was, that there should be but one standard, and that that standard should be gold; because silver was liable to undergo such changes, that it might sink in value below gold, and thus occasion the greatest confusion; but his hon. friend had formerly contended, that the adoption of two standards would be attended with advantage.[3] Now, however, his hon. friend advanced another idea, which, he confessed, did strike him with astonishment. His hon. friend seemed disposed to admit all the advantages of a fixed currency, and that gold should be adopted as the standard, but also thought, that the Bank should be allowed, at their option, to pay in silver, at

---

[1] Mr. Baring.

[2] *The Times* reports 'a *purist*, and a theorist'.

[3] The *British Press* reports more plausibly: 'The Hon. Member had called him (Mr. Ricardo) a theorist, but those who called out in that manner were generally the greatest theorists themselves. His Hon. Friend had proposed some great theories, and his own opinion of them had changed within a very short space of time. When he was examined by that Committee, of whose labours he (Mr. Ricardo) thought so highly, as to the double standard, he then said, he should prefer one standard, and that of gold. Being asked the reason for that preference, he said that from the machinery which had gone to South America, it was probable the working of the mines would be so much facilitated, that a great fall might probably take place in the value of silver.'

5*s*. 2*d*. per oz. for ten years to come, still retaining gold as the sole standard, and then adjust the price of silver to the standard of gold. Now, suppose the silver to sink to 4*s*. or to 3*s*. 6*d*., before the ten years had expired, at the end of that term it would be necessary, on the principle of his hon. friend, to raise it to 5*s*. 2*d*. thus adjusting it every ten years. This would unquestionably be one of the most variable standards that could possibly be devised. His hon. friend had stated, that representations were sent from all parts of the country complaining of the prevalence of distress. This was unfortunately too true; but it was worthy of remark, that his hon. friend, who was no theorist, had nevertheless a theory respecting the cause of these distresses, by which he imputed them all to the state of the currency. Now, it appeared to him that they might with more truth be referred to a great many other causes. They might arise from an abundant harvest, from the vast importations from Ireland, which had not taken place formerly, and from the late improvements in agriculture, which, he apprehended, would be felt hereafter more severely. These causes his hon. friend entirely over-looked, and laid the whole blame on the alteration which had been made in the currency; while he (Mr. Ricardo) contended that this alteration could not be said to amount to more than 5 per cent. He admitted, that gold might have altered in value; that was an accident against which it was impossible to provide; but, supposing that silver had been adopted as a standard, would it not also have varied? His hon. friend contended, that if silver had been made the standard, it could never have fallen so much in value; but his hon. friend argued all along on the assumption that the whole difference between gold and silver was owing to the rise of gold. This, however, was not fair; for when a difference arose in the relative value of the two metals, he had just as good a right to say that silver had fallen, as his hon. friend had to say that gold had risen. The surest test was the rate of the foreign exchanges; and if his hon. friend looked at what a pound sterling was worth in 1816 in the silver coin of France, and what it was now worth, he would find it difficult to make out a variation of more than 10 per cent. He begged the House to recollect, that in 1817 wheat sold at 109*s.* and bullion was then at 3*l.* 18*s.* 6*d.* Would his hon. friend say, that that price was owing to the depreciation of the currency? and if not, was he calling on his hon. friend to concede too much, by admitting that the present price of grain might be owing to many other causes? His hon. friend had said, that a great deal of capital had been expended during the war. Now, he doubted whether this was a sound proposition: for, he believed that the savings of individuals during the war, would be found to have more than counteracted the profuse expenditure of the government, and that the capital of the country at the end of the war was greater than it was at the commencement of it. His hon. friend had asked, why we should have a purer standard than the rest of the world?—a question which might be very properly answered by asking, why we should not? If other countries chose to adopt an error, was that any reason why we should follow their example? The attempt to procure the best possible standard had been characterised by his hon. friend as a piece of coxcombry to which he attached no value; but, in a question of finance, if we could get a better system than our neighbours, we were surely justified in adopting it. [1] He undoubtedly did wish for a better system, and it was for that reason that he wished to

---

[1] *The Times's* report, which up to this point agrees closely with *Hansard's,* here runs: 'The hon. gent., after several observations, which with even the most pain- ful attention, we were unable to catch, proceeded' etc. The rest of the speech is more briefly reported in *The Times.*

see one metal adopted as a standard of currency, and the system of two metals rejected. With respect to the adoption of a gold token, he thought it would be attended with great danger; if by a gold token was meant a token materially less in value than the gold coin which it represented. The necessary consequence of such a system would be, that the tokens would be imitated in foreign countries, and poured into this country in such quantities as would very speedily produce a depreciation of our currency, equivalent to the difference between the value of the sovereign and that of the token which represented the sovereign. If he could be induced to give his consent to the introduction of a gold token, it must be of such a value as nearly to equal the value of the sovereign. He would permit no more alloy in the token than what would be sufficient to cover the actual expense of coining the bullion into money. Such a plan would afford a sufficient security against the inroads of forgers[1], and might be advantageously adopted.—It had been said, that if one metal were adopted for a standard of currency, it would be in the power of speculators to raise or lower the standard, and consequently place the Bank in an awkward predicament; but the power which the Bank had of regulating its issues, would always be sufficient to prevent any inconvenience of that kind. With respect to the suggestion of the right hon. gentleman opposite[2] for diminishing the issues of Bank-notes as a security against forgery, he entirely concurred with his hon. friend[3] that such a plan would be wholly ineffectual as a remedy against forgery. It was perfectly clear, that whether the issues consisted altogether of Bank-notes, or half in Bank-notes and half in sovereigns, the danger of forgery would be the same. The only effectual

[1] Misprinted 'foreigners' in *Hansard*.

[2] The Chancellor of the Exchequer.

[3] Mr. Baring.

remedy against forgery would be, to hasten the period at which the Bank might commence payment in specie. He should be perfectly ready to abandon his own plan, if by so doing that most desirable object could be effected; and he was quite satisfied that the Bank was at this time in such a state of preparation, that in a very few months they might provide the best and only effectual security against the imitation of their notes, by returning to the system of currency which existed in this country previous to 1797. The right hon. gentleman had dwelt upon the tendency of his measure to prevent the accumulation of coin in the Bank; as if the coffers of the Bank were overflowing with coin. Now, the fact was, that the Bank had a great deal of bullion and very little coin. To propose a measure, therefore, for preventing the accumulation of coin in the hands of the Bank, was to provide against a danger, which was not at all likely to occur. With respect to the laws relating to usury, he should be extremely glad to see them repealed; and he thought no time more proper for the repeal of those laws than the present, when the rate of interest had actually sunk below 5 per cent. The rate of interest in the market had been invariably under 5 per cent since 1819. It would be a great advantage to the mercantile interests, that the Bank of England should discount the notes presented to them, not at one invariable rate of interest, but varying according to the alteration of the rate of interest in the market.[1]

[See further p. 105.]

---

[1] In the *British Press* the conclusion reads: 'If he might advise the Bank, they would, instead of discounting at the invariable rate of 5 per cent. alter the rate of interest according to the changes of the market. During the war those merchants who could discount at the Bank, raised money at 5 per cent. whilst those who were not so favoured paid 7 per cent. for it. That was the case in the war, but at present it would be wise for the Bank to lower the rate of interest to 4 per cent.'

BANK CASH PAYMENTS[1]

28 *March* 1821

Mr. GRENFELL, referring to the alleged refusal of the Bank of Ireland to receive coin of the realm as deposits [see above, p. 70], said that he had now been assured by the principal director of the Bank of Ireland that there was not the slightest foundation for the statement. Mr. IRVING thought 'that, situated as the Bank of Ireland was, they might have regulated the exchanges better by the distribution of their issues in a more suitable manner than they had done'. Mr. ELLIS stated 'that 500,000*l.* was voted for the service of those who, having property, could not immediately turn it into specie; but so increased was the liberality of the Bank of Ireland on that occasion, that it actually rendered necessary the application of only 100,000*l.* of that sum.... With respect to the statement that the low rate of exchange arose from the small quantity of circulating medium in Ireland it appeared to him that that could not justly be cited as the true cause, when it was on record that the exports of corn from Ireland were three times greater in the last than in the former year. That was the circumstance to which the low rate of exchange was attributable, and not to any deficiency in the Bank of Ireland issues.'

Mr. RICARDO was very much gratified at what he had heard from the hon. gent. (Mr. Irving)[2] this night. The hon. gent. was now of opinion that the circulation of the Bank regulated the state of the exchange, and he (Mr. Ricardo) was very happy that the hon. gent. was at last a convert to that doctrine. Those gentlemen who imagined that a lucrative trade could be carried on by exchanging coin for Bank-notes, were, as it appeared to him, very much mistaken, because it was impossible for Bank notes to be more valuable than the coin of the country. It was impossible for a man, who was

---

[1] This debate is not mentioned in *Hansard*. Ricardo's speech is here reprinted from the report in *The Times*.

[2] The original report in *The Times* has 'Sir H. Parnell' instead of 'Mr. Irving' and accordingly, here and below, 'hon. bart.' instead of 'hon. gent.' The correct name was given in an *Erratum* the following day.

called on in the course of trade, to purchase any commodity to carry on his trade more profitably with Bank notes than with the coin of the realm. Therefore there was no sort of inducement, as it appeared to him, for any person to exchange his bullion at the Bank for their notes. The Bank of Ireland was, however, placed under very different circumstances from the Bank of England; and they did seem to him to have acted with a degree of energy, which, if it had been the case of this country, they would have found the Bank of England not ready to have adopted. What was the case of the Bank of Ireland? The stoppage of a number of private banks in the country rendered it absolutely necessary that a very great increase in the circulation, of some sort or another, should be provided. Either the diminution of the circulating medium must be supplied by coin, or a powerful effort must be made by the Bank of Ireland to make up the deficiency by an issue of notes. The Bank of Ireland did make that great effort to the amount, he believed, of 50 per cent; and, from what he had himself heard from the Governor of the Bank of Ireland,[1] that issue would have been increased still farther if those securities had been offered on which the Bank of Ireland usually made their advances; but, from the state of Ireland, those securities could not at the moment be found; and the Bank, however willing to increase their issues, had not the power so to do. It was very evident that the Bank of Ireland would not have increased the circulation if they had taken in sovereigns and issued paper. That would have been merely to decrease one circulation, and to increase another. With respect to the management of the debt of Ireland, an hon. gent. had observed that there was a compensation given to the Bank for the care of that debt. Undoubtedly there was a species of remuneration; but when he contrasted that

[1] Arthur Guinness.

remuneration with what the Bank of England received for the management of our debt, the latter appeared to him to be enormous. At the same time he was one of those who did not think that banks should be called on to serve the public gratis. The word 'liberality' had been used, with respect to the conduct of the Bank of Ireland, and, in his opinion, such a phrase was not properly applied, merely because they had issued their Bank notes; because a bank never increased its paper issue without receiving some advantage from it. He fully concurred in the opinion of those who held that the circulation of the Bank of Ireland was, at the time the distress occurred, very deficient; and he looked upon the exchange to have been affected, not by the great increase of the exportation of corn, but as arising from the issue of the Bank of Ireland not being so high, in notes or money, as it ought to have been.

PUBLIC ACCOUNTS[1]

29 *March* 1821

Mr. RICARDO begged to know from the Secretary of the Treasury whether the annual accounts which were produced respecting the public expenditure, by order of the house, might not be printed in a more perspicuous and simple form. The hon. gent. particularly referred to one branch of the accounts; but he spoke so low, that we could not hear to which he referred.

Mr. LUSHINGTON expressed his readiness to adopt any suggestion for the purpose of having the accounts more clearly understood.

[1] This matter is not mentioned in *Hansard*. The report is here reprinted from *The Times*.

AGRICULTURAL HORSES TAX

5 *April* 1821

Mr. CURWEN moved for leave to bring in a bill for the repeal of the tax upon horses employed in agriculture.

Mr. RICARDO said, he should certainly give his support to the motion. He should do so on the same principle on which he had voted for repealing the last duty on malt[1], not because it was in itself a bad tax, or pressed with peculiar hardship on the landed interest, but with a view of compelling the observance of strict economy in the administration of government. It was his belief that the whole amount of the malt tax might be saved by measures of economy; and as he looked upon the sinking fund to be utterly useless—to be at this moment unproductive of one single good effect—he was quite disposed to abrogate every tax so long as any portion of that fund remained in existence.[2] The hon. mover had stated, that foreign monarchs were embarking in the corn trade, that they were becoming merchants, and that the king of Sweden was importing oats into this country. Now if this were the fact, he for one should rather rejoice at it, because he should expect to make much better bargains with kings and

---

[1] On 21 March 1821 Mr. Western's motion for the repeal of the additional Malt Duty imposed in 1819 had been carried against the Government by 149 votes to 125; but the bill was lost on the second reading, on 3 April, by 144 to 242. In both cases Ricardo voted for repeal.

[2] *The Times's* report here adds: 'According to the representations of an hon. bart. (Sir T. Lethbridge) the whole pressure of taxation fell on those classes of the community interested in agriculture; but to this proposition he could by no means assent. The fundholders had a very large share, a share which, if fairly examined and compared, would be found to constitute a full proportion. If foreign corn were imported, the landowners' means might be diminished; but the property and industry of the country would find another and more profitable channel of employment.'

princes than with their subjects. The hon. gentleman, however, need not be under any alarm; for if, as he represented, these trading potentates would not take back our hardware and pottery in exchange, and would receive nothing but bullion, there was a sufficient security for our continuing to grow our own corn.

Mr. BARING 'expressed his regret at hearing this question argued with reference to the conflicting interests of different classes of the community. It gave him some surprise to find his hon. friend treating a great national subject [the sinking fund] in a way which, practically considered, he must pronounce extraordinary and almost absurd.'

The motion was withdrawn.

TIMBER DUTIES[1]

5 *April* 1821

Mr. WALLACE, the Vice-President of the Board of Trade, moved a resolution for reducing the duty on timber from the Baltic and increasing that on timber from the British colonies of North America, thus diminishing the protection of the latter. Sir H. PARNELL moved an amendment to equalize all duties at the end of five years. Mr. SYKES, opposing the amendment, pointed out that 'the American timber trade was carried on by British shipping, but three-fourths of the Norway timber trade was carried on by foreign ships'. Mr. BARING remarked that 'the general principle of political economy which ought to regulate the conduct of a great country ... would lead us to purchase an article wherever it could be had of the best quality and at the

[1] On 9 Feb. 1821, speaking on a petition from the merchants of New Brunswick against any alteration in the timber duties, presented by Mr. Marryatt, 'Mr. RICARDO expressed his astonishment that any class of merchants in the city should show themselves averse to the principles of a free trade; but still he found that gentlemen could advocate the continuance of severe restrictions wherever they thought that their own interests were likely to be benefitted from them.' (*The Times's* report.)

cheapest price'. But in this particular case 'some sacrifice of the 5 April 1821 several interests of the public to those of the ship-owners was necessary'.

Mr. RICARDO[1] said, he was anxious to deliver his opinion on the present proposition, as it involved a principle of infinitely greater importance than the question immediately under consideration. They had been told that they ought to go to the best, and cheapest market, and also that the timber of Norway and Russia was better and cheaper than that of America; and yet they were recommended as a practical measure, to take the worst timber at the dearest rate! His hon. friend (Mr. Bennet), in a speech full of the soundest argument, and as yet totally unanswered by the gentlemen opposite, had shown, in the most convincing manner, that by buying our timber from the northern powers of Europe, we should save 400,000*l.* annually on the purchase of that article, and consequently that we were yearly incurring a debt to that amount, in order to put this money into the pockets of the ship-owners. If a bill were introduced for the specific and avowed purpose of granting a sum to that amount to the ship-owners, he would much rather agree to it than to the resolutions now before the committee, for in that case the capital thus given to them might be more usefully employed. At present it was a total sacrifice of 400,000*l.* a year, as much so as if the ships engaged in the coasting trade should be obliged to sail round the island in order to give employment to a greater number. He was of opinion that, according to the true principles of commerce, it ought to form no part of the consumer's consideration to enter into the distribution by the seller, of the money or labour which he (the consumer) exchanged for any commodity which he wanted. All the consumer had to consider was, where he could get the article he

---

[1] *The Times's* report opens: 'Mr RICARDO, who had frequently attempted, in vain, to catch the eye of the chairman'.

wanted cheapest; whether the payments were to be made in money or in manufactures was matter quite of minor importance. In this, as in all other branches of commercial policy, it was useless to urge partial views in behalf of one set of men or another. That House ought not to look to the right or the left, but consider merely how the people of England, as a body, could best employ their capital and labour. Wrong notions of commercial policy had too long prevailed; and now that the country had begun to recognize sounder principles, the sooner they acted upon them the better. There were exceptions to be made in cases of very old established arrangements; but this American trade was not one of them; was of new date, and mainly sprung out of a quarrel between England and the Baltic powers[1]: it was then said that the latter would withhold their timber, and that the colonial trade must necessarily be encouraged in Canada. What once occurred, might again happen it was said. Well, then, his reply was—if ever it should happen, it would be time enough to pay the high price: at present let more economical arrangements be attempted. It was strange that inconsistency always marked the progress of monopolists. One set of men now called out for this colonial trade in behalf of the shipping interest, and the very same set of men, if they were spoken to about the West India Dock system, would call it partial and oppressive. So, respecting the Irish linen monopoly, it was said, why not be allowed to go to Germany, where the same manufacture might be had cheaper? He certainly concurred in the hon. baronet's view of this question.

Sir Henry Parnell's amendment was lost by 15 votes to 54. Ricardo voted for the amendment.

[See further p. 110 below.]

[1] The duties had been imposed in 1810.

BANK CASH PAYMENTS BILL

9 *April* 1821

On this debate [cp. above, p. 91] being resumed Mr. BARING moved as an amendment that a select committee be appointed to reconsider the whole subject: 'the more he considered this question, the more he felt it to be ... "*the*" one in which were involved all the distresses experienced by the country and their remedy.' Mr. ATTWOOD, seconding, said that the value of money since 1819 had risen 20 or 30 per cent., and not 3 per cent. as predicted by Mr. Ricardo. The CHANCELLOR OF THE EXCHEQUER opposed the amendment.

Mr. RICARDO said, he would not have troubled the House if he had not been so pointedly alluded to in the course of the debate. He was not answerable, he said, for the effect which the present measure might have upon particular classes; but he contended that if the advice which he had given long ago had been adopted—if the Bank, instead of buying, had sold gold, as he recommended[1]—the effect would have been very different from what it was at present. It was impossible, on any system of metallic circulation, to guard against the alterations to which the metals themselves were liable; yet all the complaints they had heard that night referred to the changes in the value of the metals. When the measure of 1819 had been adopted, they had known that the alteration that it would make between gold and paper would be 4 per cent: yet with that knowledge, they had, in all the difficulties with which they were surrounded, recommended the measure. The hon. member for Taunton[2] had entered into a speculation on the subject, as if a gold standard had been an innovation of 1819. But that standard had been adopted some time between 1796 and 1798. Up to that period, gold and silver had been the standard. The chancellor of the exchequer had laboured

---

[1] See above, p. 13. [2] Mr. Baring.

under a mistake when he had said that silver had been a legal tender only to the amount of 25*l.* It was true that that had been the utmost amount in the degraded currency of the country; but a man might have gone to the Mint with his silver, and 100,000*l.* might be paid in silver of standard value. This, however, had never been any man's interest. But gold had been carried to the Mint, and gold had, in fact become the standard. The change in the relative value of the metals had taken place in the period he had mentioned between 1796 and 1798; and large quantities of silver had been carried to the Mint, in order to profit by the state of the law, and the relative value of silver and gold. If government had not interfered, a guinea would not have been found in the country, and silver would have been the standard. The government, aware that there would be one silver currency of degraded value, and another of standard value, had by an act of parliament, he believed, shut the Mint against silver; and he asked whether gold had not then become the standard? If the Bank had not bought gold, contrary to his opinion and recommendation, gold would not have risen. But it was only an assumption that gold had risen. When the relative value was changed, what criterion could they find, to show, whether the one rose, or the other fell? His hon. friend (Mr. Baring), who had been examined before the committee[1] with the attention which his high authority demanded, had strenuously recommended a gold standard as less variable than a silver standard. Yet he now stated, from his experience in France, that silver varied very little. His hon. friend's theories thus changed very often; his own were unchanged, though he had been represented as moving with the vibrations of a pendulum, and entertaining views of placing the currency in a degree of perfection not suited to

---

[1] The Committee of 1819 on the Resumption of Cash Payments.

our situation.[1] His hon. friend had himself the same views of the perfection of the currency; and he regretted that his hon. friend had not continued to entertain those opinions. His hon. friend had spoken of the danger of keeping men's minds in a state of uncertainty; yet he constantly came down to the House with new speculations. The evil of uncertainty and alarm could only be got rid of by parliament being determined to adhere to the measure they had adopted. Such speculations coming from so great an authority as his hon. friend, were calculated to do much mischief. It had been stated, that we could not get labourers to consent to a fall of wages, and that they ran away with the capital of their employers. By altering the value of money, it was very true that they altered the distribution of property. By increasing the value of the currency, the stockholder received greater value, and another paid more. With rents it was the same: the landlord received more value, and the farmer paid more. Thus the distribution of property was always altered by the alteration of the currency. It was quite possible that this alteration might occasion a glut of certain commodities in the market. For instance, a clothier might bring to market a certain quantity of superfine cloth when prices were at a certain rate; if the clothiers[2] should come to receive more money than before, and their labourers[3] to pay more, it was not likely that the labourers should require so much superfine cloth as those whose property was diminished by the change in the currency had required: the consequence would be a glut of cloth in the market. By altering the distribution of property thus, an alteration would be made in the demand for some commodities; there would be a deficiency of supply to the

---

[1] See above, p. 77.
[2] Should be 'labourers', as reported by *The Times*.

[3] Should be 'employers'; *The Times*, here, is uniform with *Hansard*.

new taste which came to the market, with the increase of
property: and there would be too much for the taste whose
resources had fallen. The hon. member for Callington (Mr.
Attwood) had ascribed the variations of prices in all commodities to the currency. He begged the hon. member to
look at the variations in the prices of corn during the last
century, and connect them if he could with the currency.
Corn had risen or fallen forty or fifty per cent when no alteration had taken place in the currency. The low price of corn
was to be ascribed to the very large importation from Ireland,
to the productive harvest, to the very great abundance of
corn that was in the country. The demand was limited, because no man could eat more than a certain quantity of
bread. If there was more than the usual and ordinary
quantity in the market, the price must of necessity fall. We
had no outlet for corn, because our prices were higher than
in any other country. If the variations in prices were owing
to the money standard, which he denied, all countries must
have been affected by similar variations, and he wondered
that his hon. friend[1] had not told them his experience in that
respect in France, America, Russia, Spain, and other
countries. But if the variations were owing to what he (Mr.
Ricardo) had stated, it was not fair to impute them to the
act of 1819. The chancellor of the exchequer had said gold
had not risen before the peace of Amiens. This was not quite
correct. It had begun to rise in 1799; in 1800 it had been
4*l.* 5*s.*

Mr. Baring's amendment was negatived.

[See for the third reading below, p. 110.]

[1] Mr. Baring.

USURY LAWS

12 *April* 1821

Mr. Serjeant ONSLOW moved for leave to bring in a bill to repeal the Usury Laws. In the course of the discussion Mr. R. GORDON 'deprecated the theory which this proposition had in view, cautioning the House to beware of theories from the sad experience of the measure for the resumption of cash payments. This, however, was the age of theories, and nothing was heard of but a recourse to first principles.' Mr. CALCRAFT, opposing the motion, said that none of the advantages expected from the repeal of the assize of bread had been realised: the present measure would upset mortgages and persuade lenders that they ought to have obtained better terms.

Mr. RICARDO thought the House and the public were very much indebted to the learned gentleman, for the measure which he had proposed; and expressed his astonishment at the apprehensions of members, that its adoption would operate to the prejudice of the landed gentry, by raising the rate of interest; for the fact was, that the lenders of money would not have more power to raise the rate of interest than the borrowers[1] would have to keep it down; and the competition between both would serve to bring it to a reasonable standard. As to the allusion of his hon. friend to the assize of bread, that case had no analogy to the present question, because the maximum upon bread was merely meant to keep the price of that article in due relation to the price of corn. An hon. friend had taken occasion, in referring to the resumption of cash payments, to reprobate what he called that theory. But his hon. friend should consider that the restriction upon cash payments was a departure from the old and established theory of the country, to the sound currency and wholesome practice of which it was now proposed to return. His hon. friend had deprecated change in such a strain, as would really

---

[1] Misprinted 'lenders' in *Hansard.*

12 April 1821 form an argument against any improvement. He had had great experience in the money market, and could state the usury laws to have always been felt as a dead weight on those wishing to raise money. With respect to those concerned in the money market itself, the laws had always been inoperative; and during the war indirect means had been found of obtaining seven, eight, ten and fifteen per cent interest. The laws therefore occasioned inconvenience, but did no good.

Leave was given to bring in the bill. In the course of the session the bill was postponed several times and finally abandoned.

BANK CASH PAYMENTS BILL

13 *April* 1821

13 April 1821 On this bill [cp. p. 105] being brought in for the third reading,

Mr. RICARDO said, he should not have blamed the Bank if they had only increased their issues to an amount sufficient to replace the gold coin that had been removed from the country; but they had extended their issues far beyond what was necessary for that purpose, and to this increase of circulation he ascribed all the depreciation which had followed.

The bill was read a third time and passed.

TIMBER DUTIES BILL

16 *April* 1821

16 April 1821 [See above, p. 102.] Mr. J. P. GRANT moved as an amendment that the drawback allowed on Russian timber be repealed. Mr. WALLACE opposed the amendment because the effect of such a measure would be to give Norway the monopoly of the trade.

Mr. RICARDO[1] was much surprised at the course of argument adopted upon this question. Norway was said to be benefitted by the new arrangement, merely because she had before suffered a still greater injustice than it was now proposed to inflict upon her. The proposition made by his learned friend went only to place Russia and Norway, as respected the importation of their timber and deals, on the same footing; yet this had been described by the right hon. gentleman, as giving a monopoly to Norway; and it had been contended that such a regulation would cause a proportionate rise in the price of Norwegian timber. Now, a slight degree of attention must convince every one, that the higher the price of Norwegian timber rose, the more able must Russia be to compete effectually with Norway. It was contended, that the interest of the producer ought to be looked to, as well as that of the consumer, in legislative principles. But the fact was, that in attending to the interest of the consumer, protection was at the same time extended to all other classes. The true way of encouraging production was to discover and open facilities to consumption. An hon. gentleman[2] had observed, that timber of a superior quality might be had by those who chose to pay a higher price, and that there was therefore no compulsion on the purchaser. But it was a little too much to raise the price of the best article by means of import duties, and then tell the consumer that he was not obliged to buy the cheap and inferior one. The practical effect of these duties was to raise as much compulsion as could be introduced into commercial affairs.

The amendment was negatived.

[1] Ricardo wrote to Trower that this debate was briefly and badly reported in the newspapers (see below, VIII, 371). *Hansard's* report is uniform with *The Times's*; the *Morning Chronicle* gives no report of Ricardo's speech.
[2] Mr. Marryat.

REFORM OF PARLIAMENT

18 *April* 1821

On 17 April Mr. LAMBTON moved for a committee of the whole House, 'to consider the state of the representation of the people in Parliament.' He said that he had prepared a bill extending the franchise to all householders and certain classes of leaseholders, and limiting the duration of parliaments to three years. The debate was continued on the following day.

Mr. RICARDO observed, that the subject of reform was the most important question which could come before that House. He was anxious, therefore, to declare his opinion with reference to it. He agreed with the hon. member for Durham,[1] that it was quite necessary the House of Commons should truly represent the people. It was not necessary for him to have the proof of the recent votes of the House to be convinced that the people at present were not represented. From the manner in which that House was constituted, he was quite certain before of that fact. He would, therefore, embrace any plan which was likely to give the country an efficient representation, and should consequently support the measure now proposed. There was only one thing respecting it which he regretted; and here he was sure that what he was about to declare would be very unpopular in the House: he regretted that his hon. friend did not propose the introduction of voting by ballot, which he thought would be a greater security for the full and fair representation of the people than any extension of the elective franchise. The people would then vote for the man whom they should consider as best calculated to support their interest, without any fear of the overwhelming influence of their superiors. It might be said, that if this were to take place, the effect would be, that in time the people would get rid of the Lords. He

---

[1] Mr. Lambton.

denied that this would be the effect. The people would never, when left to their own free and unbiassed choice, be anxious to get rid of that which they considered the instrument of their good government; and unless gentlemen were prepared to assert that the Lords were an instrument of bad government, which he believed nobody would assert, they could not entertain any rational fear that the people would be anxious to get rid of them.[1]

The House divided on the motion: Ayes, 43; Noes, 55. Ricardo voted for the motion.

POOR RELIEF BILL

8 May 1821

Mr. SCARLETT moved for leave to bring in three measures to amend the Poor Laws: 'the first was, the establishing the [poor rates] assessments for the last year as a maximum; the second, the preventing parochial relief where the parties merely grounded their claim upon being unable to obtain work; and the third, the abandonment of the power enabling justices to order the removal of paupers.'

Mr. RICARDO expressed his surprise that any apprehension should be entertained of the tendency of his hon. and learned friend's bill to create embarrassment in the law of settlement, as the great object of that bill was, to remove all difficulty and litigation with respect to that law. It had been observed that labour, instead of being paid in wages by employers, had been paid out of the Poor-rates. If so, why then should not the amount of such payment be deducted in fairness from those rates? This was one of the objects of his hon. and learned friend's bill; because that bill proposed to have the

---

[1] Cp. the same argument, in nearly the same words, in James Mill's article 'Government', Sect. IX (*Supplement to the Encyclopaedia Britannica*); also below, p. 286 and VII, 320.

8 May 1821   labourer paid in just wages by his employer, instead of having
him transferred to the Poor-rates. The effect, indeed, of his
hon. and learned friend's measure would be, to regulate the
price of labour by the demand, and that was the end peculiarly desired. With respect to the pressure of the taxes and
the national debt upon the poor, that pressure could not be
disputed, especially as it took away from the rich the means
of employing the poor: but he had no doubt, if the supply of
labour were reduced below the demand, which was the
purpose of his hon. and learned friend's measure, that the
public debt and taxes would bear exclusively upon the rich,
and the poor would be most materially benefitted.

Leave was given. Later in the Session the bill was withdrawn.

ORDNANCE ESTIMATES [1]

31 *May* 1821

31 May 1821   During the debate Mr. LOCKHART complained that ministers,
wishing to gloss over agricultural distress, had purposely delayed
the report of the Agricultural Committee.

Mr. RICARDO thought it right to say, in justice to his
Majesty's ministers, and to the agricultural committee, that
the charges made against them were not well-founded. (Hear,
hear.) No unnecessary delay had taken place in the formation
of the report of that committee. (Hear.) The delay had
arisen entirely from the peculiar nature of the subject, and
could not be attributed to any want of diligence on the part
of the members of the committee. (Hear, hear.) He expected
and believed that the report would be made before the
prorogation of parliament. [2] (Hear.)

[1] The report of this debate in
Hansard does not contain Ricardo's speech, which is here

reprinted from *The Times*.
[2] The Report was presented on
18 June 1821.

THE BUDGET

1 *June* 1821

The CHANCELLOR OF THE EXCHEQUER brought forward the   1 June 1821
Budget.

Mr. RICARDO said, that the chancellor of the exchequer
always gave a most flattering account of the state of the
country. Last session he had declared that the funds which
would be applicable to the expenditure of the present year
would be much greater than what he had now stated them to
be. He had stated that the addition to the sinking fund
would have been 1,700,000*l.* instead of 950,000*l.* had it not
been for the additional interest on exchequer bills. Now, he
wished to know whether the interest of those exchequer bills
had not been provided for in the preceding session? He
thought a sum was voted for that purpose, because he took
occasion, on the last budget, to remind the right hon. gentleman that he had made no provision whatever for the interest
on the exchequer debt; and he stated in answer, that provision had already been made out of former votes. If that
were the case, he must place this payment against certain
debts which should be liquidated in the present year, and not
against that which fairly belonged to the budget of former
years. From the papers which were in the hands of members,
it appeared that the account might be correctly stated thus:—
By the annual accounts, the amount of the unfunded debt
appeared to be 17,292,544*l.* There were funded, during the
last year, 7,000,000*l.* exchequer bills, which, added to the
former amount gave a total of 24,292,544*l.* There was a
deficiency arising on the consolidated fund, which the right
hon. gentleman had entirely left out of view. That deficiency
amounted to 517,232*l.* during the present year, and this being

added to the enormous deficiency which existed before, might be stated, in fact, at 8,990,000*l.* And here he could not help remarking, that these accounts, from the way in which they were made up, did not give the committee that correct view of the state of the finances which it was desirable that it should be furnished with. If he wished to consult them for information, he could find no part from which he could clearly discover what the annual deficiency upon the con-solidated fund really was. A paper having been moved for some time since, he was enabled to ascertain that on the year ending the 5th Jan. 1821, that deficiency was 8,850,327*l.* and in the year ending 5th Jan. 1820, 8,321,000*l.* The difference between the sums was 429,327*l.* Now, this being the case, what was the reason that in the annual printed accounts which were delivered to the House, the amount of the deficiency upon the consolidated fund for the very same period[1], was stated at 517,232*l.* instead of 429,327*l.?* making a difference between those accounts and the return which he spoke of, of 87,905*l.* He did not mention this difference upon account of the magnitude of the sum, but for the purpose of showing how little reliance could be placed on these public accounts, under their present shape. But, to return to the matter of those accounts. It seemed that, during the last year, we had contracted loans to the amount of 24,292,544*l.* to which must be added, for the deficiency upon the con-solidated fund, 517,232*l.,* making together 24,809,776*l.* Against this amount they must put that part of the debt which had been paid off. It must be shown how much money had been devoted to that purpose; and then, what-ever balance appeared, by so much had our debt increased or decreased. We had a sinking fund last year of 17,510,000*l.*

---

[1] *The Times's* report adds: 'that is, from the 5th of January, 1820, to the 5th of January, 1821'.

The amount of treasury bills paid off was 2,000,000*l.* The difference between the amount of exchequer bills upon the 5th January, 1820, and the 5th January, 1821, was 5,934,928*l.* So that we had devoted, in truth, to the payment of the national debt, whether funded or unfunded, during the current year, the sum of 25,444,928*l.*, and reckoning, as he did, the amount of the debt contracted to be during the same period, 24,809,776*l.*, the difference would be 635,152*l.* The actual amount, therefore, of difference, between the debt on the 5th Jan. 1820, and the debt on the 5th Jan. 1821, did appear to be no more than 635,152*l.*, although the right hon. gentleman by some other species of calculation, made it amount to 950,000*l.* The House was told by the right hon. gentleman, that there would be a sinking fund next year, of 4,000,000*l.* Now, assuming the revenue for the current year to be as stated by the right hon. gentleman, and supposing that there should be such a sinking fund, it was to be remembered that the right hon. gentleman had included in his calculation a sum of 500,000*l.* which he said he was to receive from France, and which was applicable towards the payment of the national debt during the present year. But if this 500,000*l.* was so applicable during the present year, it would not be in the next, or any future year. He (Mr. Ricardo) wished to know what funds could be made of general and permanent application in this way; and therefore it was of little avail to bring forward such a sum as this in such a statement. He took it that the sinking fund would really amount to 2,809,000*l.;* and the sinking fund on exchequer bills, to 290,000*l.*, making the sinking fund 3,099,000*l.* instead of 4,000,000*l.*[1] He confessed he was one of those who

---

[1] *The Times* adds: 'as estimated by the Chancellor of the Exchequer. He certainly wished, however, that the event might turn out according to the statement of the right honourable gentleman. But he did not think that the house or the country

thought a sinking fund very useless. He did not mean to say that he was not favourable to such a fund in the abstract. Upon the principle of the thing there could be hardly any doubt; but, after the experience which they had had, he did not expect to see that principle acted upon. He did not expect that it would ever be made applicable to the reduction of the national debt. The hon. gentleman then briefly recapitulated the history of this fund from the time of sir Robert Walpole. When Mr. Pitt came into power, he was desirous of establishing a sinking fund upon the safest and most permanent principles, so as to secure it from all intermeddling of ministers. What had become of this sinking fund, and where were all these boasted securities? First of all, the present chancellor of the exchequer came down to the House boasting (as if he were going to confer a great obligation on the country and the fund-holder) of his intention to take about 7,000,000*l.* of the annual income of this sinking fund; and he then talked of the greatness of the treasure with which we should be incumbered. That right hon. gentleman's alarms ever seemed to arise, not from any prospect of our poverty but from the great increase of our wealth; and accordingly he was always telling the House of the various mischiefs that resulted from excess of capital. Had that right hon. gentleman considered the true principles of capital, he would have seen that there never could be much danger of its excess. Upon the subject of this sinking fund,[1] he would take the liberty of calling the attention of the House to a pamphlet which had been written under the

had much reason to congratulate themselves, when it appeared, that all which the right honourable gentleman had to tell them was, that the revenue in future years would be the same as in this.'

[1] From this point the *Courier* reports: 'He begged leave to read a passage from a pamphlet written by another Right Hon. Gentleman opposite. [Mr. Ricardo read the passage he alluded to, which re-

auspices of a right hon. gentleman opposite he believed. [The hon. gentleman here read an extract from a pamphlet.] This was the system of which it had been gravely observed that no departure from the original measure, and no violation of the act of 1792, had taken place in the subsequent appropriation of the fund. Now, the principle of Mr. Pitt's system was professedly this—that thereafter, every war should carry in itself the seeds of its own destruction. In every word of the reasoning of this pamphlet upon this question, he (Mr. R.) did most cordially agree; and hence he inferred, that such appropriation as had been made of the sinking fund, was a violation of the public faith. It was the violation of that fund which had entailed upon us a large increase of debt; and they who expected to see it preserved inviolate hereafter, did, in his opinion, deceive themselves. The right hon. gentleman had ventured to apply, in payment of the interest of a new debt, almost all the sinking fund that remained to us. Almost all, did he say! The right hon. gentleman had, in effect, applied the whole of it. He had lately increased the taxes by 3,000,000*l.*, a sum which was more than the sinking fund actually amounted to. He (Mr. R.), therefore, was rather disposed now to say, "Let us have no sinking fund; let the money remain in the pockets of the people. When the ministers want supplies, whether for carrying on a war, or for any other purpose, let them come down to the House and ask for them, without having any such fund to resort to." Ministers were accustomed to tell the House that they must have a sinking fund to meet exigencies, to second the efforts of our armies and generals, and to inspire the enemy with a salutary respect for us. But the legal and the original inten-

probated any departure from the system established by Mr. Pitt, with respect to the Sinking Fund.]

In every word of that passage he (Mr. Ricardo) entirely acquiesced.'

tion of the sinking fund was, to pay off the national debt; in proof of which he might refer the House to a well known speech of Mr. Pitt's. [Here Mr. Ricardo read a passage from it.][1] After this declaration of Mr. Pitt, and after all which they had seen in late years, could they place any confidence in ministers as to their being likely to act upon such a principle? Under all circumstances, whenever a motion should be made for the repeal of any tax that was within the actual amount of the sinking fund, he, for one, would support such repeal. He knew it would be objected that the revenue would sometimes fall short in particular branches, which would make it difficult to supply the deficiency. If so, let government impose new taxes to raise the full sums necessary for the state; but he would never consent to this sort of misapplication of a fund created for the specific purpose of liquidating the debt of the country. But this sum had been appropriated and fresh taxes imposed likewise. The people consented to fresh taxes on that occasion, in the hope that they should the more speedily experience some relief; and but for this reasonable expectation, parliament too would never have been induced

---

[1] The *Courier* reports more fully: 'He begged leave to read a passage from the speech of Mr. Pitt on the first establishment of the Sinking Fund. It was to the following effect:—"To recommend that a Sinking Fund of a million a year should be allowed to accumulate; to state that in twenty-eight years that fund would amount to four millions a year; to declare that that ought not to be broken in upon, for that such a violation had been the bane of former efforts of a similar kind; and that to prevent a recurrence of that evil, the million so set aside should be vested by Act of Parliament in Commissioners, to be applied quarterly in the purchase of stock, which would have the effect eventually of relieving the country from the burdens with which it was struggling, as being so vested in Commissioners, it could not be taken by stealth, and as it was not probable it would be touched by any Act of Parliament, it not being probable that any Minister would have the confidence to come to the House and propose such an Act"'. See the full quotation from Pitt's speech of 29 March 1786, above, IV, 191–2.

to impose them. Unfortunately, the people of England were at this moment much more in debt than they would have been if there had been no sinking fund in existence. He should offer but a word or two relative to saving banks. He highly approved of them; but a plan had been suggested by a gentleman in the country, to which he thought the House would do well to pay some attention. The name of this gentleman, he believed, was Woodrow,[1] and his plan was one by which a life-annuity income might be obtained in these banks. The plan was, that persons at an early age might be willing to make a trifling sacrifice, which, by the operation of compound interest, would in the course, say of thirty or forty years, increase to a considerable sum. At the birth of a child, a father might be disposed to put by a small sum of money, for the purpose of procuring to the child an annuity hereafter: a plan of this kind would be productive of great benefits.[2]

---

[1] See below, p. 128. On 7 June 'Mr. RICARDO presented a petition from the County of Glamorgan, on the subject of Savings Banks. The petitioners recommended a new plan, by which, if persons made deposits in early life, they might afterwards have an annuity.' (*Morning Herald;* the matter is not mentioned in *Hansard.*)

[2] *The Times* reports further: 'The hon. gent. then adverted to what had fallen from the Chancellor of the Exchequer, relative to the different effect of paying a debt to the Bank of England, and a debt in any other quarter. In the former case it was said that the notes did not come into public circulation; but it was the amount only of circulation which it was material to look at; and it made little difference to the public from whence it came'.

ILL-TREATMENT OF HORSES BILL

1 *June* 1821

On this bill, which was brought in by Mr. RICHARD MARTIN,

Mr. RICARDO said, that when so many barbarities prevailed in fishing and hunting, and other species of amusement, it was idle to legislate without including all possible cases. [1]

[The session closed on 11 July 1821.]

[1] The bill seems to have been dropped this Session. The Ill-Treatment of Cattle Bill, also introduced by Richard Martin ('Humanity Martin'), was adopted in 1822.

SESSION 1822

ADDRESS ON THE KING'S SPEECH
AT THE OPENING OF THE SESSION

5 *February* 1822

The King's speech was delivered this day. On the motion for the address, Mr. HUME moved an amendment recommending a reduction of expenditure, on the grounds that the excessive taxation was 'a principal cause' of the agricultural distress.

Mr. RICARDO, though he agreed with everything that had fallen from his hon. friend, the member for Aberdeen,[1] in favour of economy and retrenchment, could not vote in favour of his amendment, as he differed widely from his hon. friend as to the causes of the existing agricultural distress. His hon. friend stated, that the cause of that distress was excessive taxation; but the real cause, it could not be denied, was the low price of agricultural produce. That taxation should be the cause of low prices was so absurd and so inconsistent with every principle of political economy, that he could not assent for a moment to the doctrine. Agreeing, however, as he did, with his hon. friend, as to the necessity of economy and retrenchment, and as to the impropriety of making loans to the occupiers of lands, he was sure they would be frequently found, in the course of the session, pursuing together that necessary object, a reduction of expenditure and taxation.

The amendment was negatived.

[1] Mr. Hume.

MR. BROUGHAM'S MOTION ON THE
DISTRESSED STATE OF THE COUNTRY

11 *February* 1822

11 Feb. 1822   Mr. BROUGHAM moved 'That it is the bounden duty of this House, well-considering the pressure of the public burthens upon all, but especially the agricultural classes, to obtain for the suffering people of these realms such a reduction of the taxes as may be suited to the change in the value of money, and may afford an immediate relief to the distresses of the country.' The Marquis of LONDONDERRY [1] opposed the motion.

Mr. RICARDO denied that taxation was the cause of the present agricultural distress. A country might, he said, be totally without taxes, and yet in the exact situation that England was at present. It was consistent enough in those who thought that the restoration of the currency had made a change of 50 or 56 per cent. in the value of money, and had consequently increased the actual value of the taxes in that proportion, though their nominal amount still remained the same, to say that taxation was the chief cause of the distressed state of agriculture; but it was impossible for those who held that the restoration in the currency had not created any thing like so great a change, to accede to such a statement. From the line of argument which his hon. and learned friend had pursued in one part of his speech, he was afraid that his hon. and learned friend was going to prove, that the very taxation which he wished to reduce was a source of benefit to the nation. His hon. and learned friend had stated, that the manufacturers of leather, on account of the tax on it, largely increased its price to the consumer, and derived so much benefit thereby as to be ready to represent it to parliament

---

[1] Lord Castlereagh had succeeded as Marquis of Londonderry on the death of his father, 8 April 1821.

as a very useful and beneficial tax. Surely, by a parity of analogy, the agricultural interest, burdened as it was by taxation, might petition parliament against a reduction of it, since it was as much in their power as in that of the leather-manufacturer, to make it useful in enhancing the price of their commodity to the consumer. His hon. and learned friend had, however, drawn a very nice distinction—so nice indeed, that, for his own part, he was not gifted with ability to discern it—between the circumstances in which the leather-manufacturer and those in which the agriculturist was placed. He had said, that, in the case of the manufacturer, the taxation was paid by the consumer; but that in the case of the agriculturist, it was paid by the seller, and could not be charged to the consumer.[1] He could wish his hon. and learned friend had stated to the House his reasons for such an assertion. If he were to be called upon to declare what he conceived the cause of the present depressed state of agriculture, he should say, that the cause of it was the abundance of produce now in hand, arising from the late abundant harvest, the quantity of land recently brought into cultivation, the importation of corn from Ireland, and various other causes, which it was not material for him at that time to mention. Indeed, the House would deceive both itself and the country, if it should come to a resolution that taxation was the cause of the distresses of the agricultural interest. He perfectly concurred in the opinion of his hon. and learned friend, that the present state of things could not last long: that was an unnatural state of things, in which the farmer could not obtain a remunerative price for his produce, and the landlord could not obtain an adequate rent from his tenant. His hon. and learned friend had stated, that unless something were done to relieve the farmer, much of the land

[1] Cp. *Protection to Agriculture,* above, IV, 239.

Speeches

would be thrown out of tillage. He said so too; and it was to that very circumstance that he looked forward as a remedy. His hon. and learned friend, among the other observations which he had made, had made some upon a set of individuals whom he stated to be anxious to transfer the whole landed property of the country into the hands of the public creditor. For his own part, he could not help observing, that he knew of no persons who entertained such wishes; neither could he imagine any cause which could, under such a measure,[1] be necessary. He himself thought that the landholder might be enabled to receive an adequate rent, without any breach of faith being committed towards the stock-holders. With regard to the stock-holders, it might be supposed, from the language which had been used that evening, that it had been proposed to transfer to them the property of the land-holders, and to leave the land-holders entirely without resources. Now, such a proposition never had been, and never could be, seriously propounded. But though he said that, he was prepared to assert, that it would be most advisable, both for the land-holder and stock-holder, that the former should surrender to the latter a part of his property, in liquidation of the debt that had been contracted. Indeed, as the stock-holder received, in the shape of interest, taxes from the land-holder, it might be said that a part of the land did at this moment absolutely belong to him. [Cries of "Hear" from both sides of the House.] He would suppose, that during the war the ministers had come into the House, and, after stating the necessity of the case, had called upon the country gentle-men to give up a certain portion of their property in a direct manner to the exigencies of the state. Must they not, in that case, have absolutely parted with a portion of it? And if at

[1] Should probably read 'any case under which such a measure could'.

that time others advanced for them that capital which they had not in an immediately tangible shape, was it not right that the capital so advanced should now be repaid to them? He was not demanding for the stock-holder more than he was entitled to receive; he was merely demanding that, in a compact such as he had described, the terms should be fairly and honourably fulfilled towards him. If the alteration in the value of the currency had given to the stock-holder more than he was entitled to, which he (Mr. R.) did not believe, let it be shown and let the deduction be made openly and without disguise. These were all the observations which he should obtrude at present upon the House. On a future occasion, he should explain the reasons why he thought that the alteration produced in the value of money by the restoration of the currency, had been greatly over-stated; and then he should endeavour to show, that if proper measures had been taken at the time of passing Mr. Peel's bill, the resumption of cash payments would have produced no greater effect on the price of corn and other agricultural produce, than a fall of five per cent; whatever greater fall might have taken place, would have been attributable to other causes.

Mr. BROUGHAM replied that he had been misrepresented. What he had said was, that the large capitalists interested in the leather trade derived a benefit from the tax on leather because it prevented men with small capitals from competing with them.

The previous question being put the House divided: for Mr. Brougham's motion, 108; against it, 212. Ricardo voted with the minority for the motion.[1]

[1] Mallet, after reporting this debate in his MS Diary (20 Feb. 1822) writes: 'The Ministers immediately perceived the great advantage they were likely to derive from Ricardo's support, and from his opinions as to the influence of taxation on prices; they cheered him throughout; and Lord Londonderry came up to him after the debate to express his concurrence in his view of the subject. The opposition were annoyed and angry in the same proportion; particularly when they saw that several persons who

SAVING BANKS

18 *February* 1822

18 Feb. 1822   Mr. RICARDO presented a petition from Mr. John Woodrow[1] who, he observed, had taken a great deal of pains in
examining into the best mode of relieving the poor, and who
was of opinion that the principle on which the Saving banks
were at present conducted was not the most beneficial that
could be devised. He conceived it would be much better, if
those who vested their money in these banks were paid by

would have voted with them, they
say as many as 30, walked away,
partly influenced by Ricardo's
opinion and partly by Brougham's
unprincipled attempt to catch the
country gentlemen.'
    Cp. a letter from Whishaw to
Thomas Smith, 26 Feb. 1822:
'Much blame is cast on Ricardo,
who, though he voted with the
Opposition, is considered as
having spoken in favour of Ministers, by countenancing their principles and opinions. I think,
indeed, that, considering the
audience whom he addressed, he
spoke too much as a theorist, and
in a manner likely to be misrepresented. But though his speeches
may have served as pretexts, I
cannot think that they operated
as the true motives of many votes.
Mackintosh, however, represented
the number thus influenced, or
professing to be so, as nearly
forty, but they were all willing to
be satisfied with the measures of
Government, and would have
found good reasons for being so

if Ricardo had never opened his
lips.' (*The 'Pope' of Holland
House,* p. 244.)
[1] Misprinted 'Woodson' in *Hansard;* given correctly in *Journals
of the House of Commons* and
cp. p. 121 above. See John
Woodrow, *Remarks on Banks
for Savings and Friendly Societies;
with an Original Plan combining
the Principles of both Institutions;
a Friendly Loan Fund, and other
Important Advantages,* London,
Taylor, 1818; another issue, under
the same title-page dated 1818,
contains a Supplement dated
March 1821. Ricardo's copies of
both issues are in the Goldsmiths'
Library of the University of
London. See also, by the same
author, *Some Suggestions for the
Improvement of Benefit Clubs, and
Assurances for the Lower Classes;
founded on the Reasoning of a
Petition presented by the late
D. Ricardo, Esq., to the House of
Commons, for the Author,* London,
Simpkin & Marshall, 1824.

way of annuity, but at a less rate of interest than was now given. Their money might be allowed to accumulate, and thus a comfortable provision would be insured to them, when they arrived at an advanced age.[1] He (Mr. R.) thought the plan deserved the attention of the legislature.

MOTION FOR A COMMITTEE ON THE AGRICULTURAL DISTRESS

18 *February* 1822

On 15 February the Marquis of LONDONDERRY announced the policy of the Government on the 'Agricultural distress and the financial measures for its relief;' he then gave notice that he would move for the revival of the agricultural committee and that the Chancellor of the Exchequer would bring forward a measure for enabling the Bank to issue 4,000,000*l*. on 3 per cent. Exchequer Bills in loans to different parishes on the security of the poor rates, to be used for the relief of the agriculturists. Accordingly, on 18 February, the Marquis of LONDONDERRY moved that the report of the committee on the agricultural distress, presented in 1821, be referred to a select committee. Mr. J. BENETT, Mr. STUART WORTLEY and several other members having spoken on the motion,

Mr. RICARDO[2] began by observing, that the hon. member[3] had stated, that the operation of the sinking fund in the purchase of stock, would have the effect of reducing the interest of money, thus benefiting mortgagers and other borrowers, and in that way relieving the landed interest. But

---

[1] The *Morning Chronicle* reports 'at sixty years of age'.

[2] On 19 February Ricardo wrote to McCulloch: 'The House listened to me with attention, and appeared to follow and understand my arguments, but I am sorry to say that the reporter of the Times does not appear to have understood me. I have seen no other paper' (see below, IX, 164). *Hansard's* report has little in common with that of *The Times;* its general excellence suggests that it may have been revised by Ricardo.

[3] Mr. Stuart Wortley.

he begged to say, that the interest of money depended upon
other causes. The rate of interest depended upon the profit
that could be made upon the employment of capital; and that
again depended upon the wages of labour, which were
regulated, in a great measure, by the price of food. While a
sinking fund was fairly applied, it might and would raise the
price of stock; but it by no means followed, because the price
of stock rose, that, therefore, the rate of interest would
generally fall. He would not be understood to be adverse to
the principle of the sinking fund, if he could be assured that
it would be really applied to the liquidation of the public
debt: but he found from experience, that, while the people
were called upon to pay a large proportion of taxes for the
maintenance of this fund, in the hope that it would be
applied to the discharge of their debt, they experienced
nothing but disappointment, through the manner in which
that fund had been appropriated by the ministers. The
existence of this fund would serve only to encourage ministers
to engage in new wars, by facilitating the contraction of new
loans. Such, indeed, had been the destination of every sinking fund which the country had known, from the plan of
Walpole to those of the ministers who followed him. Mr.
Pitt, notwithstanding the experience he had derived of the
fate of all sinking funds, established by his predecessors in
office, had been unable to secure his own. What a variety of
expedients had been resorted to in order to keep up that
system, and to secure the application of it to the purpose for
which it was professedly designed at the outset. But they
had all been ineffectual against the attacks of the present
chancellor of the exchequer; a sinking fund which ought to
be now above 20,000,000*l.* was so reduced that with the
addition of 3,000,000*l.* of new taxes it only amounted to
5,000,000*l.;* and he had no doubt, whatever, that within a few

years this grant would be found quite as inefficient as any that had preceded it. The hon. member for Wiltshire,[1] had pronounced great praise upon the speech of his hon. and learned friend (Mr. Brougham); which was the more extra-ordinary, as the hon. member differed from all the main positions laid down by his hon. and learned friend; for, in opposition to the views of the hon. member, his hon. and learned friend had maintained, that it was impossible to raise the price of agricultural produce: that the producer could not transfer the taxes imposed upon him to the consumer, in the same manner as manufacturers could; while the hon. member for Wiltshire had maintained, that taxation did tend to increase the price of raw produce, his doubt only being as to the time that would be requisite for such purpose. His hon. and learned friend had observed, that if a man embarked any large proportion of capital in manufactures, he might, by the use of improved machinery, and other means, contrive, not only to overcome any discouraging prospect which might appear at the outset to damp his speculations, but even to advance his profits beyond any thing upon which he could originally calculate. But the agriculturist, upon in-vesting his capital, had no other remedy for any discouraging prospect, excepting time alone, while he was oppressed with certain taxes; for he would never make the consumer pay them. The hon. member for Wiltshire's observation, as to the time required to transfer taxes on raw produce to the consumer, was not applicable to the matter under discussion, because no new taxes had been laid on agricultural produce. If his observation had been applied to any taxes now for the first time proposed to be adopted, it would no doubt be entitled to attention. But it was to be recollected, that the taxes to which the hon. member had alluded, were, it might

[1] Mr. J. Benett.

almost be said, interwoven with our general system of taxation, having existed for several years; yet that which had so
long existed, was now by many persons set down as the
cause of the low price of agricultural produce; and hence it
was argued, that taxation was the cause of the public distress.
But to the agriculturists he would say, that the only effectual
remedy for their case was, to regulate their supply by the
public demand: and, if they did not take special care of that,
all other efforts must be unavailing. He had been represented
by the hon. member for Wiltshire as to having said, that the
land was mortgaged for the whole of the public debt. But
he declared that he should have been quite ashamed to have
made any such observation, as he only meant to say that
which was his opinion, namely, that the land-owners were,
as well as the other classes of the people, responsible to the
fund-holders for the payment of their share of the debt
[hear, hear!.] From the responsibility the fund-holder himself was not wholly exempted: towards the payment of his
own debt he must himself be a large contributor. He did
say, that it was for those who contended that the fund-holder
received more than his fair share, to show the House how
this had happened; and that if such were really the case, a
proportionate abatement ought to be conceded. His hon.
and learned friend (Mr. Brougham) in his last speech had
remarked, that to raise the price of corn was impossible; and
that, therefore, the remedy for the present depression must
be by reducing taxes: but that, if this reduced taxation should
not have the effect of placing the gentlemen of landed
property in affluence—[cries of "No."]

Mr. BROUGHAM observed, that the case he put on a former
evening was that of the distress of the landed interest becoming intolerable.

Mr. RICARDO said, he might in some degree have misunderstood his hon. and learned friend, but he would offer a word or two on the subject of this distress. It was not very long ago since they were all in a state of the greatest alarm, on account of the distressed manufacturers. It was conceived that our manufacturers were declining and the most gloomy apprehensions were indulged on their behalf. But he then took the liberty of intimating his opinion, that those distresses were not permanent; and, happily, his predictions had been fulfilled. He was disposed to hope equally well of the agricultural interests; but not while such a system of corn laws as the present existed. He thought it was most desirable to fix some system by which the prices of corn might be rendered less variable, and by which a proper and adequate compensation might be secured to the grower. One of the measures of relief proposed was, an advance of four millions by the Bank at three per cent interest. This was an hazardous experiment, unless the Bank had issued four millions more[1] than was necessary for the circulation of the country. The House would do him the favour to recollect, that, in the session of 1819, he expressed an opinion on the Bank question, for which he received a reproof at the time from an hon. director, that the Bank should not then buy gold, but rather sell it.[2] His fears, he would confess, were now the other way. Vast quantities of gold had been obtained by them to supply the circulation of this country; and he now begged the directors to consider whether they had more than was sufficient for that purpose; for if they had not, he was quite sure that the measure which they were about to adopt could not be expedient, for four millions could not be absorbed in our circulation. It was quite impossible that four

[1] Should read 'had amassed four millions more gold'. Cp. below, p. 143–4. [2] See above, p. 13.

millions could be added to the circulation, without affording a great inducement to export the gold. If the Bank had no greater quantity of gold than sufficed to carry on the circulation of the country, no measure could be more injudicious than this, as it respected them. If, on the other hand, having large quantities of gold in their possession, they issued four millions of additional currency, the effect would be, to promote the exportation of gold, to lower its value all over the world, and to turn the foreign exchanges against us. He gave the directors of the Bank full credit for their good intentions; he believed that men of higher honour or integrity could not exist; but he thought they had not a sufficient degree of talent for the management of so vast a machine as that with which they were intrusted. Once more he would intreat them to consider the matter well, in all its probable consequences, before they increased the present currency, by so large a sum as four millions. And here he would beg the House also to reflect what might have been the effect of the bill brought in by the right hon. gentleman (Mr. Peel), had it been fully acted on. He (Mr. Ricardo) had ventured to say, that its effect upon prices would be about five per cent. To that opinion he still adhered; and he thought he could demonstrate the fact. The state of our money system at that time was this:—gold was five per cent higher in value than paper; that was, a man having an ounce of bullion could perchase the same quantity of any commodity as another man could do with 4*l.* 2*s.* in Bank notes. The question was, how to make these two denominations of money coincide in value? It was quite clear, that if nothing was done to alter the value of gold, it was only necessary to raise the value of paper to the same level, and that then the sum of 3*l.* 17*s.* 10$\frac{1}{2}$*d.* in paper would purchase as much as the ounce of gold. After the right hon. gentleman's bill was brought in and had passed, he (Mr. Ricardo) regretted that it was not carried into effect in the method at first proposed; he referred to the intended payments in bars of[1] gold bullion. If that plan had been acted upon, the Bank would have been competent to have answered all demands upon it with the gold then in their possession, how small soever that sum might have been. As they therefore, in that case, would not have affected the general value of gold in Europe, by making large purchases in other countries, the change could not possibly be greater than the difference between gold and paper, at the time of the passing of the bill. The bill of the right hon. member (Mr. Peel), he did not conceive to be materially different from the plan proposed by himself, for it established an intermediate system of payments in bullion, and did not make the payments in cash imperative till the 1st May, 1823. He could not imagine the reasons which had induced the Bank to commence cash payments at so early a period. He had always blamed them for being too hasty in their preparations; for if they had contented themselves with bullion payments, and the country had seen the advantage of that system, it might have been continued—as undoubtedly it would have been wise to continue it—and payments in cash might have been deferred some years longer. If the affairs of the Bank had been conducted with skill, the directors, instead of forcing so great an importation of gold, should have kept the exchange as nearly as possible at par. He repeated then, that the consequence of the law, if skilfully acted upon, was only to cause a rise of 5 per cent. But the Bank had acted very differently, and had imported a great quantity of gold; as much perhaps as twenty millions. This, of course, had created a change in the price of commodities, in addition to the apparent difference between paper and gold.

---

[1] Misprinted 'and' in *Hansard;* correct in *The Times.*

The buying up of this quantity of gold must have affected a change in the value of it (as compared with other commodities) throughout Europe. What the amount of this change was, it was impossible to say—it was mere matter of conjecture. But when they took the quantity of gold in circulation in Europe into the calculation, and all the paper also, for that too must be reckoned, he did not conceive that it could be great, and he should imagine that 5 per cent would be an ample allowance for the effect. [Hear, hear!].—With respect to the 4 millions of Exchequer bills, and the mode of their application which the noble lord had made a part of his plan, he was really astonished to find the right hon. member for Chichester (Mr. Huskisson), in a speech which contained many sound observations,[1] supporting a system for lending the public money on the security of corn and poor-rates. Such a system was decidedly contrary to every established principle of political economy and common sense.—As to the effect and operation of taxes, he wished to make one or two observations. There were two descriptions of persons, producers and consumers, likely to complain to that House of the pressure of taxation. Against the producers he was prepared to say, he would shut the doors of that House. He would tell them they had the remedy in their own hands; that they must regulate their own price, by making the supply square with the demand. But to the consumers on whom the taxes really pressed, he would say, the doors of the House should be always thrown open. When they said that their income was unequal to their expenditure, and that taxes prevented them from procuring the comforts and enjoyments to which they were accustomed, he would say, that their prayers were entitled to the utmost attention, and that

[1] On 15 February in the debate on 'Agricultural Distress and the Financial Measures for its Relief.'

the taxes should as far as possible, be removed. Now, he
would ask gentlemen, to whom they supposed the repeal of
the malt tax would be a benefit—to the farmer who produced
it, or to the general consumer? He should say to the consumer. And so on of the salt, the soap, and other taxes, which
affected articles of general consumption. That would be his
reason for calling for the repeal of these taxes; but not at all
from the impression that those taxes were duplicated or
triplicated by dealers or sellers. His hon. and learned friend[1]
seemed to think, that if a commodity changed hands two or
three times, each dealer would charge 10 per cent on the
amount of the tax; so that, after various changes, it might be
increased to an almost indefinite amount to the consumer;
but, if these two or three changes took place in the course of
one year, 10 per cent, supposing that was the ordinary rate of
profit per annum, would satisfy all the persons through
whose hands it passed. He had been represented, very erroneously, to have stated that reduction of taxes was not a
benefit. But the contrary was the fact. He always thought
that taxes were injurious, but they affected all classes of
consumers, and the repeal of any one of them would not be
particularly serviceable to the agricultural class. His hon.
and learned friend observed, that if the quantity of capital
were increased, it was an axiom in political economy, that
profits would be diminished. Far from that being the fact, he
denied the position altogether. If the capital of the country
were doubled and the price of provisions lowered, he would
have no doubt that the rate of profits would not be reduced.
But with the continually increasing population of England,
they could not have low prices of corn, if they did not import foreign corn. He would not at this moment propose an

[1] Mr. Brougham; the reference is to his speeches of 11 and 15
February.

importation free of all restraints, but he would agree to a protecting duty (the amount he was hardly capable of fixing), gradually declining till the duty was equal to the peculiar burthens to which the farmer was liable. The hon. member after a recapitulation of his remarks, and characterising in strong terms of reprobation the impolicy of the system of lending the public money upon the security of corn or poor's-rate, concluded with observing, in reference to what had fallen from the hon. member for Wiltshire as to the increased amount of taxation which the landowners and farmers had now to pay in consequence of the depreciation of the currency, that the fundholders were subjected to the same advance upon the taxes, although that class of proprietors had not derived any additional advantage from the war or its consequences, as Mr. Mushett had most satisfactorily demonstrated.[1]—[The hon. member sat down amidst loud and general cheering.]

A committee was appointed, consisting mostly of the same members as the committee of 1821 [see above, p. 86–7] including Ricardo: among the new members were W. W. Whitmore and Sir J. Newport.

WAYS AND MEANS[2]

22 *February* 1822

Col. DAVIES called the attention of the House to certain discrepancies between the finance accounts for the year and the statement of income and expenditure of the country up to 5 Jan. 1821. Mr. HUME moved that 'the Chancellor of the Exchequer should be requested to reconcile the two accounts'.

---

[1] *A Series of Tables, exhibiting the Gain and Loss to the Fundholders, arising from the Fluctuations in the Value of the Currency, from 1800 to 1821,* by Robert Mushet, 2nd ed., corrected, London, Baldwin, 1821.

[2] This debate is not contained in *Hansard.* Ricardo's speech is here reprinted from the report in the *Morning Chronicle.*

Mr. RICARDO thought it necessary that some explanation should be given; and he begged leave to call the attention of the Chancellor of the Exchequer to a question which he (Mr. Ricardo) had put to him last year, when he had brought forward his Budget.[1] The sum which had actually been devoted to the repayment of Exchequer Bills up to January 15, 1821, had been only 950,000*l.*, while the Chancellor of the Exchequer had said it would be 1,700,000*l.*, it appearing that 700,000*l.* had been expended in the payment of interest on Exchequer Bills. Next year the Chancellor of the Exchequer had promised that the surplus would be 4,000,000*l.* But when it came to be ascertained, it had turned out to be only 2,600,000*l.* How was the Right Honourable Gentleman to reconcile these differences. The interest on Exchequer Bills had amounted to 1,380,000*l.* and this, with some other matters not well explained, made a total of 1,700,000*l.* If the accounts were to be kept in this way, it was impossible that the Members of that House could come to any knowledge of the real state of the country. They had been told of large surpluses, which, from year to year, were to be available to purposes of economy, but when they came to count those sums, they found that the greater part had vanished. If they were told that 1,700,000*l.* would be available in one year, and instead of that had only 950,000*l.;* if they were told that in the subsequent year there would be four millions, and it had turned out that there were only two millions, what security was there that next year they might not have only two millions instead of the five millions, of which the Right Honourable Gentleman had boasted? The whole of the boasted surplus might thus, it was evident, be absorbed in a quarter of which the House had no knowledge. It had been said that the expences were to be but 18,210,000*l.* but

[1] Above, p. 115.

upon casting up the four items of which they were composed, the amount proved to be eighteen millions five hundred and fifty thousand pounds. If the expenditure of the year was to exceed the estimate by half a million; if they were to be told of a surplus of four millions, and then in place of that to have a surplus only of 2,600,000*l.* Then what security had they that there would be a surplus of five millions next year? He thought that the matter stood in much need of explanation.

NAVY FIVE PER CENTS

25 *February* 1822

The CHANCELLOR OF THE EXCHEQUER introduced a measure for the commutation of every 100*l.* of Navy five per cents into 105*l.* of a new four per cent stock. The time allowed for holders resident in Great Britain to signify their dissent was limited to the 16th of March; for those who lived out of Great Britain and in Europe, the 1st of June; and for those who lived out of Europe, twelve months from the present time.

Mr. RICARDO thought the plan very desirable, and the terms proposed by ministers extremely fair. With regard to the time allowed for option, he thought it amply sufficient. But, suppose persons were to purchase stock in the name of others residing abroad, with a fraudulent intention, would they be entitled to the extended term, or would they be obliged to give their answer by the 16th of March?

The CHANCELLOR OF THE EXCHEQUER said, the case supposed by the hon. member would be precluded by some resolutions which would be subsequently read at the table.

Mr. RICARDO said, it would very much facilitate the plan, if such holders of five per cents as assented, could know at

what time the transfer to the four per cents was to take place.
The question of the dividends might at first sight offer some difficulty, but this difficulty was more apparent than real, because the very same dividend which was given to a person holding 100*l.* in the five per cents might be given to a person holding 105*l.* in the four per cents. If this stock were quickly transferred, the natural consequence would be, to raise the price of it in the market; and as persons would be induced to speculate in it from the advantage of a small but quick profit, the operation from this circumstance would be much facilitated. The right hon. gentleman would do well if he explained the mode in which the money was to be paid off to persons who dissented. It was evident that persons having an option, and who were in doubt whether they might or might not have made a bad bargain, would not decide till the latest moment. He should like to know then, if many thousand letters came in on the 16th of March, how these applications were to be disposed of.

The resolutions were agreed to.

AGRICULTURAL DISTRESS

5 *March* 1822

Mr. SCARLETT, in presenting a petition from Peterborough, said that a superabundance of produce could not of itself have caused the agricultural distress. 'Supposing the farmer were to pay all the demands made upon him—for instance, his rent, tithes, and taxes—not in money, but in kind—would it not be clear that, in such a case, an abundance of produce would be of considerable advantage to him? How, then, could it be maintained, that abundance of produce, under the existing state of things, was the chief cause of the evils by which the agriculturist was now oppressed?'

Mr. RICARDO said, it was true, that, if the produce of the land was divided into certain[1] proportions, every party would be benefitted by an abundant crop; but his learned friend having come to that conclusion, left his argument there, instead of extending it a little farther. Now, he would ask his learned friend whether, if the quantity of commodity were excessively abundant, that was to say, the double, treble, or quadruple of an ordinary crop, it would not be a cause of poverty to the agriculturist? He maintained that it would be so; for the farmer, after having satisfied the consumption of himself and family, would find, upon going to exchange the surplus of his commodity for other commodities[2], such a competition in the market as would compel him to dispose of it upon very low terms; and thus abundance of produce would be to him a cause of distress. It was true that, from the alteration of the currency, the evil had been aggravated; for it was clear that it rendered it necessary to sell a greater quantity of corn to answer the demands of the government and the landlord. But he now contended, as he had at all former times contended, that, up to a certain point, for instance, 10 per cent, great loss had been derived from the change in our currency; but that the rest of the distress was to be attributed to the increased quantity of produce.

[1] The editors of *Letters to Trower* (p. 125) suggest that this should read 'equal'; but 'certain', as opposed to varying with the price of produce, seems correct.

[2] Misprinted 'commodity' in *Hansard.*

BANKS OF ENGLAND, AND OF IRELAND

8 *March* 1822

Mr. MABERLEY'S motion for an account of the interest paid to the Bank of Ireland having given rise to some discussion on the comparative charges made by the Banks of Ireland, and of England, Mr. PEARSE (a Bank director) rebutted 'the insinuations thrown out against the Bank of England' and said: 'The hon. member for Portarlington had, upon a former occasion, asserted, that the directors had scarcely ability enough to perform the duties with which they were intrusted:[1] but he (Mr. P.) preferred the opinions of the proprietors of Bank-stock, who elected them annually, to all the theories of modern philosophers on the subject.'

Mr. RICARDO said, that whenever the conduct of the Bank was brought before the notice of the House, he should think it his duty to speak of it as he thought and felt. With regard to the directors, he was willing, at all times, to give them full credit for honesty of intention; but he could not help thinking, that they had at different times involved the country in considerable difficulties. He persisted in saying, that the Bank restriction act which was passed in 1797, might have been unattended with detriment to the country, had the directors known how to manage their own concerns. But, not knowing how to manage them upon true principles, they had issued a quantity of paper so large as to depreciate its own value; and to recover from that depreciation, the country had found it necessary to undergo a painful process, which had been the cause of a great part of the present distress. Ever since the year 1819, the Bank had committed a great error in its eagerness to provide gold. That error they confessed themselves, when they offered to lend government 4,000,000*l.* Such an offer he took to be a specific confession

---

[1] See above, p. 135.

of error, inasmuch as it was a declaration that they had amassed more gold than was necessary, and by so doing had aggravated the evils under which the country suffered. As to the plan of the Bank lending 4,000,000*l.* to the government, he viewed it with some degree of fear, because the directors had convinced him by their conduct that they did not know what they were about. If they thought they could issue either 4,000,000*l.* of gold coin, or even of paper, without withdrawing the gold coin from circulation, they were mightily mistaken.[1] He was quite sure that the currency could not absorb it, and therefore it must go abroad.

DISTRESS IN CANADA

13 *March* 1822

Mr. MARRYAT presented a petition from the House of Assembly of Lower Canada complaining of the distress caused by the restrictions imposed on their trade by the British legislature.

Mr. RICARDO thought the House bound to attend to the complaints of the petitioners. The Canadians suffered serious hardships which ought to be removed; they complained, 1st. That we did not take timber from them on the same terms as we did before. 2nd, that we refused to admit their corn. And 3dly, that they were subjected to the inconvenience of purchasing all articles in our markets. As to the first, we had a right to go to any market we pleased for our timber; but, on that very principle, the second cause of grievance ought to be done away, and their corn ought to have access to our markets. With respect to the forcing the

[1] In the *Morning Chronicle* this reads: 'If they thought they could issue 4,000,000*l.* either in paper or in coin, and keep it in circulation, they were very much mistaken.'

colonies to purchase in our markets, when they might be
more conveniently supplied elsewhere, it was an inconvenience to which they ought not to be exposed. He would
always oppose that principle, not only as applied to Canada,
but to every other colony.

MOTION RESPECTING THE SIMPLIFYING
AND BETTER ARRANGEMENT OF THE
PUBLIC ACCOUNTS

14 *March* 1822

Mr. MABERLY, in moving for a select committee on the public
accounts, observed that the various public accounts, when compared with one another, were full of errors; for instance, the
balance-sheet account presented by the Marquis of Londonderry
on 15 February last, differed from the finance accounts of 1821,
and the Chancellor of the Exchequer's account differed from
both. Mr. LUSHINGTON, in the course of his reply, said that
'the balance-sheet form was adopted at the suggestion of an hon.
member (Mr. Ricardo), and was deemed to be the most com-
pendious way of stating the accounts.'

Mr. RICARDO said, that the public accounts ought to be so
stated, that every member, upon referring to them, might be
able to make a balance-sheet from them, and see at once
what was the actual revenue, and what the expenditure of the
country.

The motion was withdrawn. On 18 April on the motion of
the Chancellor of the Exchequer a select committee was appointed
'to investigate the manner in which the public accounts are at
present kept, and to suggest such improvements in the system
as might appear necessary.' Ricardo was appointed a member of
the committee.

MR. CURWEN'S MOTION RESPECTING THE
DUTIES ON TALLOW AND CANDLES

20 *March* 1822

Mr. CURWEN moved for a committee to take into consideration the propriety of augmenting the duty on imported tallow
and of repealing the duty on candles. Mr. ROBINSON (President
of the Board of Trade) opposed the motion; 'he could not agree
to a proposal which could only benefit agriculture by throwing
a burthen on the whole body of consumers, or by impeding the
trade of the country.' Besides, 'the just complaint of foreigners,
was, that the trade of this country was so restricted, that all their
ingenuity was required to get an article into this country on
profitable terms; and now that one article was found on which
they could get a profit, the state was to step in and take it in the
shape of a tax. If this was to be our rule of commercial policy,
we might as well shut up shop at once.'

Mr. RICARDO said, he had heard with great pleasure the
principles avowed by the president of the board of trade, and
hoped the right hon. gentleman would hereafter act upon
them; for if they had hitherto been followed up, the right
hon. gentleman could never have proposed the duties upon
cheese and butter [Hear!!.] The hon. mover was a great
friend to agriculture, and was ready to go a great way in
support of it. The length to which he had gone that night
was really surprising, for he had told them exactly the
quantity of tallow produced in this country, the quantity
produced abroad, and the effect which the tax operating on
this quantity would have upon the price, which he told them
was precisely 5*l.* 10*s.*, the rest of the proposed tax being to be
paid by the foreign producer. How the hon. gentleman got
at this result was surprising. He believed the fact would turn
out to be very different; that the producers in all foreign
countries furnished their articles on the average, at the price
at which they could afford them; and that a tax now im-

posed, would on the average of future years, be added to the price. He could not consent to tax the whole community for the benefit of one class. As he anticipated that his hon. friend's motion would meet with the fate it deserved, he should not detain the House longer, but to observe on a remark of the hon. member for Hull.[1] The hon. member for Hull had said, that he was a friend to a surplus revenue beyond expenditure, but that he was an enemy to a sinking fund. Now to what purpose was a surplus revenue applicable but as a sinking fund? The hon. member had said, that he found from the experience of history, that a sinking fund was always seized by the ministers. He (Mr. R.) agreed with him, and it was on this account that he objected to the proposal to maintain a surplus revenue. In principle nothing could be better than a sinking fund. He was so great a friend to the principle, that he was ready to consent that the country should make a great effort to get out of debt; but then he would be sure that the means taken would effect the object. He would not trust any ministers, no matter who they were, with a surplus revenue, and he should therefore, join in any vote for a remission of taxes that might be proposed, so long as a surplus revenue remained. The taxes on candles and on salt had been proposed for reduction, but though that on salt was undoubtedly very burthensome, it did not appear to him to be that which most demanded reduction. The taxes on law proceedings seemed to him the most abominable that existed in the country, by subjecting the poor man, and the man of middling fortune, who applied for justice, to the most ruinous expence [hear!]. Every gentleman had his favourite plan for repealing a particular tax, and this tax upon justice, was that which he should most desire to see reduced.

The motion was negatived.

[1] Mr. Sykes.

EXTRA POST—PETITION OF MR. BURGESS

2 *April* 1822

2 April 1822   Mr. STUART WORTLEY moved to refer to a select committee the petition of Mr. H. Burgess for remuneration for the expenses which he had incurred in the preparations for an extra post,[1] which had been encouraged by government and eventually prevented by decisions of parliament. The CHANCELLOR OF THE EXCHEQUER supported the motion.

Mr. RICARDO said, the ground on which the chancellor of the exchequer had put the case would have induced him to vote against the motion if he had known nothing else of it. The right hon. gentleman had called on them to accede to the motion as a matter of compassion or indulgence. Now, they were not entitled to vote away the public money from their own sentiments of compassion. If the Treasury had given Mr. Burgess encouragement to incur expence, they should take on themselves the responsibility of remunerating him.

The motion was negatived.

AGRICULTURAL DISTRESS

3 *April* 1822

3 April 1822   On 1 April Mr. GOOCH brought up the report of the select committee on the distressed state of agriculture: it was then agreed that the report should be taken into consideration at the end of the month [see below, p. 155].

On 3 April, however, Mr. J. BENETT presented a petition from the distressed agriculturists of Wiltshire, and this was made an occasion to anticipate the debate upon the report. Mr. WESTERN expressed his dissent from the conclusions of the select committee and said that 'an immense proportion of the present difficulties

[1] The project was to substitute a two-wheeled for a four-wheeled carriage in order to increase the speed.

arose from the alteration in the currency'. 'During the depreciation we had contracted an enormous debt, which was now to be
paid by the industrious classes in a currency of increased value.
This had made such a havoc in the property of the country, as
was never made by revolution or civil war. It was true, during
the depreciation of money, the rents of estates had been doubled,
but incumbrances had doubled and taxes had quadrupled, so that
the situation of landlord had not been a whit better. But what
was the state of the landlord now? His income was again reduced
to one half, and all their fixed payments remained.'

Mr. RICARDO said, that no one could be more aware of the
great difficulties which had been occasioned by alterations in
the currency than himself. He had given the subject the
greatest attention in his power, and had laboured hard to
show the necessity of a fixed and unvariable standard of
value. At the same time, he could not agree with the hon.
member for Essex,[1] as to the operation of the changes in the
currency upon agriculture. Let them suppose the utmost
extent of the operation of[2] the changes in currency on
the pressure of taxes. They must deduct from the whole
amount of taxation, the amount of those taxes which were
employed in expenditure, as they had been diminished in
proportion as the value of money had been augmented.[3]
Supposing, then, 40,000,000*l.* to remain, on which the operation of the currency on taxation was to be calculated. What
proportion could possibly be paid by the tenantry of this
amount? Suppose one fourth. He did not include the landlords in this calculation, but only the tenantry. Suppose one-
fourth paid by the tenantry, their proportion would be
10,000,000*l.* Suppose, according to the extravagant calcula-

---

[1] Mr. Western.
[2] *Hansard* has a dash in place of
the word 'of', here adopted from
The Times (whose report however continues less plausibly 'both
the changes in currency and the
pressure of taxes').

[3] In place of this sentence *The
Times* reports: 'They must deduct
the taxes which were not raised
from property or labour connected with agriculture.'

tion of the hon. gentleman, that 25 per cent was the real amount of the alteration operated by recurring to a metallic standard of value. Then 2,500,000*l.* was the whole extent of its operation on the tenantry. Was it possible that the distress which was now felt could be owing to 2,500,000*l.?* Such a sum was totally inadequate to such an effect. Let them look again at the landlords. The alteration could affect them only as it took more from them in the shape of taxation. No person was more ready than he was to admit, that it occasioned an increase of burthen in this shape as in every other; but he must be allowed to ask, whether, if the tenant paid the rent demanded, the landlord must not be benefited by receiving the same rent which he had exacted in the depreciated currency? He admitted that landlords did not receive the same rent, but had made an allowance equal to the depreciation. But, if he received the rest of the rent, whence arose the distress? He had given up 25 per cent, and received 75 per cent, equal to 100. How, then, was he injured? But the landlords did not receive 75 per cent. They told them that they could not receive any rent—that the distress was so great, that the surplus could not pay any thing but the taxes. He asked, then, whether the depreciation could possibly have occasioned this? He did not believe that the changes in the currency since 1819, had been more than 10 per cent. But did he say that the landed interest suffered only to the extent of 10 per cent? No such thing. The greatness of the distress he was most sensible of, and the causes which had been assigned he thought amply sufficient to account for it— namely, the abundance of several successive harvests, the importation of corn from Ireland, and other similar causes. It was utterly impossible that this country could be reduced to that situation that the surplus produce of agriculture should be only sufficient to pay the taxes, without affording any rent to the landlord, or any profit to the cultivator. This was a situation to which the country could not possibly come.— He wished here to say a few words of the report which the agricultural committee had made. The former report[1] contained some most admirable propositions. If he might divide it into two parts, he would say, the first half was as excellent a report as had ever emanated from any committee of that House, and was well worthy of being placed beside the bullion report and the report on the resumption of cash payments by the Bank. It contained most sound and excellent observations on the corn trade, and on the corn-laws. It most justly pointed out two great evils arising from the corn-laws, which affected the present distress. The first was, when there was a scarcity, and corn rose to 80*s.,* then the ports were opened, and we were deluged with foreign corn, whatever might be the price in the countries from which it came. The ports were open for any quantity. This was a great evil, and operated at the very time when the short harvest ought to be compensated by high prices. The second evil was felt when in a season of plenty we habitually produced corn at an expense very considerably above other countries. If there were successively good harvests, the farmer could obtain no relief from exportation, and was thus ruined by the abundance of produce. What was the inference from this, but that they should take measures, to enable our farmers, in seasons of abundance, when they could not obtain prices to compensate the expense of culture, to get relief by exporting to other countries, and for this purpose a duty on importation of foreign grain should be imposed, equal to the peculiar taxes which fell on the farmer, such as tythes and a part of the poor-rate; and a drawback of the same amount should be

[1] The Report of the Agricultural Committee of 1821, the first part of which had been drafted by Huskisson.

allowed on exportation. If such a regulation were adopted, after a small fall of prices, the farmer would then export to other countries, and relieve the glut of the corn market at home. Another part of the report was totally incorrect. It spoke of countervailing duties, not, as all countervailing duties ought to be, as imposts upon the importer in order to subject him to all the burthens of the home-grower of corn, so that the taxes might fall equally on grower and importer, but as duties which should be equal to the additional expense of growing corn in this country over other countries. Countervailing duties on this principle, would thus be some-times 20*s.*, and sometimes 30*s.* There appeared to him to be no principle more clear, than that there could not be a fixed remunerating price in any country. Before there was a dense state of population in a country, they would cultivate the very best lands, and they could then compete with any country, and export their surplus produce. There would then be no occasion for countervailing duties. But when popula-tion became more dense, poorer lands would be cultivated, and an increase of charges would arise from the greater ex-penses of cultivation. As population went on, the cultiva-tion would go on to still poorer lands, and the price would continue to rise. If, then, the rule should be, for a counter-vailing duty, the difference of charge in the growth, no limit could be affixed to the amount. He could not conceive any system of duties more destructive to the best interests of the country.—He would now advert to the present report. He had gone into the committee under a deep impression of the great distress which the agricultural interest suffered, with a most unfeigned desire to find some means of relief, not upon the general and absolutely true principles of legislation, but with every inclination to give every facility to measures of immediate effect in alleviating distress. All he required was, that there should be something in the report, pledging them, when the distress should have gone by, and the farmers should be rescued from their suffering—for he was the advocate of the farmer, and not those who pretended to be the exclusive friend of agriculture—all he had required was, that the report should promise a return to proper principles when the present dangers should have been removed. But, although the report recognized the evil which produced low prices, and the apprehension of still lower prices, it did not hold up the slightest purpose of ever returning to sound principles. It expressed hopes of better principles being adopted, and the House would be astonished to hear what those principles were. It was to have recourse to the counter-vailing duties which he had explained. If on this plan they attempted to give a monopoly to grapes reared in hot-houses, countervailing duties might be imposed on wine, to make it as dear as the produce of the hot-houses. In the same way with sugar. In this way all branches of foreign commerce would be lost to this nation, and to every nation which adopted countervailing duties. The only true policy was to allow us to go to the country where the article required was most easily and abundantly produced. He was ashamed to occupy the time of the House so long [Cheers]; he would not go into detail, but he felt called upon to throw out a few observations. The hon. member for Essex had alluded to the West Indian cultivators. If he wanted an argument, he would take that very case, and he asked how the currency could be supposed to have affected them? Was it not notorious that their distress was entirely caused by over production? Were not the measures adopted for their relief calculated to give them a market for their produce which they had not before? In the same manner, the agriculturist of this country must be relieved by increased demand, or diminished supply. He had not said that taxes contributed not to the distress. On that point he had been misunderstood. They who were exposed to exclusive taxes ought to receive protection from those taxes. But on this subject he would give his opinions in greater detail on a future occasion.

Mr. H. G. BENNET 'rose to protest against the doctrine, that taxes had nothing to do with the distresses of the agricultural interest'. The Marquis of LONDONDERRY in reply said, 'that hon. gentleman might take a lesson from his friend near him, the member for Portarlington, who had shown how small a portion of that distress now complained of had been thrown on the suffering individuals by taxation.... The distress was caused by the operation of the seasons, and the state of the markets; and therefore could not be cured by the remission of taxation, even though that were pushed to the length of national bankruptcy.... Though abundance was desirable, yet carried beyond a certain point, it occasioned evils like those now felt. He was not prepared to go into this view of the question, and to show how they suffered by abundance: but if the hon. member for Portarlington turned his intelligent mind to it, he could make the House understand this part of the subject.'

Mr. RICARDO corrected the error which appeared to have prevailed in the mind of his hon. friend, the member for Salisbury,[1] that he (Mr. R.) was an advocate for taxation. On the contrary, he had voted for every reduction of taxes that had been proposed in the course of the session, because he was anxious for the repeal of taxes, feeling that every tax must prove a burthen upon the public.

---

[1] Should probably be 'the member for Shrewsbury', that is, H. G. Bennet. The member for Salisbury (Lord Folkestone) did not speak in this debate.

AGRICULTURAL DISTRESS AND THE
FINANCIAL AND OTHER MEASURES
FOR ITS RELIEF

29 April 1822

The Marquis of LONDONDERRY in pursuance of the report from the committee on the agricultural distress (which had been presented on 1 April 1822) moved a series of resolutions on agriculture and at the same time announced various financial measures which the government would shortly bring forward. He repeated the opinion which he had formerly expressed that the remission of taxes could only be a palliative, but not an effectual remedy for the agricultural distress; an opinion which had received sanction and confirmation 'in the able work[1] which has recently been published by the hon. member for Portarlington (Mr. Ricardo), than whom it is impossible for the House on such questions to have higher authority'. Lord Londonderry's resolutions provided that, once the ports had been opened to the importation of corn on the price reaching the limit fixed by the existing law (80s. per quarter for wheat[2]), that limit should thereafter be lowered to 70s.; the importation however instead of being free of duty as it was under the existing law would be subject to a duty of 12s. per quarter for wheat when the price was between 70s. and 80s., of 5s. when the price was between 80s. and 85s., and of 1s. when above 85s. An exception was made for foreign corn already in the warehouses. It was also proposed to advance up to 1,000,000*l.* on the security of British corn when the price of wheat was under 60s. Mr. WESTERN spoke next.

Mr. RICARDO said, that, having a proposition which he wished to submit to the House, he offered himself thus early to the committee. He was desirous of laying his proposition before the House, as the noble lord had laid his, in order that the House might have an opportunity of judging of their several merits. The hon. member for Essex[3] had said, that the

---

[1] *On Protection to Agriculture.*
[2] The market price was at this time 50s.

[3] Mr. Western.

noble lord's plan[1] would have the effect of extending the paper currency. He cared not whether it would or would not; for he knew full surely that they had at present as extended a currency as the state of the country required. The present plan—however it might be disguised—was an attack upon the sinking fund.[2] The sinking fund was in principle relinquished. He cared not whether the ultimate accumulation was to be 7,000,000*l.* or 9,000,000*l.;* the present plan was a breach of public faith, so far as the application of the sinking fund could be a breach of faith. There was, in fact, no longer any sinking fund. He solemnly protested against prolonging the charter of the Bank. They had repeatedly called on the chancellor of the exchequer not to enter into any engagement with the Bank for a renewal of their charter. Yet it was now said, that there would be an extension for 10 years, for an object for which it was totally insufficient.[3] It would be a great improvement that the public should be allowed to enter into partnery concerns for supplying their own money transactions, instead of having them intrusted for 10 years longer to the Bank. He had hoped never to have heard of their charter being renewed. The benefit of the paper currency ought to belong to the public. No advantage could ever be derived from the Bank lending money to the public.—With respect to what the noble lord had said of their plans differing very little, he thought there was the most essential difference between them. He (Mr. R.) proposed that a duty of 20*s.* per quarter should be imposed on the importation of wheat when the price rose to 70*s.* The noble

[1] The proposal to prolong the power of country banks to issue notes under £5.

[2] Lord Londonderry had outlined in his speech the pensions plan, on which see below, p. 160.

[3] The Government proposed to extend the charter, which was due to expire in 1833, in order to induce the Bank of England to consent to a relaxation of its provisions so as to allow joint stock banks to be established in the country.

lord supposed that he (Mr. R.) had adopted this of choice; but instead of that, he considered it as forced upon him, and he consented reluctantly to this duty, on account of the distress which now existed, and only on that account. There was another very important difference. He proposed that this duty should be imposed when wheat rose to 70*s.*, because agriculture was at present so extremely depressed. But the noble lord proposed 80*s.*, 85*s.*, 70*s.*, and brought nearer all of them to the importing price, while he (Mr. R.) differed upon that point, and by imposing a duty of 20*s.* when the price was lower at home, afforded a greater relief to the farmer. He thought the farmers the most distressed class in the country, and the most cruelly used. When the prices rose in consequence of a short harvest, and when the farmers ought to have compensation, they diminished their profits, and let corn in from all parts of the world.[1] This great evil the noble lord did not propose to remedy. If the price rose to 85*s.*, it was only required to pay a duty of 1*s.*, and the poor farmer might be inundated with foreign corn. But another difference between him and the noble lord was this—he (Mr. R.) contended, that there could be no security to the farmer while the price of corn was kept higher in this country than in foreign countries. This had been ably shown in the last year's agricultural report. Did the noble lord propose to relieve the agriculturists from this evil, or to afford any mitigation of it? No. Therefore they would be fully as ill off as now.[2] According to his (Mr. R.'s) plan they would be

---

[1] Lord Londonderry referring to the opinions of the agricultural committee on this particular effect of the corn laws had said: 'No member of that committee went further in allowing the extent of that danger than the hon. member for Portarlington.'

[2] From this point *The Times* reports more fully: 'According to his (Mr. Ricardo's) plan they would be sure that the prices here could not be more than 18*s.* higher than abroad. He proposed to give them therefore 18*s.* of a duty. But there could be no pro-

sure that the prices here could not be much higher than they were abroad. He would read the propositions, which he hoped the noble lord would be prevailed on to admit with his own; if not, he hoped the House would decide respecting it. They were as follow:

1. "That it is expedient to provide that the foreign corn now under bond in the United Kingdom may be taken out for home consumption, whenever the average price of wheat, ascertained in the usual mode, shall exceed 65s. a quarter, upon the payment of the following duties:—Wheat 15s. a quarter; rye, peas, and beans, 9s. 6d. a quarter; barley, bear, or bigg, 7s. 6d. a quarter; oats, 5s. a quarter.

tecting duty unless there should be a drawback to the same amount. [The hon. gent. here made a reference to the member for Renfrewshire (Mr. Maxwell), which, as he turned his face away, we were unable to catch.] He did not accuse landlords of being hard-hearted or regardless of the situation in which other classes might be placed; but under the system of corn laws which now existed, their interests must be opposed. He was surprised to hear it often repeated in that house, that the landlord had the same interest as all other classes, and to find this declaration loudly cheered as often as it was made. If this were so, it would be quite sufficient and amply satis-factory to all, to appoint 5 or 6 gentlemen in the manufacturing interest to retire into one room. The hon. chairman of the agri-cultural committee might be their chairman, and they might be left to arrange plans for the relief of the agriculturists. Unfortunately, however, some prejudices existed on the subject; and there were manufacturers who did not think that their interests were the same as those of landlords. If not, why should not the members of the city, or for Liverpool, or the representatives of any other manufacturing or commercial places, make the law which was to relieve the farmer. He imputed no blame for this state of feeling, but he stated it as a proof that they greatly mistook this question. The hon. member for Essex had stated what the demand had been in 1819, and how much it had fallen in 1822. It was very odd that not one word had escaped from the hon. member respecting the supply. If he had attended to this, he would have found that the increased quantity had occa-sioned a diminished demand. He would read the propositions,' etc.

2. "That whenever the average price of wheat, ascer- tained in the usual mode, shall exceed 70*s.* a quarter, the trade in corn shall henceforth be permanently free, but subject to the following duties upon importation:—Of wheat, 20*s.* a quarter; rye, peas, and beans, 13*s.* 3*d.* a quarter; barley, bear, or bigg, 10*s.* a quarter; oats, 6*s.* 8*d.* a quarter.

3. "That at the expiration of one year from the time at which the above duties on corn imported shall be in operation, they be reduced as follows:—On wheat, 1*s.* a quarter; rye, peas, and beans, 8*d.* a quarter; barley, bear, or bigg, 6*d.* a quarter; oats 4*d.* a quarter.

4. "That a like reduction of duties be made in every subsequent year, until the duty on the importation of wheat be 10*s.* a quarter; rye, peas, and beans, 6*s.* 7*d.* a quarter; barley, bear, or bigg, 5*s.* a quarter; oats, 3*s.* 4*d.* a quarter, at which rates they shall henceforth be fixed.

5. "That a drawback or bounty be allowed on the exportation of corn to foreign countries, On wheat, 7*s.* a quarter; rye, peas, and beans, 4*s.* 6*d.* a quarter; barley, bear, and bigg, 3*s.* 6*d.* a quarter; oats 2*s.* 4*d.* a quarter; and that such drawback or bounty in like manner as the importation duty be fixed."

Mr. HUSKISSON moved a series of resolutions to the effect that three months after the price of wheat exceeded 70*s.* per quarter, or so much sooner as it exceeded 80*s.*, the ports should be permanently open to the importation of foreign corn, subject to the same duties as proposed by the Marquis of Londonderry.

[See further p. 162.]

NAVAL AND MILITARY PENSIONS

1 *May* 1822

The Chancellor of the Exchequer moved a series of resolutions recommending a plan for spreading the burden of pensions, which arose principally from the war, equally over a period of 45 years; it was proposed to offer a fixed annuity of 2,800,000*l.* for that period to contractors who would undertake to pay the pensions. The pensions amounted at present to 5,000,000*l.* annually and they would probably be reduced to 300,000*l.* after 45 years, by 'the natural decrement of human life'. 'The transaction', he said, 'would stand completely clear of the sinking fund.'

Mr. Ricardo was astonished how ministers could come down with grave faces, and propose such a measure, after all the anxiety they had expressed on the subject of the sinking fund. This plan was nothing more nor less than an invasion of that fund. The chancellor of the exchequer had said, that these annuities were a part of the debt of the country. This he (Mr. R.) admitted. But, supposing the object of ministers was, to relieve the country from taxation to the amount of 2,200,000*l.,* and they took that sum from the sinking fund, he would ask them to compare the situation in which the country would be placed at the end of 45 years, with that in which it would stand at the expiration of the same period by adopting the plan now proposed. In both cases the object would be to raise 2,200,000*l.* per annum; but, at the end of 45 years, acting on the plan now introduced, would not the country be more in debt, than it would be if the sum were taken immediately out of the sinking fund? Now, if this proposition were true—and it could not be controverted— was it not, he demanded, an invasion of the sinking fund? He, however, had no objection to it on that account: but it was the greatest inconsistency in the right hon. gentleman to say that the sinking fund was to be held sacred, while he came to the House with a proposition that would leave the country more in debt 45 years hence than if 2,200,000*l.* were taken from it at once. He agreed with his hon. friend (Mr. Gurney), that the debt which was the object of this proposition carried a sinking fund along with it. Year by year, as lives dropped off, it was decreasing; and what was the object of the sinking fund but to place all public debt in the situation of this particular debt? Thus, if 30,000,000*l.* were owing in one year, to reduce it to 29,500,000*l.* in the next; then to 29,000,000*l.*, then to 28,500,000*l.;* and so on progressively, until at last the whole was liquidated. A less beneficial effect would be produced by prolonging the debt beyond the term to which it would extend, but for this plan, which he could not help considering an entire fallacy.

The resolutions were agreed to.

3 *May* 1822

On the report stage, Mr. HUME moved as an amendment that the contract be made with the Commissioners for the Redemption of the National Debt.

Mr. RICARDO said, that the proposition of the hon. member for Montrose was the same as that of ministers, only he wished the contract to be made on the most advantageous terms. Whatever *bonus* the private contractor obtained, would be a clear loss to the country. There could be no doubt that, if the sum required were now taken from the sinking fund, at the end of 45 years the country would be in a better situation than if the money were borrowed of individuals. He was an enemy to all complicated schemes, and was for avoiding a crooked path when there was a straight one before him leading to the same end. The obvious course was to take the sum from the sinking fund.

The House divided: for the amendment, 56; against it, 135. Ricardo voted for the amendment.

[See further p. 191.]

AGRICULTURAL DISTRESS REPORT

7 *May* 1822

7 May 1822 The Report [see p. 155] was further considered. Mr. ATTWOOD opposed all the resolutions that had been moved [see pp. 155 and 158–9 above] because, under the pretence of relieving agriculture, their real object was to pave the way for the introduction of foreign grain. The true causes of the agricultural distress were the alterations in the value of currency and the enormous burden of taxation. But it was surprising to find that 'in the present day, when that new school, or new science as it was called, of political economy, was supposed so greatly to flourish, and was certainly so widely extended,' doubts should exist as to what the effect of taxation was. 'The hon. member for Portarlington—(and if he referred so repeatedly to the opinion of that hon. gentleman, it was because he was the only individual of equal authority, who had given any consistent exposition at all of the causes of agricultural distress, and he thought that the agricultural interest was on that account indebted to the hon. gentleman, at least, for his intentions, although he (Mr. Attwood) did not agree with him, in scarcely any one of the opinions he entertained; and was convinced that those opinions had produced extensive mischief and were calculated to occasion still more);— that hon. member had taken a survey of the condition of agriculture, and he found it suffering under great embarrassments; he had found that corn could not be produced in this country, at the present time, for the same monied cost at which it had been formerly produced here; and at which it could now be produced in the countries around them; and what was the explanation that he gave of the causes of this change? He told them that to feed an augmenting population, they had been driven to the cultivation of inferior soils; that those soils could be alone cultivated by the application of additional labour; that they yielded a smaller surplus produce; that none but a higher monied price could be a remunerative price for corn so grown; that this was the main source of the difficulties of agriculture, and that the relief from those difficulties was to be found in abandoning the cultivation of those poorer soils. But as this was the main ground on which the whole system of the hon. member rested, he would beg to state his opinions in his own words, as they were found in a pamphlet recently printed by him on that subject. [Mr. Attwood then read from a pamphlet of Mr. Ricardo]—"The words remunerative

price, are meant to denote the price at which corn can be raised,
paying all charges.—It follows, from this definition, that in proportion as a country is driven to the cultivation of poorer lands
for the support of an increasing population, the price of corn to be
remunerative must rise. It appears, then, that in the progress of
society, when no importation takes place we are obliged constantly to have recourse to worse soils to feed an augmenting
population, and with every step of our progress the price of corn
must rise."[1] This was the hon. gentleman's theory, by which, as
applied to this country, he explained the cause of the rise of corn
since 1793, and why it was, that corn could not now be grown in
this country at a low price. Now he (Mr. Attwood) was convinced,
that there was no foundation, in fact, for the assertions here
maintained, and on which this system was founded. He believed,
that the fact thus assumed was directly the reverse of that which
did in reality exist; that, so far from the average quality of land
becoming poorer as population and wealth advanced, it became
richer; and he had no doubt, but the average quality of the land
under cultivation in this country, at the period of its highest
prices, and of the greatest prosperity of agriculture, at the period
prior to the close of the late war—that the average quality of land
was then more fertile; that it produced more corn on an average
by the acre, and with less positive labour; that it yielded a greater
surplus produce, than at any former period. It was not true, that
the cultivation of any country, proceeded in the manner, and
according to the calculation here assumed. It was not the best
land, which was first cultivated; nor the worst land which was last
cultivated. This was determined in a great measure by other
circumstances; by the rights of proprietorship, by locality, by
enterprize, by the peculiarities of feudal tenure, its remains still
existing; by roads, canals, the erection of towns, of manufactories;
all those and other obstacles of a similar nature interfered with the
calculations of the hon. member; and bad land when it was once
brought into cultivation, and subjected to the operations of agriculture; by draining, by watering, by the application of various
substances, frequently became the best land, and was afterwards
cultivated at the least expense.' Mr. Attwood illustrated his contention by reference to various periods of history and continued:
'Adam Smith, the greatest of authorities on the subject of political
economy, would tell them, that the operation of excessive taxation
on agriculture, was precisely similar to that which the member
for Portarlington traced to an imaginary poverty of the land. The
effect of taxation on agriculture, as explained by Dr. Smith,

---

[1] *On Protection to Agriculture;* above, IV, 210.

might be stated in these words; that it was an effect similar to
that which would be produced,—by an increased barrenness of
the soil; by an increased inclemency of the sky.' Mr. Attwood
then proceeded to show that the burden of taxation was increased to the same extent as the value of the currency had been
raised. But this was not to be estimated from the price of gold.
'The hon. member for Portarlington, who had chiefly insisted on
that mode of calculation, had never hitherto been induced to
explain, why gold, taken as a commodity, in the market, by the
ounce, was to be considered as a better criterion than any other
commodity.' He (Mr. A.) contended that 'it was undoubtedly a
worse.... The most proper commodities to determine the extent of that change, were those in which agriculture was principally interested, corn and cattle.' The prices of corn and cattle, as
compared with the average of the last five years of the war, had
fallen one half; 'the pressure of taxation upon agriculture, therefore, had been doubled.'

Mr. RICARDO said, he rose, impressed with great admiration for the speech which the House had just heard. He
thought the hon. gentleman had shown a very considerable
degree of talent, much research, and great knowledge of the
subject upon which he had spoken. [Hear.] Notwithstanding
these circumstances, he could not help thinking, that the hon.
gentleman had committed a great many errors. The hon.
gentleman had spoken of him (Mr. Ricardo) as if he had
always been a favourer of a paper circulation [cries of "No,
no"]—as if, in fact, he had not been one of the first to point
out the evils of a currency, in the estimation of which the
House could have no guide, and which was at all times liable
to be increased or diminished, as it might suit the convenience
or the pleasure of the Bank. The hon. gentleman appeared to
have founded the whole of his speech upon a passage in a
pamphlet that he (Mr. Ricardo) had written, respecting what
were called "remunerating prices." To the test of the doctrine
and reasoning of that pamphlet, he should be very willing to
trust the whole of the argument in this case. It could make no
difference to the farmer how he obtained those remunerating

prices, provided he got them; although it was very true (as had been asserted by the hon. gentleman), that in order to obtain such prices, he must be content to be paid in money or value of very different descriptions. But the important fact was, that it was impossible a man could long go on, producing any one particular commodity, unless he could obtain for it a remunerating price.—The hon. gentleman had spoken as if he (Mr. Ricardo) were alone responsible for the alteration which had lately taken place in the value of money. He would, however, beg the House to recollect the state in which the currency stood in the year 1819. At the time of the passing of the bill of 1819, the difference between the paper currency and gold was only 5 per cent. What he had then suggested was, that measures should be taken which, while they restored the value of the paper currency to an equality with gold, and thus put an end to the depreciation, would make any purchases of gold unnecessary. Under those measures, as there would have been no additional demand for gold, there could have been no increase in the value of that metal. But as that suggestion was not followed, but another which rendered the purchase of gold necessary, and which (as it had been carried into effect by the Bank) had made a considerable change in the value of gold, how was he (Mr. R.) responsible for the effects of it? If the change in the value of money had been 20 or even 50 per cent he should not have been responsible for it. Undoubtedly, as the hon. member contended, the burthen of money taxation was increased, in proportion to the increase in the value of money: the only difference was as to the amount of that increase. He (Mr. Ricardo) contended, that it was at the utmost about 10 per cent, and nothing like what had been contended by the hon. gentleman. The hon. member had said that he (Mr. Ricardo) measured depreciation solely by the price of gold; and the same observation had been made in various parts of the House, and repeated elsewhere[1] under an entire misconception of the meaning of the word depreciation. Depreciation meant a lowering of the value of the currency, as compared with the standard by which it was professedly regulated. When he used the word, he used it in this obvious and proper sense. The standard itself might be altered, as compared with other things; and it might so happen that a currency might be depreciated, when it had actually risen, as compared with commodities, because the standard might have risen in value in a still greater proportion. When he said, that the currency was relieved from depreciation to such and such an extent, did he say that the currency had not altered in value? The question of the value of the currency was quite a different thing from the question of depreciation; and if the hon. member could prove that gold had changed in value 40 or 50 per cent, he (Mr. R.) would allow that there was a proportionate increase of value in the currency. The hon. member asked why gold was a better standard than corn or any other commodity? He (Mr. R.) answered, that gold had always been the standard of the country; and if we had not passed the fatal law of 1797, we should have continued to this moment with a metallic standard. But, would it have been said on that account, that gold had not altered in value? If, while we had continued a metallic currency, any other country which had had a paper currency had been returning to a metallic standard, the hon. gentleman might have come down, as he did now, and said, that on account of the purchase of gold that had been made, the value of that metal had been enhanced and that the pressure of money taxes had been proportionately increased. But, did the hon. member mean seriously to contend, that

[1] By Cobbett; cp. below, IX, 123, n.

corn was less variable in value than gold [Hear, hear!]? Let
him propose, then, that the Bank directors should pay their
Bank-notes at a certain rate in quarters of corn instead of
sovereigns; for that was the bearing of his assertion [Hear!].
The hon. gentleman talked of the impossibility of the cultivators of the soil having recourse to land of inferior
quality, but the hon. gentleman did not correctly state the
argument. It was not that cultivators were always driven by
the increase of population to lands of inferior quality, but
that from the additional demand for grain, they might be
driven to employ on land previously cultivated a second
portion of capital, which did[1] produce as much as the first.
On a still farther demand a third portion might be employed,
which did not produce so much as the second: it was mani-
festly by the return on the last portion of capital applied, that
the cost of production was determined. It was impossible,
therefore, that the country should go on increasing its
demand for grain without the cost of producing it being increased and causing an increased price. If the hon. member
saw in the present state of things only the consequence of the
change in the value of money, he gave no reason for the
amount of the distress. Let them suppose his (Mr. Ricardo's)
own case. He was possessed of a considerable quantity of
land, the whole of which was unburthened by a single debt.
Now, according to the hon. member, he and the tenants on
that land would have only been injured to the amount of the
increase which the change in the value of money had made in
the burthen of taxation. But they were, in point of fact,
injured much more. The hon. gentleman was mistaken as to
the fact, when he said there was little variation in the price of
grain in the last century. In the first 62 years of the last
century the average price of the quarter of wheat had been

---

[1] Should be 'did not'.

32*s.;* but, in the years from 1784 to 1792 it had been 45*s.*—a very considerable increase on the value of corn. But, he would not rest on any scattered facts what was so evident in principle, as that the extension of cultivation must extend the cost of production of corn. The hon. member had said, that the effect of taxation laid on the land was the same as if the farmer had to support an additional man from whose labours he reaped no benefit. That he (Mr. R.) acknowledged was the effect of all taxation [Hear!]. The hon. member had seemed to think that he would deny this. On the contrary, no one could assert the mischievousness of taxation more strongly than he would. He would never consent that one sixpence should be taken out of the pockets of the people that could be avoided. But he was not, therefore, so blind as to say that taxation was the cause of all the present distress [Hear, hear!]. It was truly said, that the effect of taxation on the landholder was the same as if he had to maintain an additional man: but was not this also the case of the merchant and the manufacturer? [Hear!] If taxation, then, were the sole cause of distress, the distress would press on all alike. The theory of the hon. member was, therefore, totally insufficient to account for what they now witnessed. The hon. gentleman had asked, whether the price of corn would not be doubled if the currency were paper, and taxation were doubled? If tithes were doubled, poor-rates doubled and all taxes affecting especially the growth of corn were doubled, the effect would certainly be to increase the price of corn to that amount; but the country might be taxed generally without producing that alteration. The hon. gentleman had said that he (Mr. Ricardo) advised the abandonment of the land. Now he did not advise the abandonment of it while it was profitable; but he did undoubtedly advise farmers not to grow a commodity that would not yield them a remunerating price.

He would give similar advice to the clothier and to the ship-owner, if their circumstances were similar. He would not now enter into a discussion of the particular propositions about to be brought before the committee. He was content to have answered, however inadequately, the very able speech of the hon. gentleman, and he sat down with declaring that he did not entertain the slightest doubt of the validity of the principles he had maintained.

The House having resolved itself into a committee, the Marquis of LONDONDERRY said that personally he should feel no alarm if the resolutions of either Mr. Huskisson or Mr. Ricardo were adopted; the former had shown a disposition to modify his general principles and 'the hon. member for Portarlington, too, had acted with as much accommodation as could be expected from a person who held so high the principles to which he gave his authority.' But the great mass of the committee thought that the ports should not be opened when wheat was under 80*s.*, and they ought not to legislate against the sentiments of the country; he would propose that the ports should open at 65*s.* with a duty of 15*s.* and a fluctuating duty of 5*s.* per quarter of wheat [cp. his previous proposal p. 155]. Sir T. LETHBRIDGE proposed a duty of 40*s.* per quarter on wheat; he trusted the House would not be led away by 'the abominable theories of political economists.' Sir F. BURDETT attacked the government for having brought forward a measure against their own conviction, and withdrawn it when they saw that it was not well received. He thought that there ought to be no duties at all. 'He could not agree with the hon. member who spoke last in his denunciation of the principles of political economy; nor could he comprehend what the hon. member meant by political economy, when he so abused it, unless he thought that it meant low prices.' The fall of prices was not due to the superabundance of produce or to importation, but to the diminution in the quantity of currency occasioned by the Act of 1819, 'the most fraudulent transaction that ever disgraced any country.' His argument was this: 'A decrease in the quantity of an article might raise its price beyond the proportion of that decrease. But the currency had been diminished to a great extent. During the war the bank circulation rose to about 30,000,000*l.*, and the circulation of country paper amounted, on calculation, to 40,000,000*l.* more, making together 70,000,000*l.* Taking the circulation of the country to be about a tenth part of its income, then a diminution of one per cent in the value [? quantity] of the circulating medium would depress prices 10 per cent.'

Mr. RICARDO, being of opinion that the sufferings of the agriculturists were in a great degree owing to the corn laws, considered the present a fit opportunity for saying a few words upon that subject. Even if he were fully to agree with gentlemen who ascribed the present distresses to the change in the value of the currency and the weight of taxation, still he thought those gentlemen must admit that the corn laws, considered abstractedly without any reference to those two questions, were calculated to produce great evils. One of the principal of these evils was, the unnaturally high price of corn in this country over all other countries. The hon. baronet[1] had admitted, that superabundance would occasion a great fall in the value of corn as well as all other articles. And here he must observe, that there appeared to be a little inconsistency in the arguments of the hon. baronet. In one part of his speech the hon. baronet admitted that a super-abundant production of corn would occasion mischief to the extent in which it was at present experienced. [Sir F. Burdett dissented.] The hon. baronet now said he did not admit this; but he certainly understood him to do so, and to apply the argument to the change in the value of the currency; for he said that those who contended, that the increase of an article beyond a certain limit, would occasion a fall in price greater in proportion than the increase which had taken place, must admit that an alteration in the value[2] of the currency will produce a change in the value[3] of commodities, greater in proportion than the alteration in the value[4] of money. Although he (Mr. R.) was of opinion, that a superabundant

---

[1] Sir F. Burdett.
[2] (?) 'quantity'.
[3] (?) 'prices'.
[4] (?) 'quantity'.

supply of an article produced a sinking in the value of the article greater than in proportion to the additional quantity, yet he did not apply this argument to money. He would put a case to the House, to show how a superabundant supply of an article would produce a sinking of its aggregate value much greater than in proportion to the surplus supply. He would suppose, that in a particular country a very rare commodity was introduced for the first time—superfine cloth for instance. If 10,000 yards of this cloth were imported under such circumstances, many persons would be desirous of purchasing it, and the price consequently would be enormously high. Supposing this quantity of cloth to be doubled, he was of opinion that the aggregate value of the 20,000 yards would be much more considerable than the aggregate value of the 10,000 yards, for the article would still be scarce, and therefore in great demand. If the quantity of cloth were to be again doubled, the effect would still be the same; for although each particular yard of the 40,000 would fall in price, the value of the whole would be greater than that of the 20,000. But, if he went on in this way increasing the quantity of the cloth, until it came within the reach of the purchase of every class in the country, from that time any addition to its quantity would diminish the aggregate value. This argument he applied to corn. Corn was an article which was necessarily limited in its consumption: and if you went on increasing it in quantity, its aggregate value would be diminished beyond that of a smaller quantity. He made an exception of this argument in favour of money. If there were only 100,000*l.* in this country, it would answer all the purposes of a more extended circulation; but if the quantity were increased, the value of commodities would alter only in proportion to the increase, because there was no necessary limitation of the quantity of money. The argument of the hon. baronet, to which he had before alluded, was therefore inapplicable. With respect to the subject more particularly before the House; namely, the evils of the present corn laws, he was of opinion that the farmer would suffer an injury from having too abundant crops. But to look at the other side of the question. Suppose the farmer should have scarce seasons, and that his corn should rise; just at the moment when he would be about to reap the benefit of this circumstance, the ports would be opened, and corn would pour in in unlimited quantities. These evils had been pointed out in the most able manner in the agricultural report, and in the resolutions of his right hon. friend (Mr. Huskisson), to some of which he should be sorry if the House did not agree. In his opinion, not the resolutions of the noble marquis, nor even those of his right hon. friend, and still less those of hon. members on his own side of the House, were at all adequate to remove the evils complained of. How was the evil of an habitually higher price in this country than in foreign countries to be remedied? By making the growing price in this country on a level with that of other nations. If his propositions should be agreed to, for imposing a duty of 10*s.* upon imported corn, and granting a bounty of 7*s.* upon exported corn, he thought it impossible that the price of wheat in this country could ever be materially higher than that of foreign nations. If abundant harvests should occur here, the farmer would have his remedy in exportation. In fixing the duty of 10*s.* upon imported corn, he had been guided by what he thought the circumstances of the case required. He did not intend that the House should adopt the duty of 10*s.* all at once. In the present distressed state of the agriculturists in this country, and taking into consideration the abundant supply of grain on the other side of the water, he was willing to give the farmer protection up to 70*s.*, and then open the ports for importation, commencing with a duty of 20*s*. In his own opinion, this duty of 20*s*. would amount to a total exclusion of foreign corn, but he selected it, because, under the existing laws, all importation was prohibited, and therefore he was not making the situation of the consumer worse than at present, at the same time that he was securing a gradual approach to what he considered right principles. He would state the grounds upon which he calculated the duty of 10*s*. He found it stated in the evidence given before both Houses, that the whole of the charges which the farmer had to pay, which were principally tithes and poor-rates, amounted to about 10*s*. per quarter. The hon. member for Wiltshire[1] said last night, that he desired no more than to have a duty placed upon the importation of corn, calculated on the taxes which fell on the landed interest. He did not understand the calculations of that hon. member, but he called upon him to refute his if he could. If the hon. member admitted their correctness, he should expect the support of his vote. He recommended the imposition of the duty upon imported corn, for the reasons he had before stated, namely, the protection of the farmer in the event of a bad harvest. He contended that he was vindicating the cause of the farmers more effectually than many gentlemen who called themselves their friends.—It was necessary for him to make a few observations upon that part of his plan which provided for the introduction of foreign corn, now in bond, into the home market, subject to a duty of 15*s*. whenever the price of wheat should reach 65*s*. The hon. member for Oxford[2] had said, that this measure would be destructive of the agricultural interest, and that it would reduce the price of corn to 47*s*. But the farmer had the remedy in his own hands. When the price of wheat should arrive at 64*s.*, if he apprehended the

[1] Mr. J. Benett.　　　　[2] Mr. Lockhart.

influx of foreign grain, he would be in possession of the market, and might dispose of his corn to advantage. He had selected 65*s*. in order to secure the farmer from being placed in competition with the holders of foreign corn in bond and in foreign countries at the same time; he would first have to cope with the former, and if the price should afterwards rise to 70*s*. he would then compete with the latter. It might be right to observe, that a duty of 10*s*. would be fully adequate to protect the farmer even when the ports were opened. According to the evidence before the committee, there appeared to be little danger of the country being over-whelmed by importations. The noble marquis had stated, that the expense of bringing corn from abroad to this country amounted to 10*s*. per quarter. But Mr. Solly, in his evidence, calculated that the expense of growing of corn in the interior of Germany, together with all the charges consequent upon its carriage to this country, would amount to 2*l*. 16*s*. The duty of 10*s*. upon importation would increase this sum to 3*l*. 6*s*. Now, the member for Cumberland[1] was of opinion, that 65*s*. was a fair protecting price; and if so, why did he and other members object to the duty of 10*s*., which would secure them against importation until the price of wheat should be at least 65*s*.? He could not understand upon what principle the agriculturist could object to his propositions. He was willing to give them not only a remunerating price of 70*s*., but a duty of 20*s*., and yet they thought that was not adequate protection. He would take this opportunity of in-forming the House, that Mr. Solly, to whose evidence he had referred, understanding that the noble marquis had asserted, that the last harvest in Silicia had been so very abundant that it was not considered worth while to reap it, had instructed him (Mr. R.) to state, that so far from having had an abun-

---

[1] Mr. Curwen.

dant harvest, the inhabitants were reduced to the necessity of buying seed-wheat. The noble marquis's propositions did not appear calculated to remove the existing evils, but rather to confirm them. They would tend to encourage the agriculturist in speculating upon high prices, and would thus produce the same round of evils. He also objected, though in a less degree, to the propositions of his right hon. friend.[1] His right hon. friend proposed a duty of 15*s.* on imported corn without any drawback upon exportation, the consequence of which would be, to make the price of corn in this country habitually 15*s.* higher than in foreign countries. Nobody had more clearly shown the evil of such a circumstance than his right hon. friend, and therefore he was exposed to the charge of inconsistency for having proposed a measure calculated to produce it. The drawback which he (Mr. R.) proposed, would operate in favour of the farmer when he would stand most in need of assistance. He declined entering upon the question of the currency, but he could not avoid making one observation on that subject. Some gentlemen seemed to think that the contraction of two or three millions of the currency had never before the present time taken place. In the report of the committee of 1797, it was stated, that in 1782—at which time the Bank paper in circulation did not amount to more than 8,000,000*l.* or 9,000,000*l.* in addition to coin—an actual reduction of 3,000,000*l.* of the amount of the money in circulation took place.

The debate was resumed on 8 May when Mr. J. BENETT proposed a duty of 24*s.* on foreign wheat. Mr. LOCKHART said, 'he conceived the proposition of the hon. member for Portarlington was altogether unsound. It would have the effect of throwing much of the poor land out of cultivation; a measure so destructive to those interested in it, that had he not known the amiable

---

[1] Mr. Huskisson.

7 May 1822

disposition of that hon. member, he should be disposed to question his motives.' Mr. WESTERN said that it would be in vain to seek any remedy until they had repealed the Act of 1819. 'He could not too often repeat that the higher the money price of corn the lower would be the labour price in real effect. By raising the money price of corn, they would practically lighten the weight of taxation, and reduce the real price upon the labourer.' He would not refuse permission to import foreign grain, if the state of the country required its introduction; but it was most important not to be dependent upon other powers for any considerable share of the supply. Mr. BANKES said that a free trade 'might be right, but it was not the system under which the country had acquired its wealth and power. That system was one of restriction, upon all articles of home produce, and upon none more than corn. They might be much wiser than their ancestors; but he was not disposed to consider them such fools as modern philosophy would make them out to have been.' He thought 'the country was more manufacturing than was good for it already' and deprecated 'the liberal doctrines of the day'. He concluded by reminding the House of the fable of the bundle of sticks; 'if they became disunited, and suffered the political economists to pull one out of the bundle, they would all be broken. Let them look to agriculture as the chief stick, and protect it as far as lay in their power. But above all, let them continue to follow in the course by which their ancestors had made a small country become a great one'. Mr. BROUGHAM had no objection to the principle of Mr. Ricardo's resolutions, but he thought his permanent duty of 10s. too small. That duty was calculated on the ground that the farmer was peculiarly burdened to that amount by the tithes and poor-rates; but this was not all, because 'the agriculturists, more than any other class, were affected by the taxes imposed on those commodities which were consumed by the labouring classes, because more labour was used in producing the same amount of produce in value by the farmer, than by the manufacturer, or any other individual.'

9 *May* 1822

9 May 1822

The debate being resumed, Lord ALTHORP moved as an amendment to Mr. Ricardo's resolutions that a fixed duty of 20s. per quarter be imposed on the importation of wheat (instead of 20s., decreasing in ten years to 10s.) and a bounty of 18s. per quarter be allowed on exportation (instead of 7s.).

Mr. RICARDO was surprised at his noble friend's proposing such an amendment. He could not see upon what
principle his noble friend could justify raising the bounty on
exportation to 18*s.* a quarter. For his own part, he did not
think that any bounty would often be called into operation.
Whenever it should, 7*s.* would be quite enough. His noble
friend, the learned member for Winchelsea,[1] and the hon.
member for Corfe-castle,[2] both agreed in one objection
against his resolutions—that he had not made sufficient
allowances for the effect of indirect taxation on the agricultural interest, which, according to their statement, was more
affected by it than any other interest. Their statement to a
certain extent, might be true; still he thought they had exaggerated. The principle upon which he had made his calculations was, that the price of every commodity was constituted by the wages of labour, and the profits[3] of stock.
Now, the noble lord's argument was, that in manufactured
commodities the price was constituted of only a small
portion of wages, and a large portion of the profits of the
stock; whilst, in agricultural commodities, the case was
exactly the reverse. If the noble lord could substantiate such
a proposition, he would agree that he was entitled to the
allowance he demanded.[4] All that he doubted was, whether
the fact were so. He doubted whether the proportion of
labour was greater in agriculture than in manufactures. The
right way of coming to a sound determination upon that
point was, by considering in what the dead capital of both
consisted. If he could show that the dead capital in

[1] Mr. Brougham.
[2] Mr. Bankes.
[3] Misprinted 'produce' in *Hansard,* here and three lines below;
correct in the *Morning Chronicle.*
[4] The *Morning Chronicle* reports
more fully: 'If that argument

could be substantiated by a reference to facts, it would certainly
prove that a larger allowance
should be made in the calculation
for that indirect taxation which
fell on labour. There could be no
doubt of that.'

agriculture bore the same proportion to its whole capital, that the dead capital in manufactures did to its whole capital, then he thought that his noble friend's proposition would no longer be valid. His learned friend, the member for Winchelsea, had said, that almost all the produce of the land was made up of labour. His learned friend, however, seemed to have forgotten that there was a great deal of capital in buildings, in horses, in seed in the ground, besides in labour. It was true that the manufacturer had a great proportion of his capital in his machinery; but, even though that were taken into consideration, he must still say, that the proportion of his noble friend was not made out so clearly as it ought to be; and that he was therefore only entitled to a small allowance. Now, in allowing a duty of 10*s.,* he thought that he had made an ample allowance; and he had made that allowance, too, on the principle, that all the poor-rates as well as all the tithes fell exclusively upon the agricultural interest. He now stated, however, that the agricultural interest was not entitled to the full allowance of all the poor-rates, inasmuch as a part of them was paid by the manufacturers, although much the greater part, he would allow, was paid by the agricultural classes. He was persuaded that if he had kept to that principle, the allowance to the agricultural interest would not have been more than 7*s.* Now, he had allowed them a duty of 10*s.,* and therefore, in the 3*s.* that there was over, he had made ample compensation for any errors that he might unintentionally have committed. He would now say one word to the hon. member for Corfe-castle (Mr. Bankes), regarding the lecture which he had read him (Mr. R.) upon political economy. The hon. member had talked much of the wisdom of our ancestors. He willingly allowed that there was much wisdom in our ancestors: but at the same time he must ever contend, that the present generation had all their wisdom and a little more into the bargain. [Hear, hear.] If the argument of the hon. member were to be considered as valid, there was an end at once to all hopes of future improvement. The present generation had invented steam-engines and gas-lights, and had made several other useful and beneficial discoveries, and he trusted that they would never be stopped in their progress to knowledge by being told of the wisdom of their ancestors, or be convinced that they were in the most flourishing condition possible because the system of their ancestors was called most wise and excellent. Undoubtedly this country was a great country, and had of late years increased its capital to a great extent. But in arguing upon that point, the hon. member for Corfe-castle might as well have employed this argument as the one which he had used; he might as well have said, "We have increased in wealth, whilst we have been contracting a great national debt; therefore, the national debt is a great blessing, and it would be a bad thing to get rid of it." [Hear, and a laugh.] That argument was quite as valid as the argument which the hon. member had actually used.—The hon. member then proceeded to state, that one argument urged against a free importation of corn, which appeared to him not to deserve the slightest attention, was this—that England ought not only to be a self-supplying, but also an exporting country. Now he wished to press one point upon their consideration, and that was—that it was the great interest of a country which grew a commodity for the use of another, to keep the market open for the sale of it. Now, if we were to raise a large supply for the purpose of sending our raw produce to a foreign country, in what a situation should we be placed if the market were to be shut against it? What a glut would then be forced into the home market! He would contend, that the ruin which such an event would produce, would be so great that no minister,

nor sovereign, would be able to remedy it. The hon.
member for Corfe-castle had also lamented that we were
becoming too much of a manufacturing country. The hon.
gentleman might, perhaps, think that a manufacturing
country could not be so happy as an agricultural country.
But he might as well complain of a man's growing old as of
such a change in our national condition. Nations grew old as
well as individuals; and in proportion as they grew old,
populous, and wealthy, must they become manufacturers.
If things were allowed to take their own course, we should
undoubtedly become a great manufacturing country, but we
should remain a great agricultural country also. Indeed, it
was impossible that England should be other than an agricultural country: she might become so populous as to be
obliged to import part of her food; but instead of lamenting
over that circumstance, he should think it a proof of prosperity and a subject of congratulation. There would always
be a limit to our greatness, while we were growing our own
supply of food: but we should always be increasing in wealth
and power, whilst we obtained part of it from foreign
countries, and devoted our own manufactures to the payment
of it. The hon. member for Corfe-castle had asked, whether
our farmers were to be transformed into manufacturers, and
our ploughmen into mechanics? From that question, any
stranger who had walked into the House might have supposed that a proposition had been actually made to throw
open our ports, and to change all at once our entire course of
policy. But had any proposition of that nature been even
hinted at? The hon. member for Oxford (Mr. Lockhart) had
done him the honour of stating, that he believed that he
(Mr. R) would not willingly inflict misery upon his country;
but had added that he believed his resolutions would have
such a tendency. But when he proposed a monopoly for the

agriculturist up to 70*s*. (and the hon. member for Wiltshire[1] admitted that 67*s*. was a remunerative growing price), and a duty of 20*s*. on the first opening of the ports, and a gradual reduction of it to a fixed and permanent duty of 10*s*., could it be fairly said that he was proposing a scheme to turn the capital of the country from agriculture to manufactures? It had been well observed by an hon. member, that it was totally impossible that the direction of our capital could be changed in that manner. The security against it was to be found in the necessity of our growing our own corn—a necessity which would always prevent us from becoming too much of a manufacturing country. The fact was, that his resolutions, if adopted, would gradually employ a small portion more of the capital of the country in manufactures, of which the result would be beneficial to all classes of the community, as it was only by the sale of our manufactures that we were enabled to purchase corn.—He had never heard any answer attempted to his argument respecting the miserable situation into which the farmer would be plunged under a system of protecting duties. The high prices of corn exposed the farmer to great and peculiar risks. Now, none of the representatives of the agricultural interest in that House had ever ventured to assert that the farmer was not liable to the risks which he had pointed out as likely to arise from the variation of prices: none of them had attempted to show that his view of the danger was absurd and chimerical; and, as they had not done so, he was greatly confirmed in that view which he had originally taken. The hon. member for Wiltshire had stated, that we could obtain a large supply of foreign corn at 25*s*. per quarter. Now, he held in his hand a letter from Mr. Solly,[2] in which that gentleman declared, that in all

---

[1] Mr. J. Benett.

[2] This letter has not been found. Cp. below, VIII, 374.

the evidence which he had given before the committee, he
had not spoken of the then accidental price, but of the remunerating price, on the continent; and his learned friend
(Mr. Brougham) had justly observed, that it was the remunerating price on the continent that regulated the price here.
Now, he believed that his learned friend had understated
that remunerating price. His learned friend had stated it at
45*s.;* he believed it to be 10*s.* more; for his learned friend had
made no allowance for the profits of those who brought it
here, which, in the opinion of Mr. Solly, were at least 6*s.* a
quarter. The chief reason, however, for his mentioning the
letter of Mr. Solly was, that Mr. Solly had said that Memel
(from which one of the witnesses before the committee had
derived his information) was not a port from which any
great quantity of corn was shipped—not above 20,000
quarters a year, and that of inferior quality. Now, he wished
to ask the House, if not more than 20,000 quarters were
shipped from Memel, and those too of an inferior quality,
whether such a fact would justify them in passing such a
legislative measure as his hon. friend had proposed? The
assertion, therefore, that foreign corn could be obtained at
25*s.* per quarter, was unworthy of attention for a single
moment.—The only farther observation which he had to
make was, with regard to what had fallen from the noble
marquis.[1] The noble marquis had said, that the measures
which he had recommended to the House had been carried in
the committee, almost without a dissentient voice. Now, he
(Mr. R.) had stated his opinions in the committee, and for the
sake of his own character and consistency, he would take the
liberty of restating them to the House. He had gone into
that committee with the opinion that the agricultural classes
were in a state of great and overwhelming distress—that any

[1] Marquis of Londonderry.

relief which could be held out to them, ought to be held out —and that he would give them such relief; but on condition, that he should, in his turn, receive a pledge that some better measures of legislation should be instantly resorted to. He had been disposed to give the agriculturists every thing they required. They had a prohibition at present; and they could not have more. Indeed, he had been ready to adopt any proposition that the committee might originate, so long as the committee expressed a willingness to propose some more salutary measures of legislation to the consideration of parliament. The committee had held out to him a hope that they would do what he advised; they told him that they would insert something in their report which would satisfy him upon that point; and, in consequence of that declaration, he had given a conditional assent to the measures they had proposed. When he saw the report, and found that it contained no such clause as he had anticipated, the conditional assent that he had given to their propositions was immediately dissolved; and he refused to concur in the report of the committee, because it contained nothing of the nature which he had hoped it would contain. The hon. member for Hertford[1] had said, that the evidence of those persons who imported corn was to be taken with some allowance, because their views of interest, however honest the individuals might be in intention, were likely to bias them. He did not mean to quarrel with that observation; for in most cases he allowed it to be well founded. He wished, however, to be permitted to apply it to those who had to decide in that House upon this most important subject. Let him remind them, that they had a great interest in it; let him caution them not to be led away—not to be improperly biassed—by any views of their own personal advantage. Let him implore them to recollect

---

[1] Mr. N. Calvert.

that they were legislating for the happiness of millions, and that there was no evil so intolerable as the high price of human food. [Hear!] He was astonished to hear the hon. member for Essex[1] declare, that it was matter of indifference to him whether prices were high or not; and that he wanted to have corn for little labour and for low prices. He went along with the hon. member in that sentiment; but then he was astonished to find, that the hon. member, when they came to a measure that was calculated to give them low real prices, flew off in an opposite direction, and declared that we ought to grow our own corn, and that it was only upon particular occasions that we should suffer it to be imported. Such a declaration, if acted upon would render it impossible to obtain low prices in a country increasing in population like our own: indeed, the only way of getting low real prices, with which he was acquainted, was, to divert part of the capital of the country in such a way as to increase its manufactures.

After further debate. Mr. WESTERN said that in the present state of the currency he would refuse to legislate on the question of corn. 'Were not the prices of corn on the continent, for the last twenty-five years, estimated in our paper currency, and, therefore, liable to all its fluctuations?… Would it not, then, be unwise to look at those prices as the foundation of any prospective regulation?'

Mr. RICARDO denied that the price of corn on the continent was liable to the fluctuations of our currency.

The committee then divided on Lord Althorp's amendment, to fix a permanent duty of 18*s.* on wheat: For the amendment, 24. Against it, 201.

A second division took place on Mr. Ricardo's propositions for a duty of 20*s.* per quarter of wheat, when the price shall rise above 70*s.,* to lower 1*s.* a year for ten years, and for 10*s.* being the permanent duty, and 7*s.* the bounty afterwards: Ayes, 25. Noes, 218.

[1] Mr. Western.

Athorp, lord	Evans, W.	Philips, G.
Birch, Jos.	Haldimand, W.	Rumbold, C. E.
Brougham, H.	Hume, J.	Robinson, sir G.
Barnard, lord	Lamb, hon. G.	Smith, G.
Beaumont, T. W.	Lamb, hon. W.	Scarlett, J.
Becher, W. W.	Langston, J. H.	Thompson, W.
Carter, J.	Marjoribanks, S.	Whitmore, W. W.
Davies, col.	Maberly, J.	TELLER
Denison, W. J.	Newport, sir J.	Ricardo, D.

The committee then divided on the Marquis of Londonderry's resolutions: Ayes, 218; Noes, 36.[1]

13 *May* 1822

When the report of the committee on the Marquis of London- derry's resolutions was brought up, Mr. WESTERN referred to 'the hasty and peremptory contradiction he had received on a former night on the subject of prices from the hon. member for Portarlington.' Mr. PHILIPS hoped 'that his hon. friend (Mr. Ricardo) would bring forward his resolutions year after year; convinced that time would prove the correctness of his positions. The more his hon. friend was known, the more he would be respected, and the more universally recognized, by all who had sense or candour, as one of the most original and wisest writers, and one of the soundest thinkers on the subject of political economy.'

Mr. RICARDO, in explanation of the allusion which had been made to his statement of the average prices of foreign corn, by the hon. member for Essex, begged the House would bear in mind, that there were two authorities on that subject that were quoted from, who differed much in their items. The calculations of Mr. Solly were made in conform-

13 May 1822

---

[1] Neither Ricardo nor any of the others in the list above voted against Lord Londonderry's re- solutions (only the list of the minority is given in *Hansard*).

ance with the variations of our paper currency, and were, therefore, always higher than those of Mr. Grade, who made his calculations upon a fixed exchange. He had built his argument on the latter, and it would be found that whilst he was quoting from one paper, the hon. gentleman was quoting from another, and thus the misunderstanding arose. He therefore hoped he should be acquitted of any intention to mislead.

Mr. ATTWOOD controverted in detail Mr. Ricardo on this point, and launched into another attack upon Peel's Act of 1819. Mr. PEEL replied to Mr. Attwood's attempt to 'overwhelm him with his sarcasm' that 'as he was to share that sarcasm with his hon. friend, the member for Portarlington (if he might be permitted, on account of the respect which he felt for that hon. gentleman's great talents and high character, to use a term which he certainly had no right to use from long intimacy with him), he would only observe, that he was willing to share it, so long as he shared it in such company.'

Mr. Ricardo then submitted his resolutions for the sake of having them recorded on the Journals. Mr. Ricardo's resolutions were negatived; the resolutions of the Marquis of Londonderry were then agreed to.

[See further, on the corn bill, below, p. 195.]

ABSENTEES

16 *May* 1822

Sir T. LETHBRIDGE presented a petition from 600 respectable inhabitants of Somerset, praying for a tax on absentees who had taken up their residence in foreign parts. He said that it was calculated that in Paris alone there resided 10,000 families of English, Irish and Scots; they were spending large sums and by transferring the money to France they gained an advantage of 25 per cent.

Mr. RICARDO wished to set the hon. baronet right, as to the state of the exchange, which was now, he could assure him, very nearly at par; and it was impossible it could be far otherwise, because with a metallic circulation in this country and in France, the exchange could never vary more than from $\frac{1}{2}$ to $\frac{3}{4}$ per cent. As to the petition, he should be sorry to see its prayer granted; because a tax on the property or income of absentees, would hold out a direct encouragement to them to take away their capital, as well as their persons. Now, we had at any rate their capital, which was useful, though not so useful as if they also stayed at home. What most surprised him was, that the hon. baronet should bring such a petition forward, at the very time that he was proposing in the agricultural committee a resolution which might make all the articles of life, and provisions in particular, attainable at the dearest rate.[1] The hon. baronet was for high duties; the imposition of which would be the readiest means of compelling people of small fortunes to quit the kingdom. Of all the evils complained of, he (Mr. R.) was still disposed to think the corn laws the worst. He conceived that were the corn laws once got rid of, and our general policy in these subjects thoroughly revised, this would be the cheapest country in the world; and that, instead of our complaining that capital was withdrawn from us, we should find that capital would come hither from all corners of the civilized world. Indeed, such a result must be certain, if we could once reduce the national debt—a reduction, which, although by many considered to be impracticable, he considered by no means to be so. That great debt might be reduced by a fair contribution of all sorts of property—he meant, that, by the united contribution of the mercantile, the landed, and he would add, the funded interest, the national debt might be certainly got rid of. If this were done, and if the government would pursue a right course of policy as to the corn

---

[1] See above, p. 169.

laws, England would be the cheapest country in which a man could live; and it would rise to a state of prosperity, in regard to population and riches, of which, perhaps, the imaginations of hon. gentlemen could at present form no idea. [Hear, hear.]

COLONIAL TRADE BILL

17 *May* 1822

This bill had been introduced by the President of the Board of Trade in order to remove some of the restrictions on the trade of the West Indian and North American colonies: it allowed American ships to trade with certain ports, and it allowed British ships to export from the colonies direct to foreign countries, instead of through the United Kingdom. The debate however turned on the sugar duties, which favoured the West Indies against the East Indies. On the second reading Mr. ELLICE spoke in support of the bill and referred to the injustice to which the West Indian planters and settlers had been subjected by the alteration in the currency.

Mr. RICARDO rose, in the first instance, to make one observation on the subject of the currency. Though the facts were not known to him, he could not help suspecting the correctness of his hon. friend, respecting the payments in the West Indies. That persons in the West Indies who, in 1815 paid a debt of 100*l.* with 155*l.* of their currency, should now have to pay 227*l.*, while that currency was not itself altered in value, seemed to him incredible. He would go on, however, to another subject. If he had wanted an argument in favour of a free trade, he should not have gone farther than the speech of his hon. friend. He had painted the system exactly as it was. He had told them that the ship-owners were burthened with peculiar charges; that to compensate themselves for these charges, the ship-owners were allowed to saddle unnecessary expenses on the West Indians; that the West Indians were not allowed to refine their sugar, but were obliged to send it over with a quantity of mud, in order to employ and encourage our shipping; that they, in their turn, had a monopoly given them of the supply of the home market, where the consumer got his sugar burthened by the cost of all these charges. The system throughout was of the same nature. Vexatious and unnecessary burthens were cast upon one class, and that class was allowed to relieve itself by preying upon some other. An hon. member[1] had put a very proper question; when he was told that the people of England were taxed for the sake of the West Indians, the hon. member had asked, who got this million and a half, when the West Indians could barely keep their estates in cultivation? No one got it. That was what he (Mr. R.) complained of. The people of England paid grievously for their sugar, without a corresponding benefit to any persons. The sum which they paid was swallowed up in the fruitless waste of human labour. The hon. member for London[2] had said, that they should pay the same price for their sugar, whether they taxed it or not. Now it was not possible this could be the case. The hon. member might as well have said, that if they did not lay a tax on tea, the Chinese would raise the price of it equal to the present price burthened with the tax. The general principle that regulated price where free competition operated was, that a commodity would be sold as cheap as the producers could afford. Unless, therefore, our admission of the East India sugars could add to the cost of producing them, there could be no increase of price. The case of the West Indies was precisely similar to that of the corn laws. As in the latter case we were protecting our poor soil from the competition of the rich soil of other countries, so were

---

[1] Mr. Barham.

[2] Mr. T. Wilson.

17 May 1822   we to protect the poor soil of the West Indies from the competition of the rich soil of the East Indies. The mischief in such cases was, that there was much human labour thrown away without any equivalent. He fully agreed, that there would be the greatest possible injustice in sacrificing the vested interests of the West Indies; but it would be cheaper to purchase our sugar from the East Indies, and to pay a tax directly to the West Indies for the liberty of doing so. We should be gainers by the bargain; because there would be no waste of human labour. As he thought a monopoly was a disadvantage on either side, he saw no reason for opposing the present bill, which approached, to a certain degree, to free trade. We could not too soon return to the sound principle; and if we once arrived at it the House would no longer be tormented with these discussions, and with constant solicitations to sacrifice the public good to particular interests.

NAVIGATION BILL

20 *May* 1822

20 May 1822   Early in the Session Mr. WALLACE (Vice-President of the Board of Trade) had introduced the Navigation Act Amendment Bill, which removed many of the restrictive provisions of the Navigation Laws. On the report stage,

Mr. RICARDO considered it a happy omen that so many gentlemen were now of opinion that our system admitted of improvement. The only complaint he had against the bill was, that it did not go far enough.

[See further, below, p. 197.]

NAVAL AND MILITARY PENSIONS

24 *May* 1822

No contractors having come forward for the pensions plan approved by Parliament [see above, p. 160] the CHANCELLOR OF THE EXCHEQUER introduced a modified form of that plan. He proposed that the fixed annuity should be paid to trustees accountable to Parliament; that the trustees should undertake to pay the pensions; and that they should be empowered in each year to sell as much of the annuity (or otherwise borrow from the public) as was necessary to make up the deficiency. He announced that the sums released would be used for reducing the duties on salt (from 15*s*. to 2*s*. per bushel) and on leather, and for repealing the Irish window tax and the tonnage duty on ships. Mr. HUME moved as an amendment to the financial measures that the sums required be taken from the Commissioners of the National Debt instead of being raised by loan or annuities [cp. above p. 161].

Mr. RICARDO said, he was most ready to commend the conduct of ministers where he found it prudent and proper; and in the proposed remission of taxes he thought they had acted judiciously in listening to the general prayer of the people. But, when he offered this commendation, he must decline concurring in any terms of excessive gratitude. He confessed, that he owed no gratitude to ministers for giving the people what was, in fact, their own money. If, indeed, the ministers had framed any plan for giving the people any portion of money which did not really belong to them, then would be the time to offer them fervent gratitude. But he thought that ministers, in coming down with all that earnestness to announce the remission of taxes, had not dealt quite fairly with the House. It looked as if they wished to induce the House to assent to those parts of their proposition which were bad, under the cover of those parts which were good. Now, he thought it was the duty of that House to separate the bad from the good, and by its vote to get rid of the former altogether. Under that view, he should support the amendment. He regretted much that any portion of the salt tax was continued, he did not wish that any nucleus should remain, because they well knew with what vigour, under the management of the exchequer, it would spread. [Hear, hear.] As to the present plan for meeting the dead expenditure, it was nothing more or less than an annual loan, in the contracting for which either a profit or a loss, as in all other loans, must follow. To the public, then, at last they must go for that loan; and as there was no ascertained stock in which it was to be funded, it would be of course less marketable, and consequently a greater profit must be held out to the contractor. Why then not keep that advantage to the country? There was another fallacy: for as the period of 45 years approached to a termination, what was to prevent the chancellor of the exchequer of the day, from converting these annuities into a perpetuity? He did expect the vote of the hon. member for London.[1] That hon. member had qualified his support to the former plan, by hoping that the chancellor of the exchequer would take advantage of the present high price of the funds, in making his bargain for the public. Now, by the proposed scheme, the sale of the annuities was to be annual, and of course the purchases. Being thus made from year to year, such sales and purchases must be subjected to the contingency of war, and the depreciation of the price of stocks. Besides, if the market failed the right hon. gentleman, he must issue Exchequer bills, and add to the unfunded debt. If war subsequently occurred, he would then have to fund at a greater expense.

Mr. Hume's amendment was lost on a division and the resolutions were agreed to.

[See further p. 193 below.]

[1] Mr. T. Wilson.

BANK CHARTER

31 *May* 1822

Mr. GRENFELL presented a petition against the proposed 31 May 1822 renewal of the Bank of England charter [cp. p. 156, n. 3, above] and remarked on the 'immense profits' made by the Bank during the last twenty years and 'their tyrannous conduct towards government and towards the public'.

Mr. RICARDO did not complain of the Bank directors for making the concern as profitable as possible; but he complained of ministers for having made such improvident bargains with the Bank, as to enable that establishment to make those enormous profits. He should oppose to the utmost the renewal of the Bank charter, because he was satisfied that every farthing made by the Bank ought to belong to the public. Even if a paper currency were wanted, ministers could accomplish the object more advantageously for the public without, than with the assistance of the Bank of England.[1]

NAVAL AND MILITARY PENSIONS

3 *June* 1822

On the report stage of the revised measure, Mr. HUME having 3 June 1822 again moved his amendment [cp. above, p. 191], Mr. GRENFELL said that should the amendment be rejected he would propose a clause empowering the Commissioners for the National Debt to purchase the proposed annuities. The CHANCELLOR OF THE EXCHEQUER acquiesced in this suggestion.

---

[1] In place of the last sentence the *Morning Chronicle* reports: 'He could not agree with the authorities that had been quoted to prove that the Bank of England was any great advantage to the country. Its only use was to establish a paper currency, and that object could be attained in other modes without the loss to the public that had actually been incurred.'

Mr. RICARDO said, that the plan was neither more nor less than sending one set of commissioners into the market to sell stock, and another set into the market to buy stock; and even the chancellor of the exchequer now understood that fact so fully, that he was about to support a clause which would enable these two sets of commissioners to deal with one another. And here he would remind the House of an expression used by the right hon. gentleman on first bringing forth his plan. The right hon. gentleman then assured the House, that he was not so young in office, as to make a proposal to parliament unless he had good ground to believe that he could make a bargain upon the terms which he stated. And what had the right hon. gentleman done since? Why, he had been forced to tell the House, that there had been an error in his calculations—that he had never supposed that he could make a bargain with any body for 2,800,000*l.*, but that the bargain would cost considerably more. Then look at the present situation of the country. The chancellor of the exchequer said, that the sinking fund was 5,000,000*l.* Yes; but he had for a long time maintained the delusion of its amounting to 16,000,000*l.* Now, as he had tardily acknowledged that the 16,000,000*l.* was a delusion, and that the real fund was only 5,000,000*l.*, so he might hereafter acknowledge that the 5,000,000*l.* was a delusion, and that the fund was in reality only 3,000,000*l.* The plan of the hon. member for Aberdeen,[1] was simple and easy to be effected; then why not adopt it, in place of such a complicated operation as that proposed by the chancellor of the exchequer?

Mr. HUME's amendment was negatived. Mr. CURWEN then moved as an amendment that the whole duty on salt be repealed. The CHANCELLOR OF THE EXCHEQUER opposed it and said that if the salt tax were repealed, either some new tax must be imposed or 'the integrity of the sinking fund must be invaded [A laugh!].'

---

[1] Mr. Hume.

Mr. RICARDO said, it was asserted by ministers that the 3 June 1822 annuity scheme was no infringement on the principle of the sinking fund. If so, instead of forty-five let the period of that scheme be extended to fifty or sixty years, and that would afford a sufficient sum to enable parliament to remit the whole of the salt duty.

Mr. Curwen's amendment was negatived and the original motion agreed to. The bill was then passed.

[See further below, p. 281.]

CORN IMPORTATION BILL

3 *June* 1822

The new corn bill based on Lord Londonderry's resolutions 3 June 1822 [cp. above, p. 155], having been brought in, Mr. CANNING proposed the addition of a clause to allow the taking of foreign corn out of the warehouse for being ground into flour for exportation. Sir T. LETHBRIDGE opposed the clause as likely to promote the introduction into the home market of foreign corn in the shape of flour.

Mr. RICARDO agreed, that if the clause could not be introduced with a full security against the flour coming into the home market it ought not to be admitted; but, if that security could be found, it would be most unjust to deprive the holders of foreign corn of it. He thought the bill of the noble lord would be a great improvement on the present law. The hon. member for Cumberland[1] founded all his arguments on the value of corn in pounds sterling; but he (Mr. R.) did not regard the pound sterling. He was anxious that the people should have an abundant supply of corn and an increase of their comforts, and he thought a greater freedom in the trade calculated to produce those effects. He

---

[1] Mr. Curwen. His speech is not reported in *Hansard*.

differed entirely from the hon. member, as to the ill effects which it would have upon the demand for labour.

The clause was agreed to.

On the question that 70s. be the permanent price at which wheat shall be imported, Mr. WHITMORE moved to substitute 64s.; Mr. WODEHOUSE moved to substitute 75s.

Mr. RICARDO[1] expressed his surprise at the proposition of the hon. member for Norfolk;[2] since the most active supporters of the agricultural interest had declared that 67s. would afford adequate protection to the farmer. He thought the proposition of the hon. member for Bridgenorth[3] deserving the support of the House. High protecting prices would only benefit the landlord at the expense of the rest of the community, not excepting even the farmer.

The original clause was agreed to.

[1] This speech is reported more at length in the *Morning Chronicle:* 'Mr. RICARDO observed, that it had been not long ago admitted by the Member for Wiltshire (Mr. Benett), who could not be supposed too favourable to his views, that 65s. or 66s. was a fair protecting price. His Honourable Friend, however, did not propose that the import price should be reduced to 64s. till the price had previously reached 80s.; for such would be the effect of the Amendment engrafted on the Bill. When that had happened the markets of the world would be restored to that state in which such an import price would be perfectly safe. The Amendment, therefore, was not rash or theoretical, but a sound and well matured proposition, and was to be received with the greater attention, as it came from a Gentleman whose property entirely consisted of land. All they had hitherto heard of the necessity of raising prices was very well if they legislated only for the landlords; but they could give nothing to them without taking it out of the pockets of the people, and unfortunately, for every one pound they gave the landlord they took two or three from the consumer, the difference being swallowed up in the cost of production. He had hitherto asked in vain what protection this measure would afford to the farmer? To the farmer it must be ruinous. When his crop was defective he was deprived of his high price, and when his harvest was abundant it was impossible for him to get anything like a remunerating price.'

[2] Mr. Wodehouse.

[3] Mr. Whitmore.

10 *June* 1822

On the report stage, Lord LONDONDERRY said that as there was so strong an opinion against the clause for grinding foreign wheat, he would oppose it.

Mr. RICARDO said, that unless the agriculturists could show that injury would arise to them from the adoption of the clause, parliament should not hesitate to give to the foreign importer the proposed relief.

The house divided on the clause: Ayes, 21; Noes, 116. Ricardo voted for the clause. The bill was then passed.

NAVIGATION BILL[1]

4 *June* 1822

Mr. WALLACE moved the third reading of this bill [cp. above, p. 190].

Mr. RICARDO said the Right Honourable Gentleman opposite (Mr. Canning) had adverted to the improving state of the silk trade with Bengal, in consequence of the protecting duties afforded to it. If a partial impulse were given to the trade from such a cause, he (Mr. R.) should consider it rather a subject of regret than of satisfaction. It was curious to hear the contradictory statements which were advanced in that House; for it was at once contended that it was necessary to protect Agriculture, because the Manufacturers were protected, and that to take off protecting duties from the Manufacturers, was a measure highly detrimental to the Agricultural interest. It was impossible that both these propositions could be true.

---

[1] This debate is not mentioned in *Hansard*. Ricardo's speech is here reprinted from the *Morning Chronicle.*

He should vote for the present Bill, and he gave his sincere thanks to the Right Honourable Gentleman opposite for the pains he had taken during its progress.

The Bill was read a third time and passed.

MR. WESTERN'S MOTION CONCERNING
THE RESUMPTION OF CASH PAYMENTS
12 *June* 1822

On 11 June Mr. WESTERN moved that a committee be appointed to consider the effect which the resumption of cash payments had had in producing the present agricultural distress. He concluded his speech by recommending a revision of the standard and the adoption of 'a system which should give to the products of industry of every description the same relative money price, which they commanded during the suspension of cash-payments, and secure a fair and reciprocal remuneration for the general industry of the country.' Mr. HUSKISSON moved as an amendment a resolution which had been adopted by parliament in 1696: 'That this House will not alter the standard of gold or silver, in fineness, weight or denomination.'

The debate was adjourned to the following day when, after other speakers, Mr. LEYCESTER said he would support the motion for a committee, although he must protest against any attack upon Mr. Peel's bill, which he regarded as 'a measure founded in wisdom.' Mr. HALDIMAND noticed that many charges had been brought against the Bank, and said that 'all of them appeared to him unfounded, save one;' which was, 'that the Bank of England, looking forward to the resumption of cash payments, had accumulated a large quantity of gold in its coffers, and by so doing had, as the hon. member for Portarlington observed, appreciated the currency.' On the circulation of Bank paper he remarked, 'that so long as the Bank was ready to pay its notes in gold, the House had no reason to complain whether there were five millions more or less of their notes in circulation.'

Mr. RICARDO[1] said, that he agreed in a great deal of what

[1] The report of this speech was published separately as a pamphlet under the title *Mr. Ricardo's Speech on Mr. Western's Motion,* *for a Committee to consider of the Effects produced by the Resumption of Cash Payments, delivered the 12th of June, 1822,* London,

had fallen from his hon. friend[1] who spoke last, and particularly in his view of the effect of the preparations made by the
Bank for the resumption of payments in specie; it was undeniable, that the manner in which the Bank had gone on
purchasing gold to provide for a metallic currency, had
materially affected the public interests. It was impossible to
ascertain what was the amount of the effect of that mistake on
the part of the Bank, or to what precise extent their bullion
purchases affected the value of gold; but, whatever the extent
was, so far exactly had the value of the currency been increased, and the prices of commodities been lowered. His
hon. friend had said, that whilst the Bank was obliged to pay
its notes in gold, the public had no interest in interfering
with the Bank respecting the amount of the paper circulation, for if it were too low, the deficiency would be supplied
by the importation of gold, and if it were too high, it would
be reduced by the exchange of paper for gold. In this
opinion he did not entirely concur, because there might be
an interval during which the country might sustain great inconvenience from an undue reduction of the Bank circulation. Let him put a case to elucidate his views on this subject.
Suppose the Bank were to reduce the amount of their issues
to five millions, what would be the consequence? The foreign
exchanges would be turned in our favour, and large quantities
of bullion would be imported. This bullion would be ultimately coined into money, and would replace the paper-
money which had previously been withdrawn; but, before it
was so coined, while all these operations were going on, the
currency would be at a very low level, the prices of com-

---

printed by G. Harvey, 1822. The
pamphlet's report differs only
slightly from *Hansard's;* but
where the two disagree the latter
seems more accurate and has been
followed in the text.
[1] Mr. Haldimand.

modities would fall, and great distress would be suffered.—
Something of this kind had, in fact, happened. The Bank
entirely mismanaged their concerns in the way in which
they had prepared for the resumption of cash payments;
nothing was more productive of mischief than their large
purchases of gold, at the time to which he alluded. They
ought to have borne in mind that, until the year 1823, the
bill of his right hon. friend (Mr. Peel), did not make it imperative on the Bank to pay in specie.—Until the arrival of
that period, the Bank were only called upon to pay in
bullion, and in 1819, when the bill passed, their coffers contained a supply amply sufficient to meet all demands, preparatory to the final operation of the right hon. gentleman's
bill. That bill he had always considered as an experiment, to
try whether a bank could not be carried on with advantage to
the general interests of the country, upon the principle of
not being called upon to pay their notes in coin, but in
bullion; and he had not the least doubt that, if the Bank had
gone on wisely in their preliminary arrangements—if, in
fact, they had done nothing but watch the exchanges and the
price of gold, and had regulated their issues accordingly, the
years 1819, 1820, 1821 and 1822 would have passed off so
well with the working of the bullion part of the plan, that
parliament would have continued it for a number of years
beyond the time originally stipulated for its operation. Such,
he was convinced, would have been the course, had the
Bank refrained from making those unnecessary purchases of
gold which had led to so many unpleasant consequences.
But it was said by his hon. friend (Mr. Haldimand), that the
Bank had since 1819 kept up their circulation to the same
level as before 1819, and that, therefore, they had not caused
the favourable exchange, and the influx of gold. He denied
this—he denied that their issues were now as large as in

1819; but allowing, for the sake of argument, that they were so, he should still make it matter of charge against the Bank, that they had not increased their issues, so as to operate on the foreign exchanges, and prevent the large importations of gold. With reference to the conduct of the Bank on that occasion, it had been said on a former evening, by an hon. Bank director, (Mr. Manning), in the way of justification, that they were not left masters of their own proceedings— that the numerous executions for forgery throughout the country, had made the public clamorous for a metallic cir- culation so as in a measure to compel the Bank to precipitate the substitution of coin for their one and two pound notes; but the Bank lost the benefit of this argument, by the opposition which they made throughout the discussions of the committee and the House in 1819, against every descrip- tion of metallic payments.—He believed, indeed, that after they had accumulated gold in large quantities, they thought it expedient to substitute it in the form of coin for the one and two pound notes, and also for the reason which they had given; but this consideration did not lead them to limit their issues and to purchase the large quantities of gold; and it was of the effect of such limitation and of those purchases which he complained, and against this charge they had made no defence, nor could they make any. After their remonstrances to the committee, and to the chancellor of the exchequer, on the subject of the ill consequences of restricting their issues, why did they promote the evil which they deprecated—why make those purchases for amply filled coffers—why take a step so inevitably leading to mischief? He could ascribe it to one cause only, namely, that they were ignorant of the principles of currency, and did not know how, at such an important moment, to manage the difficult machine, which was intrusted to them. He was surprised, after what had

been said by the hon. member for Shaftesbury (Mr. Leycester), of the character of Mr. Peel's bill, that he should have
come to the conclusion of voting for the appointment of a
committee. If the past measures, so far as parliament had
acted in this bill, were right, for what purpose was the committee? The declared object of the motion was to alter the
standard, and he could not see, how, after the hon. gentleman's argument in favour of adhering to the present standard,
he could vote for a motion tending to such an alteration. It
had been said by his hon. friend the member for Newton
(Mr. H. Gurney), that they had begun at the wrong end—
that they should in the first instance, have called on the
private bankers to pay their notes in specie, and afterwards
on the Bank of England to pursue the same course. Such
a proposition, he thought, would have been absurd. The
Bank of England had the power, by regulating its issues, of
depreciating or increasing the value of the Bank note just as
they pleased—a power which the country banks had not. The
Bank of England could depreciate, as was the case in 1812 and
1813, their one pound note to the value of 14s., or they could
increase it to the value of two sovereigns by an opposite
course, provided the Mint, by coining, did not counteract
their operations. It was impossible, therefore, and if even
possible, it would be most unjust, to require private banks to
call in their notes and to pay in specie, leaving at the same
time this great Leviathan, the Bank, to continue its paper
issues at will, and not subject to the same metallic convertibility.

In touching upon this subject, he must say that his opinion
had been much misunderstood, both within and without the
walls of parliament; and if it were not too great a trespass
upon the indulgence of House, he should wish to take this
opportunity of explaining himself. In doing so he could not

do better than refer to an observation which had fallen from the hon. alderman (Heygate) in the course of the debate. He had said, that if gold were the index of the depreciation of the currency, then his (Mr. Ricardo's) argument founded upon it might be good, and that the sacrifice of 3 or 4 per cent in establishing the ancient standard was small in the estimate of the advantages attending it: but he (the hon. alderman) did not concur in the opinion, that gold was the index of the depreciation of the currency. Now, the whole difficulty in reference to this part of his opinions was, as to the meaning of the word "depreciation:" it was quite evident that the hon. alderman and himself attached a different sense to that word. Suppose the only currency in the country was a metallic one, and that, by clipping, it had lost 10 per cent of its weight; suppose, for instance, that the sovereign only retained 9-10ths of the metal which by law it should contain, and that, in consequence, gold bullion, in such a medium, should rise above its mint price, would not the money of the country be depreciated? He was quite sure the hon. alderman would admit the truth of this inference. It was quite possible however, that, notwithstanding this depreciation, some of those general causes which operate on the value of gold bullion, such as war, or the mines from which gold is annually supplied becoming less productive, that gold might be so enhanced in value, as to make the clipped sovereign comparatively of greater value in the market than it was before the reduction in its weight. Would it not then be true that we should possess a depreciated currency, although it should be increased in value? The great mistake committed on this subject was in confounding the words "depreciation" and "diminution in value." With reference to the currency, he had said, and he now repeated it, that the price of gold was the index of the depreciation of the currency, not the index of the value of the currency, and it was in this that he had been misunderstood. If, for instance, the standard of the currency remained at the same fixed value, and the coin were depreciated by clipping, or the paper money by the increase of its quantity, five per cent, a fall to that amount and no more, would take place in the price of commodities, as affected by the value of money. If the metal gold (the standard) continued of the same precise value, and it was required to restore the currency thus depreciated five per cent, to par, it would be necessary only to raise its value five per cent, and no greater than that proportionate fall could take place in the price of commodities. In these cases he had supposed gold always to remain at the same fixed value; but had he ever said that there were not many causes which might operate on the value of gold as well as on the value of all other commodities? No, he had not, but just the contrary. No country that used the precious metals as a standard, were exempted from variations in the prices of commodities, occasioned by a variation in the value of their standard. To such variations we had been subject before 1797, and must be subject to again, now that we have reverted to a metallic standard. In the plan which he had proposed, there was nothing which could cause a demand for gold, and therefore he had been justified in anticipating a variation in the price of commodities, from adopting it, of only five per cent, the then difference between the value of gold and of paper. If, indeed, it had been necessary to purchase gold in order to revert to a metallic standard, then he would allow that a greater difference than 5 per cent would take place in prices, but this was wholly unnecessary; because we had adopted a gold standard, were we therefore to be exempted from those variations in the prices of commodities which arose from the cheapness of their production at one period compared with

another? Was the discovery of new improvements in machinery, or a superabundant harvest, or any of those general
causes which operate to reduce price, to have no effect? Were
the injudicious purchases of the Bank to have no effect on
the value of gold? Did he deny that in the present state of
the world, the occurrences in South America, might have
impeded the regular supply of the precious metals to Europe,
have enhanced their value and affected the prices of commodities all over the world.

It had been imputed to him that he entertained the extravagant idea, that if a metallic standard was adopted, from that
moment commodities were never to vary more than 5 per
cent. A proposition so absurd he had never maintained—his
opinion on that subject had never changed, and, if not intruding too much on the time of the House, he would quote
a passage from a pamphlet he had published in 1816, on the
subject of his plan of bullion payments, to show the House
what that opinion had then been:—

"When a standard is used, we are subject only to such a
variation in the value of money as the standard itself is
subject to; but against such variation there is no possible
remedy; and late events have proved that, during periods of
war, when gold and silver are used for the payment of large
armies, distant from home, those variations are much more
considerable than has been generally allowed. This admission
only proves that gold and silver are not so good a standard as
they have been hitherto supposed; that they are themselves
subject to greater variations than it is desirable a standard
should be subject to. They are, however, the best with which
we are acquainted. If any other commodity less variable
could be found, it might very properly be adopted as the
future standard of our money, provided it had all the other
qualities which fitted it for that purpose; but while these

metals are the standard, the currency should conform in value to them, and, whenever it does not, and the market price of bullion is above the Mint price, the currency is depreciated."[1]

Such were the arguments he had always used, and he still adhered to them. He hoped the House would pardon this personal reference to his own opinion: he was very averse from intruding on their patience; but he was as it were put upon his trial—his plan had not been adopted, and yet to it was referred the consequences which were distinct from it; and he was held responsible for the plan that had been adopted, which was not his, but was essentially different from it. Such was the singularity of his situation, and if the House would indulge him by permitting one more reference to his opinions expressed in that House in the year 1819, he should have done with that part of the argument which was strictly personal. What he had said in his speech, during the former discussion of Mr. Peel's bill (and he quoted it now from the usual channel of information—the Reports), was this, "If the House adopted the proposition of the hon. gentleman (Mr. Ellice),* another variation in the value of the currency would take place, which it was his wish to guard against. If that amendment were agreed to, an extraordinary demand would take place for gold, for the purpose of coinage, which would enhance the value of the currency three or four per cent in addition to the first enhancement."[2] "Till October, 1820, the Bank need make no reduction, and then a slight one; and he had no doubt that, if they were cautious,

* Mr. Ellice's proposal was, to allow the Bank to make payments in coin instead of bullion if they should think it expedient. [*Hansard's* note.]

[1] *Economical and Secure Currency;*   [2] See above, p. 11.
above, IV, 62–3.

they might arrive at cash payments without giving out one guinea in gold. The Bank should reduce their issues cautiously, he only feared they would do it too rapidly. If he might give them advice, he should recommend to them not to buy bullion, but even though they had but a few millions, he would boldly sell."[1] Such were his expressions in 1819. Had his recommendations been adopted? No. Why, then, was he to be held chargeable for results over and above the effect of raising the currency from the actual state of depreciation at which it stood at the time?

Having explained these personal allusions, he should now say a little upon the general question, which had not, in his opinion, been very fairly argued. A constant reference had been made to the extreme point of the depreciation in the currency, which they knew occurred in the year 1813; and Mr. Peel's bill had been argued upon as if it had been passed in that year, and had caused all the variation which it was acknowledged had taken place in the currency from that period to the present time. This was a most unfair way of arguing the question, for to Mr. Peel's bill could only be imputed the alteration which had taken place in the currency between 1819 and the present period. What was the state of the currency in 1819? It was left entirely under the management and control of a company of merchants—individuals, he was most ready to admit, of the best character, and actuated by the best intentions; but who, nevertheless—and he had declared plainly his apprehensions at the time—did not acknowledge the true principles of the currency, and who, in fact, in his opinion, did not know any thing about it. This company of merchants were, then, invested with the management of the great and important concern on which the welfare of the country, and the stability of its best in-

[1] See above, p. 13.

terests, materially depended. They were the men who had
the power of making their one pound note worth 14*s.* or
17*s.* or 18*s.* or 19*s.*, as it had successively been, under their
guidance, between the years 1813 and 1819. In the latter
year, and for four years previous to it, the system had so
operated as to bring the currency within something like
5 per cent of its par value. The time was then favourable for
fixing a standard which was likely to save the country from
the vacillation of such a system as that which had previously
so much affected it. The time had then arrived (in 1819) for
fixing a standard, and the only consideration was as to the
selection of the particular standard which ought to be
adopted. They had two courses of proceeding open to them
on that occasion; one was either to regulate the standard by
the price of gold at the moment, or to recur to the ancient
standard of the country. If, in the year 1819, the value of
the currency had stood at 14*s.* for the pound note, which was
the case in the year 1813, he should have thought that upon a
balance of all the advantages and disadvantages of the case,
it would have been as well to fix the currency at the then
value, according to which most of the existing contracts
had been made; but when the currency was within 5 per cent
of its par value, the only consideration was, whether they
should fix the standard at 4*l.* 2*s.*, the then price of gold, or
recur at once to the old standard. Under all the circumstances,
he thought they had made the best selection in recurring to
the old standard. The real evil was committed in 1797, and
the opportunity of mitigating its consequences was lost by
the conduct subsequently pursued by the Bank; for even
after the first suspension, they might, by proceeding upon
right principles in managing their issues, by keeping the
value of the currency at or near par, have prevented the
depreciation which followed. It might be asked how they

could have done so? His reply was, that *quantity regulated* 12 June 1822
the value of every thing. This was true of corn, of currency,
and of every other commodity, and more, perhaps, of
currency, than of any thing else. Whoever, then, possessed
the power of regulating the quantity of money, could always
govern its value, and make the pound note, as he had said
before, worth fourteen shillings or two sovereigns, unless
the mint, by opening to coin for the public, counteracted the
operation of the Bank issues. By pursuing a wise and prudent course, the Bank might have so regulated its affairs, as
to have prevented the currency from sustaining any depreciation from 1797 downwards; they might, in fact, have
governed the market-price of bullion, and the foreign exchanges; but, unfortunately, they had not taken the steps
necessary for that purpose.

With respect to the bill of 1819, he must say, that he never
regretted the share which he had taken in that measure.—
[Hear, hear.] Remarks had frequently been made upon an
opinion which he (Mr. Ricardo) had given of the effect
which had been produced on the value of gold, and therefore
on the value of money, by the purchases made by the Bank,
which he had computed at five per cent, making the whole
rise in the value of money ten per cent. He confessed that he
had very little ground for forming any correct opinion on
this subject. By comparing money with its standard, we had
certain means of judging of its depreciation, but he knew of
none by which we were able to ascertain with certainty
alterations in real or absolute value. His opinion of the
standard itself having been raised five per cent in value, by
the purchases of the Bank, was principally founded on the
effect which he should expect to follow, from a demand
from the general stock of the world of from fifteen to twenty
millions worth of coined money. If, as he believed, there

was in the world twenty times as much gold and silver as England had lately required to establish her standard on its ancient footing, he should say that the effect of that measure could not have exceeded five per cent. The hon. member, who had brought forward this motion had disputed the propriety of the standard recognized by Mr. Peel's bill, and contended, that the value of corn would have formed a better and more fixed standard. His reason in support of such an opinion was, that the average price of corn, taken for a series of ten years, or for longer periods, furnished a standard less liable to variation than the standard of gold. He did not perfectly comprehend that part of the hon. member's argument. Either he meant that the country ought to have a fixed metallic standard, regulated by the price of corn each year, as deduced from the average of the ten previous years, or else by an average for ten years, determinable at the expiration of every ten years. Now, in any way in which the average could be taken, according to either plan, there would be a sudden and considerable variation in the value of the currency. To-day, for example, the standard might be fixed with reference to the price of corn, when its average price was 80s. per quarter, and to-morrow, if that were the period for correcting the standard of money by such a regulation, it might be necessary to alter it to 85s. or 90s., thus causing a sudden variation in all money payments from one day to another. [Mr. Western here signified his dissent.] He was extremely sorry to have mistaken the hon. member, and he would not press this part of his argument. He must, however, say, that to take the average price of corn, as the best measure of value, was a most mistaken principle. The hon. member had, indeed, quoted in support of such a measure of value, the concurring authorities of Locke and Adam Smith, who had asserted that the average price of corn, during a period

of ten years, was a less variable standard than gold; and in
support of the opinion, the prices taken according to such an
average were quoted. But the great fallacy in the argument
was this—that, to prove that gold was more variable than
corn, they were obliged to commence by supposing gold invariable. Unless the medium in which the price of corn is
estimated could be asserted to be invariable in its value, how
could the corn be said not to have varied in relative value? If
they must admit the medium to be variable—and who would
deny it?—then what became of the argument? So far from
believing corn to be a better measure of value than gold, he
believed it to be a much worse one, and more dependent
upon a variety of fluctuating causes for its intrinsic value.
What was the real fact? In populous countries, they were
compelled to grow corn on a worse quality of land than they
were obliged to do when there was not the same demand for
subsistence. In such countries then, the price must rise to
remunerate the grower, or else the commodity must be
procured from abroad by the indirect application of a larger
capital. There were many causes operating on the value of
corn, and therefore making it a variable standard.—Improvements in husbandry; discoveries of the efficacy of
new manure; the very improvement of a threshing-machine,
had a tendency to lower the price. Again, the different
expense of production, according to the capital necessary for
cultivation, and the amount of population to be supplied
with food, had a tendency to augment the price. So that
there were always two causes operating and contending
with each other, the one to cheapen and the other to increase the price of the commodity; how, then, could it be
said to furnish the least variable standard?—[Hear, hear.] It
was a part of Adam Smith's argument that corn was a
steadier criterion, because it generally took the same quantity

to furnish one man's sustenance. That might be; but still the cost of production did not the less vary, and, that must regulate the price. Its power of sustaining life was one thing: its value was another. He fully agreed with the hon. member for Essex,[1] that there were various causes operating, also, on the value of gold, some of which were of a permanent, and others of a temporary nature. The more or less productiveness of the mines were among the permanent causes; the demands for currency, or for plate, in consequence of increased wealth and population, were temporary causes, though probably of some considerable duration. A demand for hats or for cloth would elevate the value of those commodities, but as soon as the requisite quantity of capital was employed in producing the increased quantity required, their value would fall to the former level. The same was true of gold: an increased demand would raise its value, and would ultimately lead to an increased supply, when it would fall to its original level, if the cost of production had not also been increased. No principle was more true than that the cost of production was the regulator of value, and that demand only produced temporary effects. The hon. member (Mr. Western) had entered into elaborate statements of the amount of taxation at different periods, estimated in quarters of wheat, and from this statement he inferred an enormous fall in the value of money. Now, if these calculations, and the mode of applying them, were of any value, they must apply at all times as well as at the present. Let the hon. member, then, extend his calculations a little over former times, and see how his reasonings applied. If reference were made to three particular years which he should name, the hon. gentleman's calculation would look a little differently to what it did at present. The price of wheat was, in 1796, 72s.

[1] Mr. Western.

per quarter; in 1798 (only two years afterwards) it fell to
50*s.*; in 1801 it rose as high as 118*s.*—[Hear!]. This was the
enormous fluctuation of only three years. Here, then, the
House had the experience of so short a period as three years,
and of the variations of price in that time. The hon. gentleman, in his argument, had assumed, that the price of wheat
was to be permanent as it now stood. He (Mr Ricardo)
thought it was by no means likely to be permanent; he
anticipated that it would rise; and, indeed, if the present was
not a remunerating price, it was impossible that it should
not rise; for in no case would production go on, for any
considerable length of time, without remunerating prices.
The alteration in the price of the quarter of wheat, then, in
three years, was as the difference between 50*s.* and 118*s.* But,
in 1803, the price fell again to 56*s.* In 1810 it attained 106*s.*
and in 1814 was reduced to 73*s.* The variations, in short,
were infinite and constant—[Hear!]. Then, with regard to
the price of flour, he had ascertained, that in the year 1801,
in the month of July, the Victualling office at Deptford paid
124*s.* for the sack of flour. In December of the same year
they paid only 72*s.* In December, 1802, they paid for the
same commodity and quantity, 52*s.*; in December, 1804,
89*s.*; and in subsequent years the price per sack was successively from 99*s.* to 50*s.*, in short, as uncertain as possible. All
these details tended to show that the price of corn was perpetually fluctuating and varying; and it would only be
wonderful if such were not the case. The hon. gentleman had
said, that he hoped no member of that House would, with a
contrary conviction on his mind, refuse, from motives of
mistaken pride or prejudice, to acknowledge any former error
into which he might have fallen in the consideration of these
subjects. He (Mr. R.) could assure the hon. gentleman, that
so far as he himself might be supposed to be concerned, he

would not allow any foolish pride of the sort to operate with him. The hon. gentleman had remarked, at some length, on the evidence which had been furnished to that House by Mr. Tooke, with respect to the effect of an abundance of commodities lowering prices. Those prices were said to have fallen considerably more than ten per cent; but Mr. Tooke expressly said, that of the commodities he mentioned, there was not one, for the depreciated value of which, when it exceeded ten per cent, he could not well account.[1] The quantity of all articles of consumption which had been brought into our markets, during the time of which that gentleman spoke, exceeded the quantity furnished in any former period; and there were some of the imported articles, the prices of which had continued to fall ever since, as sugars and cotton. But surely this could not be matter of surprise, when the House looked at the augmented quantity. The hon. gentleman had dwelt much on the injury which he conceived the country had sustained in consequence of loans that had been contracted for, at periods when the prices of the public funds were low, and which were now to be redeemed when the prices were high; and to make the disadvantages still more apparent, the calculation of the hon. gentleman was made in quarters of wheat at the corn prices of those times. The hon. gentleman said, "in order to pay that stock at the present value of money, I require such an additional number of quarters of corn." Any body who heard the hon. gentleman's speech would naturally have supposed that the rise in the price of the funds was necessarily connected with the increased value of the currency. But this could not be so; if the value of the currency had any thing to do with it, the contrary effect would take place. But the alteration in the

[1] See 'Report of the Select Committee on the Agriculture of the U.K.', 1821, p. 297.

value of the currency had nothing to do with this question; if the dividends were paid in a more valuable medium, so was the price of stock estimated in the same valuable medium; and if the dividend were paid in the less valuable medium, so also was the price estimated in the like medium. During the American war, the three per cent consols were as low as 53; and afterwards they rose to 97. At that time there had been no tampering with the currency. What, therefore, could the value of the currency have to do with the price of the funds? If a man wanted money upon mortgage now he could raise it at four per cent; whereas, during the continuance of the late war, he not only gave seven or eight per cent, but was obliged to procure the money, after all, in a round-about manner. The whole of the argument might be reduced to the statement of a single fact, which was this—they who invested sums of money in the funds at this day would get a low interest in return; those who had invested during the war had obtained a large interest.—With respect to an argument which had been advanced by the hon. member for Shrewsbury (Mr. Bennet) he could not concur in it. It was contended by his hon. friend, that the whole loss on the recoinage of money in king William's reign, when it was restored from a depreciated to a sound state, was about two millions and a half; and he estimated the inconvenience and loss to individuals at that sum. But his hon. friend forgot that contracts in all countries existed in a much larger proportion than money, and consequently the loss must have been much greater than his hon. friend had estimated. The contracts might, in fact, be twenty or fifty times the amount of money, and therefore the interests of particular parties would have been affected accordingly. It was quite clear, that any alteration effected in the value of currency must of necessity, now as well as at all other times, affect one party or the other to such contracts; but this was an effect perfectly natural and inevitable.

To recur to the question before the House, he must say, that the motion of the hon. member for Essex was calculated to awaken and renew the agitation, which he had hoped would, ere this, have subsided. It was calculated to do much mischief—[Hear!]. If there were any chance of the hon. gentleman's motion obtaining the support of the House, its success must be attended with the effect which, on the preceding evening, his right hon. friend (Mr. Huskisson) had ably pointed out. Every person would be eager to get rid of money which was to be rendered liable to an excessive and immediate depreciation. Every one would be anxious to withdraw it, as it were, from a currency of which he must anticipate the fate; he would be directly embarking it in gold, ships, goods, property of any kind that he might deem more likely to retain a steady value than money itself. He (Mr. R.) believed that the measure of 1819 was chiefly pernicious to the country, on account of the unfounded alarms which it created in some men's minds, and the vague fears that other people felt lest something should occur, the nature of which they could not themselves define. That alarm was now got over; those fears were subsiding; and he conceived, that as the depreciation in the value of our currency, which a few years ago was experienced, could not possibly return upon us in future, if we persevered in the measures we had taken, it would be the most unwise thing in the world to interfere with an act, the disturbance of which would unsettle the great principle we had established. He did flatter himself, that after the suffering which the country had undergone, in consequence of the Bank Suspension bill, a measure of a similar character would never again be resorted to. His hon. friend (Mr. Bennet) had stated, that the depreciation in the

value of the currency was in 1813 about 42 per cent. He
thought his hon. friend had much overstated the amount of
the depreciation. The highest price to which gold had ever
risen, and that only for a short time, was 5*l.* 10*s.* per ounce.
Even then the Bank-note was depreciated only 29 per cent,
because 5*l.* 10*s.* in Bank-notes could purchase the same
quantity of goods as the gold in 3*l.* 17*s.* 10$\frac{1}{2}$*d.* of coin. If,
then, 5*l.* 10*s.* in Bank-notes was worth 3*l.* 17*s.* 10$\frac{1}{2}$*d.* in gold,
100*l.* was worth 71*l.,* and one pound about fourteen shillings,
which is a depreciation of 29 per cent, and not 42 per cent, as
stated by his hon. friend. Another way of stating this proposition might make it appear that money had risen 42 per
cent; for if 14*s.* of the money of 1813 were now worth 20*s.,*
100*l.* was now worth 142*l.;* but as he had already observed,
nothing was more difficult than to ascertain the variations in
the value of money—to do so with any accuracy, we should
have an invariable measure of value; but such a measure we
never had, nor ever could have. In the present case, gold
might have fallen in value, at the same time that paper-
money had been rising; and therefore, when they met, and
were at par with each other, the rise in paper-money might
not have been equal to the whole of the former difference.
To speak with precision, therefore, of the value of money at
any particular period, was what no man could do; but when
we spoke of depreciation, there was always a standard by
which that might be estimated. Another argument of his
hon. friend[1] greatly surprised him: he objected to the amendment of his right hon. friend (Mr. Huskisson), because it did
not give him sufficient security that the standard would not be
at some future time altered. He appeared to fear that recourse might, on some supposed emergency, again be had to
the measure of 1797. In short, his hon. friend was for ad-

[1] Mr. Gurney.

hering to the standard fixed by Mr. Peel's bill; and yet, in the same breath, added, as it appeared to him (Mr. R.) most inconsistently, that he would vote for the motion of the hon. member for Essex, which professedly went to alter that standard.

After several other speeches, the House, at three in the morning, divided: for Mr. Western's motion, 30; against it, 194. Mr. Huskisson's amendment was then agreed to.

LABOURERS' WAGES

17 *June* 1822

Mr. LITTLETON presented a petition 'from the miners, ironmakers, and coal-masters of Dudley, praying that the House would enjoin a more strict observance of the law, which directs that labourers should be paid only in money, and not in provisions or other commodities.'

Mr. RICARDO thought it impossible to renew so obnoxious an act. Mr. Owen prided himself upon having introduced the provision system. He had opened a shop at New Lanark, in which he sold the best commodities to his workmen cheaper than they could be obtained elsewhere; and he was persuaded that the practice was a beneficial one.

IRISH BUTTER TRADE

20 *June* 1822

Sir N. COLTHURST moved 'that an additional duty of 10*s.* per cwt. be imposed on foreign butter imported into this country.' Mr. ROBINSON opposed the motion.

Mr. RICARDO said, the Irish gentlemen complained of want of protection, but what their rule of protection was he could not imagine. In this instance they had a protecting duty of 25*s.* per cwt.; but he supposed they would not be satisfied unless they had a complete monopoly of the trade. In his opinion, the proposition ought to have been the other way. Parliament ought to be called on to get rid of this protecting duty by degrees[1], by which means the trade would be rendered really beneficial to the country. The House was assailed on all sides for protecting duties. One day they were assailed by the butter trade, then by the dealers in tallow, then the West India planters complained, and the shipping interest also demanded legislative interference. But what did Adam Smith, that great and celebrated writer, say on this subject? His words were—"Consumption is the sole end and purpose of all production; and the interest of the producer ought to be attended to, only so far as it may be necessary for promoting that of the consumer. The maxim is so perfectly self-evident, that it would be absurd to attempt to prove it. But in the mercantile system, the interest of the consumer is almost constantly sacrificed to that of the producer; as if production and not consumption were the end of all industry and commerce."[2] No man could doubt the truth of this proposition. With respect to the application now made to the House, it was founded on a petition from the city of Dublin, which falsely stated, that the trade in butter had fallen off considerably. So far from that being the fact, it was, with the exception of one or two years, one of the greatest years of exportation that had ever occurred.

The motion was negatived.

[1] Misprinted 'decrees' in *Hansard.*
[2] *Wealth of Nations,* Bk. IV, ch. viii; Cannan's ed., vol. II, p. 159. Inaccurately quoted in *Hansard;* it is here corrected.

WAREHOUSING BILL

21 *June* 1822

Mr. WALLACE moved that the consideration of this bill [see below, p. 275] be postponed till next session.

Mr. RICARDO expressed his regret, that the right hon. gentleman had been induced to postpone this measure. He hoped he would take into his serious consideration the state of the silk trade, which was now labouring under peculiar disadvantages, and which might compete successfully with foreign countries, if the present high duties, which gave so much encouragement to contraband traffic, were reduced. The Spitalfields act was another grievance to which this trade was exposed, which he hoped government would see the necessity of repealing.[1]

THE BUDGET

1 *July* 1822

The CHANCELLOR OF THE EXCHEQUER having brought forward the Budget,

Mr. RICARDO said, that the chancellor of the exchequer had held out great hopes of what was to be expected from the sinking fund, and had stated, that a mere accident only had prevented all those hopes from being realized this year, but that next year we should receive its full and effective benefits. He (Mr. R.) feared, however, that we should go on as we had done, and that some accident or other would continue to prevent us from enjoying those benefits which the chancellor

[1] See below, p. 292.

of the exchequer had so flatteringly held out. If the committee took the account in the way in which the chancellor of
the exchequer wished them to view it, there would appear a
surplus of 5,000,000*l.* this year, and, that in 1824 there would
be a surplus of 6,000,000*l.* The right hon. member had, however, come at last to that point from which he (Mr. R.)
wished to start, namely, that without a surplus of revenue
over expenditure there could be no real or effective sinking
fund. Now let the committee observe the manner in which
the chancellor of the exchequer had made out the existence
of such a surplus in the present year. He said that we had a
surplus of 4,961,000*l.* But, how stood the fact? Taking the
total exchequer deficiency at 14,144,000*l.* and deducting it
from 15,481,000*l.*, the sum to meet it, there would remain
only 1,400,000*l.* as a real and effective sinking fund this year.
"Oh!" said the chancellor of the exchequer, "We have by
accident to pay the Bank 530,000*l.* this year, but next year we
shall have no such incumbrance, and therefore our surplus
will be complete." He wished to know by what process of
calculation the chancellor of the exchequer could make out
his 5,000,000*l.* this year? The revenue of the country was
53,087,000*l.*, the expenditure was 51,119,000*l.* making a
surplus of 1,968,000*l.*; this appeared to be the entire surplus
of the year; but "No," said the chancellor of the exchequer,
"we have 700,000*l.* saved by the alteration of the five per
cents.; we have also to make allowance for 2,600,000*l.* received." How this could be brought in under the head of
surplus revenue he could not perceive. A sum of five millions
might be easily made out; but would the committee call it a
surplus of revenue? Then, again, the right hon. gentleman
stated, that in 1824 there would be a surplus of 6,000,000*l.*
But how was it to be obtained? It was to be obtained by
taking credit for 4,875,000*l.* which was to be received from

the trustees of half-pay and pensions. Now he would ask, whether there were no payments to be made on the other side of the account? The chancellor of the exchequer must know, that money so obtained could not be looked upon in the light of receipts at all. The receipts in 1824 were calculated at 52,400,000*l.* and the expenditure at 50,600,000*l.* so that the real surplus on the 5th Jan. 1824, would be 1,800,000*l.* He agreed, with his hon. friend (Mr. Ellice) respecting the impolicy of diminishing our funded, while we increased our unfunded debt. He should recommend a diametrically opposite course of proceeding. Adverting to what had been said relative to the Bank having reduced its rate of interest,[1] he expressed his satisfaction at having heard the chancellor of the exchequer say, that the usury laws were unfair.[2] There was no period at which an alteration in those absurd laws could be so properly and effectively introduced as the present, when they were, in fact, a dead letter, the market price of the loan of money being lower than the legal price. But he could not believe, that the reduction of interest made by the Bank had any general effect upon the value of money in the market, or upon the price of land, or of any commodity. If the Bank had doubled its circulation, it still would have no permanent effect upon the value of money. If such a thing had taken place, the general level of interest would be restored in less than six months. The country only required, and could only bear, a certain circulation; and when that amount of circulation was afloat, the rate of interest would find its wholesome and natural level. Undoubtedly he was very glad to hear that the Bank had at length begun to discount at 4 per cent.; and

[1] The Bank rate had been reduced from 5 to 4 per cent. as from 21 June.
[2] The Chancellor of the Exchequer had described himself as 'fully concurring in the principle that the regulation of a particular rate of interest by law was quite contrary to the principles of political economy'.

he thought they should have done so long before. Had they persisted in demanding 5 per cent, they would have been without a single note to cash.[1]

MR. WESTERN'S MOTION RESPECTING THE ALTERED STATE OF THE CURRENCY

10 *July* 1822

Mr. WESTERN, pursuant to notice, introduced his resolutions on the state of the currency; but, several members being absent, he proposed to move the first seventeen now, without debate, and to bring forward the last one on a future day.

Mr. RICARDO said, he could not agree to any of the resolutions in their present form; several of them contained mistakes in fact, and all of them were pervaded by an erroneous principle.[2]

Mr. HUSKISSON strongly objected to the postponement of the discussion. Mr. WESTERN then proceeded with his motion.

---

[1] In place of the last two sentences, the *Morning Chronicle* reports: 'He was glad that the Bank had determined to reduce its rate of interest to four per cent.; indeed, they would have done wrong in declining to do so, as by that means only could they bring their notes into circulation. If the Bank had not reduced its interest to four per cent. the country must necessarily resort to a metallic currency, or else notes must be issued from some other quarter, as it would be impossible for the Bank of England to put a single pound note into circulation. In conclusion, he could not help observing, that he felt much commiseration for the unfortunate Gentleman who was induced to give 5000*l.* more for an estate in consequence of the Bank having lowered its interest to four per cent. [a laugh].'

[2] *The Times's* report adds: 'It had been his intention to have pointed some of them out, but if the debate were again deferred, he feared that he should not be able to attend.' Ricardo was leaving for the continent on 12 July.

[*The text of Western's Resolutions given below is taken from Ricardo's copy of the original parliamentary paper, which was annotated by him apparently for use while speaking, and which is preserved among his papers; Ricardo's underlinings and the marginal comments written on this copy are also reproduced.*[1]]

PROPOSED RESOLUTIONS

1st *true*
2^d *—not true*
3^d:

Descriptive of the distressed state of the Agricultural part of the country;—the effects of the altered state of the Currency on the general amount of Taxation; and the relative situation of the Public Creditor and the Public, under such altered state of the Currency.

True, but by what caused.

1.—THAT the Select Committee appointed last Session to inquire into the petitions complaining of the distressed state of the Agriculture of the United Kingdom, reported, That it was with deep regret they had to commence their Report by stating, that in their judgment the complaints of the petitioners were founded in fact, and that at the price of corn, at that time, the returns to the occupiers of arable farms, after allowing for the interest of their investments, were by no means adequate to the charges and out-goings; and that a considerable portion thereof must have, therefore, been paid out of their capitals:—

What suffering would there have been had there been no taxes.

That the price of grain having experienced a still further depression, viz. from 55s. 6d. per quarter of wheat to 45s.; and all other grain and all other articles having undergone a similar or greater decline, the insufficiency of the receipts of the farmers to cover their charges must be proportionably increased, which is further confirmed by the numerous petitions on the table of the House, representing in the strongest terms their aggravated and excessive distress; and that in consequence thereof, the labourers in many

---

[1] There is also among Ricardo's papers a printed proof of an earlier and somewhat different version of Western's resolutions, with Ricardo's comments jotted upon it, some of which are given in the footnotes below.

districts are destitute of employment and the consequent means to purchase food, and have broken out into acts of violence and aggression, and for which the lives of some have been forfeited under sanction of the law.

2.—THAT it appears by the papers relating to the state of Ireland, laid before this House by His Majesty's command, that serious disturbances had broken out in that country, of which the demand and collection of rents had been, on the part of the insurgents, the alleged causes; and subsequent information has been received, that the labourers in agriculture, from a partial failure in the crop of potatoes, together with a total want of employment, and consequent means to purchase other food, are in the most calamitous and deplorable situation; and that many have died from the want of nourishment, whilst the price of provisions still continues so low, as not to afford to the occupiers of land the means of defraying the various charges to which they are subject.

Is it possible justly to ascribe the distress in Ireland to any thing connected with the currency.

3.—THAT in the same Report of the Select Committee of last Session, it is stated, "that the measures "taken for the restoration of the currency have con-"tributed to lower the price of grain and other com-"modities generally, and consequently to cause a "*severe pressure upon the industry of the country,* and "not only to have occasioned a proportion of the fall "of prices *here,* but to have produced a similar, "though not equal, effect in other countries; and, in a "degree, to have deranged the markets of every part "of the civilized world."—That in proportion as *all* commodities, whether the produce of the soil, manufactures or commerce, have experienced a depression of their money value; so must the proprietors have suffered a direct injury; and whatever may be the degree, it is impossible that the commercial and manufacturing classes of the community can long continue to prosper, whilst the cultivators of the soil are rapidly sinking into ruin and decay, and the labourers suffering in consequence of the want of their usual employment.

No such words in the Report.

} not true

Not before
1800

4.—THAT soon after the passing of the Act of 1797, by which the Bank of England was restricted from paying its notes in specie, the antient metallic standard of value having been thus departed from, the currency of the country, composed of bank notes, became depreciated, which depreciation was evinced,

An important
admission.[1]

and may be estimated by the amount of bank paper money above 3*l.* 17*s.* 10½*d.* necessary to purchase an ounce of gold; and which fluctuating from that sum to 5*l.* 11*s.* was, on the average of eighteen years to

4. 6. 8—10 p.c.
4. 11. 2.
or 15 p.c. de-
preciation.—

1816, 4*l.* 10*s.* 10*d.* thence to 1819, 4*l.* 1*s.* and the last 10 years of the war, 4*l.* 16*s.* 1*d.* That this depreciation may be further and more accurately estimated by the price of commodities, particularly of wheat, at different periods, by which it will also appear, that the value of gold was reduced by the issue of paper, which became its nearly exclusive substitute; that the price of wheat, according to the Eton College tables, upon the average of 150 years prior to the commencement of the late war, whether calculated in periods of 10 or 50 years, had not exceeded 46*s.* per quarter, and an ounce of gold would consequently, during all that

13½ bushels

time, exchange for 13 bushels and a half; that from 1797 to 1816, the average price of wheat fluctuated from 50*s.* to 125*s.* per quarter, the average of the last eight years of the war being 101*s.* 9½*d.* and the average of the whole period 81*s.* 10*d.* and an ounce of

1797 to 1816
8 bushels ⅞
bushel

gold would therefore only exchange for 8 bushels seven eighths; that the price of grain thus became, in its nominal or money value, nearly double its amount at any former period; the rent of land and commodities acquired a similar additional value, and consequently all possessors of fixed incomes sustained an injury to the extent of such alteration.

Wheat 10
years ending
1735—1.15.2
1745—1.12.1
1755—1.13.2

5.—THAT the average price of wheat between the years 1797 and 1819 having been, therefore, in that currency about 80*s.* per quarter, existing leases were formed according thereto; that the average price since 1819 has been 55*s.* 6*d.* and last year and this, about 50*s.*; that, upon the supposition of rent being

[1] On the earlier version of this resolution (cp. above, p. 224, n. 1) Ricardo writes: 'Here it is ac- knowledged that depreciation is measured by the price of gold and not by the price of corn.'

estimated at one fourth, or two eighths of the gross produce, it is evident, at the price of 50s. being a reduction of three eighths, that so much of the money value of the gross produce is annihilated, as constitutes the present entire rental of the kingdom, and likewise so much of the receipts of the occupier as amount to one eighth; that the tenant is, therefore, liable to utter ruin if held to his engagement, or the landlord to the loss of his income, subject, at the same time, to the payment of all charges and settlements increased in their amount in the ratio of the increased nominal or money price of grain and other commodities; and in case of mortgage to the extent of half the value, at that period, a reduction of rent in proportion to the fall in the money price of produce, places the mortgagee in full possession of the estate.

1795—2.14.3

Rental annihilated

Paying off debt.

6.—THAT, from the year 1797 to 1816, the country was, with short intervals, engaged in a war of unprecedented expense; the taxes were quadrupled, as well as county and parochial assessments, and a heavy public debt created: That this period was at the same time distinguished by extraordinary efforts of national industry, applied to its agriculture, manufactures and commerce, by a facility and extension of credit in all those branches, giving more immediate activity to capital, and a consequent extent and complication of money engagements beyond all former precedent: That the national debt, which on the 5th of January 1793, was 227,989,148*l.* at an annual charge of 8,911,050*l.* progressively increased to the amount of 795,312,767*l.* of capital of various denominations, on the 5th of January 1822, at an annual charge, inclusive of terminable and life annuities, of 30,015,785*l.*; and the total of taxes, which on the 5th of January 1793, amounted to 17,656,418*l.* 11s. 3*d.* progressively increased, till in the year 1815, it amounted to 78,431,489*l.*: That, subsequent to the war, it has been reduced; and the total on the 5th of January 1822, was 60,671,025*l.*

—doubled.

—That war increased taxes, very true, but what is the inference were they increased to the injury of a particular class

7.—THAT this taxation has acquired an additional weight by the Act of 1819, and the measures preparatory thereto, the degree of which can in part be

Why calculate
this in money
at any other
rate than
£3. 17. 10½

£4. 10. 10.[1]

ascertained by a comparison of the price of gold, but more justly by the money price of commodities, by which the real value of all payments must be determined: That the equivalent in gold to 60,671,025*l.* was, in the former period, 13,358,934 ozs.; and, in the present, 15,657,246 ozs.; or in current money of the former period, 71,109,992*l.;* and that taxation is therefore further and unjustly increased, as paid in gold, 2,298,312 ozs. or 10,438,067*l.* in money.

8.—THAT the average price of wheat of the former period having been 81*s.* 10*d.* per quarter, the equivalent of the taxes in wheat was 14,228,155 quarters; and the price, since 1819, having been on an average 55*s.* 6*d.* the equivalent at that price is 21,863,720 quarters; or, in money, 89,459,050*l.* and the increase of taxation paid in wheat is consequently 7,035,565 quarters, equal to 28,787,233*l.*

9.—THAT it appears from various evidence, given in successive Committees appointed to consider the petitions of the agriculturists, that the wages of labour of an able husbandman, did, during the former period, amount to 15 or 16*s.* per week; and that, at 15*s.* the labour of 5,000,000 of persons for 15 weeks, was then equivalent to the discharge of the present taxes: That the price of labour being now reduced to about 9*s.* per week, the labour of 27 weeks of the same number of persons is now necessary; and which, at 15*s.* per week, amounts to 101,150,000*l.;* and that taxation paid in labour is consequently increased to the amount of 40,468,175*l.*

10.—THAT it appears by a comparison of the official and declared value of exports of British commodities, that in the year 1814, the declared value of the exports was 47,859,388*l.* and the official value 36,120,733*l.* being 32½ per cent. of the declared above the official value; and that in 1821, the quantity in official value amounted to 40,194,893*l.* and the declared value to 35,826,083*l.* being 11 per cent of the official above the declared, making a total decline in

---

[1] On the earlier version of this resolution Ricardo writes: 'not unjustly because 10 millions might be necessary to pay the public creditor for the loss he had previously sustained.'

value of $43\frac{1}{2}$ per cent, and the general price currents exhibit a similar decline: That the total amount of taxation in commodities, is therefore equivalent to 87,003,397*l.* of the former period, and the increased taxation paid in commodities to 26,331,572*l.*

11.—THAT the further reduction of wheat from 55*s.* 6*d.* to 45*s.* and other agricultural produce, together with any further decline in the money wages of labour, and price of commodities, additionally increases the burden of taxation, as well as all other charges, both public and private, upon the property and industry of the country to an extent proportionate to such further reduction;—and that as wheat never exceeded, upon the average, the present rate in the old money standard, it must be expected that it will on an average there remain, unless enhanced by scarcity; and that the price of commodities, and wages of labour will continue at the money value they now bear, or be further reduced. *Report allows the depreciation* — *read this* +

12.—THAT <u>such effects</u> could not by possibility have been in the contemplation of the legislature, still less of the people of England, at the time of the passing the Act of 1819:—That its destructive consequences are now visible—that individuals held to their contract, either have been or must be ruined; an unexampled revolution of property follow, and the burthens of taxation become absolutely intolerable. *What effects? why those which have been enumerated.*

13.—THAT by the Parliamentary Paper, No. 145, of the present Session, columns 1 and 2, it appears, that from the 5th of January 1798, to the 5th of January 1816, the sum of 459,630,826*l.* of money, including bills funded, was paid into the Treasury on account of loans, for which an annual charge for interest and annuities was created of 23,860,020*l.* which sum converted into a three per cent capital, is equal to 795,334,000*l.* *154 millions paid for Sinking fund.*

14.—THAT the average price of gold having been during that period 90*s.* 10*d.* the equivalent in gold to the money so lent and capital created, was 101,203,117 ozs.; and the 3 per cent stock being now at 80, the said capital is equal to 140,095,550 ozs. of gold, at the *Outrageous* before-mentioned average price of 90s. 10d. and that

Undue gain!
Why undue?
When land rose
was that an un-
due gain?

at the present price of gold of 77s. 6d. to 163,407,306 ozs.: the difference, being 23,311,836 ozs. constitutes an <u>undue gain</u> to the public creditor, at the expense of the public, equal in money to 110,974,694l.

15.—THAT the average price of wheat having been during the above period 81s. 10d. the equivalent in wheat to the money so lent was 112,333,400 quarters; and the price of 3 per cent stock being now 80, and wheat at the same average, the equivalent would now be 155,533,185 quarters; but at 55s. 6d. the average price since 1819, it is equal to 229,285,478 quarters, or in money, 938,159,330l. being an increased gain of 73,782,215 quarters by the alteration of the currency,

£301,892,228.

or in money 301,892,228l.

Annual charge
not 23 but
13 mill.

16.—THAT the annual charge of 23,860,020l. created in the period above stated, was equal to 5,253,502 ozs. and is equal to 6,127,174 ozs. being an increase of 874,192 ozs. or 3,403,886l.: That the

Is this true?
Yes, on the sup-
position that the
loans were made
in the same
medium.

above annual charge in wheat was equal to 5,831,370 quarters; is, at the average since 1819, equal to 8,600,000 quarters, or in money 35,196,666l. being an increased gain of 2,799,000 quarters, or in money of 11,328,311l. and that by comparison with commodities and labour, in the proportion of difference of their money value in those two periods, an equally undue advantage to the public creditor is proved to have been given at the charge of the public.

17.—THAT all public creditors prior to 1798, and others subsequent, have suffered in proportion to the depreciation that followed their respective loans; that they are therefore entitled, in strict justice, to be paid in money, of value equal to that of those periods, and be indemnified for the diminished value of their income during the interval: That many of those

Here is an
admission.

creditors having probably in such a length of time, sold their stock and purchased property, have since undergone another and more fatal injury, by the restoration of the old currency, and consequent diminution of the value of their property so bought; —on the other hand, those who lent their money when the currency was depreciated below the average $\frac{1}{4}$ *of a century* of the whole period, gained a further undue advant- *1809. £4.—.8.* age than is shown by the foregoing statements; and the depreciation was at its greatest extent during the latter years of the war, when the largest proportion of money was lent, and capital created; in addition to which the public have, upon very advantageous terms to the stockholder, redeemed a larger capital debt than existed prior to 1797.

18.—THAT under all these circumstances, it is evidently and indispensably necessary to take into immediate consideration the destructive effects that have arisen out of the alterations made in the currency, by the Acts of 1797 and 1819, as well respecting the enormous public burthens created and *so augmented* by the Act of 1815, as the revolution of property in the vast and complicated intercourse of individuals throughout this country occasioned thereby; in order that, by a final arrangement of the currency, as equitable to all parties as circumstances will admit, or by a reduction of taxation equal to the advance occasioned by the Act of 1819, together with the establishment of some principle for the adjustment of private contracts, justice may, as far as possible, be administered to all, and the country saved from a revolution of property, and also from a pressure of taxation beyond the ability of the people to sustain.

[*The speech is printed below for the first time from the original* 10 July 1822 *transcript in Ricardo's handwriting, which has been found in the Mill-Ricardo papers. It is four times as long as the corresponding report in* Hansard. *It must have been written on 11 July, since early on the following day Ricardo left on his Continental Tour.*[1] *The transcript is unfinished and the conclusion, as indicated below, is here taken from* Hansard.]

The first Resolution having been put,

Mr. RICARDO said that if he failed to expose all the errors and fallacies in the Resolution which the honb^{le} gent had

---

[1] It cannot have been written in advance, as it contains references to Western's speech which immediately preceded Ricardo's.

submitted to the attention of the House it would be from his inability to give clearness to his thoughts and not because they did not contain errors and fallacies, for he had seldom seen so many contained in so small a compass. The honb^{le} gent. appeared to think if he could shew that prices had undergone a considerable variation during the last 8 years that such alteration must necessarily be imputable to the act of 1819 for restoring the ancient standard of our money. He appeared to think that there was not, nor could be, any other cause for the variation of prices and that it was sufficient to shew that there had been a considerable fall in the prices of various commodities to justify him in proposing a revision of the standard of our currency with the express view of raising such prices. Even according to the Honb^{le} gentleman's principles he was bound not only to shew that prices had fallen but that they had fallen in consequence of the measures which had been pursued to give us the benefits of a fixed standard. He had forgotten that at all times we had been liable to fluctuations of prices when we had not meddled with our standard, and what proof did the honb^{le} gent offer that the present fall of prices might not be imputable to some of those general causes which operate on the value of commodities. Because the fund holder received the value of $13\frac{1}{2}$ bushels of corn now for every sum of £3. 17. $10\frac{1}{2}$ in which his dividend was paid, and had only received $7\frac{1}{2}$ bushels for the same sum formerly was it to be inferred that the currency had varied in that proportion? If the argument were good for this country it was valid also for every other, but what would the hon^{le} gent. say if it were now proposed in the legislature of France to alter the standard of the currency because a given number of francs received by the public creditor would now purchase 50 or 100 pc^{t} more of wheat than it would purchase in former years. He Mr. Ricardo

would follow the honb.^{le} gentleman thro' all his resolutions
and he would with the indulgence of the House advert to them
in their order. With respect to the distressed state of those
connected with the agriculture of the country and which was
stated in the first resolution there was no difference of opinion;
unhappily it was too well established that such distress existed, but what they differed about was the cause of such
distress—the honb.^{le} gentleman imputed the whole of it to
the alteration in the value of the currency, whereas he and
those who agreed with him without denying this as one cause
of the distress mainly attributed it to the abundance of the
quantity of produce. Corn might fall from various causes,
from abundance, from improvements in agriculture which
would lower the cost of production, from a deficient supply
of the precious metals from the mines,—these were causes
which might operate generally in all countries but they never
had yet been made the foundation of a proposal for altering
the standard of a currency. It must be remembered that the
altering the standard of the currency could not affect the
agriculturists as a class if they had no taxes to pay. The
alteration might be beneficial or injurious to tenants during
the continuance of their leases, contracted when money was
of a different value, but in the same proportion would it be
injurious or beneficial to the landlord with whom such agree-
ments were made, and therefore the whole together would be
as rich and no richer than before. This would be the case if
we were an untaxed people but that not being the case the
raising of the value of money was injurious to this class in
proportion as the increased value augmented the taxation of
the country. This effect however was general and not
partial, and would operate on all classes alike. In his
character of a payer of taxes it would operate on the stockholder equally as on all other classes. If then great as our

taxation was we deducted the increased amount paid by the Stockholder, the increased amount paid by Merchants, Manufacturers and the possessors of all other property he left it to the house to determine whether the increased amount of taxation which fell upon the agriculture of the country in consequence of any probable alteration in the value of money was adequate to account for the very general distress of that class—to him it appeared impossible that such great effects could follow from such an inadequate cause, but the whole was explained on the supposition of a too abundant quantity of agricultural produce.

The second resolution of the Honb.^{le} gentleman referred to the distress in Ireland and he actually ascribed the famine which prevailed in that country to the alteration in the value of the currency. Could the honb.^{le} gent. seriously argue that the failure in the potatoe crop which he himself did not deny, to an altered value of currency? But says the honb.^{le} gent^{n} the people are dying for want of food in Ireland, and the farmers are said to be suffering from superabundance. In these two propositions the honb^{le} gent^{n} thinks there is a manifest contradiction, but he Mr. R. could not agree with him in thinking so. Where was the contradiction in supposing it possible that in a country where wages were regulated mainly by the price of potatoes the people should be suffering the greatest distress if the potatoe crop failed and their wages were inadequate to purchase the dearer commodity corn? From whence was the money to come to enable them to purchase the grain however abundant it might [be]^{1} if its price still far exceeded that of potatoes. He Mr. Ricardo should not think it absurd or contradictory to maintain that in such a country as England where the food of the people was corn, there might be an abundance of that grain and such low

---

^{1} Omitted in MS.

prices as not to afford a remuneration to the grower, and yet
that the people might be in distress and not able for want of
employment to buy it, but in Ireland the case was much
stronger, and in that country there could be no doubt there
might be a glut of corn, and a starving people. So much for
the second resolution.

The third resolution of the Honb^le gent^n was founded on
something which he said appeared in the report of the
Agricultural committee, and he had marked it by inverted
commas, which naturally led those who read it to conclude
that the passage was an extract from the Report. A few
words in the passage to which he was referring were written
in Italics in order as it appeared to give them greater force;
after speaking of the effects of the altered value of currency
on the price of grain and other commodities the words in
italics were these, "and consequently to cause a severe pressure upon the industry of the country". He Mr. Ricardo was
sure the honb^le gent would not knowingly make any mis-
statement and therefore he concluded it was the mistake of
some one who had assisted him in drawing up these resolutions. It appeared that there were no words in the Report
which answered to the quotation in this resolution—to much
of it the spirit of the Report was at variance and in no part
could he find any words which could justify even the inference of the words emphatically written in Italics. Mr.
Ricardo here read a passage from the Agricultural Report.
But he Mr. R had another observation to make on this
resolution[;] it said "That in proportion as all commodities,
whether the produce of the soil, manufactures or commerce,
have experienced a depression of their money value, so must
the proprietors have suffered a direct injury." In this proposition he could not agree. It is not in proportion to the
fall in the money value of commodities that the parties

alluded to would be injured, but in proportion as the taxation which they may be called upon to pay shall be really increased by the rise in the value of money. Nothing can in itself be a matter of greater indifference to a producer of commodities than their money prices provided every thing alters at the same time and in the same proportion, and therefore the inference which the honb^{le} gent^{n} draws and which he would have this house also draw is wholly without foundation.

I now come to the 4th Resolution which is an important one, because in it the honb^{le} gent admits that gold is the standard of this country and that the depreciation of paper money is to be estimated "by the amount of such paper money above £3. 17. 10$\frac{1}{2}$ necessary to purchase an ounce of gold" a doctrine which I have always maintained but which is now very often in this house and out of it called in question. In this Resolution it is asserted that "soon after the passing of the act of 1797 by which the Bank of England was restricted from paying its notes in specie, the currency of the country became depreciated". It is only essential to examine into the correctness of this statement because the honb^{le} gentleman in his speech founds an important argument upon it. He was fully aware that to his proposal for altering the standard on account of the benefit which the fundholder of a recent date derived from the increase in the value of money it would be objected to him that the fundholder of 1797 had been a loser in consequence of having received his dividend in a depreciated medium for several years and if compensation was to be made to one party who was the payer of taxes so also should it be made to the old stockholder who had suffered so great an injury. How does the honb^{le} gent^{n} answer this objection? by denying the justice of his claim? no he admits it but he represents it as so old that it has be-

come antiquated—a strange answer this and I should think
that if his claim be a just one the circumstance of its being of
25 years standing does not weaken it. It can never be too
late to do justice, but the fact is not as this resolution represents it, the paper money of the country did not become
depreciated immediately after the act of 1797—it only began
to be depreciated in 1800 and the average depreciation from
1797 to 1809 did not exceed $2\frac{1}{2}$ pc^t, as measured by the average price of gold £4. —. 8. If then there was any weight
in this argument of time, I think I shew that in this case
length of time cannot be pleaded and if justice is to be done
to one party injured so must it also be to another. On the
whole I am prepared to shew that the account between
the payers of taxes and the Stockholder is pretty nearly
balanced, and that in reality the country is now no more
loaded with taxes than it would have been if we had never
departed from our metallic standard, but had uniformly
adhered to the system which we so regularly followed up to
1797. But of this I shall have occasion to speak hereafter.
I shall consider the real question to be this—Is the agricultural interest in a worse situation than it would have been
if neither of the 2 acts that of 1797 and that of 1819 had never
been passed. Did he not in fact gain as much by the effects
of the first of these acts as he has lost by the subsequent one?
To the solution of this question I shall pay attention before
I sit down. In this 4th Resolution I see it asserted that the
price of gold on an average of 18 years was £4. 10. 10.
I believe this to be incorrect and that the average was about
£4. 5. or £4. 6.—After having admitted that the price of
gold was the measure of the depreciation, the honb^{le} gent,
in this resolution, recurs to the price of corn as measuring
the depreciation. The honb^{l} gent in his speech said that he
hoped he should not be answered by any attempt to shew

that he might have been a little inaccurate in his statements of the price of corn, as he knew there would be a difference in the result whether the price was estimated from the Eton tables or otherwise; he, Mr. R, could assure the honb.^{l} gent that he had taken no pains to discover such inaccuracies because he considered the price of corn as having nothing to do with this question. Corn was not now nor never had been the standard of the money of this or any other country. If it were a better standard than that which we possessed it might be a good reason for adopting it in future but hitherto it had not been the standard but gold had and therefore we were bound to measure our payments by gold and by nothing else. As he Mr. R had already observed if the argument from the number of q^{rs} of corn paid the public creditor now as compared to former years were valid here, it was also valid in France, and therefore tho' France had uniformly maintained a metallic standard she might now justly alter the standard and pay the public creditor with a smaller number of ounces of silver because they were now equivalent to a greater number of bushels of wheat. Surely the House would not listen to such an argument, nor give countenance to so dangerous a principle. If the agriculturist thought wheat the proper standard, why might not another man think sugar such, or indigo, or cloth. Why might he not say I formerly paid the public creditor with so many pounds of sugar or yards of cloth and now I am obliged to give a greater number. What security have we that these various commodities may not vary in different directions some of them rising others falling. In such case by what rule should we determine to adopt one in preference to the other? But is the honb.^{le} gentleman prepared to go through with the standard which he himself proposes? I believe that the stock-holder might safely close with the proposal if such were made to him. The average price of wheat for 30 years ending in 1755 was £1. 13. 4, but since 1755 the public creditor has not received within 50 pc.^{t} of the quantity of wheat to which he would have been entitled if wheat had been the standard. If the Honb^{le} gentleman['s] argument be a good one why should not the fundholder have made up to him the value of the amount of corn of which he has been defrauded since 1755 together with compound interest on the same. If corn is to be the measure now so ought it always to have been since the contraction of the public debt and if the honb^{le} gentleman is not willing to admit this he should shew why he would have corn the standard when it is against the Stockholder and in favor of the agriculturists, and why he rejects the same measure when it is in favor of the Stockholder and disadvantageous to the landed interest.

Mr. Ricardo said that the 5th Resolution also contained a fallacy because it supposed that from the circumstance of the fall in the price of corn and other produce being equal to that amount which formerly constituted rent, that therefore there could not by possibility be any rent at the present moment. This would indeed be true if all the charges of production as well as taxes were to remain at the same money value as before. But could this be the case? Was it possible to believe that with so immense a fall in the value of corn, the cost of production should not be reduced? Would not labour fall with the fall of raw produce? Would not seed and many other expences be also reduced? In fact the price of corn as affected by the currency was of no importance whatever to the agriculturist excepting as he was burthened with fixed money taxes, because all the charges on production would be in proportion to the variations in price from such a cause. This resolution speaks also of the increased charges on the land in consequence of mortgages and other debts being to

be paid in money of an increased value. This was undoubtedly true but had not the landholder derived a benefit
from this source when money was depreciating and if justice
was to be done to all parties would he not have as much to
pay on this account as he would have to receive. The Honb^{le}
gent kept his eye steadily fixed on the injury which the landed
interest had recently sustained,—he wholly forgot the advantage which they had derived from the fluctuating value
of money at no very remote period. The 6th Resolution of
the Hon. gent. Mr. Western told us that during the war the
debt had most enormously increased. No one could deny
this fact: The war had been a most expensive one, but it left
undecided whether that debt had been increased injuriously
or unjustly to one particular class: That was the only point
in dispute between the hon^{le} gent and himself.

In the 7th resolution the honb^{l} gent only asserts what is
true that an increased debt must be paid with an additional
number of ounces of gold, but in order to ascertain what
amount of money such an additional quantity of ounces of
gold is equivalent to, why should they not be estimated at
the present value of gold, why should the honb^{le} gentleman
calculate it at the value of gold of a former period? He Mr.
Ricardo must again observe that in proportion as the value
of gold had been increased by the act of 1819, he acknowledged taxation had also been increased, but the question
here again offered itself on which he should have to observe
presently, had it been increased so as on the whole to impose
an undue weight on the landed interest? On the 8th Resolution he Mr. Ricardo should say little, because the honb^{le}
gentleman had laid no foundation whatever for his favorite
standard of wheat, but if he had, he Mr. Ricardo was at a loss
to know on what principle the additional quantity of wheat
which the tax payers had to contribute should be estimated

in the money price of a former period and not in the money
price of the present time. Neither should he Mr. Ricardo
make any remark on the 9th Resolution because as wheat
formed a material part of the value on which the wages of
labour were expended it was to be expected that labour
would vary with the price of wheat. In making labour the
standard therefore the honb^{l} gent. had in fact repeated his
former argument respecting a wheat standard. It was not a
distinct commodity, affording an additional proof of the
alteration in the value of money, but was most particularly
governed by the price of wheat almost necessarily rising and
falling with it.

In the 11th Resolution the honb^{le} gentleman assumes that
wheat though not a remunerating price is to remain at its
present price, but on what ground he has not indeed stated
to the house. He Mr. Ricardo was wholly at variance with
the honb^{le} gent. on this point, he could not conceive it
possible that corn would remain at its present depressed
price if it were true as stated by the honb^{l} gent. that if it did
it could neither afford rent to the landlord nor profit to the
farmer. He Mr. Ricardo was fully assured that on such conditions corn could not permanently be grown, and therefore
the honb^{le} gentleman's premises were unfounded or his conclusion must be an erroneous one.

In the 12th Resolution the House was told that in 1819
when it passed the act for the resumption of cash payments
it could not foresee the effects which the former resolutions
had enumerated. It would indeed have been strange if it
could have foreseen effects which had previously occurred.
These resolutions speak of the depreciation as being at its
height in 1814. Much of the sufferings of the agriculturist
had taken place before 1819 and could not have been the
consequence of the act of that year. The question for the

House to consider was the effect of the act of 1819. All the former variations in the currency the evils of which no one was more willing to admit than himself had taken place under a system which this act went to put an end to, and it was for putting an end to such a system that it had his warm approbation. —

He Mr. Ricardo had now to animadvert on the 13th resolution which contained only the trifling error of 154 millions. He was ready to forfeit all the little credit which he might have with the house if he did not prove his assertion. —The honb^{le}. gentleman in this resolution has stated that from the 5th. of Jany. 1798 to the 5th. Jany. 1816 the sum of 459 millions of money had been paid into the treasury on account of loans, for which a capital of £795,334,000- 3 pc^{t} stock was created, — that in payment of this sum a value equal to 101,203,000 ounces of gold was received and to pay the same capital in 3 pc^{t} stock valued at 80 at the present moment 163,407,306 ounces of gold would be necessary: the difference being 23,311,836 ounces, which the honb^{le}. gent. goes on to say constitutes an *undue gain* to the public creditor at the expence of the public equal in money to 110,974,694£. The annual charge created by the debt contracted from 1798 to 1816 the hon^{l}. gent states at 23 millions. In the first place 459 millions were not raised from the public between 1798 and 1816 but 154 millions less than that amount. It is true that the loan contractors or stockholders paid the public 459 millions in a depreciated money during that period, but they received in payment of debt in that same money, during the same time, 154 millions, consequently only 305 millions was received, and an additional debt to that amount only was contracted. It was now acknowledged on all sides that the sinking fund was only a nominal one if it did not arise from a surplus of revenue above expenditure. Suppose that the

Chancellor of the Exchequer of those days had acknowledged the delusion of the sinking fund, and had listened to the advice often given by his hon.[l] friend Mr. Grenfell of making the sinking fund commissioners subscribe to the loans of the year how much would the contractors have then paid into the treasury? 305 millions and not 459 as stated by the honb.[l] gent. But the increased charge on the debt between the two periods is 23 millions says the honb.[l] gent. but what is the fact? it is only 13 millions. But in addition to these errors, and to swell the loss to the public, the hon.[l] gent.[n] calls that an undue gain to the stockholder which arises from the difference between the price at which he contracted for the various loans during the war, and the present price of 80 to which the 3 pc.[t] have risen after several years of peace. It is something new to hear this called an undue gain made by the stockholder. If the honb.[l] gent.[n] had bought an estate for £100,000 which he could now sell for £130,000 would he call the £30,000 an undue gain? If he had purchased French stock at 58 which has now risen to 90 would he call that an unjust gain? and [what][1] would he think of a French legislator who should seriously propose to diminish the payment to the stockholder on account of such rise? If such a plea was listened to there was an end of all security and good faith, and no man could safely for a moment enter into a contract if government were to consider the profit if he made any an unjust gain.

He Mr. Ricardo would only mention the 14 and 15 resolutions to shew the extravagant conclusions to which the honb.[l] gentleman had come. He had really submitted to the house a proposition that the stockholder had gained by the alteration in the value of the currency £301,892,000 between 1798 and 1816. The honb.[l] gentleman first states that the

[1] Omitted in MS.

whole amount of money paid for loans during the above period was £459,630,000 which I have proved was in fact only 305,000,000 and yet on this sum he states him to have gained £301,000,000

[*Ricardo's own transcript breaks off here. The conclusion of his speech is reported in* Hansard *as follows.*]

The hon. gentleman seemed to insinuate, that certain individuals were in the habit of making public attacks upon the landlords of this country. The charge could not be brought against him. It was true, he looked upon rents in the same light as he did every other article in the market, liable to fluctuations, and to be regulated according to the demand for the produce of the soil. He had never said that the country would be ruined by a superabundant supply;[1] on the contrary, that the country would greatly benefit by that supply; the greater the supply the greater the comfort. Great supply induced low prices; low prices injured the grower, but gave an advantage to the country. It was not, however, that kind of advantage which he should wish it to possess. On the contrary, he would always wish to see the grower receive a fair remunerating price; because he was convinced, that all classes in the country would go on better and more prosperously when the farmer received a fair remunerating price. But a remunerating price had nothing to do with the state of the currency. If corn were down so low even as 20s. and the price of labour and all other outgoings were regulated by that price, the grower could go on paying his rent as well perhaps as when he received 80s. and when his outgoings were in proportion

---

[1] Mr. Western in his speech had said: 'When did any man before, see, hear, or read of a country ruined by superabundance? Such a thing had never entered into the head of any but modern philosophers!'

to that price.—With respect to the advantage that one class had gained over the other by the bill of 1819, he would say, that it certainly was impossible to tamper with the currency of a country, without producing such effects. The payers of taxes had lost at one period and gained at another, in consequence of the fluctuations of the currency; but it was quite remarkable to see how nearly at par stood the loss and gain. In his opinion, the great mischief sprung out of the original error, he meant the bill of 1797.—That was the great error— the measure of 1819 was the remedy. The House acknowledged the mischief of the measure of 1797, and they were bound to support the bill of 1819, which was only intended to remedy the original error. If the House at a fatal moment interfered with that bill, what would be the consequence— what would be the state of London the next day? What wild speculation—what ruin would follow! So strong were the evils that would follow such a step, that he anticipated from that House its decided negative to the motion of the hon. member.

After several other speeches, of some of which, 'from the lateness of the hour, no report has been preserved' (*Hansard*), the resolutions were negatived; and at four in the morning the House adjourned.

[The session closed on 6 Aug. 1822.]

SESSION 1823

The King's speech on the opening of the session was delivered on 4 Feb. 1823.

FOREIGN TRADE OF THE COUNTRY

12 *February* 1823

Mr. WALLACE (the retiring Vice-President of the Board of Trade) moved for the revival of the committee on foreign trade of the previous session.

Mr. RICARDO rose for the purpose of paying his tribute of respect to the merits of the right hon. gentleman, who had so lately filled the office of vice-president of the Board of Trade. He would say this; that, much as the right hon. gentleman's plans had benefitted the commerce of the country, they would have benefitted it still more, had all of them been fully carried into effect. They had met, however, with too many obstacles from interests that were hostile to his improvements; and, though he regretted the circumstance much, he must still observe, that those interests ought to be tenderly dealt with. He thought it would be wiser to make a compensation to any parties who might be injured by the alteration, than to persist in a system which was proved to be detrimental to the commercial interests of the nation at large. He had heard with the greatest pleasure, the very liberal speech which the right hon. gentleman had made that evening; nor was it with less satisfaction that he had heard his flattering account of the export trade of the country. It had been said, that the exports were greater now than they had been during the most flourishing year of the war. It ought likewise to be stated, that during the war our great foreign exports went to meet our great foreign expenditure; whereas

at present we received valuable returns for every thing we
exported. In looking at the general state of the country, it
was satisfactory to find that, amid the gloom and distress in
which the agricultural interests were involved, its foreign
commerce was in a flourishing condition. He was sure that it
must be the wish of all who heard him, that it might long go
on, prospering and to prosper. His only reason for rising
was to bear his testimony to the extraordinary merits of the
right hon. gentleman.

BANK BALANCES

18 *February* 1823

    Mr. GRENFELL, in moving for a return of the balances of
public money in the hands of the Bank of England, observed that
the services rendered by the Bank to the public were overpaid.
The new CHANCELLOR OF THE EXCHEQUER (Mr. Robinson)
declined entering at present into the subject. Mr. BARING said
that the advantage of holding the public balances 'had been
estimated and paid for by the Bank on the renewal of their
charter.'

    Mr. RICARDO said, it was true the Bank had made a com-
pensation for the grant of the charter; but it was not sufficiently great for the advantages they had so long possessed.
If, during his continuance in office, the Bank of England
should apply for a renewal of the charter, he hoped the
chancellor of the exchequer would be particularly careful that
they did not overreach him. Before any such bargain should
be made, it would be the duty of the right hon. gentleman to
consult the House as to the terms of it. If it should be open
to public competition, much more would be given for it than
had ever yet been offered. From the advantages which the
Bank had derived, it was impossible not to see, that the terms
had been very much in their favour.

FINANCIAL SITUATION OF THE COUNTRY

21 *February* 1823

The new CHANCELLOR OF THE EXCHEQUER (Mr. Robinson), anticipating the Budget, made an exposition of the financial situation of the country; he expected a surplus of more than 7,200,000*l.* and proposed to reduce or repeal several of the assessed taxes. Mr. MABERLY intimated his intention to propose a plan for hastening the operation of Pitt's land tax redemption act [on this plan, see p. 259 below].

Mr. RICARDO said, he remembered, that at the termination of the last session, he had frequently to repel the attacks which were made upon the science of political economy. He had been delighted, however, to hear the plain, sound, practical, and excellent speech, which had been delivered by the right hon. gentleman opposite; and he thought that the science of political economy had never before had so able an expositor as it had now found in that House. He thought that there never yet had been in that House a minister filling the situation which was held by the right hon. gentleman, who had in that capacity delivered sentiments so candid, so wise, and so excellent. In all the statements which he had made, it was impossible not to follow him with the greatest ease and safety; for it was in all these quite clear, that each of them was, in fact, as the right hon. gentleman had put it. But, there was this one difference—an important one, certainly—between him and the right hon. gentleman. The right hon. gentleman had stated the surplus of our income over our expenditure at 7,000,000*l.* Now he (Mr. Ricardo) had contended last year, and did still contend, that the transaction respecting the commutation of the pension charge, was only a transfer from one hand to the other.[1] This evening the right hon.

[1] See above, p. 194.

gentleman had introduced into his surplus of 7,000,000*l.* a sum of 2,000,000*l.* to be received; he would like to know from whom? Could the right hon. gentleman himself tell? On the one side of the account he had put an amount of 2,800,000*l.* to be paid for pensions and half-pay; and on the other side, he had stated, that he was to receive 4,800,000*l.* from the trustees, whoever they might be, who were to pay such pensions and half-pay; and of these two items, the balance was 2,000,000*l.* to be repaid, of course, to these trustees or commissioners themselves. Undoubtedly, therefore, from this assumed surplus of 7,000,000*l.* of actual income over expenditure, there must be deducted these 2,000,000*l.,* which the sinking fund itself was to supply. If this view of the subject was correct, the right hon. gentleman when he should have carried his plan into effect, of giving the proposed relief to the country, would actually leave them with a clear sinking fund, not of 5,000,000*l.,* but of 3,000,000*l.* This was the only difference in point of statement between him and the right hon. gentleman. But he could go along with the right hon. gentleman in every principle that he had applied to the sinking fund; as applicable to the diminution of our debt in time of peace. But, this was always in the supposition, that we did actually possess such a sinking fund, and that it could be so applied to pay off our debt. So convinced was he of the necessity, the indispensable necessity of getting rid of this tremendous debt, that he had before ventured to suggest the expediency of a general contribution from the capital of the country for that purpose. He would contribute any proportion of his own property, for the attainment of this great end, if others would do the same. If this proposition should be thought extravagant, or if it should be supposed that the contribution he should suggest was excessive, why not ask for a smaller contribution of

capital for the same object? As to the other parts of the right
hon. gentleman's speech, he considered that taxes raised in
order to pay off debt, ought to be looked upon in a very
different light, from those that were raised for the immediate
services of the state. The one, we might be considered as
paying to ourselves; the other was for ever lost to us. As to
the plan proposed by the hon. gentleman who spoke last, he
had few or no remarks to offer upon it. His scheme for the
reduction of the debt, by paying off the land tax, was, as far
as he (Mr. R.) understood it, quite practicable. It did exist,
indeed, to some extent, at the present moment; but the hon.
gentleman's plan would, perhaps, increase its facilities. The
hon. gentleman, however, in his plan for the reduction of
taxes, went much too far; for he seemed to consider, that the
clear surplus, which they had to dispose of, after allowing for
the 2,200,000*l.* which the right hon. gentleman proposed to
remit in taxes, would give a sinking fund of 5,000,000*l.* Now,
he said, that the hon. gentleman went too far, on this
ground—that we could not have such a sinking fund applicable to such a purpose. And here he would beg leave to call
the attention of the House to a pamphlet which had been
lately published under the auspices of ministers themselves.[1]
[Hear, hear! from the Treasury Bench.][2] Well, he did not
know how that might be; but this he knew, that it contained
arguments which were constantly in the mouths of ministers.
In this pamphlet the sinking fund was made applicable to two

[1] *Administration of the Affairs of
Great Britain, Ireland, and their
Dependencies, at the Commencement of the Year 1823. Stated and
Explained under the Heads of Finance, National Resources, Foreign
Relations, Colonies, Trade, and
Domestic Administration* [Anon.,
attributed to J. S. Copley, the So-
licitor-General, afterwards Lord
Lyndhurst], London, Hatchard,
1823. Cp. below, IX, 269. Ricardo's copy of the pamphlet, 3rd
ed., is in the Goldsmiths' Library
of the University of London.
[2] The *Morning Chronicle* reports
'[cries of "No, No", on the
Treasury Benches, and most emphatically by Mr. Canning and
Mr. Robinson]'.

or three different objects: and first of all, it was efficient for
paying off debt. If so, it was clearly efficient for no other
object. If a man applied the surplus of his income to the
payment of debts, he surely could not apply it to any other
purpose. But the pamphlet proceeded to say, that the fund
was efficient for carrying on war in case of an emergency, if
allowed, in the mean time, to accumulate at compound interest. This was as if the real object of the fund was, in the
event of any aggressions by an enemy, to enable us to fight
that enemy, in case of a war. But if so, why did not ministers
confess it? Let them at once openly avow their object. But
he thought that the more constitutional course would be, in
case we should be required to repel the aggressions of an
enemy, for the ministers of the crown to come down to the
House and acquaint it with the necessity of providing for the
expenses of a war that was about to be undertaken, rather
than to retain the sinking fund at its present establishment,
with the view of making it available on such an emergency.
He did think that there was something mysterious in this
doctrine of making that which was supposed to be applicable
to paying·off our debts applicable to the expense of a war.

AGRICULTURAL DISTRESS—SURREY
PETITION

26 *February* 1823

Mr. DENISON, in presenting a petition from the freeholders of
Surrey, referred to the mischief produced by tampering with the
currency in 1797 and 1819, and expressed the opinion that 'some
amicable adjustment was necessary throughout the country.'

Mr. RICARDO would not have risen upon this occasion, if
the hon. gentleman had not declared, that he wished some
amicable arrangement could be made by which that part of
the country which was now profiting on account of the loss

of the others, might be made to bear its share in the burdens. He complained that the words which had been used at that and at other public meetings, had been vague as to the advantage of the public creditor. For his part, he was at a loss to see what advantage the fundholder had gained. The argument appeared to him to be made use of rather upon the principle, that by giving your adversary's argument a bad name, you give your own a good one. Upon such grounds it was contended that the stockholder had met with nothing but gain; but those who had attended to the question, were of a different opinion. If only that which the fundholder was gaining now upon the sums which he had lent after the depreciation, was to be taken into the account, then there would no doubt be a balance in his favour; but, this view of the question would be most unfair. It would be stating the profit on the one side, without the corresponding loss on the other. If both of these were to be taken into the account, it would be found that the stockholder had had nothing more than was just; and that if the interest which he had been paid in depreciated currency, upon capital which when lent had not been depreciated, were to be set against the interest which he was receiving in undepreciated currency now, upon capital which when lent had been depreciated, then, not only would the loss in the one case compensate all that had been hitherto paid in the other, but would actually be equal to a perpetual annuity to that annual amount, which he was at present receiving. Mr. Mushett, of his majesty's mint, than whom nobody was better able to understand the subject himself, or to afford clear views of it to others, had, in a very luminous publication, demonstrated that this was the fact.[1] A parade was made in the speeches at public meetings, of the 800,000,000*l.* of debt which had been lent in depreciated currency, and the vast amount of the difference of interest

[1] See above, p. 138.

upon it; but it was well known, that about 400,000,000*l.* of this debt was borrowed before the Bank Restriction bill had operated any depreciation whatever; and another hundred millions had been lent to the government before any considerable depreciation had taken place. Hence there had been 500,000,000*l.* lent to the public in capital which was not depreciated. Interest in the depreciated currency had been paid upon this for twenty years; and the loss arising therefrom, according to the calculation of Mr. Mushett, was, allowing simple interest, about 27,000,000*l.;* or, allowing compound interest, and that was the fair allowance, about 12 or 13 millions more. It would appear, that the whole loss which the stockholder had sustained, in consequence of having been paid in a depreciated currency the interest on the sums borrowed, previous to and immediately following 1797, was about forty millions.—Having thus stated the disadvantages to the old public creditor, he should next state what was the calculation of the same authority, as to the advantages since the depreciation had ceased, by the alteration of the currency. That he calculated at two millions per annum. Compare that with the previous loss of forty millions, and by converting that amount into perpetual annuity, we should have the sum of two millions a year. So that the profit and loss would be found to balance each other. Taking, therefore, the respective interests of the stockholder and the payer of taxes, it would be seen, that no injury had occurred to either. Whether his opinion was right or wrong, as to the depreciation that existed at the period of the alteration of the currency, still, on the calculations of Mr. Mushett, it was evident, that to the public creditor, the profits at the one time, though greater, would be balanced by the corresponding losses at the other. He stood not there to defend the alterations that had taken place in the currency. No man had taken greater pains than himself, either within or without that House, to show the absolute necessity of a fixed standard. His hon. friend expressed his regret, that what was called an amicable adjustment had not taken place in 1819, at the restoration of the standard. Why, then, had he not proposed it? It was suggested at that period by a noble lord (Folkestone), in place of reverting to the old standard, to alter it to 4*l.* 1*s.* being the amount of the variation between the paper and the price of gold at that time. But, supposing that suggestion to have been adopted, was it to be argued, that a loss of 3 or 4 per cent could have produced all those distresses to agriculture, which the most extravagant opposers of the alteration of the currency attributed to that measure? Their opinions, even as to the amount of the depreciation, were irreconcileable: some stated it at 20 per cent, others contended it was 100; while the most extravagant went the length of asserting, that it amounted to 300 per cent. Suppose, however, that in place of reverting to the ancient standard, it had been increased 100 per cent, did they think no evils would have followed? Would the result, after doubling the amount of all the taxes, have left what now existed—an increasing revenue and a thriving trade? It was not his intention to renew the discussion on that hackneyed topic, Mr. Peel's bill; but, as such a variety of contradictory opinions had been given on its effects, he would state what was the opinion of a bank director on its efficacy, as it operated on the proceedings of the Bank. Mr. Turner, who had been in the direction for two years, decidedly said, that as to the operations of the Bank, Mr. Peel's bill remained a dead letter.[1] It had neither accelerated nor retarded payments in specie; except by the payment of ten millions of exchequer bills to the Bank, which enabled it to expend that

---

[1] See Samuel Turner's *Considerations upon the Agriculture, Commerce, and Manufactures of the British Empire,* London, 1822. Cp. below, IX, 197.

amount in the purchase of bullion. Taking into consideration the rule by which the bank directors generally admitted they regulated their issues, namely, the application for discounts, and coupling with that the low rate of the interest of money, the circulation would have been the same, and consequently the distress of agriculture as great, even if that bill had never passed.

Lord FOLKESTONE replied, and, 'with respect to the suggestion he had made, in 1819, of increasing the standard to 4*l.* 1*s.*, he confessed that now, after mature consideration, he was convinced that that amount of increase would be wholly inadequate to the state of things. That principle was limited to the variation which existed between paper and gold at the particular period. His hon. friend himself then argued on the assumption, that the amount of that variance did not exceed 5 per cent. And here he must be allowed to say, that his hon. friend had not been perfectly consistent with himself; for he had since admitted, that the variance was as great as 10 per cent. He (lord F.) maintained, however, that the depreciation was infinitely greater.'

Mr. RICARDO admitted, that the noble lord was correct, in stating that he (Mr. R.) had on one occasion computed the depreciation at 5 per cent, and that he now found it to be 10 per cent; still, he was not in error. His first computation referred to a payment in bullion; and it would have been correct if the Bank had acted precisely in the spirit of that bill: but, instead of doing so, they had got together a large quantity of gold, which they coined into sovereigns, and then they came down to the House to procure an act, enabling them to get rid of those sovereigns. If the measure of which he approved had been acted on, the depreciation would have been but 5 per cent; because it would have been measured by the price of gold.

Lord FOLKESTONE said, 'he had supposed the hon. member to have been arguing with reference to Mr. Peel's bill; but now he discovered, that his argument rested on a measure which existed only in his own imagination.'

MR. WHITMORE'S MOTION
RESPECTING THE CORN LAWS

26 *February* 1823

Mr. WHITMORE moved for leave to bring in a bill for lowering the price, at which the importation of foreign corn was permitted, by 2*s.* a year, until it was reduced to 60*s.* Mr. HUSKISSON (the new President of the Board of Trade) opposed the motion.

Mr. RICARDO said, that the right hon. gentleman, in all the arguments which he had brought forward for postponing the consideration of the corn laws, had in reality given a reason for proceeding at once to amend them. What was the danger which his hon. friend, who brought forward the present motion, apprehended? It was the danger of those very high prices, to the recurrence of which the right hon. gentleman looked forward, as the conjuncture when the corn laws might be amended. He apprehended the danger of capital being again drawn, by the temptation of high prices, to the land (and the right hon. gentleman agreed that the danger existed)—that there would again be a succession of low prices, and another loss of capital. This evil it was the object of the present proposition to prevent; yet the right hon. gentleman would wait till the evil came upon them, before he would provide the remedy. As to the motion of his hon. friend, he would not oppose it; because he should be glad of any approach to a free trade in corn. But he thought his hon. friend did not go far enough; he had left the mischief of a fixed price. Both his hon. friend and the right hon. gentleman had laid down the true principles of a corn law; namely, that a protecting duty should be imposed on foreign corn, equal to the peculiar burthens borne by the grower of corn in this country. But, when this was done, a fixed price should be done away altogether. In fact his hon. friend had seemed a little uncertain as to his fixed price. He had taken it at 60*s.;* but he had stated, that if foreign corn could be imported at 55*s.,* he should have reduced it to that. He thought he had committed a great error in taking any fixed price at all. A duty should be imposed on corn imported, equal to the peculiar burthens borne by the grower of corn; and, in his opinion, a drawback or bounty to nearly the same amount should be allowed on corn exported. Then, and then only, would corn be kept at a price nearly equal in this, to what it was in other countries. If there was an abundant harvest, it would find a vent by means of the bounty; and, on the other hand, if there was a deficient supply, under the influence of the duty, corn would be introduced as it was wanted, and not in the enormous quantities poured in under the existing law, when the price rose to a certain height. The right hon. gentleman had objected to the proposition, because of the agitation it would create out of doors. But his hon. friend's proposition did not interfere with the present law, until the price of corn was as high as 80*s*. In this, also, he differed from his hon. friend; because, before corn was so high, that encouragement might be given to extensive cultivation, which it was his object to avert. He (Mr. R.) should recommend, that the law for the amendment of the corn laws should come into operation long before corn had reached 80*s.;* and he should then recommend a system of duties and bounties, at first[,] in deference to those prejudices of which he thought they were too tender, higher than the amount of the peculiar burthens of the agriculturists; and gradually diminishing to an equality with the computed amount of those burthens. He could not in any way agree with his hon. friend, the member for Cumberland,[1] nor with the hon. member for Wiltshire,[2] who had entered into some strange calculations,

---

[1] Mr. Curwen.   [2] Mr. J. Benett.

to show that the agriculturist paid taxes to the amount of 67 per cent. But, on what did the hon. member reckon this per centage? Not on the expense of growing corn, but on the rent. This was a most unwarranted mode of calculation. They had it in evidence before the agricultural committee, that there was some land in England which did not pay above 2*s.* an acre rent; yet, no doubt, as the cultivation of that land was heavy, there were in truth taxes on the producer which did not affect the landlord, and taxes on the landlord which did not affect the producer. If a tax was imposed directly on the production of corn, the grower would remunerate himself, not by a deduction from the landlord's rent, but by getting more from the consumer. And as to general taxes, they pressed alike on all classes; on the labourer who worked at the loom, as well as on the labourer who worked at the plough. He hoped his hon. friend would not withdraw his motion. The greatest good would be done by bringing the question before the House. His hon. friend's speech abounded in excellent principles, which could not fail of producing an effect upon gentlemen in that House, and removing the delusion which prevailed out of doors. He therefore urged his hon. friend to take the sense of the House on this most important question. The object of the approach to a free trade, which he recommended, was to keep prices steady and low. He did not mean such low prices as would not remunerate the grower; for when the manufacturer ate his bread at all cheaper than the price at which the farmer could be remunerated, the greatest injury was done to the general interests of the country.

The House divided on the motion: Ayes, 25; Noes, 78. Ricardo voted for the motion.

MR. MABERLY'S MOTION FOR THE REDUCTION
OF TAXATION

28 *February* 1823

Mr. MABERLY, pursuant to notice [cp. above p. 248], moved for the removal of the exorbitant conditions which, by the Act of 1798, were attached to the redemption and purchase of the land tax; it was reasonable to expect that, once those obstacles were removed, the remaining balance of the tax to the amount of about 1,250,000*l.* would be redeemed, thus cancelling a sum of about 40,000,000*l.* of the three per cents. This would be a substitute for the sinking fund, which could then be applied to relieve the people of seven millions of taxes. The CHANCELLOR OF THE EXCHEQUER opposed the motion.

28 Feb. 1823

Mr. RICARDO thought that the plan which had been proposed by the hon. mover, could by no means be considered as a desirable substitute for the sinking fund. At the same time, it might possess those merits which should induce the House to adopt it. In the manner in which his hon. friend had proposed that plan, he certainly could not acquiesce; for he thought it would fail to accomplish the object which he conceived to be so desirable. It was, indeed, most desirable, that we should diminish the amount of our debt; and to effect that diminution, he did believe it might be available; but, in such case, it must be adopted in a different way from that in which the hon. gentleman had stated it. Its object was to purchase up a certain quantity of the land tax, by the transfer of a certain quantity of stock; and then it went on to propose, that other parties might purchase the tax, in case the proprietor of the land should not choose to do so. If this had been the extent of the plan—if it had gone simply to cancel an amount of stock—if it had left the purchaser no other right but that which a mortgagee possessed in his claim upon the land—if it had allowed the parties to claim of the landlord, without any intervention of the government or its officers, then he would say, that it was certainly calculated to accomplish the great object of diminishing the debt. But if, under this plan, there was to be a receiver-general to receive the amount of the proprietor, and to pay it into the Bank—if there was to be this sort of management and collection created—it would only be substituting one debt for another; and though there might thus be 42,000,000*l.* and upwards, of stock, cancelled, yet he should consider, that they were only creating a new stock in its place, and transferrable in the same manner. An objection had been raised by the chancellor of the exchequer, that did not seem to possess all the weight which that right hon. gentleman attached to it. He had said,—"Would it not be a great hardship to give to a stranger the right of demanding this tax of a land proprietor?" Why, what would be the hardship? The landed proprietor, it was clear, must pay at all events; and was the receiver of the taxes so merciful a gentleman, that the House was to suppose he would exercise his official functions with much more kindness and humanity than the proprietor of the land tax would manifest? He (Mr. R.) very much regretted, that the land tax was not of that description, that it might be extended further; for if those taxes which were applicable to the reduction of the national debt could be so extended, it was quite clear that they might push that most desirable object still nearer to its accomplishment. So far he concurred with his hon. friend, and no further. He could by no means agree with him, that if the land proprietor should wish to purchase, he should have the right; but if he should decline that, then a stranger might purchase; and, failing both, that it should be sold by public auction. How such a purpose was to be accomplished by public auction, he really could not see. Certainly, the result of this plan could not, by any

means, be called a sinking fund. It was totally unconnected
with such a fund. But the right hon. gentleman might say, if
he pleased, "Your plan is a very good one, and I will adopt it,
in addition to my sinking fund." If the plan was a good one,
as he (Mr. R.) undoubtedly considered it, upon the whole,
to be, he thought it might be quite desirable on its own
peculiar grounds; but not as a substitute for the sinking
fund. With respect to the sinking fund, he had already very
frequently said, that he should be willing to vote for a reduction of taxes to the amount of that sinking fund; but he
could not consent to vote any larger reduction than was
equivalent to its absolute amount. It was now universally
agreed, that the definition of such a fund was the surplus of
our income over our expenditure. That surplus, which the
right hon. gentleman estimated at 7,000,000*l.*, he (Mr. R.),
and the country in general he believed, took to be, in fact, no
more than 5,000,000*l.* How had the right hon. gentleman got
the item of 2,000,000*l.* which he made a part of that surplus?
Was it to be obtained in any other way, than by taking it
from the sinking fund itself, or borrowing it in the market?
If it was borrowed in the market, it was only increasing, by
so much, the debt. If it was taken from the sinking fund, it
was by so much a diminution of the assumed surplus. Therefore, he (Mr. R.) could not vote for remitting taxes to the
amount of 7,000,000*l.* He thought, indeed, that if due
economy and retrenchment were observed in every department of our expenditure, it might be very possible to remit
even 7,000,000*l.*, and thus add 2,000,000*l.* to the proposition
of the chancellor of the exchequer. But he greatly feared the
fact would not be so; and he must see another account
brought in by the government, before he could consent to the
remission of the additional 2,000,000*l.* Under the false
notion with which ministers seemed to be impressed about

their surplus of 7,000,000*l.*, it was much to be apprehended, that they would not prove a whit more economical than usual, were the House even to vote the remission of other 2,000,000*l.* They would say, "You only take away our surplus, and therefore there is no necessity for further economy." He hoped the House would pardon him, if he was tedious, but he desired once more to explain what he meant by an efficient sinking fund. An efficient sinking fund, in the opinion of many gentlemen who sat near him, could not exist at the same period that we were increasing our debt. In that position he did not coincide. He thought, for instance, that when Mr. Pitt first established a sinking fund, and although, during a considerable portion of his subsequent life, the country was engaged in foreign wars, by the enormous expenses of which the debt was increased in a far greater proportion than the sinking fund paid it off; yet that, in effect, we then always had a sinking fund. Of every loan that was borrowed to meet those vast expenses, Mr. Pitt provided for the interest, and reserved a fund of one per cent for the extinction. Undoubtedly, an incredible weight was added to the debt by the protracted war that ensued; but, what would have been the situation of the country, had she sooner effected a peace? All those loans which had been borrowed in war time, would have been provided for, and there would have been left an efficient sinking fund. Had this system been adhered to during the whole progress of the war, he (Mr. R.) would have been the last man to raise his voice against the sinking fund. But, what was the fact? In 1813, the late chancellor of the exchequer[1] came down to the House, took 8,000,000*l.* per annum away from the sinking fund, and in the same breath told them, that they were

---

[1] Vansittart; on his Plan of Finance of 1813, see above, IV, 158–9.

paying their debt, that the finances would be placed in the most flourishing condition; and in a short time after the peace, he told them, that they would be in possession of a greater treasure than any other nation of the earth could boast. It was at the very moment that he took away from the sinking fund 8,000,000*l.*, that the late chancellor of the exchequer had made all those splendid promises. But, unfortunately, this was not his only attack on that fund; nay, it was a trifling one, compared to those which he subsequently made upon it. The late chancellor of the exchequer, instead of providing for the annual interest of his loans, suffered compound interest to accrue upon them. Though there was placed, in the hands of commissioners, who most conscientiously and perfectly discharged their duties, a fund of 15,000,000*l.*, he said, "I have, by my expenditure, left you in a situation in which you have a deficiency of 15,000,000*l.* in your finances." Why, where, then, was the sinking fund? Would the chancellor of the exchequer have dared to come to that House, year after year, and have calmly spoken of a deficiency of between 12,000,000*l.* and 15,000,000*l.*, if he had not known all the while, that there was, in reserve, a fund of 15,000,000*l.* which he reckoned upon parliament's permitting him to apply to other purposes than those which it was originally intended to effect? Now he (Mr. R.) contended, that the sinking fund of this day would have the same fate as its predecessors. If it remained, it might go on well enough for a few years; but, should the right hon. gentleman opposite continue in power, he, or if not, then some future chancellor of the exchequer, after coming down to the House, and telling them how thriving a condition this sinking fund was in, would some day inform parliament, that a deficiency of some sort or other was discovered, or that some emergency had arisen, which rendered it necessary to appropriate the whole. The language of his majesty's ministers confirmed these anticipations in a great measure. If, however, they properly considered the matter, they ought to look upon this fund as already appropriated. It was a fund to pay off debt; and surely it was never to be considered as applicable to the expenses of a war; for if it was to pay debt, it could meet no other object. Let the House suppose the case of a private individual: suppose he had an income of 1,000*l.* a-year, and that he found it necessary to borrow 10,000*l.*, for which he agreed to give up to his creditor 500*l.* per annum. Let them suppose his steward to say to him, "If you will live on 400*l.* a year, and give up another 100*l.*, out of your income of 500*l.*, that will enable you, in a certain number of years, to get completely rid of your debt." The party listened to this good advice, lived on 400*l.* a-year, and gave up annually 600*l.* to his steward, in order to pay his creditor. The first year, let it be assumed, that the steward paid the creditor 100*l.* Then the debt would be 9,900*l.*; and therefore the income due to the creditor would be only 495*l.* But the party continuing to pay to his steward 600*l.* per annum, in the next year the steward paid over 105*l.*; and so from year to year the debt was diminished, 600*l.* being still received by the steward. At the end of a certain number of years, the result was this:— That out of a yearly reserve of 600*l.*, half the debt was paid off: only 250*l.* was due to the creditor, and 350*l.* remained in the hands of the steward; his master continuing to live on 400*l.* per annum. At this period, some object offering to the steward, which he thought might be beneficial to the gentleman, or to himself, he borrowed 7,000*l.*, and devoted the whole 350*l.* in his hands, to pay the interest on that sum. What, then, became of this gentleman's sinking fund? Originally he was in debt only 10,000*l.*; now, he found himself indebted, altogether, 12,000*l.*; so that instead of possessing a sinking fund, as he had hoped, he was positively so much more in debt. He considered that the whole mystery of our sinking fund was, in truth, just the same. He did believe, in his conscience, that the amount of the national debt would not have been near so large as it now was, if the sinking fund had been honourably adhered to. He did believe, that such a disastrous result would not have been the case, if Mr. Pitt had continued minister. No: he would have provided—as any other honest or efficient minister would have done—for debts as he contracted them. In time of war even we should have possessed a sinking fund. But, as he despaired of ever seeing such a system followed by any minister in that House —as he despaired of seeing a sinking fund strictly and inviolably sustained—he would give his hearty support to his hon. friend's motion, if he would make his proposed remission of taxes 5,000,000*l.,* instead of 7,000,000*l.* The latter amount seemed rather beyond the mark, and therefore he could not vote for it. With respect to the memorable plan of last year,[1] he hoped the right hon. gentleman was not one of those who could support such an inexplicable mystery. He hoped that the right hon. gentleman would repel the charge of having contributed to such a delusion. If the right hon. gentleman really wished to repeal 2,000,000*l.* of taxes, let him say to the House that the ministers of the crown, wishing to do so, proposed to take them out of the sinking fund. The roundabout statements, and the machinery of acts of parliament, which in recent sessions had been resorted to, were unbecoming the station of the right hon. gentleman, and unworthy of the government of a great and powerful nation.

Mr. BARING 'could not help adverting to what he considered a contradiction in the speech of his hon. friend. His hon. friend said, he was not opposed to the principle of Mr. Pitt's sinking

---

[1] Vansittart's plan for funding the war pensions; see above, p. 160.

fund; but he objected to the preservation of any surplus at all, because he was sure that somebody would take it away: he was afraid that some minister or other would take it away; and, therefore, he was resolved to take it away himself. This reminded him of the Frenchman in some play, who, upon being appealed to by a lady for his advice, as to the best mode of resisting the advances of her admirer, replied, that the best way of resisting temptation was to yield to it at once.' 'He should like to know from the hon. member for Portarlington, how, in a case of emergency, the country could effectively act without a surplus revenue? What would be the situation of the country, when deprived of credit?' Mr. Baring next adverted to the plan for an 'adjustment of property' which the hon. member for Portarlington had suggested; 'he must assert, that however specious in theory, or valid in abstract calculation,' it was 'totally inapplicable to any practical object.'

The motion was negatived.

NATIONAL DEBT REDUCTION BILL

6 *March* 1823

On 3 March the CHANCELLOR OF THE EXCHEQUER moved a series of resolutions recommending the repeal of the old sinking fund acts and the establishment of a new sinking fund of 5,000,000*l.*

On 6 March, on the report of the committee upon the bill to give effect to these resolutions, Mr. MONCK observed that the operation of the sinking fund, though it reduced the capital of the debt, raised the price of stocks, and therefore increased 'the real amount of the debt.' 'The more that was paid, the more we had to pay.' It would be better to apply the surplus revenue to the reduction of taxes. 'In this way, the Americans at the close of the war, having an expenditure of four millions of dollars beyond their revenue, raised small loans, till, in the last year, their revenue had increased so as to enable them to reduce their debt.'

Mr. RICARDO said, it was true that the government of America had borrowed 4,000,000 dollars, and that, by bringing capital from other countries, it had, in fact, improved its resources. It was also true, that the effect of the sinking fund

was at present to raise prices against ourselves. But this was
true of every sinking fund. The question was, had not the
sinking fund reduced the annual charge? It certainly would
do so if correctly applied. A real sinking fund, if properly
appropriated, was a great good. To a fictitious sinking fund
he had many objections. But there was a great difference
between the two. A real sinking fund applied to pay off the
debt, would raise the price of stocks, and enable us to borrow
on better terms. Many members had no hopes that a real
sinking fund would be preserved. They, therefore, objected
to grant a sum for a purpose, the beneficial effects of which
they were never likely to see. His hon. friend, the member
for Taunton,[1] had facetiously observed, that because he (Mr.
R.) thought ministers were going to rob the sinking fund, he
would willingly take it away himself.[2] It was, he thought,
good policy, when his purse was in danger, rather to spend
the money himself than allow it to be taken from him. He
did not, he confessed, think the national purse safe in the
hands of ministers. It was too great a temptation to entrust
them with. What he wanted was a real sinking fund, and
therefore he supported the present as far as it was real. But
there was every reason to believe it would become fictitious;
for every sinking fund had, in its origin, been real, but had
all been turned into fictitious funds. As to the Annuity bill of
last year,[3] he hoped the whole of it would be repealed, and
the amount be transferred to the sinking fund. It had been
estimated that 2,000,000*l.* of those annuities would die off
annually. Let this sum be applied to the purposes of the
sinking fund. The hon. member for Taunton had, on a
former evening,[4] been severe on him, giving him credit for
the ability of his calculations, but denying that he looked

[1] Mr. Baring.
[2] See above, p. 265–6.
[3] See above, p. 160.
[4] See above, p. 266.

sufficiently at their political and moral consequences. Now, he claimed the merit of extent in the scope of his views beyond the hon. member. He felt deep alarm at the heavy amount of the debt, and at the want of proper means to lighten it. His hon. friend, with his enlarged views, wished for a sinking fund, not to pay off the debt, but to furnish ministers with the means of going to war, in cases of extremity. But, if this fund were to be so appropriated, how was the debt to be paid off? He would tell his hon. friend, if no means were taken to pay it off, that he was sleeping on a volcano. He thought a national debt of 800 millions a very serious evil; and he thought so from the heart-burnings which were occasioned by the taxes levied to pay it, which in one year affected one interest, and the next year another interest. Taxation pressed on every interest; and did he not propose to benefit mankind when he said we ought to endeavour to get rid of the debt? By doing this, should we not get rid of the expense of collecting taxes? Should we not get rid of the immorality of smuggling, and of the excise laws? By getting rid of smuggling, should we not benefit trade? For all the profit of the smuggler was a tax on the whole community. Neither would it be a trifling benefit, in a constitutional point of view, that it would deprive ministers of a great deal of patronage. It would also confer great benefits on our commerce, by putting it in a natural state. At present, from the duties and restrictions of customs and excise, it was in a most unnatural state. Was this legislating for men, or for stocks and stones? He had before stated, that he thought a great effort should be made to get rid of the debt; and he had mentioned a plan which he thought should be adopted. The hon. and learned member for Winchelsea[1] had opposed his plan; and had said, that it would throw the

[1] Mr. Brougham; see above, p. 40–1.

whole land of the country into the hands of pettifogging attorneys; but of this there was no danger. Parliament might interfere, and give secure titles to the land which was disposed of, without the interference of pettifogging attorneys. Let it not be said, that he was not aware of the difficult situation in which the country stood. Nothing else could have induced him to recommend the measure. He could be quite easy in recommending the measure of a sinking fund, if they had a different kind of parliament—one that moved in more direct sympathy with the people. He confessed his fear of the present parliament, and its disposition to ministerial compliance. His hon. friend[1] asked, in case of applying the sinking fund, what they were to do should a new war break out? If that was the real view, they should not call it a sinking fund. They might call it a fund for ministers to divert to particular purposes, but not a sinking fund. But, suppose a new war to break out, no such thing as a sinking fund ever having been heard of—was his hon. friend ready to vote a fund prospectively to be at the disposal of ministers, in that event? Let him say yes, and they would understand each other.[2]

---

[1] Mr. Baring; see p. 266.

[2] The *Morning Chronicle* reports in addition: 'It was said that the Sinking Fund lowers the rate of interest, and benefited the landowner by enabling him to borrow at an easier rate. But he thought the Gallant Officer [Colonel Wood] erroneous in this view. It was quite possible that the Three per Cents. might be as high as 97, and yet money in all other transactions might be as high as 5 or 6 per cent. The rate of interest in the community at large was not affected by the price of any particular kind of stock, but the price of that stock depended on the general rate of interest. The general rate of interest might be the cause of a certain price of stock, but could never be the effect. Let the House only consider what a small proportion any one stock bore to the whole money transactions of the community. Let them also consider that the price of this stock must at all times depend on the rate of profit in agricultural and commercial transactions, and they must be convinced that the principles for which the Gallant Officer contended did not regulate the rate of interest.'

6 March 1823   Mr. BARING said, 'that, with every respect which he might have for his hon. friend's talents and the ingenuity which marked the speech which he had just made, he must be allowed to say he had never listened to one which led to such—(not to say absurd— that term would savour of want of courtesy), but so singular a conclusion. To begin with the plan of paying off a part of the debt, by a new disposition of the property of the country, he must be allowed to say, that it was the plan of a man who might calculate well and read deeply, but who had not studied mankind. It was ingenious in theory, and obvious enough; but not very sound for practice. He did not pretend to any thing like the reach of intellect possessed by his hon. friend, but he thought his hon. friend sometimes over-reached himself, and lost sight of man, and of all practical conclusions.'

11 March 1823

11 March 1823   On the report stage, Mr. GRENFELL said that 'many plans had been devised to pay off, by one great effort, the national debt, and the crotchet of his hon. friend (Mr. Ricardo) for accomplishing that great object by a general contribution from all the property of the country, was the wildest of them all.' Sir H. PARNELL expounded his plan for applying the sinking fund so as to replace the perpetual annuities by long annuities determinable in a fixed number of years.[1]

Mr. RICARDO highly approved of his hon. friend's plan, which, by taking the sinking fund out of the hands of ministers, would do away his great objection to it; namely, its liability to be perverted from the purpose for which it was originally intended. His hon. friend's proposition of converting what were at present permanent into determinable annuities, appeared to him to be deserving the serious attention of the House; and he must say, that he did not think his hon. friend did justice to his own plan, in stating, that it would liquidate the existing debt in 45 years; for the calcula-

---

[1] Parnell's plan is described by Ricardo below, IX, 175.

tion on which he had proceeded was made when the 3 per cents were only at 80. The House might easily conceive how beneficially public credit would be affected, if a real sinking fund were thus continually operating over the whole extent of the debt. From the adoption of such a plan, ministers, in the event of any occurrence requiring an increased expenditure, would not, as heretofore, be enabled to despoil a fund, which ought to be sacredly appropriated to another purpose; but must come down to parliament, and otherwise provide for the public exigencies. While he was on his legs, he would say a few words on what an hon. friend had been pleased to call his "crotchet" for reducing the national debt by a general contribution of capital. His (Mr. R.'s) proposition would merely carry further the principle of the income tax. His hon. friend was quite deceived, if he supposed that he ever contemplated the possibility of effecting the object he had described at once. On the contrary, the operation might be extended by numerous instalments over a period of two, three, six or twelve months. And when the immense benefits which would result from its adoption were considered, he could not think it so Utopian a scheme as his hon. friend seemed to imagine it to be.

14 *March* 1823

On the second reading (13 March) the CHANCELLOR OF THE EXCHEQUER said that 'there was only a surplus of 3,000,000*l*.', but if the plan of spreading the war pensions over 45 years was carried out, there would remain a clear surplus of 5,000,000*l*. 'That appeared to him a real *bonâ fide* surplus, applicable to the reduction of the debt. It was that surplus which, by the bill, it was proposed so to apply. In so doing there was no increase whatever made of the unfunded debt. Nor was there any mystery—any of what was familiarly called hocus pocus.'

On the third reading (14 March) Mr. H. G. BENNET moved as
an amendment that it be postponed six months. Mr. BARING intimated that if Mr. Bennet's motion was negatived, he would
move that the sinking fund be limited to three millions. With
respect to the plan of Sir H. Parnell 'he thought it would not
have been a bad one, if it had been applied to the reduction of
the 5 per cents last year; but it could not be applied to the 3 per
cents without the consent of the holders of stock; which could
not be well calculated upon, because there would be a difficulty
of selling the new stock in the market.'

Mr. RICARDO said, that he felt great delight at the ad-
missions which had at length been made, as to the real
amount of the sinking fund now in the exchequer. That
pleasure, however, was somewhat qualified, by finding that
the House was now called upon to augment this real sum of
three millions to the sum of five millions. The chancellor of
the exchequer, a few evenings ago, had said, that he did not
think there was any hocus pocus in his plan. The House,
after that declaration, could scarcely expect to be called on to
vote that there was at present a surplus of five millions. An
act of parliament could not create a surplus where it was not.
As to the objection which had been made against the plan of
the hon. baronet, that it might not be agreed to by the
holders of the 3 per cents, it had much weight. The plan of
the hon. baronet did not presume any such consent. He only
proposed, that a trial should be made whether or not the
public would consent to it. He proposed to convert a certain
sum, say 50,000,000*l.* from 3 per cents to 4 per cents. Why
should not ministers try the experiment? The public opinion
would thereby be ascertained. They did not want grounds for
estimating the probable event of that plan. There were then
long annuities in the market, of which 37 years remained un-
expired. Taking them at 4 per cent at 19 years purchase, they
would be worth 75 or 76. If ministers, therefore, could go to
market to sell the 4 per cent annuities at 37 years for 76, they

might buy 100*l.* three per cents at less than 76. It was said, 14 March 1823 that we had reduced 24 million of debt since 1816. Any one would imagine, in the way this was put, that the reduction was the effect of the sinking fund. It was no such thing. The reduction was occasioned by changing one kind of stock into another. We thus lessened the capital, but we did not diminish the charge; except to a very trifling amount. He would prefer being without any sinking fund, to one upon the plan now proposed; and he was sure, that if we were, public credit would not suffer. He would therefore support the amendment,[1] and if that were negatived, then he would support the proposition of his hon. friend (Mr. Baring.)

The House divided on Mr. Bennet's amendment: Ayes, 59; Noes, 109. The House again divided on Mr. Baring's amendment: Ayes, 72; Noes, 100. The bill was then passed.

MERCHANT VESSELS
APPRENTICESHIP BILL

13 *March* 1823

Mr. HUSKISSON moved for leave to bring in a bill enacting that 13 March 1823 every merchant vessel should have a number of apprentices in proportion to her tonnage.

Mr. RICARDO wished to know whether the sailors were friendly to the measure. He had no doubt that their employers were so; because they would be enabled to lower the rate of wages by increasing the number of apprentices. He thought the navy would not receive that benefit from it, which

---

[1] Although *Hansard* gives the list of the minority in the division on this amendment, Ricardo is not included. The list of the following division is not given.

seemed to be anticipated. Our sailors would seek employment in the merchant service of other countries, if the rate of wages was unduly lowered in their own. Should that be the case, where would gentlemen find that nursery for the navy, of which they now talked so largely?

[See further, p. 276.]

MUTINY BILL—FOREIGN RELATIONS

18 *March* 1823

In the course of the debate Colonel DAVIES referring to the meeting recently held in support of Spain[1] said that it was 'a cruel mockery' to inform them that they wished them success; and then to talk of neutrality.

Mr. RICARDO protested against the inference, with respect to those who had attended the dinner given to the Spanish minister. He felt a deep sympathy with the Spanish people; but he was very far from intending, by his attendance at that meeting, to pledge himself to engage the nation in war. He had no hesitation in declaring his opinion, that it would be wise in this country to keep out of the war. At any rate, the House ought to hear what ministers had to say, before it came to a decision on the subject. Right or wrong, it was not fair to condemn them unheard.

[1] The public dinner given on 7 March to the Spanish and Portuguese ambassadors at the City of London Tavern; Ricardo was present. (*Morning Chronicle,* 8 March 1823.)

COAL DUTIES[1]

21 March 1823

A petition was presented from owners of Collieries at Forest
Dean, complaining of the operation of the Coastwise Duty on
Coal, and praying for relief.

Mr. RICARDO said, that this was one of the many cases in
which industry was cramped by a restrictive system of
taxation. He understood that Forest Dean was as well able
as any place in its vicinity to supply coals, were it not that
it was fettered with duties, with a view to give a preference
to more favoured places. They were daily receiving petitions
upon this subject, and he was glad to find that His Majesty's
Ministers at length acknowledged the evils of the system.
He hoped they would turn their attention, not only to this,
but the many other inconveniences which arose out of the
restrictive system, as the country was entitled to enjoy every
benefit which could be derived from its capital and industry.

WAREHOUSING BILL

21 March 1823

Mr. WALLACE introduced a measure to permit foreign manufactures and produce to be deposited in British warehouses and
taken out for exportation without payment of duty [cp. above,
p. 220].

Mr. RICARDO was of opinion, that the bill was founded on
a sound and judicious principle, and one which ought to
prevail throughout our commercial code. The country was

[1] This debate is not mentioned   here reprinted from the *Morning*
in *Hansard.* Ricardo's speech is   *Chronicle.*

greatly indebted to the right hon. gentleman for his efforts to liberalize the system of trade. It was impossible to make a law which would not interfere with the interests of some classes; but the one before the House, while it was calculated to advance the public welfare, interfered as little as possible with particular interests.

On 2 April the bill was passed.

MERCHANT VESSELS
APPRENTICESHIP BILL

24 *March* 1823

24 March 1823   The report of this bill [cp. above, p. 273] being brought up,

Mr. RICARDO said, he objected altogether to the principle of the bill. He thought it was a maxim, that no person ought to be controlled in his own arrangements, unless such control was rendered necessary by paramount political circumstances. Now, no such necessity could be shown in support of this bill. In his opinion, it would not be more unjust to enact a law, that every surgeon should take a certain number of apprentices, to encourage the progress of surgical science, than it would be to pass this bill, rendering it imperative on the masters of merchant vessels to take a given number of apprentices, in order to encourage the increase of efficient seamen. He denied that this bill would cause an addition of one seaman to the number now in the service. So long as there was employment for seamen, there would be encouragement enough for them; and when there was not, those who were now here, would resort to foreign countries for employ. The only effect of the bill would be, to reduce the wages of seamen; and that alone would render it objectionable. He would move, to leave out from the word "repealed," to the end of the bill, his object being, to remove the compulsory condition for taking a certain number of apprentices from the bill.

The House divided: for Ricardo's amendment, 6; against it, 85.

List of the Minority

Bennet, hon. H. G.	Sykes, D.	TELLERS
Grenfell, Pascoe	Whitmore, W. W.	Ricardo, D.
Smith, Robert	Wyvill, M.	Hume, J.

[See further, p. 282.]

PETITION FROM MARY ANN CARLILE
FOR RELEASE FROM IMPRISONMENT

26 *March* 1823

Mr. HUME presented a petition from Mary Ann Carlile, shopwoman of her brother Richard Carlile; she had been prosecuted by the Society for the Suppression of Vice for selling a copy of *An Appendix to the Theological Works of Thomas Paine* and had been sentenced for blasphemous libel to a year's imprisonment and a fine of 500*l.* or to be imprisoned till that fine was paid. The year of her imprisonment had expired, but she was kept in gaol from her inability to pay the fine.

Mr. RICARDO trusted that the House would excuse him if he ventured to say a few words upon this petition. The hon. and learned gentleman who had just sat down,[1] appeared to conceive, that Mary Ann Carlile would have been entitled to some lenity, had she expressed contrition for her past offences, or had she stated any change to have taken place in her religious sentiments. Now, they were bound in common justice, to consider that the petitioner was expressing her own sentiments in the libel of which she had been found guilty.

[1] The Attorney General.

The demand, therefore, of the attorney-general was, that she must acknowledge that to be right, which she conscientiously believed to be wrong, before she could entitle herself to any lenity; or, in other words, that she must commit an act of the most shameless duplicity, in order to become a proper object for the mercy of the crown. While upon that subject, he must be permitted to find fault with a rule that prevailed in the courts of justice. A witness, before he was examined, was asked whether he believed in a future state: if he replied that he did not, his oath could not be taken. Supposing that an individual did not believe in a future state, and by replying that he did not, showed that he was an honest man, he was put aside as an incompetent witness; whereas, if he belied his belief, and did not act the part of an honest man, he was considered as a witness worthy of credit. He contended, that the hon. member for Devonshire[1] had by no means answered the case which his hon. friend had made out. His hon. friend had stated, that these prosecutions had aggravated the very evil which they were instituted to check. The hon. baronet asserted, that the fact was not so—and how did he prove it? Why, he read a passage which proved that the sale continued in spite of his prosecutions, and thus confirmed the very argument which he had intended to refute. Besides, it appeared to him, that the hon. baronet, in reading the opinions of which he complained so loudly, had not taken a wise course, to keep them from the knowledge of the public. He fully agreed with his hon. friend that the prosecutions of the Society for the Suppression of Vice had done much mischief. Blasphemy was an offence which it was quite impossible to define. Nobody, in committing it, was aware of what he was offending against. It was one thing in this

[1] Sir T. D. Acland, who had defended the Society for the Suppression of Vice against Hume's attack.

country, and another thing in France; indeed, that which was blasphemy here, was not blasphemy there, and *vice versâ.* Indeed, as the law was now laid down, the mere disputing the truths of Christianity was an offence; and, therefore, the moment it was shown that the individual had sold a work reflecting upon them, that moment he stood convicted. If he said that he believed in what he wrote or sold, and attempted to state the grounds on which he rested his belief, he was told immediately he was aggravating his original offence by repeating it; and being thus precluded from making a defence, and bound as it were hand and foot, was delivered over to the vengeance of the prosecutor. The attorney-general found great fault with his hon. friend for saying, that the jury would never have returned a verdict of guilty against Mary Ann Carlile if they could have anticipated the punishment that awaited her; and had argued, that the doctrines which such a sentence inculcated was most dangerous to the interests of public morality and justice. Now he (Mr. Ricardo) fully agreed in all that his hon. friend had said upon that subject; and so far from the doctrine of his hon. friend being new or unheard of, it was a doctrine that was perpetually influencing the conduct of juries. Juries were constantly taking into their consideration the consequences that were likely to follow from their verdicts. If not, why were they so often finding individuals guilty of stealing property under the value of 40s. when every man was convinced that the property was worth much more? Why, but because they knew that, if they did not return such a verdict, a punishment would be inflicted incompatible with the spirit of the times? In forgeries, too, would any man deny, that the punishment which followed on conviction did not often come within the contemplation of the jury? [Hear hear!] He should therefore dismiss the observations of the attorney-general, without any further remark. He must now inform the House, that after a long and attentive consideration of the question, he had made up his mind that prosecutions ought never to be instituted for religious opinions. All religious opinions, however absurd and extravagant, might be conscientiously believed by some individuals. Why, then, was one man to set up his ideas on the subject as the criterion from which no other was to be allowed to differ with impunity? Why was one man to be considered infallible, and all his fellow men as frail and erring creatures? Such a doctrine ought not to be tolerated: it savoured too much of the Inquisition to be received as genuine in a free country like England. A fair and free discussion ought to be allowed on all religious topics. If the arguments advanced upon them were incorrect and blasphemous, surely they might be put down by sound argument and good reasoning, without the intervention of force and punishment. He was convinced that if it had not been for the indiscreet conduct of certain societies in prosecuting Mr. Carlile and his connexions, that family would never have acquired the notoriety by which it was at present distinguished.[1]

---

[1] Wilberforce, who spoke later, said of Ricardo's speech that 'the hon. member for Portarlington seemed to carry into more weighty matters those principles of free trade which he had so successfully expounded'. And, after this debate, he made an entry in his diary which, (despite his editors' caution) it is clear, referred to Ricardo: 'I had hoped that——had become a Christian; I see now that he has only ceased to be a Jew.' (*The Life of William Wilberforce,* by his sons, 1838, vol. v, p. 173.)

CROWN DEBTORS—
CONTEMPT OF COURT

10 *April* 1823

Mr. HUME moved for returns of the numbers of persons con- fined as Crown debtors and for contempt of Court.

Mr. RICARDO objected to the imposition of a fine by a judge, afterwards to be remitted by a secretary of state. A judge might as well pass but one sentence—say death—for all crimes, and leave the government to inflict the quantity of chastisement it thought fit. The judge who tried the case was the fit person to decide what penalty the offender should endure[1].

MILITARY AND NAVAL PENSIONS BILL

18 *April* 1823

On 24 March 1823 the CHANCELLOR OF THE EXCHEQUER intro- duced a bill to amend the act of the previous session [see above, p. 191] so as to allow the trustees to sell their annuity for a term of years and not merely from year to year, the Bank of England having now agreed to receive part of the fixed annuity and to pay the pensions for five and a quarter years.

On the third reading of this bill, on 18 April, Sir J. NEWPORT contended, 'that this bargain with the Bank was a direct violation of the statute of William and Mary which prevented the Bank from becoming a dealer and jobber in public securities.'

Mr. RICARDO did not blame the Bank directors for making as advantageous a bargain as possible for their constituents. It was, however, an extremely improvident one for the

---

[1] The *Courier's* report continues 'and a Judge was bound to consider deeply, before he imposed a fine, the means which a defendant might have of discharging it'.

country. He thought that there was also a constitutional objection to the contract, founded on the nature of the charter of the Bank, and the manner in which the capital was made available to the public. It seemed to him highly impolitic, that the Bank should be allowed to make speculations in the funds. At all events, ministers ought to have delayed the conclusion of the bargain, until they had laid the papers regarding the late negotiations upon the table: had they so waited, the bargain might have been more favourable to the public. He wished to know whether the Bank was to be allowed to charge for the management of this transaction, as well as for the management of the public debt.

Mr. HUSKISSON answered, 'that the Bank was to be allowed nothing beyond the terms of the contract which were before the House. He contended, that the bargain was advantageous for the public, and that the Bank were permitted to deal in public securities.'

The bill was then passed.

MERCHANT VESSELS
APPRENTICESHIP BILL

18 *April* 1823

On this bill [cp. above, p. 276] being brought in for the third reading,

Mr. RICARDO opposed the measure, as imposing injurious restrictions on a particular trade, and interfering with the private rights of the individuals connected with that trade. The right hon. gentleman opposite was bound to show, that there were some circumstances in this particular trade which ought to take it out of the general rule. He had, however, not only failed to do this, but he had failed to prove that the measure would afford any protection to private seamen. He should therefore move as an amendment, "That the bill be read a third time that day six months."

Mr. HUSKISSON said, 'the measure had given universal satisfaction to the ship-owners, and he believed there was scarcely a man in the House, except the hon. member (Mr. Ricardo) who was not satisfied of its utility.'

Mr. Ricardo withdrew his amendment; and the bill was read a third time and passed.

LORD JOHN RUSSELL'S MOTION FOR A REFORM OF PARLIAMENT

24 *April* 1823

Lord JOHN RUSSELL moved 'that the present state of the representation of the people in parliament requires the most serious consideration of this House.'

Mr. RICARDO said, that the arguments of the hon. gentleman who had just sat down[1] had been too often repeated, and too often refuted, to have any weight with him on the present occasion. He would not admit that conclusions hostile to the cause of reform could be drawn from the practices of past ages; because he denied that the present generation ought to be bound down by all that had been done by their ancestors. He thought the present generation possessed not only as much wisdom as any of those which had preceded it, but a great deal more. The simple question for them to determine was, whether they would not purify the House, when it was notorious that it could not be considered, in the fair sense of the words, to represent the people? He perfectly agreed with all that his noble friend who made the present motion had said, with reference to the state and condition of the House. He concurred with him in

[1] Sir Edward Hyde East.

every one of his representations; but he did not think the remedy he had prescribed was the most adviseable for the purposes they both wished to accomplish. The question of reform was naturally divided into three considerations. First, the extension of the suffrage; secondly, the mode of election; and thirdly, the duration of parliaments. As to extension of the suffrage, important as he felt that topic to be, and convinced as he was that it ought to be extended much beyond its present limits, still the other two points appeared to him to be of deeper interest. In the arrangement of the suffrages, the whole of the people might be represented, and yet the House might be composed of persons whose elections had been procured by improper means. It was for this reason that he was compelled to dissent from his noble friend's proposal for transferring a portion of the representatives from close boroughs to extensive counties. He thought the whole system of election which prevailed at present was illegal. Of what use was it that the power of choosing its representatives should be given to the people, unless the free exercise of that right were also secured to them? He contended, that so long as the influence of the aristocracy possessed, as it did now, the means of biassing the votes of the people, this House could not be a fair representation of that people. Let it not be supposed, that he wished to deprive the aristocracy of that just influence which it derived from its wealth and respectability; but he thought that it became most pernicious, when it was exercised for the purpose of influencing elections. Of its practical evil, every person's own knowledge would furnish many and ample proofs. How could it be expected, that a man whose means of procuring a livelihood depended mainly upon the patronage and support of those who were in a more elevated rank—how could it be expected, for instance, that the inferior class of tradesmen—should withstand the threats and terrors which might be put into execution, to prevent them from voting according to their conscience? To look for this would be to call upon small freeholders for a degree of severe virtue which had no corresponding example in the higher ranks of society. There was but one method of obviating these difficulties; which was by altering the mode of election, and adopting the ballot instead of open votes. If this were done, they would have a house of commons which would fairly represent the people.—The other point which he wished to mention to the House was the necessity of more frequent election. And this he thought was indisputable; because it was the ready means of ensuring the attention of the House uniformly to the interests of the people.—There was another point in which he must dissent from the opinion of his noble friend. His noble friend had argued that in the event of any parliamentary reform, the House ought to take into their consideration what were called the vested rights of individuals in boroughs. Now, this really appeared to him to be a most extraordinary proposition. Could those pretended rights be considered in the light of property? Could any thing be more contrary to justice than to propose any compensation for such assumed property? Had not the people a right to be well governed? And was it to be maintained, that, because a certain set of persons had, for corrupt purposes, enjoyed the privilege for many years of preventing the people from being well governed, they should, therefore, be compensated for the loss of a privilege so unjustifiable.—The right honourable secretary (Mr. Canning) had, upon a former occasion,[1]

[1] On Lord John Russell's motion for a reform of parliament, 25 April 1822 (*Hansard*, N.S., VII, 106 ff.). Subsequent allusions are to the same speech.

stated, that if the House of Commons should fairly represent the people, it would become too powerful for the safety of the Crown and the House of Lords. This argument, he (Mr R.) contended, did not belong to the question; for it was impossible that a House of Commons fairly constituted should not consult their own interests. If, therefore, such a House should propose to dismiss the Crown and the House of Lords, it would be because they were unnecessary to the good government of the country. The right hon. gentleman must, therefore, abandon this argument, or confess, that a virtuous House of Commons would be driven to dismiss the Crown and the House of Lords.—It had also been contended, that if the general principle of his noble friend's motion were acceded to, a hundred different plans of reform would start up, and that it would be impossible to secure any thing like unanimity on the subject. That was not his opinion. He, for one, was for no alteration in the constitution of the House of Commons, unless that alteration should render it fully and fairly a representation of the people; and he was convinced that that was the object which all the friends of parliamentary reform had in view. The only difference between his noble friend and himself was, that he did not think the plan proposed by his noble friend would accomplish that object. He believed that if that plan were adopted, the House would continue to be what it now was—the representative of the aristocracy of the country, and of the aristocracy only. County elections were, in his opinion, conducted on no better principles than borough elections; and he repeated his conviction, that unless the system of ballot were resorted to, it would be in vain to attempt any reform at all of parliament.—The right hon. secretary opposite[1] had argued, when the question was last under con-

[1] Mr. Canning.

sideration, that the House of Commons, as at present constituted, operated as a check upon the Crown, and a balance
of the power of the other House of Parliament. That he
denied. To make such a proposition good, it must be first
shown that the House of Commons fairly represented the
people; otherwise, it was a farce and a mockery to say, that it
operated as a check upon the Crown and a balance of the
power of the other House of Parliament. His opinion was,
that at present the government of this country was a compromise between the aristocracy and the Crown. Instead of
the House of Commons, as at present constituted, being a
check upon the people, it was itself frequently checked by
public opinion. But, was that a convenient operation? Was
it convenient that county and other public meetings should
perpetually be called, for the purpose of affording a check to
the proceedings of the House of Commons? Would it not be
much better that the House should really represent the
people—that it should be the organ of public opinion?—
The right hon. gentleman, on the occasion to which he had
already alluded, had triumphantly asked, to what period of
our history the reformers would refer as affording the best
view of the state of the House of Commons? For himself,
he would answer, to none. He believed the people never had
been better represented. But, were we never to have a good
House of Commons, because we never had had a good one?
The people at large now possessed so much more information than they ever before possessed, that they were entitled
to be better represented in parliament than they had ever
before been.—The right hon. gentleman opposite had
allowed, that the proposition might be a beneficial one, but
that it was not the constitution under which we were born.
The same argument might be used to perpetuate every
abuse and every evil. It might be said with respect to Ire-

land, was the present state of things to be continued in Ireland, because it was the constitution under which the Irish were born? To hear the right hon. gentleman, it would be supposed that the friends of reform were proposing the establishment of a republic. But that was a gratuitous assumption: it was his conclusion, not theirs. The demands of the people might be easily satisfied. They asked only for that which was perfectly reasonable—that they might have a voice in the public councils, and the power of restraining the expenditure of their own money.—He by no means denied the assertion of the right hon. gentleman, that the aggregate of the House of Commons contained as much intellectual ability and moral integrity as ever existed in any similar assembly in the whole world. But then it must be recollected, that all men, in all situations, acted under the influence of motives. He was persuaded that the conduct of the very same gentlemen by whom he was then surrounded, if they were really chosen by the people, and were frequently returned to the people that their merits might be re-considered, would be extremely different from that which it was at present. Mr. Pitt, when he was the friend of parliamentary reform, had said, that it was impossible for an honest man to be minister of this country with such a House of Commons. He was also of that opinion. He did not say, that the ministers did not mean to act honestly; but they were obliged to consult men, and to pursue measures, opposed to the interests of the people. However they might be inclined, they could not do otherwise; feeling that, owing to the peculiar constitution of the House, they would be turned out in a week if they should venture to act honestly. That the people were competent to the task of electing their representatives, the experience of this and of every other country conclusively showed. The enlightened Montesquieu had said, "Could we doubt the natural capacity of the people to discern real merit, it would only be necessary to cast our eyes upon the continued series of surprising elections which were made by the Athenians and the Romans, which undoubtedly no one could attribute to hazard. It is well known that although at Rome the people possessed the right of electing the plebeians to public offices, they never chose to exercise that power; and that although at Athens, by the law of Aristides, they were allowed to select the magistrates from every rank of the state, yet the common people, says Xenophon, never petitioned for such employment as could possibly interfere with their safety or their glory."[1] These instances might serve to show, that instead of selecting demagogues and disturbers of the public peace, as was unjustly apprehended, the people, if left to the unrestricted exercise of their choice, would act wisely and prudently.

Mr. MARTIN, of Galway, opposing the motion said: 'His honourable friend and countryman, the member for Portarlington—(Loud laughter and cries of "No"); he begged pardon, he was sorry he had called the honourable gentleman his countryman, for he was informed he had never set foot in Ireland. That honourable gentleman had talked gravely against the influence of the aristocracy, yet, notwithstanding, he did not believe he could himself mention one of his own constituents, although they did not amount to more than twelve in all; and it was equally certain, that the honourable gentleman was either returned by that very aristocracy, whose influence he so loudly deprecated, or by an interest quite equivalent, and not less cogent.'[2]

The House divided on the motion: Ayes, 169; Noes, 280. Ricardo was one of the tellers for the minority.

---

[1] *Esprit des lois,* Livre II, ch. 11.
[2] Martin's speech is quoted from the report in the *Edinburgh Annual Register for 1823,* which is fuller than that in *Hansard.*

SCOTCH LINEN LAWS[1]

7 *May* 1823

Mr. RICARDO, in presenting a Petition from the Merchants and Manufacturers of the Burgh of Arbroath against the present regulation, which imposes a stamp, and inflicts a tax upon the manufacture of that article, stated, that in the opinion of the Petitioners, an opinion in which he concurred, this stamping afforded no security whatever as to the quality of the cloth, but had, in fact, rather an opposite tendency, being thus a severe and vexatious burthen upon the manufacturer, without the least advantage to the consumer or the revenue. As such, it ought no longer to be allowed to fetter the trade. He felt great pleasure in stating that the Board of Trade had taken the same view of the subject, and that the President of that Board was to bring in a Bill for the regulation of it, which he (Mr. Ricardo) hoped would meet with no opposition.

Mr. RICARDO then presented a Petition from the Spinners of Linen Yarn in the neighbourhood of Arbroath, praying that they might be relieved from that vexatious part of the Linen Laws which subjects their hanks to seizure, even though it be the full weight stipulated, if one of the hanks either want a few threads, or have a few threads too many; casualties which, in the making up of yarn spun by machinery, cannot possibly be always avoided.

[1] Neither of these two petitions is mentioned in *Hansard*. Ricardo's speeches are here reprinted from the report in the *Morning Chronicle*.

TALLOW[1]

7 *May* 1823

Mr. CURWEN presented a Petition from the Butchers praying
for the imposition of a duty on foreign tallow.

Mr. RICARDO was not exactly aware of the nature of the measure which the Hon. Gentleman had in contemplation; but if it was to be similar to that of last year,[2] he had no hesitation in saying, that the remedy would have no other effect than the imposing of a heavy burthen upon the people of this country without any advantage to the revenue; and therefore he hoped that the House would deal with it as before.

Sir T. LETHBRIDGE complained that British farmers could not compete with the prices of tallow imported from Russia.

Mr. RICARDO characterised this as one of the measures which aimed at putting money into the hands of the landed interest by taking it out of the pockets of the rest of the people. The landed interest had already too many regulations in their favour. For instance, the commercial interest had to pay five per cent. upon all property transferred upon the death of the owner; and this was not required of the landed interest.

[1] This debate is not mentioned in *Hansard*. Ricardo's speeches are here reprinted from the report in the *Morning Chronicle*.

[2] See above, p. 146.

SPITALFIELDS SILK MANUFACTURE
ACTS—PETITION FOR THE
REPEAL THEREOF

9 *May* 1823

9 May 1823   Mr. T. WILSON presented a petition from the silk-manufacturers of London against the Spitalfields Acts (which empowered the magistrates to fix the wages of the journeymen silk-manufacturers).

Mr. RICARDO could not help expressing his astonishment that, in the year 1823, those acts should be existing and in force. They were not merely an interference with the freedom of trade, but they cramped the freedom of labour itself. Such was their operation, that a man who was disposed to embark in the trade could not employ his capital in it in London; and, as it might be inconvenient, in many instances to carry that capital out of London, the trade was necessarily cramped and fettered.

Mr. HUSKISSON 'fully agreed in the propriety of repealing the acts' and intimated that he would bring in a bill to that effect.

[See further, p. 295.]

LAW OF PRINCIPAL AND FACTOR—
PETITION FOR AN ALTERATION
THEREOF

12 *May* 1823

12 May 1823   Mr. J. SMITH presented a petition from the merchants and bankers of London, praying for an alteration in the existing law of lien upon goods sent on foreign ventures. Mr. BARING said, that 'the great inconvenience felt from the present system was, that money could not be raised by the hypothecation of goods,

because it was not known to whom they belonged.... If money were remitted, the possession passed from the hands of the principal to the agent, and no lien was created; the same freedom was sought to be established for the circulation of merchandise.'

Mr. RICARDO[1] said, he would put the case in this way: suppose an individual employed him as an agent, to dispose of goods, and that he was dishonestly inclined, and defrauded his principal; in that case, who ought to be the loser, the man who said, "I will not pay a single penny without the goods are delivered to me;" or the man who did not make any inquiry, but lent his money upon mere representations? It was not desirable that either party should lose; but one must suffer, and the sufferer ought to be the individual who did not use proper caution.

On 15 May a select committee was appointed to enquire into the question: Ricardo was a member of the committee.

---

[1] The *Morning Chronicle* gives a fuller report of this speech: 'Mr. RICARDO said he would suppose a case. Suppose a foreign merchant, who knew nothing of him, were to consign goods to him as an agent, and suppose for a moment, that he (Mr. Ricardo) were a dishonest man [a laugh], and, having without authority from his principal deposited those goods as a security for an advance from a banker, were to disappear, —according to the existing law the banker would lose his money. Now, in point of justice, which of the parties ought first to suffer —the banker who had the precaution to take the goods as a security, or the foreign merchant who had trusted him (Mr. Ricardo) as his agent without proper precaution? It was certainly unjust that either party should suffer; but, if either, surely it ought to be the man who had not used proper precaution. It had been said that the person who lent the money ought to ask the person to whom he lent it whether he was an agent, or the principal? A very good observation, if the truth could be got; but who did not know the difficulty of obtaining it.'

IMPORTATION OF TALLOW—PETITION
FOR AN ADDITIONAL DUTY ON

12 *May* 1823

Sir T. LETHBRIDGE presented a petition from the butchers of Leadenhall-market, complaining of the glut of Russian tallow in the market, and praying for a further import duty on that article. He said, 'that the duty on Russian tallow would fall on the Russian merchant, and not on the English consumer.'

Mr. RICARDO observed, that the principle advocated by the hon. baronet might be applied to every foreign commodity. As the hon. baronet had discovered so easy a way of reducing the national debt, by throwing the burthen of taxation entirely on foreigners, he ought to become chancellor of the exchequer without delay; for he was afraid they had never yet found a chancellor of the exchequer who could impose taxes without inflicting serious burthens on the people.

BEER DUTIES BILL

12 *May* 1823

Mr. DENISON, in presenting a petition from the table beer and ale brewers of London, suggested that the tax should be removed from beer and placed on malt. 'This would place the poor man and the rich on an equality. At present, the poor man, who could not brew his beer, paid a tax from which the rich man was exempt.'

Mr. RICARDO could see no reason why the tax should not be imposed on the malt. If that were done, individuals would be at liberty to brew what quality of beer they pleased. The hardship was very great on the poor man, who was obliged to purchase his beer at a high rate from the public brewer; whereas all those who possessed facilities for brewing were exempted from the burden.

[See further, p. 301.]

SILK MANUFACTURE BILL

21 *May* 1823

The LORD MAYOR[1] presented a petition from his constituents, the working silk-weavers of Sudbury, against the repeal of the Spitalfields Acts.

Mr. RICARDO thought that this petition, coming from a district which was free, and praying that a restriction might be continued upon another district, was a most powerful argument in favour of the very measure which it opposed.[2]

Mr. F. BUXTON presented a similar petition from the journeymen silk-weavers of London; 'it stated, that the journeymen weavers had derived great benefit from the effects of the existing laws, of which he thought they were competent judges.' Mr. HUME vindicated the principles upon which the proposed measure was founded and said, the petitioners 'did not understand the operation of those principles to their own advantage or disadvantage. They thought, for instance, that the existing law had been beneficial to them, when it had, in fact, been, for the last forty or fifty years, diverting the trade to Sudbury and other places.' Mr. F. BUXTON 'admitted, that the petitioners did not pretend to understand political economy—a science, the principles of which appeared to change every two or three years.' Mr. ELLICE agreed that all restrictions on trade had probably

---

[1] Mr. Alderman Heygate.

[2] The *Morning Chronicle* reports: 'Mr. RICARDO remarked, that the Petition came from a place where labour was free, and requested the continuance of restraint upon the freedom of labour elsewhere, on the ground that the removal of such restriction would be injurious to the petitioners. He considered that nothing could be a stronger argument in favour of the Bill for repeal than such a petition [hear, hear!].'

better be removed. 'They were, however, proceeding to remove a law which, as the workmen conceived, afforded them protection, while they allowed the Combination act, and the act against the emigration of artisans, to remain in existence, which statutes, as every one knew, operated severely against certain of the working classes.'

Mr. RICARDO said, in answer to what had fallen from an hon. gentleman, that if they waited until they could, at one stroke, destroy all restrictions on trade they would never effect any useful alteration. The hon. member for Weymouth[1] had observed, that the petitioners knew nothing about political economy, the principles of which seemed to change every two or three years. Now, the principles of true political economy never changed; and those who did not understand that science had better say nothing about it, but endeavour to give good reasons, if they could find any, for supporting the existing act. He most assuredly would not utter a word that could be injurious to the manufacturing classes: all his sympathies were in their favour: he considered them as a most valuable part of the population, and what he said was intended for their benefit. But, why should this particular trade come under the cognizance of the magistrate more than any other? Why should he interfere with this particular branch of the trade when many other branches of it were not under his control? The law only applied to the weavers. With respect to all other parties connected with the trade the magistrate had no jurisdiction whatever. Why should he have the power to fix the price of labour, more than the price of bread, meat, or beer? Delay was asked for. Now, he saw no use or advantage in delaying the measure. The hon. member for Norwich[2] called on the House to delay the bill until next session. But, what reason had he given for the postponement? No one whatever. He merely said, "I

---

[1] Mr. F. Buxton.   [2] Mr. William Smith.

think the existing measure is a very bad one for the workmen,
but there is an extraordinary prejudice in its favour amongst
the weavers, and therefore I would delay the measure until
that prejudice is removed." Why, at the end of the next
session they would be in exactly the same state as at present;
the prejudice would be found to exist as strongly as before.
He therefore hoped that his right hon. friend would proceed
with the measure, and refuse any application for delay.

[See further, p. 306.]

EAST AND WEST INDIA SUGARS

22 *May* 1823

Mr. W. WHITMORE moved that a select committee be appointed with a view to equalising the duties on sugar (at present
an extra duty of 10s. to 15s. was payable on sugar from the East,
above that which was payable on sugar from the West Indies).
Mr. C. ELLIS, opposing the motion, said that 'the protection
extended to the West-India colonists had been conceded as a
compensation for restrictions to which the East-India interest
was not subject. If it were not a formal charter, it was an absolute compact with the consideration of value received, and not
less valid than positive law.' Mr. ROBERTSON contended that the
consumer was benefitted by the present state of things; owing
to the incapacity of the East Indies under their wretched system
of slavery, and the destruction caused by the white ants, 'it
would be impossible ever to make the growth of sugar in the
East Indies sufficiently productive.'

Mr. RICARDO congratulated the House upon the comfortable information contained in the speech of the hon. member
who had spoken last, and who had shown, that, what with
the white ants and other difficulties, it would be impossible
for the East-India planters ever to compete with those of the
West-India colonies. The inference from which was, that

there was nothing to fear from allowing them the advantage required. On this occasion he would take the liberty of quoting a speech of the hon. member for Sandwich (Mr. Marryat) in 1809, which was marked throughout by its strict adherence to the true principles of political economy. In that speech, the hon. member had contended for the policy of admitting the conquered colonies to an equal participation in the trade with the other colonies of England. The question at that time was, whether the colony of Martinique should be allowed to send its sugars to the British market on the same terms as the other colonies, and the hon. member had then clearly shown, by a train of the soundest reasoning, that the price of sugar on the continent regulating the price in this country, it could be no disadvantage to us that the sugar of Martinique should be sent here.[1] Here the hon. member read the passage of the speech to which he had alluded. He then went on to contend, that the same argument (substituting the East Indies for Martinique) would apply to the question before the House. The sugars of the East Indies would not exclude those of the West. He would maintain, that there ought to be no restrictions on the imports of any of our colonies—that it would be an injury, as well to the colonies as to the mother country, and that therefore we ought to get rid of them altogether. It should also be recollected, that if the proposed measure gave advantages to the East-India trade which it did not possess before, there were disadvantages under which that trade still laboured, which went to counterbalance them. An hon. member had talked of our compact with the West Indies. He would say, in reply, that if any compact existed, by which the industry, either of the colonies or of the mother country, was rendered less pro-

[1] See Joseph Marryat's speech on the Martinique Trade Bill, 15 March 1809, *Hansard*, XIV, Appendix, p. 83.

ductive, the sooner it was got rid of the better. The argument of the hon. member for Dumfries (Mr. K. Douglas)
was quite inconclusive, in supposing that we should lose a
great portion of the revenue derived from our West-India
produce. He did not think the proposed measure would have
any such effect, or that we should have the produce of either
the West or East Indies at half their present price. He wished
that could be proved; because it would render the proposition still more desirable. But he thought it was absurd to
maintain, that because our West-India planters had a large
capital embarked in the trade, we were therefore bound to
take sugars from them at double the price which we could
get them for elsewhere. Such an effect would not, however,
be the result of the proposed alteration. East or West-India
sugars would not be much lowered by it; but we should have
this advantage from it, which would be most desirable—it
would prevent sugars from rising above their value. Some
gentlemen were alarmed at the idea of exporting bullion to
India. For himself, he did not object to it; for bullion could
not be acquired without the employment of our industry,
and if a duty was levied in one case as well as in the other, it
was clear that we should not lose any part of our revenue.
With respect to the employment of our ships and sailors, it
was natural to conclude, that as the East Indies were further
off than the West, the proposed alteration would employ
more rather than fewer. As to the duty on East India sugar,
it was, by their own confession, of recent date, not having
been introduced until 1814. What then, became of the
ground of long possession? With respect to the effect the
measure recommended would produce on the negro population, he did not see any grounds for supposing that it would
be injurious. In the first place, he did not believe that we
should import East-India sugar to any very considerable

amount. But even were the competition to interfere with the sale of the produce of the West Indies, the condition of the slaves, if not improved, would not be injured by the change; inasmuch as the capital now employed in the production of sugar, would, under such circumstances, be converted to the growth of a more beneficial, because a more remunerating commodity. In the speech of the hon. member for Sandwich, to which he before alluded, there was a most extraordinary observation. It the more surprised him, as it was irreconcileable with the sound views entertained by the hon. member. In the speech, however, it was stated, that the price of any commodity did not depend on the cost of cultivation, but on the relation of the supply to the demand. Now, nothing was more unsound. In all cases, the cost of cultivation was sure to regulate the price which any commodity must bear in the markets of the world. As, therefore, the cost of production was acknowledged to be less in the East Indies in the production of sugar, the price of that article in the markets of the world must in the long run be regulated by that cost. There was another observation which was worthy of remark. The hon. members acknowledged, that the greatest advantage would attend a free trade; but, said they, "it is not a free trade, but a participation in the monopoly that the East-India advocates demand." Granted. He would accede to their object; though at the same time, he was prepared to go to a much greater extent. He was ready to allow a free trade on sugar from all parts of the world where that commodity was grown. He would allow a competition not alone of East-India sugar, but of the sugars of South America, Cuba, Brazils, and China. And so would the hon. member for Sandwich, provided he was allowed to import the sugars of the West Indies with the lower rate of duties. It was, however, of those duties which prohibited all competition, that he (Mr. R.) complained; and, with the hope of modifying the evil, he would give his support to the motion.

Mr. MARRYAT said, 'it was extremely amusing to hear hon. members, proprietors of East-India stock, declaiming in that House on the advantages of a free trade, at the very moment that they themselves were interested in one of the most outrageous monopolies that ever existed in any country in the world.'

Mr. RICARDO, in explanation, observed, that he had never possessed a shilling more than 1000*l.* East-India stock, and never given a vote in favour of monopoly in his life.

Mr. HUSKISSON 'agreed with the hon. member for Portarlington that, considering the question abstractly, and without reference to the state of things which had grown out of the colonial policy of this country for the last century—the only point worthy of notice was, where, as consumers, could we get our sugars at the cheapest rate? But, he denied that the question ought to be so abstractly considered', and opposed the motion.

The House divided on Mr. Whitmore's motion: Ayes, 34. Noes, 161. Ricardo voted for the motion.

MALT AND BEER TAX

28 *May* 1823

Mr. MABERLY moved 'That a select committee be appointed to inquire into the present mode of taxing malt and beer separately, and whether it would not be expedient to collect the same amount on malt alone' [cp. above, p. 294]. The CHANCELLOR OF THE EXCHEQUER opposed the motion.

Mr. RICARDO thought, that his hon. friend, the mover, had shown the tax on beer to be unequal, and that one class was exempted from it, while another was obliged to pay. He had shown, also, that the diminution in the expense of collecting this tax would assist the revenue. The hon. member regretted that this had been made a question between the agricultural and other classes; but, even if it were true that the tax had an

28 May 1823   unequal operation, in this respect also the sooner it was equalized the better. If the duty paid ought to attach on all persons consuming beer, it ought to attach equally. The motion should have his hearty support, because it went to accomplish that object.

The House divided: Ayes, 27. Noes, 119. Ricardo voted for the motion.

WAGES OF MANUFACTURERS—
USE OF MACHINERY

30 *May* 1823

30 May 1823   Mr. ATTWOOD presented a petition from the manual weavers of Stockport, complaining of the extremely low rate of wages: 'they complained also of certain improvements in machinery, the effect of which had been to reduce the quantity of employment of those who wove by hand, and which threatened to leave a large population without any means whatever of support.' Mr. PHILIPS contended 'that no means were so effectual for the benefit of the manufacturing class, as the introduction of machinery; and if parliament were foolish enough to comply with the prayer of those who wished to discourage machinery, they would inflict the greatest possible injury on the public, and especially on the petitioners themselves.' Mr. H. G. BENNET said, 'a very useful publication on the subject of machinery, written by Mr. Cobbett, had been extensively circulated throughout the manufacturing counties, and would, he hoped, effect a change of opinion no less extensive.'[1]

---

[1] See 'A Letter to the Luddites', first published in *Cobbett's Weekly Political Register*, 30 Nov. 1816. (In 1830 Brougham proposed to republish this tract 'in order to put an end to the outrages, then going on in the country'. See Cobbett in *State Trials*, N.S., ii, 865.) Cobbett's conclusion was: 'I think, then, that it is quite clear, that the existence of machinery, to its present extent, cannot possibly do the journeyman manufacturer *any harm;* but, on the contrary, that he must be injured by the destruction of machinery. And, it appears to me equally clear, that if machines could be invented so as to make lace, stockings, &c. for half or a quarter the present price, such an improvement could not possibly be injurious to you.'

Mr. RICARDO said, that much information might, undoubtedly, be derived from Mr. Cobbett's publication, because that writer explained the use of machinery in such a way
as to render the subject perfectly clear. He was not, however, altogether satisfied with the reasoning contained in that
pamphlet; because it was evident, that the extensive use of
machinery, by throwing a large portion of labour into the
market, while, on the other hand, there might not be a
corresponding increase of demand for it, must, in some
degree, operate prejudicially to the working classes. But still
he would not tolerate any law to prevent the use of machinery. The question was,—if they gave up a system which
enabled them to undersell in the foreign market, would
other nations refrain from pursuing it? Certainly not. They
were therefore bound, for their own interest, to continue it.
Gentlemen ought, however, to inculcate this truth on the
minds of the working classes—that the value of labour, like
the value of other things, depended on the relative proportion
of supply and demand. If the supply of labour were greater
than could be employed, then the people must be miserable.
But the people had the remedy in their own hands. A little
forethought, a little prudence (which probably they would
exert, if they were not made such machines of by the poor-
laws), a little of that caution which the better educated felt it
necessary to use, would enable them to improve their situation.

Mr. PHILIPS instanced the fact, that the wages of the artisan were
more liberal where machinery was used than where it was not used,
as a proof that its introduction was not hurtful to the weaver.

Mr. RICARDO said, his proposition was, not that the use of
machinery was prejudicial to persons employed in one particular manufacture, but to the working classes generally. It
was the means of throwing additional labour into the market,
and thus the demand for labour, generally, was diminished.

IRISH TITHES COMPOSITION BILL

30 *May* 1823

This measure (which had been introduced by Mr. GOULBURN, chief secretary for Ireland, on 6 March) 'proceeded upon the principle of endeavouring to effect a voluntary agreement between the owners and the payers of tithes.'

Mr. RICARDO observed that, by the present bill, land improved within the last 21 years was not to be tithable for such improvement; but as an adjustment was to take place every year, suppose a man possessed of poor land, to improve that land within one year after the passing this bill, he would become liable to pay upon his improved land, while his neighbour, having been so fortunate as to improve a year sooner, would be liable to no such burthen. This would be to give one person a preference, ruinous in its effect, to another. The bill might be favourable to Ireland, but it would be most injurious to the English agriculturist, as it would enable the Irish grower to grow corn cheap, and he might glut the English market, to the ruin of the English grower, unless a protecting duty was imposed on Irish corn.[1]

Mr. GOULBURN said, 'the argument just introduced by the hon. member for Portarlington, was one quite beside the present question; though it would apply to any measure introduced with a view of assisting agriculture in any part of the empire.... How would the hon. gentleman reconcile his proposition with the various instances which existed in Yorkshire and Lincolnshire, in particular, of parishes relieved from the operation of the tithe system by special acts of parliament. According to the hon. gentleman's doctrine, we must have Custom-houses erected on the borders of those counties, and countervailing duties imposed, to keep up this beautiful system of equilibrium of price.'

---

[1] In the adjourned debate, on 9 June 1823, 'Mr. RICARDO thought the composition should be regulated every three years, and that such regulation should be fixed on the average price of corn for the last three years.'

RECIPROCITY OF DUTIES

6 *June* 1823

Mr. HUSKISSON (President of the Board of Trade) moved two resolutions authorising his majesty, by order in council, to declare that the importation or exportation of merchandise in foreign vessels might take place upon payment of the same duties as were payable on similar merchandise carried in British vessels, from or to countries which allowed reciprocal conditions; and granting powers of retaliation. This, he said, 'was an entire departure from the principles which had hitherto governed our foreign commerce.... It had for a long time, indeed from the passing of the Navigation act, been our policy to impose upon cargoes, brought in foreign vessels, higher duties than those imported in British bottoms'; that policy was becoming impossible, owing to retaliatory action taken by foreign countries.

Mr. RICARDO said, that the country was much indebted to his right hon. friend (Mr. Huskisson) for the enlightened views he had taken, and the measures he had brought forward, to improve the commerce of the country. Parliament had, at length, begun to find out, that restrictions on commerce were restrictions, not on other countries, but on ourselves. It certainly was a question of policy whether England should take off the duties without receiving reciprocal advantage from foreign powers; but, if foreign powers recognised the same liberal principle, there could be no doubt that the advantage to England would be double the advantage which any other country could derive from the regulation. An hon. member had said, that it would be to his personal advantage to second the principles laid down, but that personal benefits ought to be sacrificed for the good of the navy. Now, with respect to the navy, he had no apprehension whatever. The state of that navy, the facility for building ships, the superiority of this country in that branch of art, the great capital and enterprise of the people, were so

6 June 1823 many securities, that the navy would not fall into decay. He hoped soon to see Canada deprived of the preference which she enjoyed in the timber trade, and placed, in that respect, upon the same footing as Norway and Sweden.

The resolutions were agreed to.

SILK MANUFACTURE BILL

9 *June* 1823

9 June 1823 On the report of the bill for the repeal of the Spitalfields acts Mr. F. BUXTON moved that it be referred to a select committee, so that the petitioners against the measure [see above, p. 295] might prove their case by evidence. 'It was indeed objected to the petitioners, that the bill did not rest upon disputed facts, but rested on admitted principles of political economy; but, ... it was rather hard to say to these poor people, that they should lose their bread by principles of political economy.... The petitioners also begged humbly to represent, that they had seen the greatest fluctuations, as to what the "soundest principles of political economy" were. And indeed the House must know, that certain principles of political economy were acted upon some fifty years ago, and which were then undoubted, until Adam Smith gained great credit by overturning them; and recently they had heard his hon. friend, the member for Portarlington (Mr. Ricardo), combat the doctrines of Adam Smith in many particulars, with a clearness and force which had certainly persuaded him (Mr. F. Buxton) of his hon. friend's correctness. The petitioners therefore, were certainly entitled to ask, what security there was, that some future system of political economy would not overturn the system of his hon. friend, which had overturned the system of Adam Smith, who, in his day, had overturned the system of those who had gone before him?' Mr. HUSKISSON opposed the inquiry. Mr. BRIGHT supported it and asked, 'ought the House to refuse it merely because some persons talked largely about the principles of political economy?'

Mr. RICARDO was as anxious for inquiry as any member, in cases where it was at all necessary; but, admitting all that the opponents of this bill stated they could prove, it would not change his opinion. If these acts were indeed so beneficial, they ought to be adopted all over the country, and applied to every branch of manufacture; but the question was, whether labour should or should not be free? The quantity of work must depend upon the extent of demand; and if the demand was great, the number of persons employed would be in proportion. If these acts were repealed, no doubt the number of weavers employed in London would be greater than at present. They might not, indeed, receive such high wages; but it was improper that those wages should be artificially kept up by the interference of a magistrate. If a manufacturer was obliged to use a certain quantity of labour, he ought to obtain it at a fair price. It had been said, that the weavers of Spital-fields received very little from the poor-rates. True. And why? Because there was so little to be distributed among them. Very little could be raised in the parish; and sometimes, when great distress prevailed, resort had actually been had to government, for large sums for the relief of the poor. An hon. member for Bristol[1] had talked about political economy; but the words "political economy" had, of late, become terms of ridicule and reproach. They were used as a substitute for an argument, and had been so used by the hon. member for Weymouth.[2] Upon every view which he could take of the subject, the bill would be beneficial both to the manufacturers and the workmen.

The House divided: For the Committee, 60. Against it, 68.

[1] Mr. Bright.   [2] Mr. F. Buxton.

11 *June* 1823

Mr. HUSKISSON having moved the third reading of the bill,

Mr. RICARDO contended, that the effect of the existing law was, to diminish the quantity of labour, and that, though the rate of wages was high,[1] the workmen had so little to do, that their wages were, in point of fact, lower than they would be under the proposed alteration of the law. He could not bear to hear it said that they were legislating to the injury of the working classes. He would not stand up in support of the measure, if he thought for one moment that it had any such tendency. The existing law was more injurious to the workmen than to their employers; because, at periods when the trade was brisk, it empowered the magistrates to inter- fere, and prevent their wages from rising as much as they would if the law imposed no shackles on the regulations of the trade. He was in possession of a number of cases, in which the decision of the magistrates had been resisted, either by the workmen or their masters, where counsel had been employed, and the masters had at length given up the dispute rather than incur the trouble and expense of con- tinuing it. He was perfectly satisfied that, if the present bill should pass, there would be a much greater quantity of work for the weavers in London than there was at present. With respect to wages, he was persuaded, that, in all the common branches of the manufacture, they would not fall; for at the present moment they were as high in the country, with reference to those branches, as they were in London.

The House divided: For the third reading, 53; Against it, 40. The bill was then passed.

---

[1] The *Courier* reports instead: 'the tendency of the existing law was to diminish the rate of wages; for though the rate of wages was nominally high,' etc.

On 18 July, when the amended bill came back from the Lords, Mr. HUSKISSON declared that 'it now came down in so altered a state and with so many of the old regulations unrepealed, that, in his view of the subject, it would neither conduce to the public interest, nor be consistent with his duty, to proceed further with it at present.'[1]

MR. WESTERN'S MOTION RESPECTING
THE RESUMPTION OF CASH PAYMENTS

11 *June* 1823

Mr. WESTERN (the member for Essex) moved 'That a com- mittee be appointed to take into consideration the changes that have been made in the value of the currency between the year 1793 and the present time, and the consequences produced there- by upon the money-income of the country derived from its industry; the amount of the public debt and taxes considered relatively to the money-income of the country; and the effect of such changes of the currency upon the money-contracts between individuals.'

Mr. RICARDO* observed, that the hon. member for Essex, and all those who took his view of the subject, laid down very sound principles, but drew from them conclusions which were altogether untenable. No one doubted, that, in proportion as the quantity of money in a country increased, commerce and transactions remaining the same, its value must fall. No one questioned, that the change from a de- preciated to a metallic currency of increased value must have the effect of reducing its quantity, and of lowering the price of all commodities brought to market. These were principles which he had himself on various occasions asserted; but the

*This Speech was written out by Mr. Ricardo for this Work, and sent to the Editor a few days before his death. [*Hansard's* note.]

---

[1] Cp. below, IX, 318.

difference between him and the hon. member for Essex, was, as to the degree in which the value of our currency had been increased, and the degree in which prices generally had been diminished by the bill (called Mr. Peel's Bill) of 1819. It was from seeing the evils which resulted from a currency without any fixed standard, that he had given his best support to that bill. What he sought was, to guard against the many and the severe mischiefs of a fluctuating currency; fluctuating, not according to the variations in the value of the standard itself, from which no currency could be exempted, but fluctuating according to the caprice or interest of a company of merchants, who, before the passing of that bill, had the power to increase or diminish the amount of money, and consequently to alter the value, whenever they thought proper. It was from seeing the immense power which the Bank, prior to 1819, possessed—a power, which he believed that body had been inclined to exercise fairly, but which had not been always judiciously exercised, and which might have been so used as to have become formidable to the interests of the country—it was from the view which he took of the extent of that power of the Bank, that he had rejoiced, in 1819, in the prospect of a fixed currency. He had cared little, comparatively, what the standard established[1] was—whether it continued at its then value, or went back to the old standard: his object had been, a fixed standard of some description or other. In the discussions of 1819, he certainly had said, that he measured the depreciation of the then currency, by the difference of value between paper and gold; and he held to that opinion still. He maintained now, that the depreciation of a currency could only be measured by a reference to the proper standard—that was, to gold; but he did not say, that the standard itself was not variable. The hon.

---

[1] Misprinted 'establishment' in *Hansard;* correct in *The Times.*

gentleman, and those who supported his opinions, were always confounding the terms "depreciation," and "value." A currency might be depreciated, without falling in value; it might fall in value, without being depreciated, because depreciation is estimated only by reference to a standard. He had undoubtedly given an opinion in 1819, that, by the measure then proposed, the prices of commodities would not be altered more than 5 per cent;[1] but, let it be explained under what circumstances that opinion had been given. The difference in 1819, between paper and gold, was 5 per cent, and the paper being brought, by the bill of 1819, up to the gold standard, he had considered that, as the value of the currency was only altered 5 per cent, there could be no greater variation than 5 per cent, in the result as to prices. But this calculation had always been subject to a supposition, that no change was to take place in the value of gold. Mr. Peel's bill, as originally constituted, led the way to no such change. That bill did not require the Bank to provide itself with any additional stock of gold till 1823. It was not a bill demanding that coin should be thrown into circulation, till after the expiration of four years and a half; and before that period, if the system worked well, of which there could be no doubt, parliament could, and in all probability would, have deferred coin payments to a considerably later time. It was a bill by which, if they had followed it strictly, the Bank would have been enabled to carry on the currency of the country in paper, without using an ounce more of gold than was then in their possession.

Gentlemen forgot that, by that bill, the Bank was prohibited from paying their notes in specie, and were required only to pay them in ingots on demand; ingots which nobody

---

[1] See his evidence to the Commons Committee of 1819, Question 49, below, p. 385.

wanted, for no one could use them beneficially. The charge against him was, that he had not foreseen the alteration in the value of the standard, to which, by the bill, the paper money was required to conform. No doubt, gold had altered in value; and why? Why, because the Bank, from the moment of the passing of the bill in 1819, set their faces against the due execution of it. Instead of doing nothing, they carried their ingots, which the public might have demanded of them, to the Mint, to be coined into specie, which the public could not demand of them, and which they could not pay if it did. Instead of maintaining an amount of paper money in circulation, which should keep the exchanges at par, they so limited the quantity as to cause an unprecedented influx of the precious metals, which they eagerly bought and coined into money. By their measures they occasioned a demand for gold, which was, in no way, necessarily consequent upon the bill of 1819; and so raising the value of gold in the general market of the world, they changed the value of the standard with reference to which our currency had been calculated, in a manner which had not been presumed upon.

This, then, was the error which he (Mr. Ricardo) had been guilty of: he had not foreseen these unnecessary, and, as he must add, mischievous operations of the Bank. Fully allowing, as he did, for the effect thus produced on the value of gold, it remained to consider what that effect really had been. The hon. member for Essex estimated it at 30 per cent; he (Mr. Ricardo) calculated it at 5 per cent; and he was therefore now ready to admit, that Mr. Peel's bill had raised the value of the currency 10 per cent. By increasing the value of gold 5 per cent, it had become necessary to raise the value of paper 10 per cent, instead of 5 per cent, to make it conform to the enhanced value of gold. To estimate what the effect of this demand for gold had had upon its value in the general market of the world, he contended, that we should compare the quantity actually purchased, with the whole quantity used in the different currencies of the world; and he was satisfied that, on such a principle of calculation, 5 per cent would be found to be an ample allowance for the effect of such purchases. But the hon. member for Essex had said nothing of all this. He merely came down to the House and said, "My proof that there has been an alteration of 30 per cent in the value of money is, that there is a change to that amount in the price of wheat, and of various other commodities." Every alteration, under every circumstance, in the price of commodities might so be solved, without the trouble of inquiry, by reference to the value of gold. If this argument were good for any thing now, it was good for all times; and we never had had any variations in the value of commodities: the variations in price, which had often occurred, were to be attributed to no other cause but to the alteration in the value of money.

But, suppose the calculation of the hon. member to be correct, and that all the alteration which had taken place in the price of corn had been owing to the alteration in the value of money, he (Mr. Ricardo) should ask him, whether, even in that case, the agricultural interest had suffered any injustice? It was not pretended, that money was now of a higher value than it was previous to the Bank Restriction bill, nor corn at a lower price. The favourite argument was, that they, the landed interest, had to pay the interest of the debt in a medium of a different value from that in which it had been contracted, and therefore, that they actually pay 30 per cent more than they would have paid, if money had never altered in value. He (Mr. Ricardo) had once before endeavoured to show the fallacy of this argument,[1] and had

[1] See above, p. 251 ff.

attempted to prove, that the payers of taxes actually paid no
more now, than they would have paid, if we had had the
wisdom never to depart from the sound principles of currency; and that the stock-holders, taking them as a class,
receive no more than what is justly due to them. The hon.
member would lead the House to believe, that the whole of
our immense debt was contracted in a depreciated currency;
but the fact was, that nearly *five hundred millions* of that debt
was contracted before the currency had suffered any depreciation; and the rest of the debt had been contracted in currency
depreciated in various degrees. Mr. Mushett had been at the
trouble of making very minute calculations on this subject,[1]
and had proved, that the loss to the stock-holders, from receiving their dividends in a depreciated currency for twenty
years, on the stock contracted for in a sound currency, would
amount to a sum sufficiently large to buy a perpetual
annuity, equal to the additional value of the dividends paid
on the *three hundred millions* of debt contracted for in the
depreciated currency. He should be glad to hear an answer
given to this statement. For his own part, it did appear to
him, that the success of the present motion would not
benefit the landed interest a jot: because the motion asked
for an examination as to the changes from the year 1793 to
the present moment; and, as it must be admitted, that the
landed interest had derived vast advantages from the depreciation between the years 1800 and 1819, the present motion
compelling them to make due allowance for the benefits they
had acquired during those years, would take from them an
amount equal to that which they had lost by the subsequent
change.

The hon. member for Essex said, that the currency had
altered 30 per cent in value; but his chief proof rested on the

[1] See above, p. 138.

altered price of corn. The true cause of the greater part of this alteration was, not the change in the currency, but the abundance of the supply. The stimulus to agriculture had been great during the war, and we were now suffering from a re-action, operating at the same time with the effect of two or three abundant crops. Could the agricultural interest be ruined by an alteration in the value of money, without its affecting, in the same manner, the manufacturing and commercial interests of the country? If corn fell 30 per cent from an alteration in the value of money, must not all other commodities fall in something like the same proportion? But, had they so fallen? Was the manufacturing interest so distressed? Quite the contrary. Every thing was flourishing, but agriculture. The legacy duty, the probate duty, the advalorem duty on stamps, were all on the increase; and certainly, if a raised value of money had lessened the value of property, less might be expected to be paid generally upon transfers of property. The state of the revenue was to him (Mr. Ricardo) a satisfactory proof, if every other were wanting, of the erroneous conclusions of the hon. gentleman.

The hon. member for Essex had asked, if any man would say, that under the present system of currency the country could bear the expenses of a war? would any man say now, that the country could pay, as it did in the former war, eighty-four millions per annum? Now, this question was not put quite fairly; because, as the hon. member contended, that our currency was increased in value 30 per cent, he ought to ask, whether we could now afford to pay sixty millions per annum for a war, as we paid eighty-four millions formerly? He (Mr. Ricardo) would answer, that the country would be able to pay just as much real value under the existing system, as under any system of the hon. member for Essex's recommendation; for he thought, that a change in the value of her currency could have no effect at all upon the powers of a country. An unrestricted paper currency created a new distribution of property. It transferred wealth from the pockets of one man to whom it really belonged, to the pockets of another who was in no way entitled to it; but it imparted no strength to a country.

Agreeing as he did most sincerely, with almost all the opinions of his right hon. friend, the president of the Board of Trade (Mr. Huskisson) on this subject, he still considered, that his right hon. friend had given too much currency to the opinion, that an unrestricted paper issue enabled us to meet with increased strength the public enemy. It was not useful to war—it was most injurious in peace—and could not again be put under control, without the grossest injustice to a great portion of the community. We had happily recovered from those effects; and he sincerely trusted, that the country would never again be subjected to a similar calamity.

It was singular, that the objection against the restoration of our currency from a depreciation of 5 per cent in a period of four years, should have come from the hon. member for Essex, who, in 1811, saw no danger in restoring it from its depreciated state of 15 per cent in a single day. The House might recollect that, in 1811, a bill had been brought in, to make paper money equivalent to a legal tender, in consequence of lord King having, most justly, demanded the payment of his rents in the coin of the realm, according to the value of the currency at the time the leases were granted. Suppose that bill had been thrown out, agreeably to the views of the hon. gentleman, who in a speech strenuously opposed the bill,[1] and that the law had taken its course, and that creditors had been defended, in demanding their payments in

---

[1] See Western's speech on Lord Stanhope's Bill (Gold Coin and Bank Note Bill), 19 July 1811, in *Hansard,* XX, 1079–86.

coin—what would have been the result in that case? Would not the ounce of gold have fallen the very next day from 4*l.* 10*s.* to 3*l.* 17*s.* 10½*d.?* Would there have been no inconvenience in an enhancement in the value of the currency to that amount? or was the hon. gentleman prepared to say, that a rise in the value of paper of 15 per cent in one day, in 1811, would have been harmless, but that it would be ruinous to raise it to the amount of 5 per cent only, in a period of four years from 1819?

The hon. member for Essex had not dealt quite fairly by him (Mr. Ricardo) in a pamphlet which he had recently published.[1] In speaking of Mr. Peel's bill, he acquitted his majesty's ministers of any intention of plunging the country into the difficulties which he thought that bill had caused: he paid a compliment to their integrity, by supposing them ignorant: but not so to him (Mr. Ricardo). Without naming him, the hon. gentleman alluded to him and his opinion, in a way that no one could mistake the person meant, and said, that it required the utmost extent of charity to believe, that in the advice he had given he was not influenced by interested motives. The hon. gentleman would have acted a more manly part, if he had explicitly and boldly made his charge, and openly mentioned his name. He (Mr. Ricardo) did not pretend to be more exempted from the weaknesses and errors of human nature than other men, but he could assure the House and the hon. member for Essex, that it would puzzle a good accountant to make out on which side his interest predominated. He (Mr. R.) would find it difficult himself, from the different kinds of property which he possessed (no part funded property), to determine the question. But, by whom was this effort of charity found so difficult? By the

---

[1] *Second Address to the Landowners of the United Empire,* by C. C. Western, 1822. See the extracts given below, p. 522 ff.

hon. gentleman, whose interest in this question could not, for one moment be doubted—whose whole property consisted of land—and who would greatly benefit by any measure which should lessen the value of money. He imputed no bad motive to the hon. gentleman. He believed he would perform his duty as well as most men, even when it was opposed to his interest; but he asked the hon. gentleman to state, on what grounds he inferred, that he (Mr. Ricardo) should, under similar circumstances, be wanting in his.

I beg particularly (continued Mr. Ricardo) to call the attention of the House, to the opinions which I have given on the cause of our recent difficulties, and which the hon. member for Essex now reprobates; as I think that, for every one of those opinions, I can appeal to an authority which the hon. gentleman will be the last to question—for it is to his own. I contend, that the present low price of corn is mainly owing to an excess of supply, and not to an alteration in the value of the currency. What said the hon. gentleman in this House, in the year 1816, when corn had fallen considerably, and when the causes of that fall was the subject of discussion? "The first and obvious cause, I say, has been a redundant supply beyond the demand, and that created chiefly by the produce of our own agriculture. Permit me, Sir, here to call to the recollection of the House the effect of a small surplus or deficit of supply above or below the demand of the market. It is perfectly well known, that if there is a small deficiency of supply, the price will rise in a ratio far beyond any proportion of such deficiency: the effect, indeed, is almost incalculable. So likewise on a surplus of supply beyond demand, the price will fall in a ratio exceeding almost tenfold the amount of such surplus. Corn being an article of prime necessity, is peculiarly liable to such variations: upon a deficit of supply the price is further advanced by alarm; and upon a surplus, it is further diminished by the difficulty the growers have in contracting the amount of their growth, compared to the means which other manufacturers have of limiting the amount of their manufacture."[1]

Now, I would ask the House in what these sentiments differ from those which I have had the honour of supporting in this House, and which the hon. gentleman now thinks so reprehensible? But further, the hon. gentleman contended, in the speech alluded to, that the diminution which at that time had taken place in the amount of the circulating medium was not in any way the cause of the fall in the price of corn, but on the contrary it was the fall in the price of corn which was the cause of the diminution of the quantity of the circulating medium—"I say" (continued he) "there is nothing which will prevent it" (corn) "so falling, nor are there any means to force a re-issue of this paper currency which has thus vanished in a moment: nothing but a revival of the value on which it was founded can accomplish the object."

On this point, I rather agree with the hon. gentleman's present opinions, than with his former ones, that there are means of forcing a re-issue of paper, and of raising the price of corn; but I trust that we shall not have recourse to them. The hon. gentleman proceeds to say—"Now, Sir, let us turn from the contemplation of this gloomy picture, and consider what prospect there is of remedy, or what means we have of affording relief. If I am right in attributing the primary cause of all these calamities to the effects of a surplus in the market beyond the demand, the remedy must be found in taking off that surplus; or it will remedy itself in a short time by a reduction of supply. The danger is, that the

[1] See Western's speech on his own motion for a Committee on the Distressed State of Agriculture, 7 March 1816 (*Hansard*, XXXIII, 36).

present abundant supply should be converted into an alarming deficiency." The hon. gentleman goes on to say, that it
is impossible, for any length of time, for the price of corn to
be below a remunerating price, and that it is possible for the
harvest to be so abundant as to produce loss instead of advantage to the grower. These were the opinions which he
(Mr. Ricardo) held on this subject, and which he had at
various times, though with much less ability, attempted to
support in that House. If he had learned them from the hon.
member, it was very extraordinary that at the moment he
adopted them the hon. member should turn round and reproach him for conforming to his sentiments.

The hon. gentleman proceeded to animadvert on the
arguments and statements set forth by the hon. mover in a
pamphlet recently published,[1] and particularly on one, in
which the hon. member, in making up the balance of advantage which the stock-holder had derived from the several
measures affecting the currency, entirely omitted to set on
one side of the account, the various sums which had been
paid to him in discharge of his debt by the sinking fund in the
depreciated currency, and which, amounted to upwards of
one hundred millions. If the money advanced by the stockholder to the public had been in a depreciated currency, so
had been the payments made to the stock-holder; and it was
not fair for the hon. gentleman to calculate on the sum of
such advances, but on the difference between the advances
and payments. As the hon. gentleman stated the question, it
would appear as if all the advances to government had been
in depreciated money, and all the payments from government
to the stock-holder had been in currency of the Mint value.
Nothing could be so little conformable to the fact; as the
advances and payments were made in the same medium, and,

[1] Cp. above, p. 317, n.

as far as the amounts were equal, they were equally injurious to both parties.

After going through various other objections which he took to the contents of the same pamphlet, Mr. Ricardo went on to justify the opinions which he had given before the Bank committee from an attack which had been made upon them, in another pamphlet, by the hon. member for Callington (Mr. Attwood).[1] He concluded by objecting to the motion. It was too late to make any alteration in the currency. The difficulties of the measure of 1819 were now got over. The people were reconciled to it. Agriculture, he believed, would soon be in the same flourishing condition as the other interests of the country. If it were not, it would only be on account of the mischievous corn law, which would always be a bar to its prosperity. As a punishment to the hon. gentleman, he could almost wish that a committee should be granted. He would, of course, be chairman of it; and tired enough he would be of his office, by the time he had "adjusted" all the interests relative to his new modus! He could not tell how the hon. gentleman would go about the performance of such a labour; but this he would say, that the immediate result of granting such a committee would be, to produce the most mischievous effects, and to renew all the inconveniences which had been previously occasioned by the uncertainty and fluctuations of the currency.

The debate extended to the following day, when Mr. PEEL and Mr. HUSKISSON opposed the motion. Most of the speakers for the motion attacked Ricardo; one of them, Mr. WODEHOUSE, said that Ministers 'were too ready to listen to the suggestions of

---

[1] *A Letter to Lord Archibald Hamilton, on the Alterations in the Value of Money; and containing an Examination of some Opinions* *recently published on that Subject* [Anon.], London, Ridgway, 1823. The author was Mathias Attwood.

the hon. member for Portarlington (Mr. Ricardo), whose conclusions on this head appeared to him to be utterly incomprehensible. Never could he introduce that hon. member's name without feeling what was due to his talents, and also to his character; and, as this observation from himself must carry with it an air of presumption, perhaps he might be allowed to state in explanation, that he had sat with the hon. member for weeks on the same Committee [the Agricultural Committee], had differed with him on almost every point that had been started, but was so struck with the entire absence of all illiberal imputation, and such a manifest desire on his part of establishing only that which was fair, that somehow it was impossible not to have acquired a facility of communication, even with one so infinitely his superior. But, to believe that he had a clear perception on the subject of money, was utterly impossible.'

Mr. Western's motion, with the addition of a clause for 'establishing an equitable adjustment of contracts', proposed by Lord Folkestone, being put, the House divided: Ayes, 27; Noes, 96.

BEER DUTIES BILL

13 *June* 1823

On the report of this bill (which added to the two kinds of beer, then taxed respectively 10*s.* and 2*s.* per barrel according to strength, an 'intermediate beer', to be taxed 5*s.*, and prohibited the brewing of different kinds of beer on the same premises),

Mr. RICARDO thought the bill would be inoperative and it certainly was very unjust; as it, in fact, confiscated the property of the table-beer brewers. As to the idea of preventing weak beer from being put off on the public for strong, the public might be safely left to take care of itself. No harm could be done by passing the bill without the vexatious restrictions; at least for a year, by way of experiment.

On 17 June the bill was read a third time and passed. Ricardo voted against the third reading.

USURY LAWS REPEAL BILL

17 June 1823

Mr. Serjeant ONSLOW moved that the usury laws repeal bill be committed. Mr. DAVENPORT opposed the motion.

Mr. RICARDO argued, that money ought to be placed on the same footing as any other commodity. The lender and borrower ought to be allowed to bargain together, as freely as the buyer and seller did when goods were to be disposed of. The hon. member who spoke last,[1] feared that this measure would place the borrower entirely in the power of the lender. But, did the present laws alter his situation? Certainly not. Means were found to evade the law; for though the law said, "You shall not take more than a certain interest for your money," it could not compel a man to lend at that particular rate; and, therefore, he who wished to borrow at all events, and he who wished to lend at as high a rate of interest as he could get, both conspired to evade the law. These laws operated precisely in the same way as the laws against exporting the coin of the realm. Now, notwithstanding those laws, did not the exportation of that coin take place? The only effect of the statutes in that case was, to place the traffic in the hands of characters who had no scruples against taking a false oath. They were encouraged to evade the law, and made a great profit by so doing.

The House divided: For the motion, 38; Against it, 15. On the report stage (27 June) the bill was lost.

[1] Mr. Davenport.

RELIGIOUS OPINIONS—PETITION OF
MINISTERS OF THE CHRISTIAN
RELIGION FOR FREE DISCUSSION

1 *July* 1823

1 July 1823   Mr. HUME presented the 'Christians' petition' against the prosecution of unbelievers[1] and moved 'That it is the opinion of this House, that Free Discussion has been attended with more benefit than injury to the community, and it is unjust and inexpedient to expose any person to legal penalties on account of the expression of opinions on matters of religion.' Seconding the motion,

Mr. RICARDO said, he had heard with pleasure a great part of the speech of his hon. friend who had just sat down,[2] and the remainder certainly with no inconsiderable concern. The greater part of that speech had been in support of the opinion which he (Mr. Ricardo) held, in common with his hon. friend who had introduced the motion; namely, that no man had a right to dictate his opinions upon abstract questions[3] to another, upon peril of punishment for a refusal to adopt them; and his hon. friend had further admitted, that so long as the controversy upon such topics was conducted with decency, it ought not to be prevented by force of law. Now, he lamented that when his hon. friend had thought proper to quote the sentiments of Dr. Paley, he had not given them more at length, for he would, in the writings of that eminent individual, find a more large and liberal spirit of toleration, than he was disposed to admit practically in other parts of his speech.

[1] The petition had been drawn up by an acquaintance of Ricardo, the Unitarian minister Robert Aspland; it was signed by 2,047 members of Christian congregations, of whom 98 were ministers. See *Memoir of the Life, Works and Correspondence of the Rev. Robert Aspland, of Hackney,* by R. B. Aspland, London, 1850, p. 436.
[2] Mr. Wilberforce.
[3] Misprinted 'opinions' in *Hansard.*

Mr. WILBERFORCE.—Dr. Paley distinctly excepts to the 1 July 1823 treatment of such subjects with levity and ribaldry.

Mr. RICARDO.—That, certainly, was Dr. Paley's only exception; and he, as well as the other chief ornaments of the church, for instance, Dr. Tillotson and Dr. Porteus, had asserted, in the largest sense, the right of unfettered opinion. If the validity of such opinions were admitted, who could approve of the operation of the law of this country in such matters? Who could sustain those impolitic and unjust prosecutions? What was the prosecution of Carlile for re-publishing the "Age of Reason?"[1] That was not a work written in a style of levity and ribaldry, but a serious argument upon publishing the truth of the Christian religion. Look again at the impending prosecution for eighteen weeks of the same man for publishing Mr. Hone's parodies,[2] which was not abandoned until Hone had himself secured an acquittal on the charge. But, said his hon. friend (Mr. Wilberforce),[3] in justification of these public prosecutions, there were some offences which did not directly affect private interest, although they injured the community, and which might go unpunished, were it not for general associations which took cognizance of such matters; and he had talked of obscene writings in illustration of his opinion. But, was there really any comparison between such writings and those upon speculative points of religion, which were the only topics to which this motion applied? They were all agreed that obscene writings ought to be punished. And why?— because they were obviously pernicious to the moral in-

---

[1] By Thomas Paine. Republished by Richard Carlile, London, 1818.

[2] William Hone's parodies of the Church Catechism, the Lord's Prayer, the Ten Commandments, the Litany, and the Creed of St. Athanasius, published in 1817.

[3] This and the subsequent references are to Wilberforce's speech on M. A. Carlile's petition on 26 March 1823.

terests of society, and constituted a general and disgusting
species of offence. But not so with respect to abstract
religious subjects, upon which it was quite impossible to
obtain universal assent. No man had a right to say to
another, "My opinion upon religion is right, and yours is
not only wrong when you differ from me, but I am entitled
to punish you for that difference." Such an arrogant assumption of will was intolerable, and was an outrage upon the
benignant influence of religion. They might talk of ribaldry
and levity, but there was nothing more intolerable than the
proposition which he had just stated, and which was nothing
less than the power contended for by the advocates of these
prosecutions for mere opinions upon points of faith. Then,
what an absurd and immoral mode did the law provide for
estimating the credit of a man's faith before his testimony
was legally admissible! When the question was put to a
witness, "Do you believe in a future state?" If he were a
conscientious man, entertaining seriously such an opinion,
his answer must be in the negative, and the law said he should
not be heard; but if he were an immoral man, and disre-
garded truth, and said, "I do believe in a future state," although in his conscience he disbelieved in it, then his evidence was admissible, and his hypocrisy and falsehood
secured him credibility. Now, there would be some sense in
the law, if it declined tempting the hypocrisy of the individual, or his fear of the world's hostility or prejudice, and let
in other evidence to establish, from previous knowledge of
the individual, whether or not he ought not to be admitted
as a witness; but as it stood, it was absurd and ridiculous;
and when he (Mr. R.) was charged upon this ground with a
desire to do away with the sanctity of an oath, his reply was,
"I do not desire to diminish the sacredness of the obligation;
but I do desire to get rid of the hypocrisy by which that oath
may be evaded." But then, again, was it possible for a man

not to believe in a future state, and yet be strictly moral, and impressed with the necessity of upholding credibility in the common obligations of society? For his part, he firmly believed in the possibility of a man's being very honest for all the social purposes and essential obligations of the community in which he lived, and still not assenting to the belief of a future state. He fully admitted that religion was a powerful obligation; but he denied it to be the only obligation. It was, in fact, one which was superadded to the general force of moral impressions—it were a libel upon human nature to say otherwise. Tillotson was of that opinion in the following quotation from his works:—"As for most of those restraints which Christianity lays upon us, they are so much both for our private and public advantage, that, setting aside all considerations of religion, and of the rewards and punishments of another life, they are really good for us; and if God had not laid them upon us, we ought in reason, in order to our temporal benefit and advantage to have laid them upon ourselves. If there were no religion, I know men would not have such strong and forcible obligations to these duties; but yet, I say, though there were no religion, it were good for men, in order to temporal ends, to their health and quiet, and reputation, and safety, and, in a word, to the private and public prosperity of mankind, that men should be temperate, and chaste, and just, and peaceable, and charitable, and kind, and obliging to one another, rather than the contrary. So that religion does not create those restraints arbitrarily, but requires those things of us, which our reason, and a regard to our advantage, which the necessity and conveniency of the things themselves, without any consideration of religion, would in most cases urge us to."[1] He read this passage for the purpose of showing, and from a great authority in the

[1] See Sermon LXIV, in *The Works of Dr. John Tillotson, late Archbishop of Canterbury,* London, 1712, vol. 1, pp. 465–6.

church, that the obligation of religion was not alone considered as the influential test of moral truth, and that a man might be very sceptical upon doctrinal points, and yet very positive in the control of moral impressions distinct from religious faith. For instance, there was Mr. Owen of Lanark, a great benefactor to society, and yet a man not believing (judging from some opinions of his) in a future state. Would any man, with the demonstrating experience of the contrary before his eyes, say that Mr. Owen was less susceptible of moral feeling, because he was incredulous upon matters of religion? Would any man, pretending to honour or candour, say that Mr. Owen, after a life spent in improving the condition of others, had a mind less pure, a heart less sincere, or a less conviction of the restraint and control of moral rectitude, than if he were more imbued with the precepts of religious obligation? Why, then, was such a man (for so by the law he was) to be excluded from the pale of legal credibility—why was he, if he promulgated his opinions, to be liable to spend his days immured in a prison? With respect to the exception provided according to his hon. friend (Mr. Wilberforce), for treating such subjects with levity and ribaldry, he must confess, that he thought it a very singular reservation: for what was it, but to say—"You may discuss, if you please, in the most solemn, most serious, and therefore most influential manner, any topic of religion you please; but, the moment you discuss it with levity or ribaldry, that is, in such a manner as to be sure to offend the common sense of mankind, and therefore deprive you of really acquiring any serious proselytes, then the law takes cognizance of your conduct, and makes your imbecility penal." Was not this a glaring inconsistency? The law allowed the greater evil, the serious and substantial principle of discussion; and it denounced the lesser, which after admitting the first, it ought

to have tolerated; and yet his hon. friend had, by his argument, justified and supported so singular a course. There was
one passage of this petition which was very forcible, and to
which he called the attention of his hon. friend. It was this:
— "The reviler of Christianity appears to your petitioners to
be the least formidable of its enemies; because his scoffs can
rarely fail of arousing against him public opinion, than which
nothing more is wanted to defeat his end. Between freedom
of discussion and absolute persecution there is no assignable
medium." When this subject was last before the House, unless his memory deceived him, he had heard singular opinions
propounded by gentlemen who took a different view of this
subject from himself. He thought he had heard it avowed,
that the religion which ought to be established in a state, was
not that which the majority said they believed, but that the
doctrines of which were true. He had heard an observation
like that fall from a very respectable quarter.[1] It was difficult
to argue with any body entertaining such an opinion; for
where was the test by which such an argument could be
tried? There was not in polemics, as in astronomy, one
unerring criterion to which the common credence of mankind bowed: it was not like the rising sun, or any of the other
phenomena of nature, which were bound by indissoluble and
indisputable laws; but, on the contrary, a subject open to
conflicting opinions. Who, then, was to decide upon the
truth—who was authorized to say, "My opinion is right,
yours is wrong?" If this was impossible, how was the test to
be decided? How, for instance, in such a country as Ireland
try the question of the truth of what ought to be the religion
of the state, against the opinions of the majority of the people?
How would, upon that test, the stability of the Protestant

---

[1] See Mr. Bankes' speech on the Roman Catholic franchise bill,
30 June 1823 (*Hansard*, N.S., IX, 1341).

religion in Ireland be secured? Or, if it was secured there, merely because the minority thought it the true religion, the same reason and the same duty, would authorize the extension of the principle to India; and why not supplant Mahometanism to establish the doctrines of the Reformation? Into this wide field did the gentleman enter who embarked in such fanciful notions. He begged to be understood as having argued this question, from beginning to end, as the friend of free discussion. He knew the delicacy of the subject, and was anxious to guard himself against being supposed to entertain opinions obnoxious to the bulk of mankind. He repeated, that he only contended for the general right of self-opinion, and for the unfettered liberty of discussion, and hoped that while he was doing so, he should not have, as his hon. friend (Mr. Hume) had had last night,[1] certain opinions fixed upon him which he did not entertain, and which it was quite unnecessary for him to countenance, in supporting the line of argument which the subject suggested to him, and which his reason approved.

Mr. MONEY, opposing the motion, said, that 'his principal object in rising was, to do justice to an individual who had been alluded to during the debate—he meant Mr. Owen. An hon. member had said, that Mr. Owen disbelieved in a future state. He had communicated with Mr. Owen, and he had great reason to believe that the hon. member had mistaken the opinions of Mr. Owen. He begged the hon. member to state in what part of Mr. Owen's works he found that opinion promulgated.'

Mr. RICARDO said, that the last act he would commit would be to misrepresent the opinions of any individuals. He had gathered Mr. Owen's opinions from the works which

---

[1] In the debate on the Roman Catholic franchise bill, Mr. Hume having attacked the Methodists as 'the Protestant Jesuits,' Mr. Butterworth had retorted, 'The sect to which he belonged was highly complimented by the censure of a gentleman who had defended the principles of Carlile in that House.'

he had published. After reading the speeches which Mr.
Owen had delivered in Ireland and other places, he had come
to the conclusion, that Mr. Owen did not believe in a future
state of rewards and punishments. It was one of the doctrines
of Mr. Owen that a man could not form his own character,
but that it was formed by the circumstances which surrounded him—that when a man committed an act which the
world called vice, it ought to be considered his misfortune
merely, and that therefore no man could be a proper object
for punishment. This doctrine was interwoven in his system;
and he who held it could not impute to the Omnipotent
Being a desire to punish those who, in this view, could not be
considered responsible for their actions.[1]

The motion was negatived.

[The session closed on 19 July 1823.]

---

[1] Some light is thrown on this incident by Mallet, who after re-porting the debate in his Diary adds: 'There the debate closed; but it appears that Ricardo had seen Owen in the morning and had asked him whether he had any objection to have his name and peculiar opinions quoted in support of the prayer of the petition, and that Owen had not only assented to it, but told Ricardo that it would be peculiarly gratifying to him. The fact is that Owen is extremely disregardful of established opinions and of public feeling, and that he de-lights in any opportunity of asser-ting his own principles. But being in the House during the debate, when he saw the effect produced by Ricardo's statement, and the feeling it excited in the assembly, his natural boldness forsook him and a desire of fair fame prevailed; he therefore wrote a few lines to Ricardo in pencil desiring him to explain away what he had said, and upon Ricardo's declining to comply with his request he applied to Money. Ricardo told me that he was very near stating to the House what had passed between him and Owen in the morning; but his good nature prevailed.' (J. L. Mallet's MS Diary, entry of 10 July 1823.) On the morning of the day in question (1 July) they had met when Owen had appeared before the Committee on the Employment of the Poor in Ireland, of which Ricardo was a member. (See the Committee's Report, p. 156.)

ON 12 Feb. 1824 Mr. HUME rose to move for an inquiry into the laws restricting the emigration of artizans, the exportation of machinery and the combination of workmen, and said: 'At the end of last session he had given notice that he would, early in the present, fulfil his undertaking; and he had done so by the advice, and in hopes of the assistance, of a distinguished individual, whose recent loss the kingdom had to deplore [hear, hear!]. The late Mr. Ricardo was so well acquainted with every branch of the science of political economy, formerly, and until he had thrown light upon it, so ill understood, that his aid on such a question would have been of the utmost value. When he remembered the manner in which his lamented friend had always delivered his opinions, and the candour of moderation he invariably displayed towards his opponents, he might boldly assert, that there was not a member on any side of the House, who would for a moment deny the extent of the loss the country had thus sustained [hear, hear! from all parts of the House]. The general interest of the community was the single object he ever had in view, and through good report and bad report, he had pursued it with the meekest spirit of humility, and the most liberal spirit of inquiry. With regard to the principles which Mr. Ricardo was so capable of expounding, now that time had worn away many of the ruder prejudices against them, he might say, that not a few of those opponents, who had long theoretically resisted his doctrines, would at this time, though perhaps somewhat unwillingly, allow, that many of his predictions had been fulfilled. It was doubtless presumptuous in him to touch matters which his late friend had already so ably treated; and he only had given notice originally of his intention to bring this great subject under the consideration of the House, in the hope and expectation, that he should have enjoyed the benefit of his aid and counsel.'

Mr. HUSKISSON (President of the Board of Trade), concurring in the motion, said: 'He was not at all surprised that the hon. member for Aberdeen, in proposing this inquiry, should have regretted the loss which the House had sustained by the death of his valued friend, the late Mr. Ricardo—a gentleman, whom he had also had the pleasure of reckoning among his friends. There was no man who esteemed more highly the acuteness and ability of Mr. Ricardo than he did, and no man who more sincerely lamented his loss. In all his public conduct there was an evident anxiety to do what he thought right, to seek the good of the country, and to pursue no other object; and his speeches were always distinguished by a spirit of firmness and conciliation that did equal honour to himself and to his country.'

RICARDO'S AUTOGRAPH TRANSCRIPT
OF HIS OWN SPEECH OF 24 MAY 1819

(see p. xxx)

Ricardo May 24ᵗʰ 268

Mr. *Ricardo* said, he was fully prepared of the truth of the declaration of the hon. Director that the Bank wished to resume cash payments, but he was just as fully persuaded that they did not know how to set about it. When called before the committee the Directors individually admitted that the price of bullion & the exchanges were affected by the amount of their issues;— when collected in their own Court they avowed that "they conceive it to be their duty to declare, that they are unable to discover any solid foundation for such a sentiment." And now in the Phenomena which they have made to the Chancellor of the Exchequer, they again admit that the exchanges are affected by their fears, for they condemn the measure recommended by the Committee for restoring the exchange to par, on the ground of its being calculated to force them to contract the amount of their circulation, which they represent as fatal to the public interest. When they warned such immediate opening, and after the experience which the House had had of their conduct, it would be the highest indiscretion in Parliament not to take note of their want the preparation for the resumption of cash payments. He did not think this a question only between the Bank & Ministers, on it had been argued by his right hon. friend but ——— between one & the Bank on one side, & the country on the other. He was therefore disposed to concur with his right hon. friend in any measure which might be devised to keep the minister also under control. One principle was clear, & was of the utmost importance in the consideration of this subject. – it was this; that those who had the power of regulating the quantity of the circulating medium of the country had the power of regulating the rate of the exchange, and (the price of) every commodity. This power clearly resided in the hands of the Directors of the Bank, and it was a most formidable

___

... it quite astonished him that Mr. Harman could imagine that it was in the power of an individual to influence the exchanges against the wish of the Bank; which was just as reasonable as to suppose that an individual ~~commander~~ could regulate the price of corn. This question was one of immense importance in principle, but in the manner of bringing it about was trivial, and not deserving the half an hour's consideration of the House. The difficulty was only that of raising the currency 3 per cent. in value [hear,

... or any other commodity of general consumption.

tion equal to this, without inconvenience, when in

where metal alone circulated, it could not be doubted that gold might, from various circumstances, become more or less valuable, and thus affect all contracts, though from there being no other standard to measure it by, its variations were less palpable. His particular reason — support, the measure under consideration was this. By withdrawing paper, so as to restore the note to its bullion value (an alteration, by the bye, only of 5 per cent.), the House would have done all that was required (hear, hear!). But if the House adopted the proposition of the Honourable Gentleman (Mr. Ellice), another variation in the value of the currency would take place, which it was his (Mr. R.'s) wish to guard against. If that Amendment were agreed to, an extraordinary demand would take place for gold for the purpose of coinage, which would enhance the value of the currency 3 or 4 per cent. in addition to the first enhancement (hear, hear!). As to the plan under the consideration of the House, it was that which the Bank Directors, if they were wise, should wish to fill for (hear!). They should wish to fill the circulation with paper, and so long ... they would have there would be no coin in circulation, they would have the monopoly. They had no real interest in the depreciation of the currency; it would be rather their interest to raise it, even to double the value. They were in the situation of creditors, not of debtors; their whole capital being in money or other securities representing money (hear, hear!). As to the Resolution which bore, that the Government should repay the Bank a certain sum, he could not agree with it. The House having taken a security that the currency should be of a certain value, they had done enough, and should not farther interfere with the proceedings of the Directors, who should answer to their Proprietors only for their concerns. The Bank might, if this Resolution were agreed to, feel some difficulty in putting forth the amount of currency which was required. For though what the Directors thought a check, viz. the rate of interest on money, was no check at all as to the amount of issues,

Adam

as as Smith and Mr. Hume, and others had satisfactorily proved; yet as the Bank Directors were governed by certain traditional limits, or something like limits, in discounting to individual merchants, they might have difficulty in keeping up the requisite amount of currency.

He was certainly for leaving them to conduct all such transactions according to their own discretion and pleasure, provided only that such a check was established as should guard against a redundancy. The proposed mode of resuming payments appeared to him the easiest that could be imagined. The Bank would be placed under no restraint at first, nor any sudden necessity of reducing its issues. An opportunity would be afforded of effecting the object in the most gradual manner; and even when bullion payments should be made at the Mint price, the inconvenience would be but inconsiderable.

... Till October 1820, the Bank need make no reduction, and then a slight one [hear!]; and he had no doubt that if they were cautious they might arrive at cash payments without giving out one guinea in gold. The Bank need not reduce their issues cautiously; he only feared they would do it too rapidly [hear!]. If he might give them advice, he should recommend to them not to buy bullion, but even though they had a few millions, if he had the management of their concerns, he should even boldly sell. Every sale would improve the exchanges, and till gold fell to 3l. 17s. 6d. there would be no necessity for the Bank to make any purchases. He was only sorry that the Bank was not to be obliged by the Resolutions to buy all the bullion of-might starve the circulation. The Mint, it was true, was to remain open to the public, who might coin the bullion which they obtained from the Bank. Mr. Mushett, whose evidence respecting the coinage was worthy of attention, from its accuracy and general ability, had stated, that with a capital of 12,000,000l. a 300,000l. the Mint could supply the public with 12,000,000l. a year. Yet a year was a long time to wait for twelve millions, and it might easily happen, that in the interim between the reduction of the Bank issues and the supply afforded from the Mint, the country might seriously feel the deficiency. It was on that account that he should have wished a resolution inserted, to compel the Bank to give its notes for bullion (at 3l. 17s. 6d.) on demand. With the exception of this omission, the plan was, in his opinion, perfectly safe and gentle. He was quite astonished that such an alarm prevailed at a reduction of perhaps one million in four years ... and could only ascribe it to the indiscreet language of the Bank [hear, hear!]. The Hon—ble Director ... had that night told them, not to withdraw confidence from the Bank. The House did not withdraw confidence from the Bank from ... but from a conviction of its total ignorance of the principles of political economy [hear! and a laugh]. The Bank had had ample time to reduce their issues, so as to lower the price of gold; yet in spite of the times repeatedly fixed for the resumption of cash payments, they had never done so. It was not the business of the Directors to consider the interests of the public. That was the business of his Majesty's Ministers ... and when the Hon. Director ... told them that the Directors had lost so much on the purchase of gold, and so much on the issue of tokens, his question was, why had they done so? Their business was with the interests of the Proprietors, for whom they were trustees, not with the interests of the Public. The Directors were answerable to the Proprietors for these misapplications of their funds. He (Mr. R.) had been so astonished, that the undivided profits of the Bank had been so small, which, he should have imagined, must have at least amounted to £........ ; but now, by the confession of the Hon—able Gentleman, the matter was explained. The Directors had scattered a million here and a million there, according to their views of the wants of the Ministry or the Country, without any regard to the interest of the Proprietors [hear, hear!]. The Hon—ble Director had advised them not to cramp the currency, and had referred to their experience of 1797. But that was not a parallel case. It was a season of alarm and panic, when every man had wished to have gold in his house in fear of an invasion. His Right Honourable Friend (Mr. Tierney) had asked, what, under the plan proposed, was the holder of 10l. to do; for he could not get bullion at the Bank? According to the Amendment, the Right Honourable Gentleman was in no great hurry to give this poor man either bullion or specie. But were they doing nothing by the plan for the holder of 10l.? The holder of a 10l. note would be improved in his condition; for, although he could not go to the Bank for gold, he might resort to any goldsmith, who would let him have that proportion of gold to which his note was entitled; and the difference to him would be so trifling, as not to be worthy of consideration in the decision of a great question. It had been said, on the part of the Bank, that they were ready to pay, if repaid the advances which they had made to the Government. But how came they to make those advances to Government, if not assured of repayment at a certain time? The Bank had not been forced to make those advances, but the Directors had such an extraordinary disposition to act as Ministers [a laugh, and hear, hear]. It would, however, be better if those Directors would rather attend to their own interests and those of their constituents. A most fearful and destructive depreciation had at one time taken place; but from that we had recovered, and he was happy to reflect that we had so far retraced our steps. We had nearly got home, and he hoped the right [struck] would lend them his assistance to enable them to reach it in safety. He would venture to state, that in a very few weeks all alarm would be forgotten, and at the end of the year we should all be surprised to reflect that any alarm had ever prevailed at a prospect of a variation of 3 per cent. in the value of the circulating medium. His own general opinion was, that an unfavourable state of exchange must always proceed from a redundant currency. If corn were imported and paid for in bullion, it was a proof that bullion was the cheapest commodity. Suppose all the Bank-notes [struck], would not gold become infinitely cheaper? If our paper had been of any intrinsic value, it would, having become cheap from excess, have been exported also. [struck] He thought it right here to pay the tribute of his approbation to the late excellent regulations of the Mint. He entirely approved of making gold the standard, and of keeping silver as a token currency. It appeared to him to be a solid improvement in the system of our coinage. Nothing could be clearer than that Government had the power, by limiting the quantity, to regulate the value of the silver. The hon. gent. (Mr. J.P. Grant) indeed had observed, that the silver coin might be imitated abroad; supposing this to be the fact, the value of the silver coin might be lessened, but that of the gold would not therefore be raised. The silver was not a legal tender above 40s., and gold might always be of 100l. in gold; but this could have no effect in altering the relation between gold and all other commodities. He should be happy to argue this question with the hon. member, (Alderman) of the "Old Merchant," [a laugh] on some occasion when it would be less irrelevant to the subject under consideration.—The hon. member sat down amidst loud and general cheering from all sides of the house.

Alderman HEYGATE then addressed the chair, but the impatience of the house produced a temporary confusion, in the midst of which, after one or two observations, the hon. member sat down.

Lord CASTLEREAGH suggested, that as there was but little hope of the house being able to come to a decision on this important question that night, it might be more satisfactory to the hon. member himself that the debate should be now adjourned till to-morrow, when he would have a more favourable opportunity of stating his views to the house.

The question for adjournment was then put and carried, and the other orders of the day being disposed of, the house adjourned at two o'clock.

EVIDENCE ON THE
USURY LAWS
1818

NOTE ON THE EVIDENCE ON THE
USURY LAWS

THE question of the Usury Laws was first raised in the House
of Commons, after the end of the war, by Brougham in a speech
of 1 February 1816.[1] The law then in force was an Act of Queen
Anne (12 Anne Stat. 2. c. 16) which limited the rate of interest
to five per cent. Following Brougham's suggestion, on 22 May
1816 Serjeant Onslow, M.P. for Guildford, moved to bring in a
bill for their repeal; this bill, which was later withdrawn, was the
first of a series of unsuccessful attempts to obtain their repeal.
Onslow's motion was introduced again in May 1817, when it was
postponed till the following year.

On 21 April 1818, again on Onslow's motion, a Committee
was appointed 'to consider the effects of the Laws which regulate
or restrain the Interest of Money'.[2] The Chairman of the Committee was Onslow himself and among the members were the
Chancellor of the Exchequer, Lord Castlereagh, Robinson,
Wallace, Huskisson, Sir John Newport, Sir James Mackintosh,
Baring, Brougham, Sir Samuel Romilly; Sir Henry Parnell was
added to the Committee on 28 April.

The Committee took evidence from twenty-one witnesses representing the commercial and landed interests; the first to be
heard was Ricardo. Almost every one of the witnesses declared
that the Laws were either injurious, particularly to the landed
interest, or inoperative. The Report of the Committee was presented on 28 May 1818 in the form of three Resolutions as follows:

1. That the laws regulating or restraining the rate of interest
have been extensively evaded, and have failed of the effect of
imposing a maximum on such rate; and that of late years, from
the constant excess of the market rate of interest above the rate
limited by law, they have added to the expense incurred by
borrowers on real security, and that such borrowers have been
compelled to resort to the mode of granting annuities on lives,
a mode which has been made a cover for obtaining higher interest

---

[1] *Hansard*, XXXII, 41; cp. also
ib. 381.

[2] *Journals of the House of Commons*, 1818, p. 272.

than the rate limited by law, and has farther subjected the borrowers to enormous charges, or forced them to make very disadvantageous sales of their estates.

2. That the construction of such laws, as applicable to the transactions of commerce as at present carried on, have been attended with much uncertainty as to the legality of many transactions of frequent occurrence, and consequently been productive of much embarrassment and litigation.

3. That the present period, when the market rate of interest is below the legal rate, affords an opportunity peculiarly proper for the repeal of the said laws.[1]

No action was taken till 10 Feb. 1819 when Onslow again introduced a Bill to repeal the Usury Laws; but on 9 June it was postponed once more. It was revived on 12 April 1821, when it was the occasion of a debate in which Ricardo took part;[2] after being deferred several times the bill was dropped. A similar bill was introduced by Onslow in 1823, when Ricardo again spoke in support;[3] it was however once more abandoned. Onslow renewed his attempts in 1824 and 1826 with no better success.

The repeal of the Usury Laws took place by stages over a period of years from 1833 to 1854. It began with a clause in the Bank Charter Act of 1833 (3 & 4 Wm. IV c. 98) which exempted bills of exchange, not having more than three months to run, from the operation of the Usury Laws. An Act of 1837 (7 Wm. IV & 1 Vict. c. 80) also exempted bills of exchange of not more than twelve months' currency; this measure, which was a temporary one, was prolonged by an Act of 1839 (2 & 3 Vict. c. 37) which also exempted loans of more than £10. These measures were further prolonged by Acts of 1843 (6 & 7 Vict. c. 45), 1845 (8 & 9 Vict. c. 102), and 1850 (13 & 14 Vict. c. 56). The Usury Laws were finally repealed by an Act of 1854 (17 & 18 Vict. c. 90).

Ricardo's Evidence is here reprinted from the 'Report from the Select Committee on the Usury Laws', in *Parliamentary Papers,* 1818, vol. VI.[4] Numbers have been prefixed to the questions, and questions and answers printed in separate paragraphs.

---

[1] *Hansard,* XXXVIII, 995–6.
[2] See his speech above, p. 109.
[3] See above, p. 323.

[4] The Report and Evidence were reprinted in April 1821 (*Parliamentary Papers,* 1821, vol. IV).

MINUTES OF EVIDENCE TAKEN BEFORE
THE SELECT COMMITTEE ON
THE USURY LAWS

Jovis, 30° die Aprilis, 1818.

Mr. Serjeant ONSLOW, in the Chair.

DAVID RICARDO, Esq. called in; and Examined.

[1] Has your attention been called to the laws which restrain the rate of interest?
Yes.

[2] Have you that experience, to say, or have you perceived, whether those laws are beneficial or otherwise?
I think otherwise.

[3] In what respect do you think otherwise?
It appears to me, from the experience which I have had on the Stock Exchange, that, upon almost all occasions they are evaded, and that they are disadvantageous to those only who conscientiously adhere to them.

[4] Do you think that repealing those laws, would have the effect of raising or lowering the average rate of interest?
I think that the effect would be but trifling; but if any thing, it would tend to lower the rate of interest.

[5] When the funds afford a greater rate of interest than 5 per cent, do not the usury laws injure the commercial part of the world, with regard to discounts?
Not only at that time, but at other times, for it often happens that the price of the funds afford a less rate of interest than 5 per cent, at the same time that the market rate of interest is much above 5 per cent.

[6] But however, in point of fact, during the late wars, have or have not persons engaged in commerce, sustained injuries from the operation of the usury laws?

I should think, that they had sustained injuries in consequence of those laws.

[7] Have you any doubt of it?

I have no doubt at all, as far as my experience goes, but those injuries have been diminished by the easy means of evading them.

[8] Of successfully evading them?

The evasion of the laws is the effect of the natural order in which these transactions take place.

[9] In what manner evaded?

In the particular market with which I am acquainted, namely, the Stock Market, they are evaded by means of the difference between the money price and the time price of stock, which enables a person to borrow at a higher rate of interest than 5 per cent, if possessed of stock, or to lend at a higher rate, if the difference between the money price and the time price, affords a higher rate.

[10] Has that been acted upon extensively?

Very extensively; it is the usual and constant practice.

[11] The difference between the money and the time price, is that which is called "continuation;" is it not?

Yes.

[12] Was there not a trial some time ago, as to the legality of "continuation"?

There was.

[13] For some time, did not that trial diminish the practice very considerably, at least so far as making bargains for buying and selling to the same person?

That trial did diminish such bargains.

[14] Will you be kind enough to favour the Committee with your opinion with respect to these laws?

As far as my experience goes in business, nothing is more easy than to evade them; and after that trial to which allusion has been made, the same practice was continued, by altering the quantity of stock, either for money or for time; on all former occasions, the same amount of stock was bought for one period, that was sold for another period; but some timid men, after that trial, thought they were perfectly safe by making those sums different quantities, although they differed but a trifle in amount; and they thought themselves equally safe in buying stock for money of one person, and selling it, at the same instant, for time to another.

[15] Do you think that the supposed or real illegality tends, in any degree, to increase the rate of that Continuation?

The dealing in stock, for Time, is, in many cases, an illegal transaction; and that therefore may sometimes have an effect on the Continuation. A man possessed of money, purchasing stock for ready money at one price, and selling for a future day at a higher price, may make more than the legal rate of interest by so doing; but as he may not be actually possessed of stock at the time of making the time bargain, it cannot be considered, in any shape, as a legal transaction, and he can have no legal remedy against the default of the purchaser.

[16] I beg to ask whether I am to understand that, in general, these transactions by Continuation, are not strictly legal?

In my opinion, the greater part of these transactions are not legal.

[17] And you are of opinion, that that illegality raises the rate at which the borrower obtains the money?

Exactly so; there would be more competition if it was not for that.

[18] In this manner you conceive the usury laws, indirectly, to raise the rate of interest in these transactions, by compelling persons to resort to a practice not strictly legal? Yes.

[19] Am I to understand that, in point of fact, by this Continuation, nothing is done, but that money is raised at a higher than the legal rate of interest?

The transaction never has that complexion. A man bargains either for the purchase or the sale of stock, for money or time, and the rate of interest is never spoken of; it is the effect of the transaction, but never the avowed object of it.

[20] That I understand; but I wish to ask, whether, in point of fact, the effect is not simply to obtain the use of money at a higher than the legal rate, though that is not the shape of the transaction?

That is generally the object, but it frequently happens that the difference between the money and the time price of stock, may not afford so much as the market rate of interest, and may also be below the legal rate.

[21] I am to understand, therefore, that this is a risk which the lender, so to speak, takes upon himself?

There is no risk whatever in it, as far as regards the rate at which the money is lent or borrowed, because it is known at the time what rate of interest the difference between the money and time prices affords, and because the sum to be received by the lender is thereby defined and settled.

[22] Is not that sum, or rather the profit to be derived by the lender, governed by the market rate of interest at that time?

I can only say, that I think it is not.

[23] How comes it that it is not?

When preparations are making for a loan, large sales of stock are made, of which the seller may not be possessed, but which he may expect to replace by the share he may have in the loan to be contracted for; in such case, there may be rather a scarcity than otherwise of ready money stock in the market; the seller, who is not possessed of stock, will sell it at a small addition of price for time, and sometimes even under the money price.

[24] In your opinion can the Government loans, and other public transactions in the funds, be carried on without purchasing and selling stock for Time, and will not the difference between the two prices be governed and depend on the market value of money, and not on the legal rate of interest?

The Government loans could not, in my opinion, be carried on, if Time bargains were disused. The difference between the money price and the time price, does not always depend, as I have before stated, on the market rate of interest. In general, stock is in abundance; and in that case no inconvenience arises in depositing that as a security for money borrowed; but on some occasions stock exists in a degree of scarcity, and then, although the market rate of interest may be high, it may be inconvenient to the borrower to deposit this particular security; consequently the time price will be either very little above, or even below the money price.

[25] I beg to ask if it is within your knowledge, and if it is your opinion, that what you have described as Continuation, or time bargains, embrace any dealings in money at all, or are they not rather speculations between the parties?

In many cases, indeed in most cases, it is a speculation between the parties; but it is constantly had recourse to, as a means of borrowing and lending money.

[26] In times of difficulty, do not the usury laws injure commerce by restricting discounts, and the making of loans to persons engaged in all branches of trade?

In my opinion, they do.

[27] Will you state to the Committee, if you think that any good effect is derived by the public from the usury laws?

I think no good effect is derived from those laws.

[28] Are you aware of any inconvenience that would result from the repeal of them?

None, whatever.

[29] Were there not a considerable number of persons, who formerly lent money upon Continuation, who were deterred from doing so by this trial, in which it seemed to be held by the Court to be usurious?

The trial which took place was concerning Continuation upon scrip receipts, and not on stock. The transactions are similar to each other, but the facility of proof may be different.

[30] Those were actions under the usury laws, were they not?

They were.

[31] But it was, I believe, one action to recover penalties under the usury laws?

It was.

[32] You have already said, that it did deter many persons from continuing to lend money on Continuation?

Yes.

[33] By so deterring them, had it not the natural operation to raise the rate of Continuation?

I consider that rather as a question of science, which must
require a good deal of consideration, because the money
may be lent by these parties at the legal rate of interest, and
thus it may come to the same borrowers by a circuitous
route.

[34] If you wished yourself to borrow money on Continuation, should you not be desirous that there should be
in the market a great number of persons disposed to lend
upon Continuation?

Most certainly.

[35] For what reason?

Because it is probable the terms might be somewhat
lower.

[36] Does not the power of selling stock for money, and
repurchasing it for time, afford great facility to the holders
of stock, by enabling them for temporary purposes to procure
money, without foregoing the advantage of repossessing
their stock at a distant day?

Most undoubtedly.

[37] May not this advantage be considerably more than
the excessive interest which the transaction may have obliged
them to pay?

Without any doubt at all.

[38] What effect would the abrogation of the usury laws
produce upon the financial operations of the Government,
in time of war; I mean, in the negociation of loans?

It would rather tend to facilitate them; the Government
is not bound by the usury laws, for in allowing discount for
prompt payment for a loan, they frequently give considerably
more than 5 per cent.

[39] When the legal rate of interest is 5 per cent, and the
Government are enabled to borrow at a higher rate of interest,

does it not proceed, as a necessary consequence, that they, the Government, are enabled to borrow when individuals are not?

Certainly.

[40] Does not the Government, therefore, obtain in this way, a preference in the money market, and thereby obtain a facility in the negociation of their loans?

If the law was not evaded, such would be the effect; but, as I have already observed, it is completely evaded.

[41] In the negociation of loans, have you ever known the laws for restricting interest to be taken into consideration in adjusting the terms?

Never; and frequently, when loans are raised at an interest below the legal rate of interest, the mode in which the discount on prompt payment is calculated, affords a rate of interest of sometimes 7, 8, or 9 per cent.

[42] Do not takers of loans calculate the advantages which result in Government stock transactions from the habit of evading the usury laws?

Certainly; if those laws were not evaded, the contractor would not be able to give the minister such good terms; his transactions would be cramped, if he were prevented from borrowing at the market rate of interest.

[43] What is the criterion by which you judge the market rate of interest, or is there any criterion at all?

I know of no other criterion than the prices of the public securities, and the facility of raising money for short periods.

[44] Do you not think that the price of the Government securities affords a very good criterion of the market rate of interest?

Not a very good one; their price is a good deal influenced

by speculation, and by the anticipation of political and financial events.

[45] I would mean to speak of the average price of these securities, and not of their occasional fluctuations?

I can hardly conceive any times in which these securities are not acted upon by the considerations I have stated.

[46] Would you consider the price of exchequer bills as a criterion?

As a better criterion than the price of the funds.

[47] Would you not rather consider, that discount in the market was a more just criterion than the value of the public funds?

No; because discounts are strictly regulated by the laws of usury.

[48] I mean to confine it to discounts when interest is not above the legal rate, and there are cases when discounts are inferior to the legal rate?

When the market rate of interest is below 5 per cent, then I think that the discount given on a bill is a very good criterion of the market rate of interest.

[49] You have already said, that money may be raised by borrowing on Continuation; does not this give to the holder of stock a greater facility of raising money than other persons possess, who are holders of other property?

I should think it does.

[50] Are you acquainted with the nature of foreign loans?

I never was engaged in any.

[51] You do not know what is the discount of bills, or the mode of raising loans in France, Holland and Germany?

No, I do not.

[52] What are the grounds of your opinion of the principle by which the rate of interest is regulated?

It is regulated by the demand and supply, in the same way as any other commodity; but the demand and supply itself is again regulated by the rate of profit to be made on capital.

[53] Do you think there is anything in the nature of money, or of the transactions regarding the borrowing or lending of money, which distinguishes it from other commodities which find their value in the market, according to the proportion of demand and supply?

None, whatever; the market rate of interest for money depends on the proportion between the borrower and the lender of capital, without reference to the quantity or value of the currency by which the transactions of the country are carried on.

[54] Have you, in the course of your transactions, been acquainted with a case, in which any disadvantage could have been derived to the borrower, by the abrogation of the usury laws?

None whatever; on the contrary, the abrogation of the usury laws would, upon all occasions, have been advantageous, in my opinion, to the borrower.

[55] Are you not of opinion also, that their abrogation would be equally advantageous to the lender?

I conceive there are cases in which their abrogation would not be quite advantageous to the lender, because he may exact a premium for the risk which the law imposes upon him.

[56] But except in so far as he exacts a premium for his risk in breaking the law, you are of opinion he can derive no advantage from the usury laws?

I think all his advantages may be referred to that principle.

[57] Do you think that mercantile interests will be injured or served by these restraints of the usury laws upon interest?

I have already given my opinion, that they would be much served by the abrogation of these laws.

[58] If a person who is possessed of considerable capital in this country, or in any other country belonging to the United Kingdom, should wish to make the most of his money, and if he is restrained in this country by the Usury Act, do you not think it would be the means of his transferring his capital to another country, where he would obtain a greater rate of interest, by loan or discount?

Undoubtedly, if the law be not easily evaded.

[59] Do you not believe, that many have been injured by borrowing money upon annuities at a very high rate; and do you not believe, that many have been more injured by these means, than if they could have borrowed money at the market rate of interest?

I have no knowledge of any such transactions; but my opinion is very decided, that they have been more injured by having been prevented from borrowing money at the market rate of interest.

EVIDENCE
ON THE RESUMPTION
OF CASH PAYMENTS
1819

NOTES ON THE EVIDENCE ON THE RESUMPTION OF CASH PAYMENTS

I. *The Committees*

THE Suspension of Cash Payments by the Bank of England, which had been effected by the Order in Council of 26 February 1797, and confirmed by the Bank Restriction Act of the same year (37 Geo. III c. 45), was continued by an Act of 1803 (44 Geo. III c. 1), 'until Six Months after the Ratification of a Definitive Treaty of Peace'. After the Peace of Paris however the Resumption of Cash Payments was postponed by successive Acts,[1] the latest of which, in 1818, had fixed the date for Resumption as 5 July 1819.

Early in the Session of 1819 the Chancellor of the Exchequer intimated in the House of Commons that he would bring forward a measure for continuing the Restriction Act for a short period; but, soon after, he announced that in consequence of a communication from the Directors of the Bank (who preferred to 'submit to the Consequences of a Parliamentary Inquiry' rather than consent to a temporary and inadequate measure)[2] he proposed to move for a Committee of inquiry.[3] On 2 February 1819, on the motion of the Chancellor of the Exchequer, it was agreed that a Committee of Secrecy consisting of twenty-one members should be appointed 'to consider of the State of the Bank of England, with reference to the Expediency of the Resumption of Cash Payments at the period fixed by law, and into such other matters as are connected therewith; and to report to the House such information relative thereto, as may be disclosed without injury to the Public interests, with their Observations'. On 3 February the members were chosen by ballot as follows: Lord Castlereagh, the Chancellor of the Exchequer (Vansittart), Tierney, Canning, Wellesley Pole, Lamb, Robinson, Grenfell,

---

[1] 1814 (54 Geo. III c. 99), 1815 (55 Geo. III c. 28), 1816 (56 Geo. III c. 40), 1818 (58 Geo. III c. 37).

[2] Minute of the Committee of Treasury, 20 Jan. 1819, in Lords' Report, Appendix, p. 300.

[3] *Hansard,* XXXIX, 72 and 104.

Huskisson, Abercromby, Bankes, Sir James Mackintosh, Peel, Sir John Nicholl, Littleton, Wilson, Stuart Wortley, Manning, Frankland Lewis, Ashurst, Sir John Newport.[1] Peel was Chairman.

On 4 February the Lords appointed a Secret Committee, with the same terms of reference as the Commons'. The members were: Earl of Harrowby (Lord President), Duke of Wellington, Marquess of Lansdowne, Earl Graham, Earl Bathurst, Earl of Liverpool, Earl of St. Germains, Viscount Gordon, Viscount Granville, Lord King, Lord Grenville, Lord Redesdale, Lord Lauderdale.[2]

The Commons' Committee took evidence from twenty-four witnesses between 11 February and 1 May; the Lords' from twenty-five witnesses between 8 February and 30 April. Sixteen of them, including Ricardo, were heard by both Committees.

II. *The Proceedings of the Committees*

The enquiries of both Committees soon became centred round the plan of bullion payments, which had been outlined by Ricardo in the Appendix (1811) to his *High Price of Bullion* and developed in his *Proposals for an Economical and Secure Currency* (1816). Ricardo's plan hd been intended as a permanent system of currency; but the Committees at first considered it only as a temporary device to facilitate the resumption of cash payments. And although in the later stages of the enquiry the plan was discussed as a permanent system, it was eventually as a temporary measure that it was recommended by the Committee and embodied in Peel's Act. Nevertheless, even after the Act had been passed, Ricardo and his friends retained the hope that the plan might still be adopted permanently.[3]

Also the scheme, which was adopted, of reducing the price of gold according to a fixed scale until the mint price was reached was an idea of Ricardo; he had suggested it in 1811 in a letter to Tierney[4] (now a member of the Commons' Committee), but not in his published writings.

---

[1] *Journals of the House of Commons*, 1818–19, pp. 64 and 77.
[2] *Journals of the House of Lords*, 1818–19, p. 43.

[3] See Ricardo's letters to McCulloch of May 1819, quoted below, p. 367–8, and of January 1822, below, IX, 141.
[4] Below, VI, 67.

Some account of the proceedings of the Committees in their early stages is given in his Diary by J. L. Mallet,[1] who was in close touch with some of the principal witnesses, particularly William Haldimand[2] and Alexander Baring,[3] as well as with some of the members. In the entry for 13 February 1819, he writes that he 'dined at the Marcets with Abercrombie, Sharpe, Ricardo, Mr Geo. Philips, the Rev. Sidney Smith and his wife, Mr and Miss Boddington. In the evening Mr Blake, Sir Edward Coddrington, Dr Wollaston, and other People came in'. The conversation first turned on Parliamentary Reform:

'The Secret Committees of both Houses respecting the Restriction Act, also became a subject of interesting conversation. Mr Ricardo is more at home here than in the maze of political reform. He had been closeted in the morning with Lord Grenville and Mr Grenfell; discussing various parts of that important subject. Abercrombie, who is a Member of the Committee of the Lower House, also entered with some interesting particulars of the state of opinions in the Committees; for altho' they are com-

---

[1] The editor is much indebted to the late Sir Bernard Mallet for allowing him to quote this and many other passages from the unpublished MS in his possession.

[2] A Director of the Bank, at this time out by rotation.

[3] Alexander Baring was the head of the house of Baring Brothers, the magnitude of whose loans to the French Government in 1818 and 1819 complicated the problem of the resumption of cash payments. Baring himself was in Paris during the early stages of the enquiry, when the examination of the witnesses seemed to proceed somewhat aimlessly; a focal point was provided when, on his return to London at the end of February, Baring's views in favour of a delayed resumption of payments on Ricardo's plan became known. In the subsequent debate in the Commons the Chancellor of the Exchequer referred to Baring's evidence as 'certainly the most important of any' (*Hansard*, XL, 739). And *The Times* in a leader remarked 'We wish that the Bank had been able to control Mr Baring's loans, rather than Mr Baring's loans had controlled the Bank' (18 May 1819). Mallet records in his MS Diary a conversation with Baring in which the latter described his intricate financial operations in Paris and surmises that Baring was apprehensive of an early resumption: 'Narrower means of credits, a closer system of discounts, a return to a sound currency in this great commercial country, could not fail affecting all Europe for a time; and it is *for a time,* and for that *very time,* that Baring wants facilities of every kind.' (Entry of 2 March 1819.)

mittees of *secrecy*, every thing that passes there in the morning, is known at night in the great political circles.

'The examination of William Haldimand (Mrs Marcet's Brother) before the Lords Committee, for two days successively,[1] and during five hours in each day—and the effect produced by his evidence and the information he had given the Committee, was a subject of general remark and congratulation....

'Lord King sent him a scheme this morning thro' Mr Thorpe, by means of which the resumption of cash payments would be facilitated. Supposing the period fixed for paying in cash to be 18 months; a scale would be formed of the price at which the Bank would be obliged to purchase Bullion during every week of the intervening space of time. For instance the price of Gold is £4. 4. –: during the first week they would be obliged to purchase Bullion (upon Ricardo's plan) at £4. 4. The next at £4. 3. $11\frac{3}{4}$, and so on, till by the reduction of the issues, they had brought the price down to the Mint price of £3. 18. 6. William Haldimand thinks well of King's scheme, which might in his opinion be adopted with some modifications: but he apprehends that no scheme can prevent the extreme distress which will be felt from the narrowing the discounts of the Bank. The depreciation is reckoned at about 7 per cent...Ricardo does not think that the distress will be so great but in this he differs from all other commercial men.

'Mr Dorrien, Mr Pole and Mr Harman, the two first of whom are the Governor and Deputy Governor of the Bank, and the latter one of the oldest and ablest of the Directors, have been examined before both Committees, and have made a wretched figure. Mr Pole shewed himself so totally ignorant of first principles, that Huskisson who took the lead in the examination of the House of Commons Committee, looked around him, and observing the impression, stopt short and sat down, not wishing to expose Mr Pole unnecessarily—. And yet these are the men to whom the power is delegated of regulating the currency of the kingdom, and of lowering or raising at their pleasure the market value of every species of property—.

'Lord Liverpool and Lord Grenville take the lead in the

---

[1] Friday 12 and Monday 15 February.

examinations of the House of Lords. Canning, Huskisson, and Frankland Lewis in the Commons. Lord Castlereagh asks questions which shew that he does not know the a.b.c. of the subject. Poor Vansittart sits silent and dejected at seeing all his opinions overturned. The Duke of Wellington is very attentive, and writes down all that passes: he made some very pertinent observations to William Haldimand, in a very unassuming and modest manner. Lord Harrowby and Lord Bathurst are also very attentive. Lord Lansdowne, Lord King and Lord Lauderdale understand the subject thoroughly, and afford great assistance. There cannot be a better Committee than in the Lords. The Committee of the Commons is not so good. Huskisson is the only man who understands the subject thoroughly. Mr Peel who is Chairman is very impartial and intelligent; but he knows little about it. Tierney altho' a good financier, is not up to the intricacies of the question. It is always a toss up whether good Sir John Newport is right or wrong. Abercrombie can seldom attend. Mr Grenfell is able and well acquainted with the subject; but not of the calibre of Lord Grenville.'

It was on 12 February, during the examination of Haldimand before the Lords' Committee, that the plan of bullion payments was first mentioned. He was asked: 'Does the Witness think, that gradual Reduction [in the Amount of Paper Circulation] would be secured by compelling the Bank of England to sell Bullion at the price of 82s. during the first three Months; 81s. during the next three Months and so on in Succession, reducing it in Fifteen Months to the Mint Price?'[1] Haldimand asked for time to consider the question and when recalled on 15 February he said: 'I have consulted two sensible Men, whom I consider to understand the Subject; and I do think, in Concurrence with them, the Plan well calculated to secure to the Public a gradual and certain Restoration of the ancient Value of the Currency.'[2]

The first reference before the Commons' Committee to the plan was in a question put to William Ward, a Director of the Bank, on 23 February: 'What would, in your opinion, be the effect of requiring the bank of England to sell gold and silver bullion, in quantities not less than the value of £100 sterling, to

---

[1] Lords' Report, 'Minutes of Evidence', p. 44, Q. 35.

[2] Lords' Report, 'Minutes of Evidence', p. 47, Q. 52.

holders of their notes, at the present market price, and to lower the price at a given rate weekly, until it fell to the mint price, provision being at the same time made that the bank should, in each week, buy bullion at a fraction less than the selling price of each week?' Ward objected that such a plan would not save the Bank from a run 'occasioned by panic or by politics'.[1]

It was in the evidence of Swinton Holland, 'a partner with Baring, Brothers, & Co.', before the Commons' Committee on 2 March that the plan was proposed as a permanent measure, and Ricardo named as its author: 'It having been intimated to me, some days ago, that I was likely to be called before this Committee, I turned my attention to the subject. My opinions are chiefly founded upon Mr. Ricardo's theory, reduced, as I conceive, to a practical form.' He then read a paper, which began: 'In submitting this plan to the consideration of the Committee, I must beg to premise, that the ground work of it is entirely taken from Mr. Ricardo's admirable pamphlet, "*Proposals for an economical and secure Currency;*" that if there is any merit in the plan, that merit appertains to Mr. Ricardo. With this gentleman I have not had any communication on the subject, nor have I the honour of being known to him; that I have merely reduced his system into detail and form for practice; and I can venture to assert, as a practical man of business, that there will be little, if any difficulty, in carrying it into effect'.

He proposed that the Bank should be required, within a period to be fixed (and which in a subsequent answer he suggested might be six months from the Report of the Committee), 'to pay (if demanded) all their notes large and small, if the amount presented, added together, forms a sum total of one hundred pounds; and that the same shall be paid by the ounce of gold, at the option of the bank, either in gold, in specie of the current coin of the realm, gold in ingots, bars, or gold in foreign coin...'

'Let the period at which the bank is to commence this system be made public, and declared to the world as *fixed, absolute,* and *unchangeable.*

'Instead of 3*l.* 17*s.* 10$\frac{1}{2}$*d.* per ounce, let the standard value be declared to be 80*s.* per ounce; which would require the bank to

---

[1] Commons' Report, 'Minutes of Evidence', p. 78.

deliver or pay against £.100 of its notes, exactly 25 ounces of gold of standard fineness, (or in proportion to standard fineness, if delivered in foreign coin)…

'In order to preserve the equilibrium between paper and gold, and prevent bank notes rising to a premium, the bank must be obliged to deliver its paper to the public, or to the bearer of one ounce or more of gold in bullion, (or coin in its relative proportion per ounce to standard) thereby creating a fixed and invariable market for gold, at 80s. per ounce…

'This system will require the trade in bullion to be free, unrestricted, and the import and export allowed, without any impediment being thrown in the way thereof.

'Bank notes will be required to be made a *legal tender* so long as, *and no longer* than the bank gives 25 ounces of gold for 100*l.* in bank notes.'[1]

The following day, 3 March, Alexander Baring stated before the Lords' Committee that he had 'a very favourable Opinion of the Plan of Currency suggested by Mr. Ricardo, as combining the two Desiderata of an extensive Paper Circulation, with Security against its Depreciation.'[2]

Meanwhile Ricardo had been in touch with members of the Committees and was expecting to be examined. On 28 February he had written to Trower: 'The inquiry into the state of our currency, and exchanges, is proceeding in both houses very satisfactorily. I have had many conversations with several of the Committees of both Houses—with Lord Grenville, Marquis of Lansdown, Lord King, Mr. Huskisson, Mr. F. Lewis, Mr. Grenfell and others. All have a very perfect knowledge of the subject, and all agree that the progress of the public in comprehending the question has been very great. The Bank Directors themselves have improved, and they are far behind every other person. I confidently rely on measures being taken to place our currency in a satisfactory state. I am told that I shall be examined.'[3]

On 4 March he gave evidence before the Commons' Committee and outlined his plan. It is curious that in his evidence,

[1] Commons' Report, 'Minutes of Evidence', pp. 123–4.

[2] Lords' Report, 'Minutes of Evidence', p. 107, Q. 35.

[3] Below, VIII, 19.

both to the Commons' and to the Lords' Committees (below, p. 379, Q. 21 and p. 422, Q. 21) Ricardo recommended that the Bank should have the option of paying their notes either in specie or bullion; whilst in the subsequent debate in the House of Commons he opposed Ellice's amendment which gave to the Bank just such an option (above, p. 11). Perhaps Ricardo at first took it for granted that, Bullion payments being more advantageous to the Bank, the latter would not normally exercise the option of paying in specie; and later, when the reluctance of the Bank Directors to operate the plan became apparent, he thought it necessary to make Bullion payments obligatory.[1]

Thereafter most of the witnesses before the Commons' Committee were asked for their opinion on the plan of bullion payments. N. M. Rothschild, on 8 March, to the question whether he was acquainted with 'the plan proposed by Mr. Ricardo for the regulation of the payments at the bank', replied: 'I cannot recommend it, because, in case any news comes from abroad that there is the smallest chance of a war, every one will come at once and take out gold bars; a man may fetch a hundred thousand pounds worth of gold bars out of the bank in five minutes; but if you pay in cash, the bank will find out this, and they must count the cash; and in the course of a short period the government will hear of this, and the bank may be protected.'[2] He added that there would be many other difficulties in the plan; in particular, there was the danger of silver bars cased over with gold being passed for gold bars.

Two questions put to Lewis Lloyd, a banker, on 9 March, stress the distinction drawn by the Committee between the plan of bullion payments and the 'graduated scale'.

'A plan has been suggested to this Committee for the resumption of cash payments, which is known by the name of Mr. Ricardo's plan; have the goodness to state to the Committee whether you have formed any opinion upon that plan?—It certainly has appeared to me as unexceptionable a plan as any

---

[1] It should be noticed that, in spite of Ricardo's own evidence, the Committees assumed throughout that his plan excluded payments in specie.

[2] Commons' Report, 'Minutes of Evidence', p. 160.

I have heard suggested; it seems to remove some of the difficulties which would attend a resumption of cash payments.

'There has been another modification of that plan suggested, which would have this effect, that the bank should immediately or at the expiration of three months commence the payment of its notes in cash, but that they should pay in coin at the market price of gold, and that there should be a gradual reduction of the price of the gold which they should pay, until the market price of gold was reduced to the mint price; do you conceive the adoption of that plan would facilitate the resumption of cash payments?— I have paid very little attention to that, and am not able to give an answer; as to the other, I read the work, and it seemed to me to suggest an ingenious plan to counteract some of the objections which have occurred to the resumption of cash payments.'[1]

On 11 and 12 March Alexander Baring was examined on 'Mr. Ricardo's plan'.[2] He said that 'The plan in question is, in fact, no other than that of the bank of Hamburgh, only substituting a currency of paper in lieu of a transfer of book debt; and the bank of Hamburgh has always been found, from long experience, the best institution for preserving the standard of value; the payments of the bank of Hamburgh are solely in silver bullion.

'Supposing such a plan once adopted, and the price of gold and the exchanges to have continued steady for some time, under the operation of this plan; would not such a state of things afford a great facility for the return to the ancient system of this country, if such return should still be thought more desirable?—The plan would certainly bring with it no expense, and could at any period be got rid of without difficulty; at the same time, as one of its merits is to carry on the circulation with the least possible amount of bullion, of course, the supply for returning to the system of coin, would not be very great; at the same time it is my opinion that such a system would make London the great mart for gold and silver bullion in the same manner as the bank of Hamburgh has given that advantage to the city of Hamburgh for silver.

'You have probably heard that another plan has been suggested for the resumption of cash payments, with reference to the present actual price of gold, and varying the amount at which the issues

[1] Commons' Report, 'Minutes of Evidence', p. 171.

[2] Commons' Report, 'Minutes of Evidence', p. 189.

should be made from time to time, in proportion as the price of gold shall come nearer to the mint price; setting aside the question of good faith, which is involved in the first step of such a plan, do you think in other respects that it is practicable and advisable? —I should think not; I do not think the bank could be placed in a state of cash payments much earlier, by making a small difference in the price at which they would begin to pay, than by abiding by the old standard; there might be some facility, but not sufficient to justify so great a novelty.'[1]

On 17 March John Smith, a London banker and a member of the House, questioned on 'Mr Ricardo's suggestion', agreed that it would be advantageous to country banks. Asked for his opinion of 'the merits of that plan generally' he answered that he felt 'favourably disposed towards it'.[2]

Ricardo was again examined, apparently at his own request, on 19 March, when he delivered a paper in which he suggested that, if it was decided that a currency partly made up of gold coin was desirable, a 'moderate seignorage' should be charged on gold coin.

Two more witnesses were examined by the Commons' Committee on the plan. Vincent Stuckey, a country banker, on 22 March, agreed that 'the plan for the resumption of cash payments, commonly called Mr. Ricardo's' would 'afford a facility both to country bankers and to the bank of England'. Asked further 'What are the inconveniences which you consider would arise from this change in the mode of paying the notes of the bank of England?', he replied 'I am not aware of any inconvenience which can arise; I think it would be attended with very considerable convenience to pay the larger sums in bullion: it appears to me to be a very great improvement on a well-regulated paper currency; and it has always struck me, that at the resumption of cash payments by the bank, the above would be by far the best plan I ever heard of: I think it would do away a great part of that which many dread, a great and general demand for guineas; and after a year or two, seeing how the plan answered, the circulation of coin might be introduced, if found necessary.'[3]

---

[1] Commons' Report, 'Minutes of Evidence', p. 191. When recalled on 25 March Baring confirmed this answer; see *ib.* p. 204.

[2] Commons' Report, 'Minutes of Evidence', p. 224–5.

[3] Commons' Report, 'Minutes of Evidence', p. 247.

Thomas Smith, an accountant,[1] asked on 24 March 'Have you heard and considered of a plan, which is generally known by the name of Mr. Ricardo's plan, for the resumption of cash payments?' replied 'I wrote a reply to it a few weeks after it was published'.[2] To the question 'Do you think the plan of Mr. Ricardo preferable to the one for the resumption of cash payments, in the sense in which cash payments are ordinarily used?' he replied 'I conceive Mr. Ricardo's plan to be perfectly illegal, and to be impossible to be put in practice without risking the destruction of the bank, and the ruin of the country'. He then explained his own views on a standard of value and criticised at length Ricardo's plan.[3]

The Lords' Committee recalled Baring on 10 March and asked him: 'Supposing it were now the Determination of Parliament to restore to the Country, as quickly as may be safe and practicable, the Advantages of a Circulating Medium, regulated by a Metallic Standard of Value; would it in your Opinion be advisable to adopt for the Purpose the following Proposal, either wholly, or with any and what Variations, viz.

1st, That the Bank should be subjected to the Delivery of uncoined Gold or Silver, at the Mint Standard and Price, in Exchange for their Notes, instead of the Delivery of Coin:

2dly, That the Bank should also be obliged to give their Paper in Exchange for Standard Gold or Silver, at fixed Prices, taken somewhat below the Mint Price:

3dly, That the Quantity of Gold or Silver to be so demanded in Exchange for Paper at the Bank, and the Quantity to be so sold to the Bank, should be limited, not to go below a fixed Amount:

4thly, That the most perfect Liberty should be given at the same Time to export and import every Description of Bullion:

5thly, That the Mint should continue open to the Public for the Coinage of Gold Money:

6thly, That the same Privilege of paying Notes in Bullion should either be extended to the Country Banks, or that the Bank of England Notes (their Value being thus secured) should be made a legal Tender?'

---

[1] Not to be identified with Ricardo's friend of the same name.
[2] *A Reply to Mr. Ricardo's Proposals for an Economical and Secure Currency*, by Thomas Smith, London, Richardson, 1816.
[3] Commons' Report, 'Minutes of Evidence', pp. 257–9.

Baring replied: 'the Plan which I consider as by far the most perfect, and to which I know no Objection of any Sort, and which I am not sure that I should not prefer even to the old State of Currency, if that State could be easily returned to, is the Plan alluded to in the Question.'[1]

Richard Page,[2] a general merchant, asked on 17 March 'Are you acquainted with Mr. Ricardo's plan?' answered 'I have read it' and added that under this plan 'you have got one sort of Currency for every rich Man, and another sort of Currency for a poor Man ... you give the rich Man the best, and you give the poor Man the worst.'[3]

Thomas Tooke was examined on 22 March. In reply to a question on the restoration of the value of Bank of England paper he said: 'I have heard of no Measure better adapted, than one which has been suggested, of obliging the Bank by an Act of the Legislature to sell Gold Bullion at certain stated Prices progressively downwards, till it shall have reached the Mint Price; because I conceive, that there would be very great Danger of any Measure short of this failing of its Effect, as no Words merely conveying the Promise of a Resumption of Payments in Specie can satisfy the Public that it will actually take place at the Period fixed'.[4] On being asked whether he thought it possible to effect the restoration by stages so as to reach the mint price by 5 July 1820, he expressed the hope that this might be effected in a shorter period and stressed the disadvantages attending a long interval: 'These Disadvantages are the Suspence and more or less Uncertainty in undertaking all commercial Operations, which may be influenced in their Results by the State of the Currency while they are in Progress.'[5]

Asked further: 'Have you considered whether, after the Value of Bank Paper had been brought back to the Mint Standard, it would be more expedient that the Bank should thenceforth pay in

---

[1] Lords' Report, 'Minutes of Evidence', pp. 131–2, Q. 167. Later he was questioned about the period in which 'the Plan of Mr. Ricardo' could be carried into effect (p. 136–7).
[2] Author, under the pseudonym of Daniel Hardcastle, of a series of letters to *The Times* on the Bank Restriction; see below, VIII, 3, n. 1.
[3] Lords' Report, 'Minutes of Evidence', p. 158–9, Q. 79.
[4] Lords' Report, 'Minutes of Evidence', p. 179–80, Q. 83.
[5] *ib.* p. 180, Q. 84.

Coin, on the same Footing as before the Restriction, or that their Payments should continue to be made not in Coin but in Bullion, at the Mint Standard?' he delivered in answer a written paper: 'The Plan of a Circulation of Paper, convertible into Gold Bullion only at the Mint Price, is admirable for its Ingenuity and Simplicity, and there can be no Doubt of its Convenience and Cheapness. It is particularly well calculated to serve as an intermediate Measure for limiting and regulating the Paper Circulation, till Arrangements can be made for establishing the whole Currency on a permanent Footing. But if proposed in itself as a permanent System, I cannot but consider it as objectionable. A Circulation so saturated with Paper would be liable to Abuse, and to a Suspension of the Check of partial Convertibility, on lighter Grounds than if the Currency consisted of Coin and of strictly convertible Paper. And, taken in a general point of view, it must be admitted, that a Basis of so frail a Material, resting so exclusively on Credit and Confidence, is exposed to the Danger of frequent Derangement, and in some conceivable Cases to total Destruction. But, above all, is the Objection arising from the extended Inducement to Forgery. And independent of these Objections to an exclusive Paper Currency, it strikes me that many Contingencies and Exigencies might arise, wherein an abundant Stock of the precious Metals might be of essential Advantage. Upon the whole, therefore, in as far as I might be permitted to give an Opinion, it would be in favour of a Return to Payments in Coin.'[1] The rest of Tooke's paper discussed the question of a seignorage on the gold coin. He agreed with the remark of Ricardo, in the *Principles of Political Economy*,[2] that with a seignorage of five per cent the currency might be depreciated to that extent before coin were demanded and he supported the remedy proposed by Ricardo that Bank notes should be made payable in bullion, though not in coin, at the mint price. He suggested, as an improvement, that the gold bars should be issued by the Mint, instead of the Bank, 'because, independently of other Advantages, the high Prerogative of the Crown, as the Source from whence every Thing like metallic Money should emanate, would be preserved, as in fact the Bar Gold thus stamped, and

[1] Lords' Report, 'Minutes of Evidence', p. 180–1, Q. 89.

[2] Above, I, 372.

thereby acquiring additional Value, would be the simplest and cheapest Form of metallic Money.'[1]

Meanwhile the necessary permission from the House of Commons enabling Ricardo, as a member of the House, to appear before the Lords' Committee had been asked by the House of Lords on 17 March and granted by the Commons on 19 March.[2]

On 24 March Ricardo appeared before the Committee, and his examination was resumed when they next met on 26 March.

Before concluding their hearings the Lords' Committee recalled the Bank Directors to ascertain their views on the plan, which had come under discussion since their first appearance. On 31 March Jeremiah Harman, a former Governor, said: 'The Plan suggested would be a great Change in our ancient Monetary System, without an adequate Object, as it strikes me; and no one can foresee all the Consequences it might lead to.'[3] He also objected to the adoption for a period of a scale of gradually reduced prices on the ground that it 'would be a virtual Re-opening at £3. 17s. $10\frac{1}{2}$d.' Moreover 'it would oblige the Bank to go into the Bullion Market at a very great Disadvantage, and subject it to be the Sport of Bullion Dealers and Exchange Jobbers.'[4]

Samuel Thornton, also a former Governor, recalled on 2 April, expressed himself in favour of the plan of bullion payments on a graduated scale as a temporary measure: it would facilitate the ultimate resumption of cash payments, and it would allow a considerable saving of the precious metals. He suggested January 1820 as the earliest period at which the Bank could commence bullion payments at the market price, and twelve to eighteen months from that date before payments could be made at the mint price. He thought that it would be 'a necessary Part of the Plan to pay on a graduated Scale' to relieve the Bank from the liability to pay in cash their notes dated prior to 1817.[5]

The Governor, George Dorrien, heard again on 5 April, agreed that the plan of bullion payments would be a security to the Bank and would be a check on any sudden run upon it, and

---

[1] Lords' Report, 'Minutes of Evidence', p. 182, Q. 89.

[2] *Journals of the House of Lords, 1818–1819*, pp. 147 and 157.

[3] Lords' Report, 'Minutes of Evidence', p. 221, Q. 88.

[4] Lords' Report, 'Minutes of Evidence', p. 222, Qq. 96 and 97.

[5] *ib.* pp. 225–34.

approved the principle of a graduated scale; he thought that bullion payments could not be begun before a year and a half and that a further twelve months would be required to bring down the price to the Mint standard.[1]

III. *The Reports*

The First (or Interim) Reports of both Committees, issued on 5 April, merely stated that they would shortly present a plan for the Resumption of Cash payments; but in the meantime they recommended, as a matter of urgency, the adoption of a measure to suspend the engagements entered into by the Bank, in 1817, to pay in gold coin its notes of an earlier date than 1 January 1817.

A bill to this effect was immediately brought in by Peel; it passed through all its stages in the House of Commons on the same day (5 April),[2] and in the House of Lords on the following day, when it received the Royal Assent.

By this time Ricardo knew that his plan would be recommended in the final reports of the Committees. In a letter to McCulloch of 7 April, referring to the latter's review of *Economical and Secure Currency* in the *Edinburgh Review* for December 1818, he wrote: 'You have I am sure been the means of affording the most useful instruction, to many members of the Committees of both houses, and as for myself, I am under great obligations to you, for my plan might have slumbered, or have been forgotten, if you had not rescued it from oblivion, and said more in its favour than I had been able to do. You will be pleased to know that an investigation into the probable results of adopting that plan, or some modification of it, has formed one of the leading subjects of examination, by both Committees, and from the speech of Mr. Peel, as well as from those of Mr. Canning, and the Marquis of Lansdown, I have very little doubt but that it will be recommended, as a temporary, if not a permanent measure, in both reports.'[3]

The Second (and Final) Report of the Commons' Committee was presented and ordered to be printed on 6 May, and that of the Lords' Committee on 7 May.

[1] *ib.* p. 243–4.
[2] See Ricardo's speech supporting the bill, above, p. 2.
[3] Below, VIII, 20.

Mallet in his Diary indicates how the Committees reached their decision:

'The Committee of the Lords was unanimous with the exception of Lord Lauderdale who stuck to his own theory: the Committee of the Commons unanimous with the exception of Tierney and Mr Manning. Tierney from factious motives, and ignorance of the question: Manning as a Bank Director of the old school. There were no doubt many Members of the Lords Committee and some Members of the Commons Committee who went into the measure with their eyes shut and great terror and reluctance; but the weight of talent and influence carried them on. All the first men were agreed, including Lord Wellington.—Lord Castlereagh and Vansittart lagged behind: Ned Cooke, Lord Castlereagh's right hand, was at the very time writing the most alarming pamphlets:[1] Lord Harrowby and Lord Bathurst were dragged into the measure: but Lord Liverpool, Lords Grenville, Wellington and Lansdowne, Peel and Canning being agreed, no paper administration could be formed, and the reluctant multitude were obliged to yield. It will ever resound to the credit of Peel to have taken so honourable and decided a line: he went into the Committee, as he said himself,[2] without any opinions; and if he had any bias it was against the proposed measure. He had always voted with Vansittart; and his Father Sir Robert Peel entertained so decided an opinion, that he proposed the resolutions and the Petition in the London Tavern,[3] and presented the Petition to the House, warning them of their danger, and lamenting the error of his son...

'In forming their Committees, Ministers had no plan in view: but the inclinations of the majority by the Cabinet being adverse to Cash payments, they took care (as they thought) to secure a majority in their favour: But so difficult is it to guard all avenues, when they need not be guarded, that two of the Members of the Commons Committee, who were appointed to form an anti-

---

[1] See *An Address to the Public on the Plan Proposed by the Secret Committee of the House of Commons for Examining the Affairs of the Bank,* by Edward Cooke, London, Stockdale, 1819.

[2] Speech of 24 May 1819, *Hansard,* XL, 677.

[3] The meeting on 15 May 1819 at the City of London Tavern, held to oppose the Reports of the Committees.

bullion majority, Sir John Nicholls and Mr Ashurst, were both friends to a general resumption of Cash payments. The one is a decided Ministerial Member; a sort of devoted adherent: the other a Tory Country Gentleman: they were not people likely to have either read or thought much upon the subject; and all that was expected of them was to be upon the Government side if it came to a counting of noses: but it so happened that they had read and had opinions of their own, and that those opinions were sound, so that they immediately sided in the Committee with those Members of administration who were favourable to a better system of currency.'

The recommendations contained in the Second Report of the Commons' Committee were as follows:

'That, after the 1st May 1821, the Bank shall be liable to deliver a quantity of Gold, not less than 60 ounces, of standard fineness, to be first assayed and stamped at His Majesty's mint, at the established mint price of £3. 17*s*. 10$\frac{1}{2}$*d*. per oz. in exchange for such an amount of Notes presented to them as shall represent, at that rate, the value of the Gold demanded:

'That this liability of the Bank to deliver Gold in exchange for their Notes, shall continue for not less than two nor more than three years, from the 1st May 1821; and that at the end of that period, Cash Payments shall be resumed:

'That on a day, to be fixed by Parliament, not later than the 1st February 1820, the Bank shall be required to deliver Gold, of standard fineness, assayed and stamped as before mentioned, in exchange for their notes (an amount of not less than 60 ounces of Gold being demanded) at £.4. 1*s*. per ounce, that being nearly the market price of standard Gold in bars on an average of the last three months.

'That on or before the 1st October 1820, the Bank shall pay their Notes in Gold of standard fineness, at the rate of £.3. 19*s*.6*d*.; and on or before the 1st May 1821, as before mentioned, at the ancient standard rate of £.3. 17*s*. 10$\frac{1}{2}$*d*.'[1]

Those of the Lords' Committee were:

'1. That provision should be made by Parliament for a repayment of the debt of Government to the Bank to a considerable amount, and that a part of that repayment should take place some

---

[1] Commons' 'Second Report', p. 15.

time antecedent to the first period which may be fixed for the commencement of bullion payments by the Bank:

'2. That from and after the 1st of December 1819, or at latest the 1st of February 1820, the Bank of England shall be required to pay its notes in gold bullion duly assayed and stamped in His Majesty's Mint, if demanded, in sums of not less than the value of 60 ounces, at the price of £4 1s. per ounce of standard bullion; that on the 1st of November 1820, or at such other period as may be fixed, the price shall be reduced to £3 19s. 6d., unless the Bank shall have previously reduced it to that rate, it being always understood that the price, when once lowered, shall not again be raised by the Bank; and that on the 1st of May 1821, the Bank shall pay its notes, if demanded, in gold bullion, in sums of not less than the value of 30 ounces, at the price of £3 17s. 10½d. per ounce of standard bullion:

'3. That a weekly account of the average amount of notes in circulation during the preceding week, shall be transmitted to the Privy Council; and a quarterly account of the average amount of notes in circulation during the preceding quarter, shall be published in the London Gazette:

'4. That for two years, from and after the first of May 1821, the Bank shall pay its notes in gold bullion only at the Mint price; and that whenever Parliament shall think proper to require the Bank to pay its notes in coin, notice thereof shall be given to the Bank one year before hand, such notice not to be given before the first of May 1822.'[1]

Commenting on the plan recommended by the Commons' Committee, Ricardo wrote to McCulloch on 8 May: 'The Committee have deviated in two points from the plan as originally suggested—they think that the bars of bullion delivered by the Bank, in exchange for notes, should be assayed, and stamped, at the Mint; and they have advised that after 1823, at the latest, we should revert to the old system of specie payments. Perhaps, in both instances, they have done right, for the Bank persisting in the most determined opposition to them, they were under the necessity of having the bullion stamped that it might be legally called money of a large denomination, and that the Bank might not raise a clamour against them for having imposed upon that

---

[1] Lords' 'Second Report', p. 18–19.

corporation the obligation of paying in Bullion, from which they said their charter protected them. In the second place they had to contend with public prejudice, and perhaps too with prepossessions which they themselves felt in favour of coin. If no inconvenience is suffered from the working of this plan for the next 5 years, the Bank will be amongst the foremost in contending that it should be adopted as a permanent system.'[1]

A set of Resolutions based on the recommendations of the Committees were moved by Peel in the House of Commons on 24 May[2] when Ricardo made his first important parliamentary speech; they were adopted on the following day. Peel's Bill, which embodied the Resolutions, received the Royal Assent on 2 July 1819.[3]

IV. The 'Ricardoes'

The plan came into effect on 1 February 1820 when the Bank resumed gold payments at 81s. per ounce in ingots of 60 ounces of gold of standard fineness, stamped and assayed at the Mint.

From the beginning the ingots had caught the public imagination and were referred to in the press as one of the oddities of the day. 'The proposed Ingots have already obtained a name. They are called *Ricardoes* from their inventor, as the gold *Napoleons* were named from Bonaparte.'[4] 'Mr RICARDO's *ingots* were the fashionable novelties of the day, like the automaton chess player,[5] or the fair Circassian[6].'[7] When they actually came into existence, in 1820, the market price of gold being below 81s, the demand for them was only as collectors' pieces: 'The Bank resumed bul-

[1] Below, VIII, 26–7.
[2] The text of the Resolutions is given above, p. 7–8.
[3] 59 Geo. III. c. 49. An amendment to the original bill had been adopted on Ellice's motion; see above, p. 8 and n.
[4] *The New Times*, 15 May 1819.
[5] The Automaton Chess-Player was on exhibition at No. 4 Spring Garden (Advt. in *The Times*, 6 Feb. 1819).
[6] The Fair Circassian was the name popularly applied to a lady in the suite of the recently arrived Persian Ambassador. Much curiosity had been aroused by the seclusion in which she was kept; 'hundreds of loungers and dandies' crowded outside the Embassy in the vain hope of a glimpse of her. 'The door of her room is constantly guarded by two black eunuchs, who have sabres by their sides. They are her only attendants, being selected to dress and undress her.' (*The Times*, 30 April 1819.)
[7] *The New Times*, 15 June 1819.

lion payments on 1st February, in ingots (to the amount of 300l.), commonly called Ricardos; and I understand that in the first three days only three were applied for. One for Lord Thanet, one for a country banker, from curiosity, and the other I know not for whom. The price of gold is from two to three shillings below the Mint price, which accounts for this little demand.'[1]

Some more details came to light as a result of an article on 'Ricardo's Ingot Plan' by Dr. Bonar in the *Economic Journal* for September 1923. The following number of the *Journal* (December 1923) announced the discovery in the Coins and Medals Department of the British Museum 'not indeed of the ingot itself but of an impression in bronze from the die which was used to stamp it. An undated ticket lay under it, on which were written in a contemporary hand the words:

Stamp
for striking gold
ingots according
to the suggestion of
Mr. Ricardo.

'It would have been more correct to say impression of a stamp.

'The diameter of the object is 34 mm.; that of the actual die as shown by the edge of the circular impression is 32 mm. The impression is of a G.R. crowned, as in the engraving above ... The above engraving is of the actual size.

'In the same way it has been discovered by the Bank of England, that in the early months of 1820 the Mint delivered to the Bank 2028 gold bars of 60 ounces each. Of these 13 were sold, to 12 different purchasers, viz.:

(*a*) 3 in February 1820 at £4 1*s*. per standard oz.

(*b*) 3 in October 1820 at £3 19*s*. 6*d*.

(*c*) 7 in May 1821 at £3 17*s*. 10$\frac{1}{2}$*d*.

The remaining 2015 were returned to the Mint.'

---

[1] Letter from E. B. Wilbraham, 7 Feb. 1820, in *Diary and Correspondence of Charles Abbot, Lord Colchester*, 1861, vol. iii, p. 113. Cp. Tooke's *History of Prices*, vol. ii, p. 98–9, and Ricardo's speech of 8 Feb. 1821, above, p. 76.

The plan of bullion payments virtually came to an end in April 1821, when an Act was passed (1 and 2 Geo. IV, c. 26) to anticipate by one year the operation of the clause which allowed the Bank to pay their notes either in coin or in bullion. In May 1823, under the terms of the Act of 1819, payment in coin became obligatory.

V.

The Reports of the Lords' and Commons' Committees, with Minutes of Evidence and Appendices, were printed in *Parliamentary Papers,* 1819, vol. III.[1] The Lords' Reports with Minutes of Evidence and Appendix were ordered to be reprinted on 15 February 1844, and an Index was added. These are the official editions in folio. An unofficial edition, in octavo, of the Commons' Second Report and Minutes of Evidence was published by Charles Clement, London, in 1819.

Ricardo's evidence is reprinted below from the official edition of 1819. The original arrangement and spelling have been retained; except that in the Commons' evidence (by analogy with the more convenient arrangement of the Lords' evidence) numbers have been prefixed in square brackets to the questions, and each question and answer, which in the original are printed as a single paragraph, have been separated.

---

[1] The title of the Commons' Reports is: 'Reports from the Secret Committee on the Expediency of The Bank resuming Cash Payments, Ordered by the House of Commons to be Printed, 5 April and 6 May 1819.'

The title of the Lords' Reports, as printed for the House of Commons, is: 'Reports respecting the Bank of England resuming Cash Payments: *viz.* The First and Second Reports by the Lords Committees appointed a Secret Committee to enquire into the State of The Bank of England, with respect to the Expediency of the Resumption of Cash Payments;—with Minutes of Evidence, and an Appendix:—7 May 1819:—Communicated by The Lords, 12th May 1819. Ordered, by the House of Commons, to be Printed, 12 May 1819.'

MINUTES OF EVIDENCE TAKEN BEFORE
THE SECRET COMMITTEE ON THE
EXPEDIENCY OF THE BANK
RESUMING CASH PAYMENTS

Jovis, 4° die Martii, 1819.

The Right Honourable ROBERT PEEL, in the Chair.

DAVID RICARDO, ESQUIRE;
A Member of the House; was Examined.

[1] Do you conceive that the paper currency of this country is now excessive, and depreciated in comparison with gold, and that the high price of bullion and low rate of exchange, are the consequences, as well as the sign, of that depreciation?
Yes, I do.

[2] The following is an extract from a publication of your's: "Why will not the bank try the experiment, by a reduction in the amount of their notes of two or three millions for the short period of three months? if no effects were produced on the price of bullion and the foreign exchanges, then might their friends boast, that the principles of the bullion committee were the wild dreams of speculative theorists;"[1] do you still adhere to the opinion expressed in that extract?
Yes, I do.

[3] From July to December 1817, the average amount of bank of England notes in circulation, appears to have been £. 29,210,000; from July to December 1818, the amount appears to have been £. 26,487,000; in the latter period, the

---

[1] *Reply to Bosanquet;* above, III, 195.

price of gold was higher than in the former, and the exchanges were more unfavourable to this country, so that the reduction in the issues, though carried to the extent of £. 3,000,000, produced no effect upon the exchange and on the price of gold; how do you reconcile these facts with the theory?

When I gave the opinion that has been stated, it was on the supposition, that no commercial causes were at that time to operate on the price of bullion or on the exchange, being firmly convinced, that a reduction in the amount of notes, under those circumstances, would raise their value to any point which might be desired; I am fully aware that there are other causes, besides the quantity of bank notes, which operate upon the exchanges; but I am quite sure, that from whatever cause a bad exchange arises, it may be corrected by a reduction in the amount of the currency.

[4] Then ought there not to have been an addition to the statement above referred to of words to the following effect; provided other causes do not counteract the effect of the reduction?

Clearly; I was speaking with respect to a given time; I did not mean to assert, that at all times and under all circumstances a reduction of bank notes would improve the exchange.

[5] What are the causes to which you refer?

Those causes, I conceive, are various; there may be a great increase in the capital of a country, which may so increase the quantity of commodities to be circulated, that there may be required more circulating medium at one time than at another; there may be a great diminution in the value of gold and silver, generally, in Europe, which may make it possible, with the same commerce, to maintain an increased amount of circulation; I consider, in all cases, that the

quantity of circulation must depend upon its value, and the
quantity of business which it has to perform.

[6] Then do you consider the high price of gold to be a
certain sign of the depreciation of bank notes?

I consider it to be a certain sign of the depreciation of
bank notes, because I consider the standard of the currency
to be bullion, and whether that bullion be more or less
valuable, the paper ought to conform to that value, and
would, under the system that we pursued previously to 1797:
there is an instance of the truth, I think, of the opinion which
I am maintaining, in the year 1782, when, by a return made
by the bank, it appears that there was a reduction of, I believe,
three millions of bank notes in the space of a few months;
that reduction was probably also accompanied by a reduction
in the metallic part of our currency, there being then no notes
under ten pounds in circulation, but of that we can have no
knowledge; this proves to me, that in order to make the
value of the paper conform to the value of bullion, the bank
were under the necessity of reducing the amount of their
currency.

[7] The price of gold being lower when the amount of
bank of England notes in circulation was twenty-nine
millions than when it was twenty-six millions, and you
considering the price of gold to be the criterion of the
depreciation of bank notes, to what other causes do you
attribute the rise in the price of gold when there had been
a diminution to the extent of three millions in the amount
of bank notes?

It seems to me, that when we compare two commodities
together, gold and paper for example, it is impossible to say,
when they are varying, whether the one is falling or the other
is rising. If gold was rising in the general market of the

world at the time stated, it is evident that it might exceed more than before the value of paper currency, although the latter was reduced in quantity and increased in value; they would both rise, but gold would rise most. By the operation of country banks, the whole currency might have been increased, although that part of it issued by the bank of England was diminished. Confidence and credit may have prevailed to a high degree, which are substitutes for currency. I am of opinion, that we have never sufficiently attended to the variations that may take place in the value of the metal itself, by which we estimate the value of our currency; there are a number of commercial causes, as I have already said, which I think affect the value of gold, and when I say the value, I do not mean the value as compared with paper, but the value as compared with commodities generally. I think every tax has some influence upon the value of the precious metals, and either occasions their exportation or importation. I think that every improvement in machinery has a tendency to produce similar effects; but as I have before observed, from whatever cause it may arise that paper exceeds the value of bullion, whether from the increase of paper, from the rise in the value of gold, or from any other cause whatever, it can always be corrected by a reduction in the amount of the paper circulation, and such was the uniform practice before the year 1797.

[8] Do you think that a reduction of bank of England paper will certainly produce a fall in the price of gold?

I do; I should rather say, a reduction in the amount of the whole circulation of the country; but here again it is possible that there might be a reduction of the bank circulation without a corresponding reduction in the country circulation, and it might even be possible that there might be an increase of such country circulation, not that I expect that any such result would follow, for I consider that the reduction of the bank of England circulation would be immediately followed by a reduction of country circulation; but it is not physically impossible.

[9] Do you think that the amount of country bank circulation will vary with the amount of bank of England circulation?

In all common cases I think it will; but I believe that there are exceptions to that general rule, arising from the more or less credit of the country banks; there is of course always a contention between the country banks and the bank of England, to fill as many districts as they can with their respective notes. The bank of England or the country banks may be more successful at one period than at another, but provided every thing were to remain the same in that respect, I have no doubt that a reduction of the London circulation would occasion a reduction of the country circulation. I should observe also, that with respect to the public, it is a matter of very little importance whether the whole reduction should be in the bank of England issues, or should be partly of the bank of England issues and partly of the country bank issues: it is a question of importance, as it refers to the interest of the country banks and the bank of England, but the public have no interest in it whatever: the inconvenience which they would suffer, if any, would arise from the reduction of the whole amount of the circulating medium, it being of little importance from which fund that reduction was made.

[10] The bank of England circulation has fallen, from the last half year of 1817, as compared with the present time, from £. 29,210,000 to about £. 25,000,000; that is, there

has been a reduction between that half year and the present time, to the amount of £. 4,000,000; as the diminution has been gradual, and has operated for 15 months, ought it not to have produced its effect on country bank circulation?

I think it ought in common cases, and must have done so in the present case, if no counteracting causes have particularly operated; of which I know nothing, nor can know nothing.

[11] As then there has been an actual diminution of bank of England paper, to the amount of four millions within that period, and there ought to have been a corresponding reduction in the amount of country bank paper, does it not strike you as somewhat inconsistent with the theory, that the price of gold is at present higher than it was at the period when the circulation of the bank of England was four millions greater than it is now?

It does not in the least shake my confidence in the theory, being fully persuaded that such an effect must have followed, if it had not been counteracted by some of those causes to which I have already adverted.

[12] What are the causes which have, in your opinion, practically operated to countervail the effect of this reduction of the circulating medium?

The facts are not sufficiently within my knowledge, to give any plausible explanation of them; but I am persuaded that there are other causes, besides the mere amount of paper, which will so operate, and I therefore infer, that some of them have now been acting.

[13] Then supposing the bank to make a further reduction, beyond the present amount of their issues, might not the operation of the same causes prevent the good effects to be expected from that reduction?

It is quite possible, but I do not think it probable.

[14] Have the goodness to state why you think it probable, that the same causes that must have operated to produce
that effect in the former case, should not continue to produce
it in the case assumed?

Because, in commerce, it appears to me that a cause may
operate for a certain time without our being warranted to
expect that it should continue to operate for a much greater
length of time; and being fully persuaded that a reduction
in the quantity of such a commodity as money must either
raise its value, or prevent its falling in value, I am sure that
a reduction of the quantity of currency, provided it be sufficient in degree, will operate in raising its value, whatever
countervailing causes may contribute to oppose it.

[15] Do you think there is any perfect assurance that if
the bank of England were to reduce its issues to the extent
of two or three millions below their present amount, the
consequence would be a fall in the price of gold, and the
restoration of the exchange, or might not the other causes
which affect the price of gold and the rate of exchange
possibly countervail the effect of the reduction of the issues?

Certainly, they might countervail the effect of the reduction of the issues, but provided they were sufficient in degree
the reduction would be sure to bring the two together; there
are two commodities which we are comparing with each other,
namely, bank notes, and gold; the variation in the relative
value of these two commodities may be caused by an increase
in the quantity of paper, or by a fall in the value of gold; in the
former state of our circulation, whenever it proceeded from
either of those causes, a reduction in the amount of paper was
the remedy, and must at all times I think be the remedy.

[16] Take then a considerable period, when the amount
of bank notes in circulation was very nearly the same; it was

so for three half years, from July 1815 to December 1816 namely, about twenty-six millions and a half; at the beginning of that period the price of gold was 4*l.* 16*s.* an ounce, it fell to 4*l.* 11*s.* 4*l.* 9*s.* 4*l.* 7*s.* 4*l.* 3*s.* 4*l.* 2*s.* 4*l.* 1*s.* 4*l.* 0*s.* 3*l.* 19*s.* and 3*l.* 18*s.* 6*d.;* there was no interruption in the regular gradation of the fall of gold, and there was no variation in the average amount of bank notes in circulation, do you attribute the fall in the price of gold to an alteration that took place in the value of gold?

Most undoubtedly; and by returns that have been made at different times to Parliament, we observe the relative value of gold and silver to differ very materially at different times; now to what cause can this possibly be attributed, but to an alteration in the real value of one of them? in which ever metal that alteration of value takes place, provided it be the standard, it will either warrant an increase or a diminution of paper.

[17] Do you know what have been the greatest limits of the variation in the relative value of gold and silver; within a given period, supposing three years, have they ever varied one per cent within that period?

I should say six or seven, speaking from the slight recollection I have at this moment on the subject; I only mention these circumstances to show the Committee that it is quite possible that there may be variations in the value of the precious metals, which would produce such effects, as it appears the object of the present examination to explain.

[18] But supposing there has been, during the same period, a corresponding fall in the price of silver, then, evidently, that cause which you assign as possible to account for a fall in the price of gold has not operated?

I should then say, that whatever cause had operated, had equally operated on the two metals, instead of operating on one exclusively.

[19] Do you not conceive, that the most perfect state to which a currency can be brought is, that by which the public are secured against any variations in the value of the currency other than those to which the standard is subject, and in which the circulation is carried on by the least expensive means?
Certainly.

[20] Have you turned your attention to any plan by which these desirable objects may be best attained?
Yes, I have.

[21] Have the goodness to favour the Committee with your opinions upon that subject?
My opinion is, that the bank of England should have the liberty of either paying their notes in specie or in bullion at the mint price of 3*l.* 17*s.* 10$\frac{1}{2}$*d.;* by which means the paper currency could never fall below the value at which the coin stood previously to 1797.

[22] What quantity of gold ought a person to be at liberty to demand, in exchange for paper?
That appears to be a regulation which should be left to the bank to decide on; it is, comparatively, of very little importance.

[23] Would it not be necessary to have a regulation of law?
Undoubtedly there should be a regulation of law; but whether the quantity should be 20 ounces, or 50 or 100, I have scarcely any motive for making a choice; the object would be equally effected by taking either quantity.

[24] Do you think it would be politic to impose, at the same time, upon the bank, the necessity of issuing paper in exchange for gold tendered to them?

That is a measure not absolutely necessary; but I think it would be a great improvement to the system, if that regulation were adopted.

[25] The object of it would be, to prevent a rise in the value of the bank note above the price of gold?

Exactly so; which the bank can now effect.

[26] Might not the object be answered by giving every person an option to go to the mint, and receive coin in exchange for the bullion?

Which would do just as well, if you could readily turn bullion into coin or into paper, the object would be equally effected.[1]

[27] Would you advise, that notes below 5*l.* should be continued in circulation?

Under those circumstances there necessarily must be notes of 1*l.* and 2*l.*

[28] Would you advise bank notes to be made a legal tender?

I would certainly.

[29] Would you leave to the country bankers the power of issuing notes payable on demand, in bank of England notes?

I would.

[30] And not subject them to the necessity of paying in coin?

Certainly not.

---

[1] This answer is amended below, pp. 401–3, Question 106.

[31] Would you repeal the laws respecting the exportation of coin?

Undoubtedly.

[32] And leave the trade in bullion and coin perfectly free?

Perfectly free; and also a perfect liberty to any man to melt the coin if he thought proper.

[33] What regulation would you advise to be adopted with respect to foreign coins?

When I say that the public should have the privilege of buying and selling bullion to the bank, I have in my mind bullion of the standard of England; but if allowance be made for the alloy in the foreign coins, according as they may be more or less fine than the standard of England, it appears to me of small importance whether these dealings be in those coins or in bullion.

[34] Would not that be an additional convenience?

I think it would.

[35] Could you assign any period of time, at the expiration of which this plan, in your opinion, could be safely resorted to?

I think it ought to be immediately resorted to, either at the price of $3l.$ $17s.$ $10\frac{1}{2}d.$ or at some other price; because I consider that our currency is in a very unsatisfactory state, while the bank have the power of increasing or diminishing the circulation, and altering its value at their pleasure; and therefore, whatever regulation might be resolved on, with respect to the time of paying in the standard of the country, I should certainly recommend the adoption of this plan at some other price in the interval.

[36] That is, that the bank should be under an obligation of paying their notes on demand in gold, at the present market price of gold for instance, and of making a gradual

reduction in the price of gold which they should issue, until the market price of gold corresponded with the mint price?

Precisely so; but under those circumstances the price at which the bank should be obliged to buy gold I think should not be fixed above that price, at which it should be a permanent regulation.

[37] Would you propose that price to be something below the mint price?

Exactly so; in what degree below I have scarcely the means of judging; the bank would be better able to fix that price than I should; it should be very little below.

[38] Would you propose, that the price at which the bank should be compelled to purchase gold, should be the same or something lower than that at which in succession they issue it, according to the operations that would take place in a graduated scale?

I have already mentioned, that I should rather recommend that the price at which they should buy gold, should be under the present mint price, which is $3l.$ $17s.$ $10\frac{1}{2}d.$ and fixed now once for all.

[39] Would not the bank in that case have it in their power to make a sudden change in the value of the circulation, by a more sudden reduction in the amount of their notes than might be desirable?

Within those limits they might; but after intrusting the bank with the great powers which they have had for two-and-twenty years, I should not be very fastidious in intrusting them with this small power at the present moment.

[40] But if that was objectionable, might it not be counteracted by providing that they shall purchase at, or nearly at, the same price at which they issued gold?

Certainly not at the same price, but at a price under that.

[41] If the bank, after the resumption of cash payments, continued to issue one and two pound notes, would not their issue tend greatly to diminish the quantity of gold which would be necessary for the purposes of circulation, when compared with that quantity which was necessary previous to the restriction?

Certainly; if the public liked a paper currency, consisting of one and two pound notes, better than one consisting of the gold coins, then this regulation would be nugatory; but if they did not, it would secure a power to the bank of filling that part of our circulation with one and two pound notes, and thereby preventing the public from demanding coin as substitutes for those notes.

[42] Do you think there would be any difficulty whatever in procuring such a supply of gold as, under the circumstances you have supposed, would be adequate for the supply of this country?

According to the view which I take of this question, I think there would be no provision of gold necessary beyond that which the bank must now have, however small it may be.

[43] That is, supposing they immediately commence the payment in gold, at about the present market price?

Or at any price; having a firm opinion that the bank, by the reduction in the amount of their notes, can raise their value to any assignable limit, it does appear to me that they can always keep the value of their paper on a par with the value of bullion, at whatever price the Committee might choose to fix it.

[44] Would it not be necessary, nevertheless, that they should have at all times a considerable supply of gold to meet the demands upon them, although the market and mint price of gold should correspond?

That would certainly be desirable, but the bank would be regulated by the same rules by which they were guided at the time they were paying in a metallic currency. I do not think it would be prudent on the part of the bank not to have a provision of bullion, because there are intervals during which the paper may not immediately attain that value which it finally will attain in consequence of its reduction, and during that interval they would be subject to demands for bullion.

[45] Does not that assume that the reduction of the issues of the bank of England, would necessarily and immediately lead to a reduction of country bank paper?

Undoubtedly; I have already explained to the Committee that it appears to me that there might be a greater reduction of the bank of England paper in some cases, and a less reduction of country bank paper; but it is a mere question of degree; the bank might, under some circumstances, be obliged to make a greater reduction of their paper, in order to keep the value of paper currency generally on a par with the value of bullion.

[46] Might not the circumstances of the country be such as to make a reduction of issues at some particular period, in order to have the effect of reducing the price of gold exceedingly embarrassing to trade?

It undoubtedly might be; that is an evil to which all currencies are subject; every country that carries on its circulation by means of the metals is liable to that inconvenience, and it would be no other to which the public would be exposed if the plan suggested were adopted.

[47] Are you aware that there is at present a considerable stagnation in trade, and that there has been a great reduction of prices in consequence?

I have heard so; but I am not engaged in trade, and it does not come much within my own knowledge.

[48] Would not the effect of a reduction of the issues of the bank be a further reduction in the prices of commodities?

I should certainly expect so, because I consider a reduction in the amount of bank paper to be raising the value of the medium in which the prices of those commodities are estimated.

[49] Explain in what degree you think it would take place?

I should think, to the amount of about five or six per cent; I measure it by the extent of the excess of the market above the mint price of gold.

[50] Do you think a diminution of the circulation produces a diminution of prices in exact arithmetical proportion?

I think it has a tendency so to do, but it does not act exactly so nicely as that.

[51] Does it reduce the prices of all commodities equally?

I think not, in consequence of the inequality of taxation, otherwise I think it would.

[52] Might not the reduction of prices to the amount of five per cent, consequent on a reduction of the issues of the bank, be particularly embarrassing, if it took place at a period when there appears to have been so great a reduction of prices in consequence of other causes; namely, the excess of speculation, and the stagnation resulting from that?

An alteration in value of five per cent does not appear to me very formidable; but of this matter I do not profess to know much; I have had very little practical knowledge upon these subjects.

[53] When merchants have a want of confidence in each other, which disinclines them to deal on credit, is there not a greater demand for money?

Undoubtedly.

[54] Then if this is a period when there is a greater demand for money on account of a want of confidence, does it not follow that it would be an inconvenient period for reducing the means of accommodation?

It appears to me that that very circumstance would make a smaller reduction efficacious for the purpose; a demand for currency in consequence of want of confidence, I should think a legitimate demand; it would enable the bank to keep their circulation at a higher level than they would be able to do, if there had not been a demand from such a cause.

[55] Supposing such a reduction of the issues of the bank to take place as would restore the market price of gold to the mint price, there would be, in your opinion, an improvement in the value of the currency of about five per cent?

Exactly so.

[56] Would it not be necessary to raise the same nominal amount of taxes to defray all that portion of the public expenditure which is applied to the payment of the public creditor?

Undoubtedly.

[57] Would not the increased burthen of such taxes upon the people be in proportion to the increase in the nominal value of the money?

Certainly.

[58] You are aware that by the act, providing for a new silver coinage, the act of 56 George 3, cap. 68, there has been an alteration in the relative value of gold to silver, from

15,059. 2. 1. to 14,121. making a difference of nearly six per cent in the relative intrinsic value of our gold and silver coin; do you think this difference so made, will have the effect of banishing gold coin from this country, provided silver coin be a legal tender to the amount only of 40*s.* and provided the mint retains the power in their hands of regulating the amount of silver coin?

It appears to me quite impossible, at whatever relative value these two metals might be, while guarded by the regulations which have been mentioned.

[59] Are you of opinion that it would be desirable to keep the intrinsic value of our gold coin as near the intrinsic value of bullion as possible?

My first preference is to have nothing but a paper circulation, and the expedient I have proposed had that for its object; but provided we have a metallic circulation, then I conceive nothing can be more desirable than to keep the value of the coin at as near as possible to the value of bullion.

[60] The price of gold in April 1815 was 5*l.* 7*s.* an ounce, and in April in the following year it was 4*l.* 1*s.* an ounce, making a difference of 1*l.* 6*s.;* supposing the average price of other commodities in the country, as measured in bank notes, to have been the same at those two periods, would you then infer, from that state of things, that bank notes were depreciated in April 1816, as compared with April 1815, in the proportion of the difference between the prices of gold, namely, 1*l.* 6*s.?*

Yes, I should.

[61] Though the price of all other articles remained the same as measured by bank notes?

Though the price of all other articles remained the same.

[62] You have stated, that a currency, of which gold is
the standard, is subject to considerable variations, which
arise in the variable value of gold in exchange as compared
with other commodities; can a standard of currency, more
invariable in its value than the value of a certain quantity of
gold, be established by any system yet discovered?

By none that I have ever even imagined.

[63] Would it be possible, by fixing from time to time
the amount of bank notes which should circulate, to obtain
a circulation any thing approaching in steadiness of value,
to one which was attached to the value of a metallic standard?

I do not know any means whatever by which we can
certainly ascertain the value of any one commodity; but in
practice bullion appears to approach the nearest to an invariable standard.

[64] Are not the Committee then to conclude it to be
your opinion, that the standard value of the currency, since
it has ceased to be exchangeable for specie on demand, has
been infinitely more variable than it would have been if it
had remained on the same footing on which it stood previously to the year 1797?

Yes; my opinion is, that it has undergone more variations
than it would have done if it had been regulated by a metallic
standard.

[65] As compared with gold?

As compared with either gold or silver; I have no preference for either.

[66] You have stated it to be your opinion, that the reason
why a reduction in the amount of bank notes to the amount
of three millions had not been accompanied by a corresponding fall in the price of gold and a rise in the exchange,

must have proceeded from other natural counteracting causes; you also stated that you believe, for the most part, a reduction in bank of England paper would produce a corresponding reduction in country bank paper; if country bank paper had been withdrawn, in consequence of such a panic as you describe, in the years 1816 and 1817, and if some of those districts in which country bank paper had before circulated in consequence of that operation, had been filled in a greater or a less degree by bank of England paper, is it not probable that a re-issue of country bank paper might, in consequence of restored confidence in the country, have driven that bank of England paper back into London circulation, and by that means materially counteracted the effect of the decrease in the bank of England issues, both in reducing the prices of gold and raising the exchanges, and also in limiting the amount of country bank paper circulation?

I think, undoubtedly, it would; the more contracted the circle is in which the bank of England notes circulate, the more effect must an increase or reduction of their quantity occasion. I wish also to remark, that in some of the accounts of the amount of bank notes in circulation at certain periods which I have seen, the one and two pound notes vary, very remarkably, relatively to the notes of a higher value, which may be occasioned (not that I know that it is) by the increased or diminished credit of the country banks. It appears, in 1815, that the amount of notes above five pounds was about thirteen millions, while those under five pounds were above nine millions; in January 1818, the amount of notes above five pounds is above sixteen millions, and those under five pounds about seven millions and a half, and from some of the accounts which have been laid before the House of Commons, the same sort of inequality appears to affect the notes of the amount of ten and twenty pounds, which may be supposed to be that description of notes which, as well as those of five pounds and under, are used chiefly in the country circulation, upon occasions of the discredit of the country banks. I have not examined these relative proportions, with a view to explain the difficulty that the question has now started, but I remark it as a circumstance which I do not know well how to explain; but it may be connected with the situation of the country banks.

[67] Do you believe that the issue of bank notes from the bank, upon the purchase of bullion, may be carried on to a greater extent with more security, and without producing the same effect upon the circulation, as to excess or diminution, than when issued by any other of their ordinary modes?

It appears to me to make no sort of difference, whether the issues be made in the way of discounts, by advances to government, or in the purchase of bullion; it is the numerical amount which will produce the effect.

[68] Do you conceive that a standard of value would be more variable if measured by a reference to two metals, namely gold and silver, as was formerly the case in this country, and is now the case in some other countries, than if confined to one metal only?

Yes, I think it would be more variable if measured by two metals.

[69] If then one metal is preferable as affording a less variable measure, which metal would you recommend?

I find some difficulty in answering that question; there were reasons which at one time induced me to think that silver would have been the better metal for a standard measure of value, principally on account of its being chiefly used in the currencies of other countries;[1] but as I have under-

---

[1] See *Economical and Secure Currency* (1816), above, IV, 63

stood that machinery is particularly applicable to the silver 4 March 1819
mines,[1] and may therefore very much conduce to an increased
quantity of that metal and an alteration of its value, whilst
the same cause is not likely to operate upon the value of gold,
I have come to the conclusion, that gold is the better metal
by which to regulate the value of our currency.

[70] Although the currency of other countries may be
usually measured in silver?

I think that fact is of no importance whatever in practice;
it is of no inconvenience to trade, I imagine.

[71] Does not the circumstance of the measure of value
in one country being in gold, and in another with which it
trades being in silver, occasion a frequent fluctuation of the
real par of exchange?

Not only in the real par, but in the market rate of exchange
also.

[72] It appears, by the accounts already referred to, that
the price of gold in this country in April 1815 was £. 5. 7s.
and in April 1816 £. 4. 1s. being a difference of from 25 to
30 per cent, such price being always measured in our paper
currency, do you know whether, during the same period,
any such variation, or any variation in the price of gold took
place in France, or in any other continental country?

It appears to me that in France there can be no variation
in the price of the metal which is the standard of the currency;
and with respect to the variations in the other metal which
is not the standard of the currency, it must at all times be

---

[1] Alexander Baring, too, in his
evidence to the Commons Committee on 12 March 1819, referred
to the possibility 'that the amount
of silver may be hereafter increased
by the improvement in the working of the South American mines'
('Minutes of Evidence', p. 192).
Cp. below, VIII, 3.

confined to the variations which take place in the relative value of the two metals generally in Europe.

[73] If then it should appear that, during the period referred to, no variation whatever has taken place in the price of gold in Paris, would you infer from that circumstance that the variation in the price of gold between April 1815 and April 1816 arose from the variation in the value of paper, and not of gold?

Every fall in the price of the standard metal is immediately corrected in France by a reduction in the amount of the circulation; if no similar reduction takes place under the same circumstances in our circulation, there must necessarily be a redundancy and an excess of the market above the mint price of gold; in a sound state of the currency the value of gold may vary, but its price cannot.

[74] The variation you alluded to in your answer to a former question, is what you meant by the depreciation of the paper in your answer to a question before put to you?

From whatever cause may arise the difference in the value between paper and gold (and I have enumerated several,) I always call the paper depreciated when the market price exceeds the mint price of gold, because I conceive that there is then a greater quantity of circulating medium than what there would have been if we were obliged to make our paper currency conform to the value of coin, and which we are obliged to do, whenever the bank pay in specie.

[75] Do you consider the difference between the market and mint price of gold to be the criterion of the depreciation of bank notes?

Strictly so.

[76] Then taking the three months of the last year, January, February and March, the average amount of bank-

notes in circulation was thirty millions, twenty-nine millions, and twenty-eight millions; in the three last months of the year, October, November and December, the amount was twenty-six millions, twenty-six millions, and twenty-five millions; so that the average amount in December was less than the average amount of January by five millions; in the last three months the price of gold was higher than in the first three months; do you consider that bank notes were more depreciated at the latter period than the former?

I consider they were more depreciated in the latter period than in the former, provided at that time the price of gold was higher.

[77] Do you not consider that coin or bullion are distinguishable from bank notes in this important respect, that the coin or bullion, being the medium of universal value, operates in the nature of a bill of exchange, whereas the bank note does not possess this quality; must not, therefore, the value of the coin and bullion follow the rate of the exchange, whilst the bank note cannot be influenced by such operation?

Certainly; a bank note not payable in specie is confined to our circulation, and cannot make a foreign payment; a bank note payable in specie is the same thing as coin or bullion.

[78] May not this distinguishing quality between the bank note and the bullion, explain the difference of value, without its following, that the bank note is depreciated for any purposes of measuring the value of commodities within the country?

No, I think it cannot; the term "depreciation," I conceive, does not mean a mere diminution in value, but it means a diminished relative value, on a comparison with something which is a standard; and therefore I think it quite possible that a bank note may be depreciated, although it should rise in value, if it did not rise in value in a degree equal to the standard, by which only its depreciation is measured.

[79] Are you of opinion, that the bank could have permanently continued their payments in specie, from the year 1797, when they discontinued so to do?

It appears to me, that all banks are subject to be affected by panics, against which no prudence can guard, and that in 1797 such a panic had taken place; but I have some doubts whether, if the bank had resolved to pay to their last guinea, that panic would not have subsided, and the bank have been able to carry on its transactions in the way that it had done up to that period.

[80] Would you not have thought it a very dangerous experiment to try, as the failure of the attempt would have led to an absolute stoppage of payment?

It would have led only to the crisis which has actually taken place.

[81] You have stated an opinion, that the contraction of issues of paper would at all times restore the price of gold to the mint price, and render the exchange favourable to the country, supposing the balance of payments of the country to be against us, in what manner would you have them paid?

It appears to me, that a reduction in the amount of currency may always restore the price of bullion to the mint price, but I have not said, that that will always restore the exchange to par; although, if that reduction were carried still further, I believe it would restore the exchange to par; but under some circumstances, the price of bullion would be in such cases, for a short time, under the mint price.

[82] You have stated, that you consider a very small quantity of gold in circulation, or bullion, necessary for the bank to resume its operations?

That is on the supposition of an arrangement taking place, by which the bank shall not be compelled to pay in specie, but to pay its notes on demand in bullion; I think, that in that case, a very small quantity of bullion would be necessary to enable the bank to carry on its operations.

[83] Assuming that the balance of payments should be against this country, must the payment not necessarily be made, either in specie or in bullion?

It appears to me, that the balance of payments is frequently the effect of the situation of our currency, and not the cause.

[84] You must be convinced, that between two trading countries, there must be a balance one way or the other?

Those purchases and sales appear to me to be guided a great deal by the relative value of the currencies of the two countries; that any cause which shall operate to encrease the value of one, would have an effect upon its commercial transactions with the other, and consequently the exchange would be affected by an increase or diminution in the value of the currency of either.

[85] Would you infer then, that because at the present time cotton, coffee, and various other articles, are in this country particularly low, it would be either advantageous or desirable to send them to France or to the continent?

That must depend, I conceive, upon the fact, whether those articles are higher in France and other countries than they are here.

[86] The fact being decidedly that they are lower in France?

Then of course it could not be advantageous to send them from this country to France.

[87] Then is there any other way of paying, but by bullion or by specie?

By limiting the amount of paper, we should alter the value of cottons, and those other goods which are referred to, and we might in that case make our payment by the exportation of those goods, which at their present price it appears we cannot pay in.

[88] Then do you think that it can be a prudent measure, that as circumstances may fluctuate, the trade of the country is to be so starved as to produce an operation upon the price of gold?

It appears to me, that a reduction in the price of gold can never be brought about but by a reduction in the quantity of currency, by an increased use and demand for it, or by a fall in the general exchangeable value of gold; and if it be brought about by a reduction of paper, it must always be attended by what is called starving the circulation.

[89] Do not you think that the remedy might be often worse than the disease?

Undoubtedly there are cases in which I think the remedy would be worse than the disease; but this does not appear to me to be one of that sort.

[90] Can you state any particular time at which you think it would be preferable that the bank should undertake to pay in coin or bullion at the mint price?

It is difficult for me to define strictly at what time, but I have not much apprehension of any ill consequences from their doing it in a few months; at the same time I acknowledge there will be some little difficulty in it, but a difficulty which does not appear to me very formidable, and one for which we would be more than compensated by the possession of a currency regulated by a known and fixed standard.

[91] Do you think there is any inconvenience to the mercantile world and the public interest generally, resulting

from the state of uncertainty and fluctuation in which things are now placed, and must probably remain, until the bank has resumed cash payments?

I think a very serious inconvenience results from the state of uncertainty: one of the evils attending a paper currency not convertible, is, that it encourages over-trading, and leads us into some of those difficulties into which we should not be plunged, if our paper were corrected by the issues of metals.

[92] Do you think there is any thing in the present state of the commercial world, which makes it so little desirable that it should be operated upon by a fall in prices, to the amount of five per cent, which you think must accompany the measures to be taken for the resumption of cash payments, as to make it desirable that the inconveniences which you describe to accompany a continuance of that system, should be endured for a longer period than to the first of March 1820?

I am of opinion that it should not continue longer than that period.

[93] Did not over-trading take place very frequently before the restriction on cash payments at the bank?

I believe there is always a disposition to over-trading; that it was very much encouraged by the peculiar circumstances in which we were placed during the last war, from the modes in which we were obliged to carry on trade, and that those habits have in some degree continued with us, but that they are rather encouraged by a paper system than otherwise.

[94] Do not you believe that over-trading was very much encouraged by the system of country banking, although their notes were convertible into cash on demand?

It appears to me, that the country banks can never add to the amount of circulation permanently, and therefore I think they can hold out no encouragement to over-trading.

[95] Do you mean, in case their notes are convertible into coin?

Yes; when they are not convertible, of course their level is higher, as well as the London circulation.

[96] Was there not occasionally a temporary excess of country bank notes at the time they were payable in cash, which gave occasion to speculations and over-trading?

I conceive there are never any proofs of excess, but a high market above a mint price of bullion, and I never saw such an excess previously to 1797, nor never heard of such a thing; it is not imaginable by me.

[97] Would you consider a great number of bankruptcies as any indication of over-trading?

A number of bankruptcies may be a proof of over-trading, but not a proof of a redundant circulation.

[98] Even if those bankruptcies could be clearly traced to a connection with country banks?

Even if those bankruptcies could be clearly traced to a connection with country banks, I should only say, that the issuers of country paper were not the right sort of issuers.

[99] Do you believe that the restriction on cash payments holds out a greater temptation and affords greater facilities for over-trading, than would exist, were the bank to pay in cash?

It appears so to me, because men rely more confidently on renewing the discounting of their bills.

[100] You have stated, that the stagnation of trade, and a general decline of prices, would produce a similar effect,

with a positive reduction in the amount of our circulation,
would that effect be with reference to the foreign exchanges
to bring them nearer to a par?

Certainly.

[101] May not the result of that effect now operating, be
to bring the market to the mint price of gold, without any
interference of the legislature with respect to the amount of
issues of the bank of England?

It is a circumstance that may very probably occur, but
whether it will or not, I have no sufficient facts to judge by,
although it is quite consistent with the view I take of the
general question of currency.

[102] Under a given continuance of that stagnation of
trade, and of that depression of price, do you think it more
probable that it will occur, than that it will not?

I find some difficulty in answering that question, I have
no decided opinion upon that point; the effect may already
have been produced, and therefore it may cease to operate
any further; all those causes seem to me of a very uncertain
nature, and they cannot be very easily traced or followed.

[103] When there is a tendency to a general fall of prices,
is not money locked up just as commodities are accumulated
in the opposite state of things, and for the same reason, the
expectation of profit by holding the article for a better
market?

It appears to me, that no man would willingly lock up his
money, he would endeavour to make it as productive as he
could; he would not purchase commodities if he expected
a fall of those commodities, but he would be glad to lend his
money at interest during the interval that it was necessary
for him to keep it.

[104] The exchange having been favourable to this country, when the bank suspended its payments in 1797, is it not possible that by a more liberal and extensive accommodation to trade and country bankers, by discount, the bank might at that period have afforded such aid to the country circulation, as would have checked the alarm and relieved the distress?

I have great doubts on that question; it appears to me that it was an alarm from foreign causes, and a desire to hoard, and I have some doubts whether an extension of circulation would have quieted those fears.

[105] Does not it often happen that a variety of opinions may be entertained as to the period when commodities have come to their lowest state of depression, and of course one person may be a seller and another a buyer, both on different views of the same object, namely, profit?

Certainly; but it is the balance of those opinions which either raises the commodity or lowers it.

Veneris, 19° die Martii, 1819.

The Right Honourable ROBERT PEEL, in the Chair.

DAVID RICARDO, ESQUIRE,
A Member of the House, again Examined.

[106] There are some points on which the Committee   19 March 1819
understand you have further information to give to them.

[The witness delivered in the following paper.]

"I request to be allowed to amend a part of the evidence
which I had lately the honour of giving before this Committee.

"When I was last examined, I was asked,[1] whether it
would not be an improvement of the present mint regulations, if the mint were to keep a supply of coined gold, which
they should exchange without the least delay, and without
any deduction, for equal weights of uncoined gold; to which
I answered, that it would be an improvement, that every
thing which tended to equalize the value of gold coin and
gold bullion, made the currency approach more near to
perfection, and that such a regulation could not fail of
producing a beneficial result.

"I adhere to that answer as far as regards our circulation;
but I ought to add, that by making gold bullion exchangeable
without delay, and without loss, for gold coin, there would
be a great inducement offered to all exporters of gold, to
exchange their bullion for coin previously to its exportation.
Gold coin carries on its face a certificate of its fineness; it is
divisible into small sums, and it would, for these reasons,
possess advantages as an article of merchandize over gold
bullion. Our mint would not only be called upon to coin

---

[1] Questions 26 and 59.

gold without charge, for the internal circulation of England, but also the additional quantity which might be required for exportation, and which would, in the case supposed, be acquired without any additional expense. This is the inconvenience which would attend a money absolutely free from seignorage, free even from the loss of interest, which on the present system arises from the delay of the mint in returning coin for bullion, and which may strictly be called a small seignorage. But a coin with a seignorage has also its inconveniences, for the mint is not the only place from which money is issued. The bank have the undisputed power of increasing the quantity of currency, and thereby of diminishing its value to its intrinsic worth. If silver, for example, were now the standard of our currency, and therefore a legal tender to any amount, the bank might issue their paper till they raised the price of silver bullion to 5*s*. 6*d*. per ounce, (the current value of the silver coin) without inconvenience to themselves; they might then reduce their issues, till silver fell to 5*s*. 2*d*.; and thus they might alternately raise and lower the price of silver, between the limits of 5*s*. 6*d*. and 5*s*. 2*d*. as often as to them it might appear expedient. If there were no seignorage on the silver coin, and it were immediately exchangeable for silver bullion on the demand of the holder of bullion, it is evident that the price of silver would not rise above, nor fall below 5*s*. 2*d*. the mint price; but then the mint might, as I have before stated, be called upon to coin all the silver that might be exported. If it be decided, that under all circumstances, a currency, partly made up of gold coin, is desirable, the most perfect footing on which it could be put, would be to charge a moderate seignorage on the gold coin, giving at the same time the privilege to the holder of bank notes, to demand of the bank, either gold coin or gold bullion at the mint price, as he should think best, in exchange for his notes; if he preferred gold bullion for the purpose of exportation, as he probably would on account of its greater intrinsic value, it would be exported without any disadvantage to the country; if he preferred the coin on account of its more convenient form, and its certified fineness, which is barely possible, he could not obtain it without paying all the charges of its fabrication. If this plan were adopted, the seignorage should be at least sufficient to cover all the expenses of manufacture, and might with perfect safety be extended to that point at which it would just be insufficient to make the imitating of the coins a profitable employment.[1] This appears to me to be the best plan for a currency, consisting partly of the precious metals; but I am still of opinion, that we should have all its advantages, with the additional one of economy, by adopting the plan, which I had the honour of laying before the Committee when I was last before them."

[107] What seignorage do you think would be sufficient to protect the coin of the country, according to the suggestions which have been made in the paper which has just now been read?

That is a practical question, to which I am not qualified to give an answer.

[108] Do you know what seignorage is taken upon the French gold coin?

---

[1] A similar proposal had been made on 10 March by Alexander Baring before the Lords' Committee: 'I should certainly say that it would be better to have no Gold Coin, if the Question of the Forgery of Paper can be satisfactorily settled. If there should be a Gold Coin, it must be to a restricted Amount, with a Seignorage which may be carried to any Extent, provided it be not sufficient to encourage illegal coining; the Gold Coin would in fact be a Gold Token, and could not affect the Value of the Standard.' (Lords' Report, 'Minutes of Evidence', p. 132, Q. 167.) Cp. *Principles*, above, I, 371–2.

No, I am not acquainted with the regulations of the French mint.[1]

[109] Do you think that, under a currency partly consisting of paper convertible into coin at the option of the holder, and partly of gold coin, such occasional fluctuations in the market price of gold would frequently occur, as to make it an advantageous speculation to export the gold coin?

If there were no seignorage, there could be no variation in the price of gold; but it might nevertheless be exported, on account of the exchange being unfavourable; if there were a seignorage, then the price of gold might vary to the amount of that seignorage.

[110] Must not fluctuations, from the rate of exchange or other causes, frequently happen?

The value of gold coin and of gold bullion can only differ on account of the greater intrinsic value of the one or the other; if an ounce of gold is coined into $3l.$ $17s.$ $10\frac{1}{2}d.$ and is delivered at the mint in exchange for bullion, without any delay, I think the one must be precisely of the same value as the other, there could be no preference, and therefore no rise in the price of gold; but if a seignorage be taken from the gold coin, so as to make $3l.$ $17s.$ $10\frac{1}{2}d.$ in gold coin of less weight than an ounce of bullion, then the price of bullion might rise above the mint price to the amount of that difference.

[111] May not such demands for gold occur in foreign countries, as we have heard there was lately in Russia, so as to give a higher value to gold exported to that country, than it would obtain in France or in this country?

---

[1] There are extensive extracts from the regulations of 1803 concerning French coinage, in Ricardo's hand, among his papers; these however belong to a much earlier period.

Undoubtedly; because more goods would in such case be given for gold by Russia than by France, but its price would continue unaltered in this country.

[112] If you measure gold or coin which is here taken as equivalent to gold, and the gold bears a higher value in Russia than the goods, will it not cause a draw for gold upon this country in such a state of things?

If it bears a higher value in goods, it will make the exchange unfavourable to this country, and will cause an exportation of coin or bullion.

[113] They will be sent out, if it is more advantageous to send them than woollen or cotton goods; if there is a seignorage, you keep the gold coin at home until there is a great fluctuation in the exchanges?

If there is a seignorage, it will depend upon this circumstance; namely, whether the coin be passing at its nominal or at its intrinsic value; by proper regulations the coin may be sustained at its nominal value, but by bad management, by putting too great a quantity of currency into circulation, you may sink its value to the value of the metal which is in it, and then it will be immediately exported on the turn of the exchange.

[114] Supposing the plan which you have suggested, of the bank paying in gold bullion at the present standard of $3l.$ $17s.$ $10\frac{1}{2}d.$ an ounce, all sums demanded in their notes above a limited amount, say £. 100, and supposing sovereigns to be coined at such a brassage as would raise the standard of gold coin to $4l.$ an ounce, and that such coin were made a legal tender to the amount of £. 100 only, or whatever might be the lowest amount in notes for which bullion could be demanded at the bank, would not this modification of your plan of payment in bullion, afford the double advantage

of an invariable standard in bullion, and of a gold coin for the purposes of currency, without exposing the country to the risk of such coin being melted down or exported?

Entirely; I think it would quite exempt us from any such risk, and the price of gold under such circumstances, could, in my opinion, never be above $3l.$ $17s.$ $10\frac{1}{2}d.$; but the question supposes an advantage by possessing a gold currency, which I do not consider as such.

[115] Assuming that it should be thought expedient to combine your plan of the bank paying its notes above a certain amount in gold bullion, with the maintenance of a certain proportion of gold coin in currency, would not such a modification as the former question suggests, be the most advisable mode of affecting such object?

The very best, and the one which I have, under such circumstances, recommended in the paper I have delivered in this morning. I have there said, that under such a system, I should be favourable to any amount of seignorage which did not expose the coin to the risk of being imitated in this or any other country.

[116] Do you think that the difference between $3l.$ $17s.$ $10\frac{1}{2}d.$ the standard price in bullion, and $4l.$ the proposed standard for the coin, would expose the coin to such a risk?

I think it would not.

[117] Should you be disposed to push the seignorage further than the $4l.$?

It is difficult for me to estimate what proportion of encouragement would be sufficient to set people to work upon the imitating coin; it is a thing in which I have no experience, and I cannot give a more correct opinion than any other individual.

[118] Do you see a strong objection to a seignorage approaching very nearly the present market price of gold?

I feel some difficulty in mentioning any seignorage, as being within the proper limits; many persons can give better information than I can upon that subject.

[119] Do you believe that, under such a system as you have just described, any considerable quantity of gold coin would be likely to be required for the use of this country?

That is a difficult question to answer; I should apprehend that the taste of the public for paper is now so confirmed, that they would have little inducement to demand gold coin, and in that case a very small quantity would be sufficient for all the purposes of circulation.

[120] With a gold currency upon our present mint regulations, namely 3*l.* 17*s.* 10$\frac{1}{2}$*d.* per ounce, and if the export of coin and bullion were free, would it not be likely that exporters would prefer coin of that description to bullion for their exportation?

They would prefer gold coin.

[121] Under the system of a seignorage upon the gold coin, would not coin be the last article of gold to be exported; and would not the exporters in every instance prefer bullion to coin for their exportations?

That must depend upon the current value of the money. Unless some such restriction, as has been mentioned, should be adopted, I think it is as probable that coin might be exported as bullion, because the bank might increase the amount of their issues, till they lowered the value of their paper to the intrinsic value of the gold coin.

[122] Referring to a former question respecting the demand of gold for Russia; and supposing, after that demand

shall have been satisfied, that there should be a demand in this country for gold, should we not possess the same power of bringing that gold from Russia to England in exchange for our commodities, which you have stated might have taken place by an exchange of Russian goods against gold from this country?

I think that all countries have the means of purchasing the commodities which they want, gold among the number, and therefore there is no demand for gold [that] could exist in this country, which we should not have the means of supplying.

[123] Do not you think, that a rich country possesses greater means of acquiring and retaining gold within itself, than a poor country?

I think it will require more, and it will have greater means of obtaining that increased quantity.

[124] Do you not believe, referring to the trade manufactures and products, domestic and colonial, of this country, that it possesses the means of acquiring gold to an extent greatly beyond what is possessed by Russia, Austria, or any other continental power?

I believe it has; but I consider that in some measure a disadvantage, inasmuch as we have a greater quantity of currency forced upon us than I should desire to see employed; I always consider the currency as the dead part of our stock.

[125] Supposing the system of this country be to possess a great quantity of gold, does not this country possess superior means for that purpose to the continental countries just referred to?

A manufacturing country, I conceive, has always advantages over an agricultural country, in the means of supplying itself with bullion; and as no country is so highly manufacturing as this, I of course think it has the most ample means of supplying itself with any quantity of bullion that it may desire to have.

[126] Do not our colonial possessions add to those means? Undoubtedly, as far as colonial productions are exportable commodities generally in demand in other countries.

[127] As it will require a hundred pounds to be enabled to draw any quantity of gold bullion from the bank, will not the possessor of a less sum in bank notes than £100 be placed in a worse situation, with respect to the value of the sum which he possesses, than the possessor either of £. 100 or a larger sum; assuming in the question the sum of £. 100 arbitrarily, as the lowest for which bullion may be demanded?

The object which I had in view, was to regulate the value of the whole currency, by securing a control over its quantity; and it appears to me that by giving the power to persons possessing large notes only to demand gold in exchange for them, the quantity would be always effectually reduced to the wants of circulation, and therefore it never can happen, except on occasion of a panic, when every man is striving to turn his bank notes into bullion, that the person possessed of a less sum than £. 100 can be relatively in a worse situation than the man possessed of £. 100 and more, and even in the case of a panic, I think there would be dealers ready to purchase the one and two pound notes with bullion, at a price, very little below the mint price, knowing, as they would know, that as soon as they had accumulated a hundred pounds of those notes, they could go to the bank and demand bullion for them at the mint price. As there would be competition in this trade as well as there is in all others, the difference between the value of a £. 1 note, as compared with notes of a larger amount, would be so trifling as not to be worth considering.

[128] Would not the plan exclude the possessors of notes under £. 100 from converting them into bullion?

Certainly, in any other mode than by sale or bargain.

[129] You have stated that in case of a panic, dealers would purchase the small notes till they amounted to the £. 100, for which bullion could be demanded; in what commodity would the dealers purchase those £. 100 notes?

In bullion; the supposition is, that the man possessing a large note would have the privilege of getting bullion for his note, which the man with the smaller note would not have.

[130] How is he to pay in bullion; by that being divided into parts, and given to the holders of the notes?

Yes.

[131] In what shape is a note to the amount of £. 5 to be paid in bullion?

I conceive £. 5 worth of bullion can be sold as well as £. 500 worth.

[132] Is not a state of panic precisely that state of things which baffles ordinary speculations, with respect to the circulating medium; is it not very difficult to take precautions which can guard against all the possible consequences of alarm in the public mind?

I think it utterly impossible to provide against the effect of panic, on any system of banking whatever.

[133] What would be the effect produced, if the bank, instead of paying the supposed sum of £. 100 intirely in gold bullion, were entitled, or were liable to pay a small part of it, say in the proportion of five per cent, in the silver coin with its present seignorage?

That would have partially the effect of making either of the two metals the standard, instead of one exclusively, and

which, in my opinion, would be attended with very great
inconvenience.

[134] Would not such partial payment in silver coin in
the case of panic afford relief to the holders of small notes,
and afford time to the bank to protect itself against, and to
counteract such panic?

The question supposes that silver is a legal tender as well
as gold, which alters the state of things, and would be a
worse system than that which is at present established.

[135] Either there will be an attempt to accumulate the
small notes into sums of £. 100, or there will not; if there
is not, will it not be a proof that bank notes are considered
equally valuable with gold; if there is, will not the competition
equalize the value of the small note and the great one?

If there is not an attempt to accumulate the small notes
into sums of £. 100, it will be a proof that the small notes
are equally valuable with the large; and if there is, there
could be only that small difference in their value to which
I have before alluded, the profit of the dealer.

[136] Do you think there would be as much difference
between the premium that would be required to convert the
small notes into large ones, as the difference between
£. 3. 17s. 10$\frac{1}{2}$d. the mint price for bullion, and £. 4. for
specie?

Perhaps nearly the same.

[137] You have said, that in case there should be any
strong desire, from any cause, in the holders of small notes,
to turn them into bullion, they would be enabled to do so
through dealers, who would collect those small notes in order
to carry them into the bank, when they amounted to £. 100;
is not the reason for using gold coin, that by the stamp the

person to whom it is presented is immediately aware of its quality?

That is the advantage of using coin, but an advantage superseded in modern times by the more economical use of paper.

[138] In case I were the holder of a one pound note, and wished to change it into bullion from one of those dealers, how could I ascertain that what he gave me in bullion was of the value that it purported to be; could I do it without an assay, or without the same modes which are taken to demonstrate the value of coin?

Not unless you had full confidence in the dealer; but this is a state of things which I apprehend could never happen and which it is not necessary at all to guard against.

[139] It was understood that your answer, in which you state, that the holders of small notes would get them exchanged into bullion by applying to dealers, was given with a view to show that the holders of those notes would have a remedy which would place them upon the same footing as those persons presenting a certain sum of £. 100?

Yes, in the extreme case of a panic; but I consider that a very extreme case.

[140] Is it not essential to the execution of your plan, that bank notes should be made a legal tender?

Yes, undoubtedly. I wish to make one observation here; that in the evidence I gave the last time I was examined, I think the price of £. 3. 17s. was mentioned[1] as the price at which the bank should be compelled to buy bullion; but I wish the Committee to understand, that that was an ar-

---

[1] The price is not mentioned in the earlier part of the evidence as published; cp. Question 36 ff., p. 381 ff. above.

bitrary price, not one that I fixed on, or think the very 19 March 1819
best that could be settled; my opinion rather inclines to its
being considerably more than £. 3. 17s. somewhere about
£. 3. 17s. 6d.

[141] In case your plan was adopted, and no legal coinage
of gold was to take place, would it not be probable, that there
would be a circulation, to a certain extent, of foreign gold
coin in the country?

I think not; for I can see no advantage that would attend
the introduction of foreign coin.

[142] It is understood to be a part of your plan, that the
bank should be at liberty to pay the notes of a certain value,
presented to them, either in bars of gold, or foreign gold at
its intrinsic value?

Yes.

[143] In that case would not a considerable quantity of
foreign coin be probably issued by the bank?

Certainly.

[144] Do you think that would be required only for the
purpose of exportation, or that some of it would remain in
the country?

I think it would be required only for the purpose of
exportation, or the manufacture of gold articles.

[145] Supposing the bank to be obliged to pay their small
notes, when tendered to an amount less than £. 100, in
sovereigns, at the value of £. 4 per ounce, would such a
regulation tend to facilitate the plan which has been in
contemplation?

It would, in my opinion, be no hindrance whatever to it,
though not so economical always supposing that the large
notes are to be exchangeable for bullion.

[146] How do you suppose the value of the bars of gold should be ascertained, to the satisfaction of the person receiving them at the bank, and the person to whom he may afterwards dispose of them?

There are many transactions of that sort now taking place between the public and the bank, and I do not expect there will be any more in consequence of adopting my system: the mode which the bank now follow is, to advance a certain sum immediately on the sale of the gold; a portion of the bar of gold is then sent to the mint to be assayed, and, as soon as the quality of it is ascertained, the bank pay the remainder of the money, and the seller is quite satisfied, I believe, with that process.

[147] That answer is quite satisfactory, as to the purchase of gold by the bank; but put the case of a person going to receive a bar of gold at the bank, how is the receiver to be assured that that bar of gold is of the proper assay; and still more, how is the person to whom he may dispose of it the next day to receive a similar assurance?

Every bar of gold that the bank have purchased will have been assayed, and I think that the purchaser would always take it upon that report, without any further assay.

[148] Without any stamp?

I think so; but if it were advisable to put a stamp upon it, that might be done in the roughest possible way. Dealings in bullion are not similar to a man's taking a piece of money from another, whom he cannot afterwards trace, but the transaction is with a person he knows, and if he has any suspicions that the bar is not so valuable as is represented, even when he has it in his possession he may have it assayed, and if it is found deficient in the fineness for which he agreed, he can make his remonstrance, show the stamp, and satisfy the seller that it is the very identical bar which had been delivered to him; I think there would be no more difficulty in those transactions than in those that are now daily taking place in the purchase and sale of bullion between private individuals, and I have never heard of any difficulty arising from that source.

[149] It would then have become the standard of value?

Although a standard of value, I think it would never be used as money; all our transactions in bullion would be confined to our foreign trade, and to the uses for our own manufactures, that is exactly the amount of our trade in bullion at this moment.

[150] You have admitted that a rich country has greater facility to procure a large supply of gold; will not a poor country, exporting largely, and importing few goods, necessarily produce an exchange favourable to such poor country, and naturally bring gold into the country, without reference to the country being rich or poor?

It seems to me, that exportation of goods on balance is the effect of the value of gold, and not the cause of it.

MINUTES OF EVIDENCE TAKEN BEFORE
THE LORDS COMMITTEES

APPOINTED A SECRET COMMITTEE

TO ENQUIRE INTO THE STATE OF THE BANK

OF ENGLAND, WITH REFERENCE TO

THE EXPEDIENCY OF

THE RESUMPTION OF CASH PAYMENTS

AT THE PERIOD NOW FIXED BY LAW

Die Mercurii, 24° *Martii* 1819.

The LORD PRESIDENT in the Chair.

Mr. DAVID RICARDO is called in,
and examined as follows:

24 March 1819   1. What is your Line of Business?
I am in no Business now; but I have been all my Life in
the Money Market on the Stock Exchange.

2. Would it, in your Judgment, be safe and practicable
for the Bank of England to resume Payments in Cash on the
5th of July next?
I think it perfectly safe and practicable; but not without
some little Inconvenience, which must attend the Resumption of Cash Payments whenever it shall take place.

3. State your Grounds for that Opinion?
An alteration of the Price of Commodities, to the Amount
of even Four per Cent., must be attended with some little
Inconvenience.

4. On what Grounds do you form the Opinion, that the
only Inconvenience attendant on the Measure, would be a

Reduction of the Price of Commodities of no more than Four per Cent?

I consider the Price of Commodities to depend on the Quantity and Value of the Medium by which they are estimated; and as I consider that Medium to be now depreciated Four per Cent. on Comparison with the Mint Price of Bullion, I consider that a Reduction in the Amount of the Currency to the Amount of Four per Cent., would lower the Price of Commodities to that Amount. I mean a Reduction of Four per Cent. in the Amount of all the Paper Currency now in Circulation.

5. Supposing the Amount of Bank of England Notes to be now 25 Millions, and that they were reduced One Million; and that a proportionate Reduction took place in the rest of the Circulating Medium of the Country; would that have the Effect of raising the Value of the whole Currency Four per Cent., and thereby lowering Prices to the same Amount?

I should expect such a Consequence to follow, if no Commercial Causes were operating on the Value of the Currency; if such Causes were operating, the Reduction required might be either more or less. I wish also to observe, that a Reduction in the Amount of Notes of Four per Cent. will not produce a Rise in the Value of the Currency of exactly Four per Cent., but something very near to that Amount.

6. What do you mean by any Commercial Causes operating on the Value of the Currency?

The Quantity of Currency required to circulate Commodities must depend on the Value of that Currency; if, therefore, any Causes should operate to raise the Value of Gold generally in the World, a less Quantity of Gold would be necessary for the Circulation of the same Quantity of

Commodities in England; and under such Circumstances a greater Reduction than Four per Cent. in the Quantity of Paper would be necessary; an Extension of Trade also, or an Increase of Capital, may make a greater Quantity of Currency necessary at one Period than at another, and might therefore diminish the Proportion necessary to be reduced.

7. Are you aware that there was a Reduction of Bank Notes in Circulation during the Course of 1818, to the Amount of Three Millions, without any apparent proportionate Increase in the Course of that Year of the Country Paper; how do you account, under these Circumstances, for the Exchanges being more unfavourable, and the Price of Gold higher, at the End of 1818, than at the Beginning of that Year?

Facts of this Kind I find it very difficult to account for; but I should think it might have been owing to the diminished Trade, and to a Rise in the general Value of Bullion in the World.

8. Might it not, in a considerable Degree, be accounted for by the Operations going on in the Money Markets on the Continent, and more particularly those at Paris and Petersburgh, towards the Close of last Year?

Not unless those Operations had a Tendency to increase the general Value of Bullion, which might be affected by a Reduction of the Paper Circulation of the Continent, and by the Substitution of Gold and Silver Coin.

9. Might not the Effect of these Operations at Paris and Petersburgh, and other Places on the Continent, be to induce Individuals to make large Remittances from this Country for the Purpose of assisting the Operations which were going on in those Places?

Certainly; but whether those Remittances should be made in Bullion or Goods, would depend on their relative Value; and if Gold was preferred, it proves to me, that the Value of Bullion was affected by those Transactions on the Continent.

10. Do you recollect the Fall which took place in all Prices in the Year 1816? Was not that Decline in the Prices much more considerable than any Decline you anticipate now, from an Endeavour to raise the Value of the Currency to a Par with Gold?

Much more considerable; one of the Causes which operate on the Value and the Quantity of Currency, I have omitted to mention, namely, the varying State of Credit, which considerably affects the Quantity necessary to perform the same Business, and which I think operated in the Year mentioned.

11. Paper having been, in the Middle of 1815, at upwards of 20 per Cent. Discount, and we having it in Evidence, that Gold at the latter End of 1816 would have been at the Mint Price, had it not been sustained by the Bank at the Price of £3 18*s. 6d.;* do you not think that the Pressure which the Country sustained at that Period must be much greater than what it will now sustain from Paper resuming its Value upon a Par with Gold, it being now at a Discount of only 4 per Cent; and can you state any Proportion which the Difficulties of one Period are likely to bear in relation to the Difficulties of the other?

I think the Pressure sustained at that Period was much greater than would be experienced now by a Reduction of 4 per Cent. in the Amount of the Currency. At the same Time, I do not think that the whole Difference in the comparative Value of Paper and Gold in 1815 and 1816, is to be ascribed to the Rise in the Value of Paper only, but also to a Fall in the Value of Gold, arising from some of those Causes I have mentioned. I find it quite impossible to assign a Proportion between the Difficulties of the Two Periods.

12. Do you suppose, that from the Middle of 1815 to the Commencement of 1817, a Fall took place in the Price of Gold through the World?

I am wholly unacquainted with the Fact, such is the Opinion I should form; and my Reason is, that there did not appear any proportionate Fall in the Prices of Commodities and the Price of Gold in this Country. The Value of Gold and Paper was equalized, probably by a Rise in the Value of Paper, and a Fall in the Value of Gold.

13. Can you infer a general Fall in the Price of Gold through the World, from the State of the Prices of Commodities in this Country solely?

Quite impossible.

14. The Question and Answer No. 4. are repeated; would the Fall of Four per Cent. be the only Inconvenience resulting from the Reduction of the Circulating Medium necessary to precede or accompany the Resumption of metallic Payments by the Bank?

I think it would not be the only Inconvenience; whatever affects the Value of the Currency, must affect the relative Interest of Debtor and Creditor; but I know of no other Inconvenience.

15. Do you conceive that the Amount of Trade, Capital, and Revenue, and the Amount of Currency required, must necessarily bear any fixed Ratio or Proportion to each other?

Certainly not; I think the Proportion must depend on the Economy in the Use of Money, which again must depend on the State of Credit at the Time.

16. Must not these Proportions also be affected by the general State of Wealth and Population, at any Two Periods in which the Comparison is to be made?

I think it must. The more dense the Population, the less, all other Circumstances being the same, will be the Amount of Circulating Medium required.

17. Must it not also be in some Degree affected by the Nature of the Transactions?

I do not see that that would affect it.

18. Do not different Branches of Commerce require different Proportions of Circulating Medium, in proportion to the different Quantity of Capital invested, and Profits made?

They probably may.

19. Are you of Opinion that the Circumstances to which you have alluded in your former Answer, (No. 15.) have so far operated in the Course of the last 20 Years, as to make it practicable to carry on the Business of the Country with an Amount of Currency not numerically greater than that which existed previous to the Bank Restriction, notwithstanding the apparent Increase of Trade, Capital, and Revenue?

I think the numerical Amount of Currency required at this Time is greater than what was required previous to 1797; but the Proportion of that Currency to the Transactions to which it is applied is less now than at the former Period.

20. Do you know any Practice, tending materially to economise the Use of the Circulating Medium in the Conduct of our Transactions, introduced since the Beginning of 1815?

No, not since that Period.

21. What Means would you recommend to be adopted to enable the Bank, at the earliest practicable Period, to pay their Notes in Cash or Bullion?

The Measure which I should recommend would be, to give the Bank the Option of paying its Notes on Demand in Gold Bullion, or in Coin, at the Mint Price of £3 17s. 10$\frac{1}{2}$d.; at the same Time requiring of them to purchase Standard Gold at the Price of £3 17s. 6d. to any Extent.

22. What are the peculiar Advantages which you think would attend this Plan, in preference to a simple Resumption of Cash Payments?

First, it would exempt the Bank from providing a Quantity of Gold necessary to replace all the smaller Notes which are now circulated in London and the Country. Secondly, it would obtain for the Bank, and therefore for the Nation, all the Advantages which a Capital equal to the Amount of all the small Notes would produce.

23. Referring then to Question and Answer No. 21, do you mean that the Bank should be obliged to pay each Note on Demand in Coin or Bullion, at its Option; or would you limit the Obligation to Notes of a certain Amount, and to what Amount?

I would limit the Obligation on the Part of the Bank to Notes of £50, £60, or £100 Value, or to a Number of smaller Notes amounting in the Whole to such a Sum. The Object which I have in view, is to regulate the Value of Currency, by having an effectual Controul over its Quantity. I have no Preference for any Sums I have stated, provided they may not be too small.

24. Is that Part of your Plan, which requires the Bank to purchase Gold at £3 17s. 6d., in your Judgment necessary to it; or would not the same Object be obtained by the Mint

being opened to the Public for the Purpose of coining Gold, or by Government reserving to themselves the Power of coining and issuing Gold Coin?

That Part of my Plan is not necessary. My Object would be equally effected by either of the other Modes. I prefer my own only because it is more economical, and because it would be of more speedy Operation.

25. Have you formed any Estimate of the Saving by the Plan you propose, when compared with the Resumption of Payments in Cash as before the Restriction?

The Saving must depend entirely on the Preference of the Public for metallic Circulation: if they continued to use Paper in smaller Payments, on the Supposition of the Bank paying in Coin, as it did before 1797, there would be no Saving at all by my Plan.

26. What Amount of Bullion would it be necessary for the Bank to be possessed of on your Plan, for the Purpose of regulating the Amount of their Notes; and what would be the Amount of the Coin that the Bank should be possessed of under the old System, for the Purpose of enabling them to pay their Notes in Coin?

On both Plans I think the Quantity would be the same, but what the Quantity should be, must depend on the Knowledge of the Bank of the true Principles of Currency; because they have always the Power to regulate the Price of Bullion, by limiting or increasing the Quantity of their Notes. My Answer applies to the habitual Reserve the Bank would be obliged to keep up, according as the Currency was settled upon one or the other Plan.

27. What would be the Amount of the Difference of the Bullion and Coin which the Bank would have to provide, for enabling them to open, under the one Plan or the other?

If the Bank were to limit their Circulation till they had raised the Value of their Notes to an Equality with the Value of Bullion, it would perhaps be necessary, or they might think it prudent, to provide a sufficient Quantity of Coin against the extreme Case of their being called upon to replace all the small Circulation of the Town and Country with Coin, if Cash Payments be resumed on the old Plan. On my Plan no such Provision of either Coin or Bullion to replace small Notes would be necessary. In the First Case, an Amount of 15 Millions might probably be required, merely for the Purpose of answering the smaller Notes, and a further Reserve of Coin for larger Notes.

28. What in your Judgment would be the necessary Reserve of Coin for the larger Notes according to the old Plan, and what would be the Amount of Bullion to answer the Demand according to your Plan?

I have already observed, they would in my Opinion be equal, and must depend on the Knowledge of the Bank of the Principles of Money. I should think that a Reserve of Three Millions would under good Management be amply sufficient upon a Supposition of 24 Millions of Bank of England Notes in Circulation.

29. Would not the Object of your Plan be most completely effected by there being no Gold Coin in Circulation, unless it should be necessary for the Government to issue a Proportion of such Coin, in consequence of the Bank having reduced their Issues of Paper too low?

The Object of my Plan would be most completely effected by there being no Gold Coin in Circulation; and the latter Measure would be unnecessary if the Bank were obliged to purchase Gold.

30. Would not such an Obligation be a much better Security for the Public against too reduced an Issue, than any Discretion, wherever vested and however guarded?

Much better; it can be done so rapidly, and so certainly in proportion to the Demand for Money.

31. Is not, in one Case, the Operation performed by the necessary Effect of such a Provision, constantly operating on the Interests of the Bank itself, set in Motion by the Interests of Individuals; while, on the other, it must depend on the Judgment to be formed on the particular Circumstances of the Case?

It is certainly so.

32. What Security is there that the Bank would always be able to purchase Bullion at that Rate, and therefore would always be able, by the Notes issued for such Purchases, to keep up a Sufficiency of Circulating Medium?

I am of opinion, that the Bank, by regulating the Quantity of their Paper, would either lower the Price of Bullion to £3 17s. 6d.; that is, to one of the Limits mentioned; or raise it to the other Limit of £3 17s. $10\frac{1}{2}d.$

33. If such Circumstances, as you have alluded to in your former Answer, as raising the general Value of Gold Bullion in the World, should again occur, and if other Circumstances, to which you have also alluded, in the State of Commerce between this and other Countries, should also again occur, and produce, as far as any of these Causes can effect it, a considerable Increase of the Price of Gold Bullion, and a very unfavourable State of Exchange, would it not require a Reduction of the Issue of Bank Notes proportionably great, to keep down Gold Bullion to this Price in spite of the Tendency of all these Circumstances to raise it?

Certainly, in every such Case it would be incumbent on

the Bank to raise in an equal Degree the Value of their Paper, which could only be done by a Reduction in Quantity. In 1783, there was in a few Months, on a very small Circulation of Paper, a Reduction in the Amount of Bank Notes of about Three Millions, the Bank being then compelled to make the Value of their Paper conform to the Value of Gold Bullion.

34. Can you conceive the Existence of any other real Standard of Value, besides Bullion, out of which that Inconvenience would not arise in the same or a greater Degree?
None.

35. What, in your Opinion, would be the Convenience or Inconvenience of allowing the Bank the Option of paying either in Gold or Silver Bullion, according to some fixed Proportion of Value established between them; establishing at the same Time only one of the Metals as the fixed Standard or Measure of Value, to which the other Metal should be made to conform by a Review of the Proportion at regular fixed Periods, according to the relative Prices of the precious Metals, as then ascertained in the Markets of the World?
The greatest Inconvenience would result from such a Provision. I consider it a great Improvement having established one of the Metals as the Standard for Money. The Bank and all other Debtors would naturally pay their Debts in the Metal which could at the Time be most cheaply purchased, and at certain fixed Periods the Currency might be suddenly increased or lowered in Value, in proportion to the Variation in the relative Value of the Two Metals from one of these Periods to the other. I find, from a Paper I have in my Hand, extracted from Mushet's Tables, which, I believe, will be found correct on a Comparison with Official Documents, that frequently in the Space of Two or Three Years the relative Value of Gold and Silver has varied as much as from

9 to 15 per Cent. From 1777 to 1779, the relative Proportion varied from 13·19[1] to 15·01, a Difference of 9 per Cent. From 1782 to 1785, it varied from 13·04 to 15·07, a Difference of 15 per Cent. From 1782 to 1809, it varied from 13·04 to 16·49, a Difference of 25 per Cent. The greatest Inconvenience would result in raising or lowering suddenly the Value of the Currency to so great an Extent.

36. Considering the great Variation in the relative Value of Gold and Silver, and considering that Silver is the Standard Measure in most other Countries, what will be the Advantage in our having Gold as the Standard Measure in Value in this Country, on the Supposition of your Plan being adopted, which supersedes the Necessity of a Gold Circulation?

My only Reason for preferring one Metal to the other is its being less variable in Value. I had at one Time thought Silver would be less variable; but having heard that Machinery is particularly applicable to the working of Silver Mines, and cannot be applied to increase the Quantity of Gold, I now think that Gold is the more invariable Metal.[2]

37. Supposing this Country has a Gold Standard, and other Countries a Silver Standard, shall we not experience from the Variations of Gold and Silver, in our Intercourse with other Nations, the same Difficulty in the Exchanges, which our internal Circulation would sustain if the Bank had the Option, as is supposed, of paying in either of the Two Metals?

I think we should; the Inconveniences would be of the same Nature, but the Exchanges would be regulated accordingly.

[1] Should be '13.79'. See Robert Mushet, *An Enquiry into the Effects produced on the National Currency and Rates of Exchange* *by the Bank Restriction Bill...*, London, Baldwin, 1810, Appendix.

[2] Cp. above, p. 390–1.

38. If we had a Gold Standard, and other Countries continued to have a Silver Standard, would it be possible to state the Par of Exchange for any Length of Time together?

It would be quite impossible. But that I do not think a Matter of the least Importance; and with respect to the Inconvenience before mentioned, it would not exist if all the Debts to this Country and from this Country were contracted in our Currency: they would exist only on the Supposition that they would be contracted partly in British Currency and partly in Foreign Currency.

39. If all Debts were contracted in our Currency, would it not be an Extension to Foreign Countries of our Standard?

As far as we were concerned in Trade with them.

40. Is that the Practice in contracting Debts in Foreign Countries?

I should think not; they are as often contracted in the Currency of the one Country as in that of the other; the Advantage in the Payment may be in our Favour or against us, that is Matter of Chance.

41. Would not the Inconvenience of leaving the Advantage or Disadvantage in Payments to be a Matter of Chance, be corrected by our adopting a Silver Standard?

Certainly.

42. Would not our adopting Silver as the Standard of Value, and as the general Medium of Circulation, have in some Degree an Effect, which you have stated as a Benefit attending your Plan, viz. the keeping in Circulation more Bank Notes, than our adopting a Gold Standard, and paying in Gold Coin, as before the Restriction?

Certainly.

43. Is it intended to form an essential Part of your Plan, that the Bank of England Note, and the Country Bank Note, should circulate after the Bank has begun to pay in Bullion, upon the same Footing as at present?

It is an essential Part of my Plan.

44. Would the Plan, of requiring from the Bank the Delivery of Gold Bullion in Exchange only for large Sums in their Notes, be compatible with the Circulation of a certain Quantity of Gold Coin, if that were judged desirable?

Quite compatible; the Gold Coin should, in that Case, be subject to a Charge equal to the Expence of Coinage, but not sufficiently high to afford Temptation to false Coining. The Advantage of making the Coin very perfect, and immediately procurable in Exchange at the Mint, without any Delay or any Deduction, for an equal Weight of Gold Bullion, would be considerable, as far as regards our internal Circulation; but it would expose us to an additional Charge, as all Exporters of Bullion would be desirous of exchanging their Bullion for Coin, previous to its Exportation; the coined Metal being of course more valuable than an equal Weight of Gold Bullion. All the Advantages of a metallic Circulation would be obtained by allowing such a Charge on the Coin, and giving the Option to the Holder of Bank Notes, of demanding at the Bank either Gold Bullion or Gold Coin subject to such a Charge, in Exchange for his Note. If no such Privilege be allowed, of demanding Bullion from the Bank in Exchange for Notes, the Bank, by augmenting their Issues, might sink the Value of the whole Currency, and therefore of the coined Part of it, to the intrinsic Value of the Metal of which it is composed.

45. Would it not be more convenient that the Demand for Money coined, on the Principle stated in your last

Answer, should be made at the Mint only, and not at the Bank in Exchange for their Notes; and that the Mint should keep in Readiness for that Purpose a certain Quantity of Gold already coined?

The Effect would be the same; but I think the Plan suggested by the Question would be an Improvement.

46. In that Case, would it be expedient to subject the Bank to the Obligation of paying small Sums in Coin, or would it be more advisable to make its small Notes completely a legal Tender?

Under those Circumstances, I think small Notes should be exchanged for Coin at the Bank, if required.

47. Might it not be sufficient if the Bank were discharged from the Obligation of paying Coin in any Cases for their small Notes, except when presented in large Sums; and would not the Facility which Individuals would thus have of procuring Coin for their small Notes from Bankers and others who could present them in large Sums for Payment in Bullion, and obtain Coin for that Bullion from the Mint, be sufficient to keep in Circulation a certain Quantity of Gold Coin, and to prevent any Discredit of small Notes?

Bankers would be under no Obligation to give Coin for small Notes; and I do not see any other Advantage in making large Notes exchangeable for Coin, but to give the Public the Option of using Coin instead of small Notes. I think the small Notes could never fall into Discredit, while you have the Power of regulating the Quantity of large Notes, by the Obligation imposed on the Bank to pay their Notes to a large Amount in Bullion.

48. Is it a necessary Part of the proposed Plan that the Trade in Bullion and Coin should be wholly free, and the

melting of Coin, as well as its Exportation, be permitted by 24 March 1819
Law?

It is; and on any Plan of Currency I think such a Regulation would be desirable.

49. Would it not also be necessary, that the internal Traffic as well as the Foreign Trade in all Bullion should be completely free?

Certainly.

50. If the Mint were obliged to keep in reserve a certain Quantity of Gold ready coined, would it not be necessary, in order to secure the Public against great Expence, to make a Charge upon the Coin equal, not only to the Expence of Coinage, but to the Loss of Interest upon the probable Quantity of Coin there to be kept in reserve?

I think the Charge should be as high as it could be, consistently with the Object of not encouraging false coining.

51. Supposing then that Gold Coin should be issued at 80s. per oz., that is 2s. $1\frac{1}{2}d$. above the Mint Price, of which Advance one Part should be considered as Seignorage, and the other Part as the strict Cost of Manufacture; supposing in this Proportion, 1s. 6d. per oz., viz. $4\frac{1}{2}d$. each Sovereign, be considered as Seignorage, and $7\frac{1}{2}d$. per oz. as the Brassage; will you state, in case such Coin by Wear should lose Part of its legal Weight, whether it will not be just to allow the Whole of what may be called Seignorage, subjecting the Holder only to the Loss of Weight and Cost of Manufacture?

I think it would be unjust to deduct from the Holder of light Money any thing but the mere Loss of Weight.

52. Suppose, in any Country, Gold were declared by Law the Standard of Value, and that Gold de facto engrossed the Circulation in Exclusion of all Silver Money, would not

the Course of Exchange with that Country regulate itself
with Reference to its Gold Money?

Certainly, the Course of Exchange would be regulated
with Reference to the relative Value of Gold and Silver.

53. Supposing, in any Country, Silver were declared the
Standard of Value, and Silver were de facto in Circulation
to the Exclusion of all Gold Money, would not, in such a
Country, the Exchange regulate itself with Reference to its
Silver Money?

It would.

54. With the Exception of War and Conquest, can Foreign
Commodities ever be acquired, but in Exchange for something which has been manufactured or produced at Home,
either immediately or after Two or more different Exchanges?

They can be procured in no other Manner.

55. Is it not sound Policy to encourage the Importation
of Manufactures, or Raw Materials which a Country does
not itself produce, with a View to encourage the Increase of
its own Produce and Manufactures, which must go Abroad
in Quantities similar in Value to the Value of what it acquires?

It is the soundest Policy to make the Trade both of Import
and Export as free as possible, as that will be the Means of
giving us the greatest Abundance of Articles for our own
Consumption.

56. Have you not stated, that if the Bank was to resume
Payments in Bullion upon your Plan, it would be exempted
from providing Gold necessary for circulating its small
Notes to a given Sum, say 15 Millions; and that the general
Wealth of the Country would be increased by enriching the
Bank in consequence of this Saving?

I have said so, and I think so.

57. Do you believe the following Account to be an
accurate Account of the Profits of the Bank since the Restriction, viz.

	£
In Bonuses and Increase of Dividends - -	7,451,136
New Bank Stock (£2,910,600) divided among the Proprietors - - - - - - -	7,276,500
Increased Value of Capital of £11,642,400, (which on an Average of 1797 was worth 125, and which is now worth 250), that is - - - - - - - - - - - - - - -	14,553,000
Making in all, on a Capital of £11,642,400, a Gain in 19 Years of - - - - - - -	£29,280,636

I have no Reason to doubt it; I believe it is accurate as far
as I recollect. Part of that increased Value is derived from
the increased Value of all funded Property.

58. Suppose we were to resume Cash Payments under a
Plan which required that the Bank should provide themselves
with only Three Millions of Treasure, would not there be
a Demand for 15 Millions less of the Produce and Manufactures of this Country, than would be created by imposing
on the Bank the Necessity of providing 18 Millions?

Yes, there would; but as we should export these Commodities without procuring a Return of any other which
would contribute to our Advantage, the Gold would not be
a very desirable Importation.

59. Would not the additional Demand for 15 Millions
enrich our Manufacturers, who are the greatest Sufferers by
the present State of the Circulation?

In the same Way as if we were to throw those 15 Millions
of Manufactures into the Sea, which would also create a
Demand for them.

60. Does it signify to our Manufacturers, after they have found a Sale for their Manufactures in France, whether the Purchaser uses them, or throws them into the Sea?

It is of no Importance to them, but of the greatest Importance to the Country, inasmuch as in that Case we should have 15 Millions less of productive Capital.

61. Do you mean to say, that if we sold those 15 Millions for Gold, we should not acquire a Value equal to them in Exchange?

We should acquire a Value equal to them in Exchange; but as such Gold would be a dead Stock, it would be no Advantage or Profit.

62. Do you think it would be advisable to adopt a Plan, under the present Circumstances of the Country, the Consequence of which would be to enrich the Bank, who has been such an inordinate Gainer by the Restriction, at the Expence of abstracting a Demand for 15 Millions worth of their Commodities from our Manufacturers, at a Time, when they have been the greatest Sufferers by the Restriction, and are likely to be great Sufferers by the Resumption of Cash Payments?

In whatever way Compensation was made to the Manufacturers, I should regret that we should think it necessary to make so great a Sacrifice of national Profit and Income, which I think we should be doing if we consented to make 15 Millions of our Capital totally unproductive.

63. Supposing we were to adopt a Plan which should annihilate that Demand for 15 Millions of our Manufactures, do you suppose that that Portion of Wealth would at all exist, in so far as it is composed of Manufacturing Labour?

I think it would; because the Quantity of Labour employed and Commodities produced must be in proportion to the Capital we have; and there can be no Production without occasioning an equal Consumption. In this Case, I think we should consume the Commodities ourselves; in the other Case, they would be consumed by others.

64. Do you mean to say, that an extra Demand for the Commodities of the Country would not produce any Increase of its Manufactures?

I should very much doubt whether it would; the sole Difference would be, with respect to what Commodities would be produced, and to the more advantageous Exchange we should make, by having a more extended Market.

65. Do you mean, that you doubt whether an Increase of Foreign Demand has not always a Tendency to increase the Production and Wealth of a Nation?

In no other Way than by procuring for us a greater Quantity of the Commodities we desire in Exchange for a given Quantity of our own Commodities, or rather for a given Quantity of the Produce of our Land and Labour.

66. Do you then think that it is true, as a general Principle, that the Demand does not regulate the Production of a Country, and that the Increase of the Demand does not add to its Wealth?

An Increase of Demand is serviceable to a Country, inasmuch as it procures for it a more extensive Market, and enables it to get a greater Quantity of Foreign Goods in Exchange for its own; but the Amount and Value of the Commodities produced, whether the Country possess Foreign Trade or not, is always limited by the Amount of Capital employed; and therefore Foreign Trade may alter the Description of Commodities produced, but cannot increase their aggregate Value.

67. Is it possible, then, there should exist an increased
Foreign Demand to the Extent of Five Millions, for Cotton
Goods for Example, without an Increase of their Price in
the Home Market immediately taking place?

Certainly not; but those Cotton Goods cannot be produced unless Capital be withdrawn from other Employments.

68. Do you not know, that when the Demand for our
Manufactures is great in this Country, the very Credit which
that Circumstance creates enables the Manufacturer to make
more extended Use of his Capital in the Production of
Manufactures?

I have no Notion of Credit being at all effectual in the
Production of Commodities; Commodities can only be
produced by Labour, Machinery, and raw Materials; and if
these are employed in one Place they must necessarily be
withdrawn from another. I am not denying the Advantages
of Foreign Trade; but I wish to reduce those Advantages
to what I consider their just Value.

69. Have you never known Machinery, raw Materials,
and Labour, paid for by any Individual who used them to
a greater Extent than the Capital he actually possessed, by
Means of the Credit he commanded?

Yes; but if he had not had that Credit, it would have been
in the Power of somebody else to have employed them.

70. Whence would that other Person have obtained that
Capital, if you suppose that the Capital of the Country is
always employed, and that Foreign Demand cannot therefore produce a greater Quantity of Manufacture or rude
Produce, which is limited by the Quantity of our Capital?

Credit, I think, is the Means, which is alternately transferred from one to another, to make use of Capital actually
existing; it does not create Capital; it determines only by

whom that Capital should be employed: the removing Capital from one Employment to another may often be very advantageous, and it may also be very injurious.

71. If Credit always represents an existing Capital, what Advantage does this Country derive from the Institution of Banks of Credit, which is not enjoyed by Countries who have only Banks of Deposit?

The Disadvantage to which those Countries are exposed which have Banks of Deposit only, is, that they are obliged to use a Part of their Capital unproductively; whereas those which have Banks of Credit use their whole Capital productively, except such Part as is kept in Reserve to answer Demands.

72. Am I then to understand, that in Countries which have Banks of Credit, there is never any Capital employed productively, of which there does not exist a similar Quantity of either productive or unproductive Capital, that might be applied to the same Object?

I do not understand the Question: for my Supposition is, that there is no Capital used unproductively, where Banks of Credit exist in a great Degree of Perfection: I think the whole Capital is used productively.

73. Are not the Capitals invested in Land, for Example, capable of Two Uses. 1. Is it not productively used, as vested in Land. 2. May not Money be raised by Credit on that Land, which may be applied to the Purposes of Manufactures?

The Question supposes Two Capitals, the Land, and the Instruments employed in Manufactures; the Money which circulates them forms no Part of the productive Capital, it determines only by whom it shall be employed.

74. May not a Man get Credit from a Bank of Credit on the Security of his Capital, which is profitably employed, whether vested in Stock or in Land, and may he not by means of that Credit purchase or create an additional Quantity of Machinery and raw Materials, and pay an additional Number of Labourers, without dislodging Capital from any existing Employment in the Country?

Impossible; he can purchase Machinery, &c. with Credit, he can never create them. If he purchases, it is always at the Expence of some other Person; and he displaces some other from the Employment of Capital.

75. Are you then of Opinion that there never can be made in any Country Two Uses of the same Capital; one to acquire an annual Revenue, which it produces by the Modes in which it is invested, and the other to acquire a Capital on Credit, which may also be profitably employed by the Person who acquires it, and which will be so whenever there is an increased Demand for Commodities?

Capital can only be acquired by saving. It is impossible that one Capital can be employed by Two Persons at the same Time, or for Two Objects: the greatest Advantage will be sought and obtained at all Times by the Employer of Capital.

76. Will not a great Diminution of the Demand for Commodities prevent his obtaining those Advantages from his Capital, which a great Increase of the Demand for them would secure?

It may, as far as regards the particular Commodity; but if there be a less Production of one Commodity, the Production of another would in a Degree be encouraged.

The Witness is directed to withdraw.

Die Veneris, 26° Martii 1819.

The LORD PRESIDENT in the Chair.

Mr. DAVID RICARDO is called in again, and further
examined as follows:

77. Supposing the Plan of the Bank paying its Notes in 26 March 1819
Bullion, at the Mint Price, as explained in your preceding
Examination, to be adopted by the Legislature, will you
state your Opinion as to what Period it would be most
advantageous to fix for the Commencement of such a
System?

It would be difficult to fix on any one Period as most
advantageous; but as I think the Effects of a Return to Cash
Payments have been already in a great Degree borne, I should
not think that there would be any great Difficulty attending
the commencing the Bullion Payments even as early as July
next.

78. Are you of Opinion that it would be more advantageous to require the Bank to commence this System by
Payment of its Notes in Bullion at the Mint Price, or that
any Facility would be given to the Plan, by the Adoption
of a graduated Scale, by which they should pay at first at
the present Market Price, and at Prices successively reduced
at stated Periods, until they came down to the Mint Price?

Facility would be afforded by a graduated Scale, commencing at the present Market Price. By far the most
important Consideration with me is, preventing the Currency
being depreciated, as compared with Bullion, below the
present Rate of Depreciation, and by adopting the graduated
Scale you would have complete Security upon that Point.
At the same Time, I think we should attain the ultimate
Result of reducing the Price of Bullion to the Mint Price of

£3 17*s.* 10$\frac{1}{2}$*d.,* before the Time to which the Regulation might apply.

79. Would it not therefore be necessary, in the Adoption of such a graduated Scale, to allow the Bank a Discretion to accelerate, but not to retard, the successive Reduction of Prices at which they would give Bullion in Exchange for their Notes?

I think such would be a very good Regulation.

80. Supposing the Bank had Power to accelerate the Rate of Reduction, might not those who were in the Knowledge of the Intention so to accelerate it, take Advantage of that Knowledge, which they would be precluded from doing, if it was to take place at fixed Days?

Such an Effect might possibly take place in a slight Degree. But I have already said, that I think the ultimate Effect would be anticipated, and as every Person would be certain that in a short Space of Time Gold would fall to the Mint Price, they would not be induced to make Purchases above that Price, notwithstanding a premature Reduction in the Price of Gold by the Bank, below that fixed by the Scale.

81. State your Opinion, supposing the System of successive Reduction were adopted, at what Time that Operation might be safely commenced, and how long the Interval ought to be from thence to the Period of Payment at the Mint Price?

I think it could not commence too soon; and with respect to the Interval, it appears to me a Matter of slight Importance; probably Twelve Months would be a good Period. I cannot conceive that the Fall in the Value of Commodities to the Amount of Four per Cent. would be a very formidable Operation, or one likely to be attended with serious Consequences.

82. Do you, having stated that you think that they might begin to pay at the Mint Price on the 5th of July next, suppose that there would be any Advantage derived from postponing that Obligation, by adopting a graduated Scale, other than to save the Funds of the Bank?

I think there would be other Advantages, besides saving the Funds of the Bank; for when I said that on the 5th of July next the Bank might without Difficulty commence paying in Bullion at the Mint Price, I supposed the Bank was to retain the same unlimited Power of increasing their Issues, between this Time and the 5th of July, that they now have. On the Principle of a graduated Scale, commencing at the present Market Price, I concluded that the Regulation of making them pay at the Market Price would be adopted immediately; with that Security, I think there are Advantages in deferring the ultimate Reduction to the Mint Price.

83. If the graduated Scale was to be adopted, so as to afford that Security at the earliest possible Period in which an Act of Parliament could be passed, do you think there would be any Danger to the Public from accelerating the Gradations of that Scale, so as to come to the Payment in Bullion at the Mint Price by the 5th of January 1820?

I think that no Danger would attend the coming to the Mint Price by the Beginning of next Year; in every Change of this Sort, there is some Advantage in making it as gradual as possible.

84. Do you recollect whether within these last Eight Years we have not frequently seen the Circulating Medium of the Country undergo much more formidable Changes with respect to Value than 4 per cent., within a shorter Period than Six Months, judging of the Value of the Circulating Medium by the Price of Gold?

In my Opinion it has undergone much greater Variations than 4 per Cent.; and in the soundest State of our Currency, it would be liable to such Variations.

85. From what Causes could it undergo Variations, exceeding that Amount, if the Currency were restored to its soundest possible State?

It would not undergo any Variation, as compared with the Standard; but I mean, that the Standard itself might undergo Variations exceeding that Amount; the whole Currency is of course subject to all the Variations of the Standard.

86. In that Case, would not the Currency of other Countries, in an equally sound State, undergo similar Variations?

Certainly; the Inconvenience, as far as regarded England, would not be less on that Account; I consider any Variation in the Value of the Currency as an Evil, from producing a Variation in the Prices of all Articles.

87. Is there not this Difference between the Case of a Variation occasioned by Causes peculiarly affecting England, and that of a Variation occasioned by Causes affecting equally all Countries enjoying a sound State of Currency; that in the First Case, the Exchange between this Country and those Countries would be affected; in the Second, the Exchanges between England and those Countries would not be affected?

In the First Case, the Exchanges would be affected; in the Second, they would not, if the Causes operated on all Countries at once; but Scarcity and increased Value of the precious Metals might take place in one particular Country, which would ultimately affect their Value in all; but in the Interval, the Exchange would be affected. The Circumstance of the Exchange being unfavourable, does not seem to me to be any Disadvantage to us.

88. Do you believe, that if this Plan were adopted of Payments in Bullion, according to a graduated Scale of Reduction, there are any Circumstances arising, either from the general State of the Bullion Market, or from any other Causes whatever, which are likely to create Dangers and Difficulty to the Bank in their procuring such Quantities of Gold, and at such Prices, as this Plan would require?

None whatever. The Bank would always have the Power of keeping the Price of Gold rather below that which was fixed by the Scale; and therefore the Price of Gold might gradually be reduced to the Mint Price, without the Bank being under any absolute Necessity of exchanging one Ounce of Bullion for its Notes.

89. If, contrary to all reasonable Expectation, any unforeseen Contingency of such a Tendency as stated in the preceding Question should by Possibility arise, would not the Plan of a graduated Scale, operating as above proposed for the next 12 Months from the present Time, afford to the Legislature the fullest Opportunity of meeting and providing for such a Case as its Exigency might require?

It certainly would.

90. Is it not also a great Advantage of such a Plan, that nearly the whole Progress of its Operation, and that of our Currency as connected with it, would thus be brought successively under the View of Parliament, instead of its being left to the Discretion of the Bank, until the Arrival of the Time ultimately fixed for Payment in Cash or Bullion at the Mint Price, without any such Gradation?

That would be a considerable Advantage.

91. Having stated that a Circulation of 24 Millions of Bank Notes might be conducted with Three Millions of Bullion; do you not think, that it might be injurious to the

general Credit of the Bank, for Parliament to legislate upon the Supposition that it would require one Twelvemonth for them to provide a Sum in that Proportion to any Currency which the Country may require?

The Wealth of the Bank is so well established as a Fact in the Opinion of the Public, that I do not think such a legislative Measure would in the slightest Degree affect the Credit of that Body.

92. Would not the Facility of dispensing with the Gold Coin in Circulation, according to the Plan you have suggested, operate as a Saving of the general Stock; so that a Country which adopted it might be considered, as in that Proportion, richer than a Country which did not?

That is the precise Advantage which I expect to follow from that Measure.

93. Supposing all, or most other Countries successively to adopt the same Plan of Paper Currency, regulated only by the Price of Bullion; must not that Circumstance, by occasioning a great Diminution in the Demand for that Bullion, and consequently lowering its Value throughout the World, ultimately occasion a Depression in all Currency, and a considerable Rise in the nominal Prices of all Commodities?

For a short Time the Value of Gold would be affected, and it would be lowered by such a general Regulation; but, in my Opinion, it would not ultimately be depressed; the Value of Gold and of all other Commodities depending on the Cost of Production, that is, on the Quantity of Labour necessary to produce them, which is not supposed to be either increased or diminished.

94. Supposing Two Countries in every other respect enjoying the same State of Wealth, but with this Difference

that one possesses a Circulating Medium which is conducted
with Three Millions of Bullion, and the other, over and above
the same Degree of Wealth in every Thing (except in Circulating Medium), has a Circulating Medium of Eighteen
Millions of Bullion, which of these Two Countries in your
Opinion possesses the greatest Wealth?

The Country possessing the Eighteen Millions; but if they
had any Intercourse with each other, it would be impossible
for the Twenty-one Millions, the Aggregate of the Two
Circulations, to be divided in these Proportions.

95. You have stated that a Reduction of Paper in Circulation, to the Amount of nearly Four per Cent., would be
necessary, in order to restore the Currency to the legal
Standard of the Mint; would those Reductions have any
very sensible Effect on the general Rate of Interest or
Discounts?

Reduction or Increase of the Quantity of Money always
ultimately raises or lowers the Price of Commodities; when
this is effected, the Rate of Interest will be precisely the same
as before; it is only during the Interval, that is, before the
Prices are settled at the new Rate, that the Rate of Interest
is either raised or lowered.

96. Are we to understand that, when Money is lent,
Capital is advanced, and that Interest only can be effected
by the Abundance or Scarcity of real Capital, combined with
the Opportunity of employing it?

Precisely so; Money is only the Medium by which the
Borrower possesses himself of the Capital which he means
ultimately to employ.

97. State what in your Opinion is the Difference between
that State of Things, in which a Stimulus is given by fictitious
Capital arising from an Over-abundance of Paper in Circu-

lation, and that which results from the regular Operation of real Capital employed in Production?

I believe that on this Subject I differ from most other People. I do not think that any Stimulus is given to Production by the Use of fictitious Capital, as it is called.

98. State what in your Judgment are the Effects on Agriculture, Commerce, and Manufactures of a superabundant Issue of Paper?

Under some Circumstances it may derange the Proportions in which the whole Produce of Capital is divided, between the Capitalist and the Labourer; but in general I do not think it even affects those Proportions. It never I think increases the Produce of Capital.

99. Has such Issue, in your Judgment, any Tendency to the Encouragement of the Commerce or Industry of any People?

I think none, excepting that by affecting the Proportions into which Produce is divided, it may facilitate the Accumulation of Capital in the Hands of the Capitalist; he having increased Profits, while the Labourer has diminished Wages. This may sometimes happen, but I think seldom does.

100. Has not the Increase of Prices during the progressive Depreciation of Paper a Tendency to produce Over-trading, and excessive Speculation?

I think Over-speculation has rather been encouraged by the Facility with which Speculators have been enabled to raise Money upon Discount, in consequence of the progressive Increase of Paper Issues. This Facility would be in a great Degree destroyed, as soon as the full Effect of any given Abundance of Issue on Prices was felt.

101. Is not that Facility, while it exists, wholly given at the Expence of Persons already holding Paper previously in

Circulation; or of those who may be compellable by Law to receive it at Par for Payments previously stipulated for, in Money of account?

It is only given at their Expence.

102. Are you of Opinion that the occasional Success of Speculators, and Over-traders, even when beneficial to themselves, is advantageous to the Community, or that such individual Benefits are overbalanced by the general Evils of such a System?

The Public are only interested in the Abundance of Production; these will not be increased; and therefore, if one Party gains, it must be at the Expence of another.

103. Is not the Irregularity of the Distribution, and the Inequality of the Demand, under the System supposed in the last Answer, very injurious to the Country?

Frequently.

104. From what Circumstance do you draw the Conclusion, at any particular Period, that there is a Superabundance of Circulating Medium?

From the Market Price of Gold exceeding the Mint Price in those Countries where Gold is the Standard, and the unfavourable State of the Exchanges.

105. Is not the Market Price of Gold, and the State of the Exchanges, liable to vary, when there is no Variation in the Amount of the Circulating Medium?

The Rate of Exchange is; but the Market Price of Gold I think is not.

106. Does not the Market Price of the precious Metals vary at Hamburgh, when there is no Variation in the Amount of the Circulating Medium; but Payments are made by a Transfer of Credit on the Bank, representing a given Quantity of Silver of a given Fineness?

The utmost Limits of Variation to which Silver would be subject at Hamburgh, would be the Difference of Price at which the Bank purchases Silver, and the Price at which it sold it. And if the Bank of England were to fix the Price of £3 17s. 10½d. for the Rate of Gold, and the Price of £3 17s. 6d. for the Purchase of Gold, as proposed, I think that Gold could never vary but between those Limits.

107. Are not the Rates of Exchange affected by the Balance of Payments on all Accounts?

Yes, within the Limits of the Expence attending the Transmission of Gold.

108. Must not therefore a Part of the Depression of the Exchange between any Countries, be attributable to a Cause independent of the Amount of the Circulating Medium?

Very frequently, but the real Exchange would be in favour of the Country, while the nominal Exchange is against it.

109. Can you therefore conclude, from the Degree to which the Exchange is at any Moment against any Country, that the whole Per-centage of that unfavourable Exchange is owing to the Amount of its Circulating Medium?

A Part may be owing to other Causes. There is no unfavourable Exchange, which might not be turned in our Favour, by a Reduction in the Amount of Currency; it might not however be wise to make such a Reduction.

110. If a considerable Portion of such unfavourable Exchange were at any Time owing to the Balance of Payments being against us, would not a Reduction of our Circulating Medium, grounded on a Supposition that the unfavourable Exchanges was owing to its Excess, be productive of considerable Distress?

It might; but the best Criterion of an Excess of Circulation, is the Agreement of the Market Price of Gold with the Mint Price.

111. Would you then conclude, that when such Agreement exists there can be no Excess in our Circulating Medium?

There might be a temporary Excess in our Circulating Medium, but it would be attended with such a State of Exchange, as would make it profitable for Individuals to export Bullion, or Coin, which would have the Effect of reducing the Circulating Medium to its proper Limits.

112. Can such a State of Exchange be compatible with an Equality between the Mint Price and Market Price of Bullion?

If there was no Seignorage on Coin whatever, nor any Delay in returning Coin for Bullion at the Mint, it is quite compatible.

113. Would you conclude, then, that when not only the Market Price of Bullion does not exceed the Mint Price, but the Exchanges are also favourable or at Par, that there is no Excess of Circulating Medium?

It is quite possible, that under such Circumstances there might be a Deficiency of Circulating Medium, but there could not be any Excess.

114. You have stated that you consider the abundant Issue of Paper as having given Facilities to Speculation; do you conceive, that if on the Balance such Speculations have been unsuccessful, it would have been possible for so large an Increase to have taken place in the internal and external Commerce of the Country, as has occurred within the last 20 Years?

I think the Increase of the external and internal Commerce of the Country totally independent of those Causes.

115. To what Causes then do you attribute it?

To the Discovery of improved Machinery, and to the Industry and Ingenuity of our People.

116. You have stated that the most important Consideration in the Mode of returning to Cash Payments, was preventing the Currency being further depreciated; and if the graduated Scale were adopted you think the ultimate Effect would be anticipated; and with the Security which the Adoption of the graduated Scale would give, that the Bank must ultimately pay in Bullion at the Mint Price, there were Advantages in deferring the Period of the ultimate Reduction to that Price. Do you think, on the whole, that any Inconvenience would arise from prolonging that Period beyond the Period of 12 Months from July next, with a Security that at the different Stages of it the Plan would be put into Execution, sufficient to counterbalance the Convenience which such a Prolongation would give, by giving further Time to the Bank to increase its Treasures, by allowing more gradual Reduction of its Issues, and by enabling all Persons engaged in Commerce to accommodate their Transactions gradually to the new State of our Circulation?

I think the Advantages to be derived from a Prolongation of the Period would preponderate, provided the Public had complete Security, by obliging the Bank to sell Gold at the present Market Price, against a further Excess of Paper Circulation. I say the present Market Price, because I am averse to entrusting the Bank, for even the next Three Months, with the Power of raising the Price of Bullion.

117. Would not the Danger be completely obviated by providing, that on the 5th of July next the Bank should pay its Notes in Bullion at the present Market Price, and not at the Price at which it may then be?

Nothing could prevent it but gross Misconduct on the Part of the Bank.

118. Do you think the Balance of the Advantage of Prolongation would extend to a Period of Two Years from July next?

I think Two Years an ample Time; I should say a less Period; but it may be prudent to consult the Fears of even the most timid.

119. If the Period were to be so prolonged, what would in your Opinion be the best Gradation of Scale, both in Price and Time?

I should think the Price of Gold should diminish 6*d.* per Ounce at stated and equal Intervals.

120. Do you not think, that the longer the Time allowed the Bank for the Payment of their Notes in Cash or Bullion at the Mint Price, the more necessary the graduated Scale would be, as a Security to the Parliament and to the Public for the Accomplishment of their ultimate Object?

Certainly; without it we should not have complete Security that the ultimate Object would be attained.

121. As Part of the Advantages, to which you look, as facilitating the Operation of the Plan of a graduated Scale, arise from the Certainty which Dealers in Bullion will have, that Bullion will in a short Time be brought down to the Mint Price; would not those Advantages be in some Degree diminished, even by deferring the Period of that ultimate Operation for 6 or 12 Months longer than could really be necessary?

The Advantages would be diminished by deferring the Period: and I am only reconciled to a further Length of Time by a Consideration of the Fears which I think many People very unreasonably entertain.

122. As far, therefore, as your own Judgment goes, should you prefer the Period of One or of Two Years for the Operation?

I should prefer One Year.

123. Do the Prices of Commodities conform to the Fluctuations in the Market Price of Gold, or does not a Length of Time elapse before such Conformity takes place?

They do not immediately conform, but I do not think it very long before they do.

124. If the Prices of Commodities have not already fallen to a Level with the present Market Price of Gold, is it certain there will not be a greater Reduction in their Prices than 4 per Cent., on the Market Price of Gold falling to the Mint Price?

I think the Prices of Commodities fall from a Reduction of the Paper Circulation quite as soon as Gold falls. If the Prices of Commodities and of Bullion have not already fallen in proportion to the Reduction of Paper, I should think that, to make the Value of Bullion and Paper agree, a less Reduction of Paper would be necessary.

125. If the Bank should for their own Security think proper to make a further Reduction of their Notes to the Amount of Three Millions, between this Time and the Month of July next, what Effect would this have upon the Prices of Commodities?

I think a greater Effect would be produced on the Prices of Bullion, on the Currency and on the Prices of Commodities, than what is necessary to bring Bullion down to the Mint Price. Both Bullion and Commodities might probably fall 8 or 10 per Cent. No such Fall could take place if the Mint were open, or the Bank were obliged to buy Bullion at

£3 17s. 6d. The Bank could not then reduce the Circulation Three Millions.

126. If, in consequence of large Foreign Payments, the Course of Foreign Exchanges should become more unfavourable, unless counteracted by a great Contraction of Bank Notes, would it not be necessary to make such Contraction for the Purpose of reducing the Market Price of Gold to the Mint Price?

It certainly would; but this is an Inconvenience to which our Currency was always exposed before 1797.

127. Might it not then be necessary for the Bank to make a Reduction of Three Millions between this and the 5th of July, notwithstanding the present favourable Tendency of the Exchanges?

Possibly it might.

128. Supposing the Bank not to think that they could engage with Safety to pay their Notes in Bullion at any specified Period, according to the present Market Price, without previously making a considerable Purchase of Gold, would not such Purchase have a Tendency to increase the Price of Bullion?

I think it would have such a Tendency; but I should not admit this Plea, for I should think it not founded on a Knowledge of the true Principles of Currency, the Purchase of any great Quantity of Gold being wholly unnecessary.

129. Has not the present Suspense of Commercial Transactions, in consequence of the Examination now taking place, the Effect, to a certain Extent, which a contracted Issue of Notes would have had?

I think it has.

130. If then that Suspence were relieved by a Decision one Way or the other, would not the Price of Gold have a Tendency to rise, unless it were counteracted by some further Reduction of Bank Notes?

It would very much depend on the Decision taken.

131. Would not the Danger of any improvident Diminution of Issues by the Bank during the Progress of these Operations, of which we have been speaking, be best obviated by applying to the Period of gradual Reduction the same Principle which you have proposed for Bullion Payments at the Mint Price, viz. an Obligation on the Bank to purchase Bullion at Prices bearing a fixed Proportion to those at which they are to deliver it?

It undoubtedly would; still I am inclined to recommend that the Price at which the Bank should be obliged to purchase Gold, should be at once fixed at £3 17s. 6d. The only Inconvenience that could arise from such a Regulation might possibly be a more rapid Diminution of the Amount of the Currency, than what a graduated Scale would require.

132. But if the Apprehensions of the Bank should so far exceed all just Reasoning on the Subject, as to lead them to make a sudden and excessive Diminution of the Currency, far beyond what the Necessity of the Case might require; might not such a Provision as above stated be useful, not only as a Corrective of the Evil, but also as an Indication to them of the real Circumstances of the Case?

The Provision above stated would afford a complete Security against a sudden and mischievous Reduction in the Amount of the Circulating Medium.

133. How would it afford that complete Security?

Without such a Provision the Bank might diminish their Issues till the Price of Bullion fell to £3 17s. 6d. per oz., with it they could only diminish them till it fell to the Price fixed for the Purchase on the graduated Scale.

134. Might not the Bullion Merchant under such Circumstances, by occasionally bringing forward their Gold to the Bank immediately before the Time at which the Price would be lowered for the Bank to make such Purchases, and by watching the Variations occasioned by the Increase or Diminution of the Issue of Notes, for the Purpose of meeting such Demand, throw great Confusion during the whole Time into the Market Price of Gold; and would not the Uncertainty in which the Bank would be placed, oblige them to withhold the Issue of their Notes on Discount to a considerable Extent?

I think, if the selling Price of Gold and the buying Price of Gold should be fixed too near to each other, the Bank might be exposed to this Inconvenience, but if they differ as much as a Shilling, no great Inconvenience would arise. As to the Question of Discount, the Accommodation to Commerce must depend on the whole Amount of the Circulation, and not on that Part of it which the Bank may issue in that particular Manner.

135. If the Bank were to be the only Market to which Persons would resort for Bullion, as distinguished from Coin, at a fixed Price; might there not be, under extreme Circumstances, a peculiar Run upon the Bank for that Article?

The Run upon them must necessarily be limited by the Amount of their Notes, because it is with their Notes only that the Bullion could be purchased. The Diminution of the Quantity of Bank Notes would increase their Value, and would consequently stop the Demand for Bullion. In this respect we should be precisely in the same Situation that we were previous to 1797, the only Difference would be, that we could then demand Coin, and now we should demand Bullion; as Articles of Commerce they may be considered as the same.

136. Supposing the Bank to keep no more Treasure than what you consider would be necessary, or Three Millions of Bullion, might not a Run for Bullion to that Amount be made with so much greater Rapidity, than could possibly be made for the same Amount of Coin, as to expose the Bank to greater Danger in the new State of Things, than it could ever have incurred in the former?

Bullion could be drawn out of the Bank in a shorter Space of Time than an equal Amount of Coin, as there would be no Necessity for counting.

137. Might not a Demand for Bullion be made upon the Bank to that Extent, in so short a Space of Time, as not to allow of the Effect which a Diminution of the Quantity of Notes would have in raising their Value, to operate in Time to check such a Run?

I should answer, in no greater Degree than before 1797, and this could only happen in the extreme Case of a Panic, against which no System of Banking can possibly provide.

138. Do you think, on the whole, that the Danger of any such Panic would be increased or diminished, by making Bank Notes payable in Bullion for large Amounts only, or in Coin for the smallest Amounts, as before 1797?

If there is any Difference, I should think that the Danger of Panic would be less in the former Case than in the latter.

139. Would there be, in case of a Panic, less Eagerness to demand Bullion than Coin, if that were demandable?

I think there would be less Eagerness to demand Bullion.

140. Would not such a Demand be made, without any Reference to the Market Price of Gold?

Certainly.

141. Referring to Question and Answer (No. 84), you have stated, that our Currency and Prices have undergone, during the last Eight Years, much greater Variations than what you conceive would be now produced by the Resumption of Cash Payments; was not the Inconvenience which may have resulted at any of those former Periods, from the Fall of Prices, much mitigated by the unlimited Power then possessed by the Bank of increasing its Issues, without any regard to the Price of Gold and the State of Exchanges?

The Variations in the Value of the Currency, and in Prices, have generally been in a different Direction from that at present to be provided against; the Bank having the Power to issue Paper unchecked, could certainly mitigate the Inconvenience resulting from a sudden Fall.

142. When the Bank have lost that Power, might not the same Degree of Reduction of Currency which took place in former Periods produce a greater Reduction of Prices, and of course greater Distress?

Equal Effects would follow equal Amounts of Reduction; but when the Bank was unchecked, they had the Power of arresting that Reduction; an Advantage counterbalanced by other Disadvantages.

The Witness is directed to withdraw.

SPEECHES ON VARIOUS
OCCASIONS
1811–1823

I

GENERAL COURT OF PROPRIETORS
OF THE BANK OF ENGLAND[1]

21 *March* 1811

Mr. CATTLEY, the first speaker, 'entered into a vindication of the Bank, against the attacks made upon them by the Bullion Committee, Mr. Huskisson and others. He said that the Bullion Committee should have examined into the causes of the high price of bullion, which they had wholly neglected to do—and it would not be just to require of the Bank to pay their notes in specie, whilst gold was at so high a price'.

Mr. RICARDO 'then rose, and was proceeding to make some observations on the remarks of Mr. Cattley, when he was reminded by the Governor that there was no question before the Court.'

Mr. RICARDO said, that he would have wished to set the Honourable Proprietor right, with regard to some of the facts which he had stated respecting the Bullion Committee, but as such discussion was not thought admissible he would confine himself by putting a question to the Directors. He said that in the discussion of principles, it was highly essential that the facts by which those principles were ultimately to be tried, should be correctly stated. He had observed, however, that in the papers which had at different times been submitted to Parliament, there appeared facts which were at variance with each other, and of which he hoped the Court would receive some explanation. It appeared, he said, by a paper which was published in the Appendix to the Report of the Secret Committee of the Lords, that in October of the year 1795, the Directors stated the price of gold bullion to be 4*l.* 3*s.* to 4*l.* 4*s.* per ounce,[2] although no traces of any such

---

[1] Report in the *Morning Chronicle* of 22 March 1811.
[2] See 'Report of the Lords Com-mittee of Secrecy, 1797' (reprint in *Parliamentary Papers,* 1810, vol. III), p. 84.

price could be discovered in any list that was published during that year; on the contrary, the price quoted in December of that year, in the list which Mr. Goldsmid, in his evidence, declared to be authentic, as he himself furnished the prices to it,[1] was 3*l.* 17*s.* 6*d.* That further, in 1797 Mr. Newland, in his evidence before the same Secret Committee, had declared that he had known the Bank to give as much as 4*l.* 1*s.*, 4*l.* 2*s.*, 4*l.* 6*s.*, and as high as 4*l.* 8*s.* per ounce and when asked on what occasion the Bank gave 4*l.* 8*s.* said it was about two years since, speaking then in March 1797.[2] Mr. Ricardo said that there was a paper just laid before Parliament by the Bank, in which they stated, not the lowest, not the average, but the highest price which they had given for gold bullion from 1773 up to the present period. In this account it appeared that the Bank had never given more, from 1786 to 1800, than 3*l.* 17*s.* 10$\frac{1}{2}$*d.* per ounce.[3] He found it difficult to reconcile this seeming contradiction, and he hoped the Directors would explain it.

Mr. PEARSE, the Governor, 'observed in reply, that the price being stated by the Directors to be 4*l.* 3*s.* or 4*l.* 4*s.* per ounce in the year 1795, did not afford any proof that the Directors of the Bank had purchased at that price. That 4*l.* 8*s.* being given, as stated by Mr. Newland, was, he believed, correct—it was by way of experiment in the beginning of the year 1796, and was obtained by their agent in Portugal, but which was discontinued after a small quantity had been purchased. That in a return which they had since made to the House of Commons, they had stated this and some other exceptions.'[4]

---

[1] Goldsmid in his evidence stated that the Tables 'published by Wettenhall are likely to be correct; they are made from our reports to the person who furnishes him with the prices' (Bullion Rep. p. 36).
[2] 'Report ... 1797', p. 40.
[3] See 'Bank of England, Accounts...', ordered to be printed

22 Feb. 1811 (No. 5 of these Accounts is 'An Account of the highest Prices paid by the Bank for Bullion in each Year, from 1773 to 1809, both inclusive'), in *Parliamentary Papers*, 1810–11, vol. x, No. 22. Cp. above, III, 77, n.
[4] See 'An Abstract Account of the Prices paid by the Bank of

II

GENERAL COURT OF PROPRIETORS
OF THE BANK OF ENGLAND[1]

21 *December* 1815

Mr. Bouverie moved 'that an account be laid before a General Court...of the amount of the surplus profits of this Company'. 21 Dec. 1815

Mr. Ricardo warmly supported the motion, and wished to recal the Court to the consideration of the real question before them, which appeared to him to be, whether the system to be acted upon should be that which was prescribed by the law of the land, and by the Bank Charter, or whether the Proprietors should be deprived of that participation in the profits to which they were, both by the one and the other, so clearly entitled. It had been contended by the Gentlemen who had preceded him, that on the present extended scale of the commerce of the country, the profits of the Bank, instead

England for Gold and Silver Bullion, in each Year, from 1697 to 28 Feb. 1811', in *Parliamentary Papers*, 1810–11, vol. x, No. 69.
[1] This report, taken from the *Morning Post* of 23 Dec. 1815, seems more accurate than those in the other newspapers. Ricardo wrote to Malthus on 24 December that the reporters 'were most carefully excluded from the Court', and that the *Morning Chronicle* had imputed to him what he 'neither felt nor uttered'. For Ricardo's own account of his speech see the same letter (below, VI, 335–6), and *Economical and Secure Currency* (above, IV, 106). The report in the *Morning Chronicle* of 22 December, to

which he objected, was as follows: 'Mr. D. Ricardo argued in favour of the motion; he stated that he was a great friend to publicity; that he attached no blame to the Directors, on the contrary was ready to give his testimony in their favour, but still that the law of the land was paramount to every consideration, and that no argument of advantage such as had been stated by his neighbour (Mr. Payne) could weigh against it; he would acquiesce in any distribution the Bank Directors might choose to make; that Bankers differed from every other trader, they trade with others' capital, merchants of every degree with their own.'

of being divided among the Proprietors ought to go to an increase of its capital. Now, though he might be of opinion that a Bank, deriving its profits from the capitals of others, required no such increase of capital for itself, yet it was nevertheless a matter of indifference to him in which of the two modes the accumulated profits should be applied; all he contended for was, that the Proprietors had a right in the production of such accounts as would exhibit the actual amount of such profits, and that it might be a subject of future regulation how they should be disposed of.

Mr. MELLISH, the Governor, 'then rose and said that he felt he should be betraying his duty were he to answer the topics urged by the last speaker, as well as the mover; that the Company had all along placed great confidence in their Directors; and that if any reason were harboured for wishing to withdraw it, he begged that their accusation might be spoken out.'

The question was put, and 'on a shew of hands was lost by about two to one.'

[The question was raised again before a General Court of Proprietors held on 21 March 1816 to declare a Dividend, when an amendment was moved for the adjournment of the Court until 28 March to enable the Governor and Directors to produce accounts showing the surplus profits. The amendment being defeated, a paper signed by eleven Proprietors, including Ricardo, was delivered to the Governor demanding a ballot on the motion of amendment. The ballot took place on 26 March and resulted in the defeat of the motion by 393 votes to 69.[1]]

---

[1] See the *Star*, 23 and 27 March 1816.

III

GENERAL COURT OF PROPRIETORS
OF THE BANK OF ENGLAND[1]

8 *February* 1816

Mr. MELLISH, the Governor, stated that the object for which the Court was called together, was to consider a letter from the Government applying for an extension for two years of the loan of three millions now existing without interest, and for a new loan of six millions at 4 per cent for two years. Ministers intended to propose to Parliament that the restriction on cash payments be continued for one year. The Directors proposed complying with the application of Government. The Governor reminded the Court that 'their engagements with the country, in so far as it regarded their chartered rights, were now near a termination, and therefore it was absolutely necessary that some understanding should be come to with Government', in order to effect an arrangement, based on equity and good faith.

Mr. RICARDO wished to know whether it was understood that, at the expiration of the period of the loan, the Bank would continue in the custody of the money of the government? He was led to this inquiry by a paper laid before the House of Commons, in which the Directors seemed to claim the custody of the money as a right.[2] Now, however, they seemed to have abandoned this claim.

Mr. MELLISH 'declined entering into any discussion on the topic alluded to by the hon. proprietor. He could not be expected to say what would happen two years hence. In the mean time a bargain must be a bargain.'

The motion was put and was 'carried by a very large majority, there being only two or three hands held against it.'

---

[1] Report in *The Times,* 9 Feb. 1816. Ricardo refers to this Court in ed. 2 of *Economical and Secure Currency,* above, IV, 88, n. Cp. his letter to Malthus of 7 Feb.

1816, below, VII, 19.
[2] Mr. Mellish's Resolutions, which are discussed by Ricardo and reprinted in *Economical and Secure Currency,* above, IV, 86 and 138.

IV

GENERAL COURT OF PROPRIETORS
OF THE BANK OF ENGLAND[1]

18 *March* 1819

On the motion for a dividend, an amendment was proposed that no dividend should be declared until 'an exposition of the funds, income, and expenditure of the Bank should be made to the Proprietors'. The Hon. Mr. BOUVERIE stated that the Bank had acknowledged the existence of a Reserved Fund, and the Proprietors ought to be informed of its amount. Sir THOMAS TURTON said that 'it seemed absurd to vote a given dividend, without knowing the amount of the capital from which it was distributed'.

Mr. RICARDO was of the same opinion, and expressed his confident belief that the Bank were in possession of at least 5,000,000*l.*, in addition to their known capital of 15,000,000*l.* It was not a fear of their poverty but a jealousy of their riches that had provoked inquiry. Whilst it was clear, therefore, that the proprietors had a right to know the condition of their affairs, it was equally manifest that no injury would arise from the disclosure. A letter which he had received from one of the directors of the Bank of France[2] entirely accorded with his views.

After some further discussion Mr. R. JACKSON said that demands for increased dividends might result in their restriction by Parliament, as had happened with the East India Company. While he did not doubt the motives of those who brought forward such motions, 'it was still certain that patriotism, and a desire to impair the profits of the Bank, were not necessarily connected'.

---

[1] Report in *The Times,* 19 March 1819.
[2] 'Nous pensons comme vous que l'essence d'une Banque comme de toute institution qui repose sur le crédit doit être la publicité la plus entière de ses opérations et la clarté de ses comptes.' (Letter from Benjamin Delessert to Ricardo, dated Paris, 13 March 1819; MS in *R.P.*)

'Mr. RICARDO and Mr. BOUVERIE disclaimed any such object as that referred to by the hon. and learned gent., in the conduct formerly pursued at the East India House; and the former desired also to vindicate an absent member of their body[1] from any supposed imputation of the kind.'
The amendments were negatived.

V

MEETING ON MR. OWEN'S PLAN[2]

26 *June* 1819

'A very respectable and numerous meeting of both sexes was held in Freemasons-hall, for the purpose of taking into consideration the plan of Mr. Owen.' The chair was taken by the Duke of Kent. After a speech of Mr. OWEN, who explained his plan for the employment and improvement of the poor, the names of those who were willing to be members of the committee to investigate the plan were announced.[3]

Mr. RICARDO begged to trouble the Meeting with a few observations. As his name was placed upon the Committee, he should state shortly those circumstances in which he agreed and in which he differed from the preceding speaker. He completely concurred with him in the commendations bestowed upon the illustrious personage who presided at the meeting. It was an example of zeal for the public good, and of benevolent intention, worthy of the highest praise. In a limited degree he thought the scheme likely to succeed,

[1] Probably Joseph Hume.
[2] Report in *The Times,* 28 June 1819.
[3] In a letter to Trower of 8 July 1819 (below, VIII, 45–6), Ricardo explains that he was very reluctant to let his name be on the Committee, as he dissented from all of Owen's conclusions; he was only persuaded by the entreaties of the Duke of Kent, who assured him that he was 'not bound to approve, only to examine.' See also his speech in the House of Commons on 16 Dec. 1819, above, p. 30.

and to produce, where it did succeed, considerable happiness, comfort, and morality, by giving employment and instruction to the lower classes. No person could admire more than he did, or appreciate more highly, the benevolence of his friend (Mr. Owen) to prosecute his plan with so much zeal, and at the expense of so much time and trouble. He could not, however, go along with him in the hope of ameliorating the condition of the lower classes to such a degree as he seemed to expect: nor should he wish it to go forth to the public that he thought that the plan would produce all the good anticipated from it by his sanguine friend. As a member of the Committee, he should do every thing in his power to forward the objects for which it was appointed.

At a subsequent meeting, held at the City of London Tavern on 26 July 1819, the Committee was finally appointed, Ricardo being a member. In August the Committee appealed for the subscription of £100,000 for the establishment of an agricultural and manufacturing community as an experiment on the lines of that at New Lanark. On 1 Dec. 1819, as the subscriptions amounted to less than £8,000, the Committee resigned and in a final resolution urged that the Government should facilitate the experiment by granting a portion of the Crown lands and using the funds raised for the relief of the poor.[1]

---

[1] See *The Life of Robert Owen, written by himself,* London, 1858, vol. IA, pp. 237–50.

VI

GLOUCESTER COUNTY MEETING[1]

30 December 1820

30 Dec. 1820

'One of the most numerous and respectable meetings of the County of Glocester which has been held for several years took place at the Shirehall, Glocester'. The object of the meeting was to consider an address to the King on 'the illegal and unconstitutional measures' taken by the Ministers in the late proceedings against the Queen. Lord Sherborne was called to the chair. The address having been unanimously adopted by the meeting,

Mr. RICARDO came forward and was received with marks of approbation. He said he was sure this meeting felt as he did respecting the conduct pursued on a late occasion in the House of Peers by their noble Chairman and by Lord Ducie[2] (Loud cheers). The county he was sure could but feel one sentiment upon that conduct; it was entitled to their fullest and most unqualified approbation (Reiterated cheers). These noble Lords had in an independent and manly manner opposed his Majesty's ministers during the prosecution of the Queen. It became the county to express their opinion of the conduct of the noble lords who had acted in so independent a manner, and his object at present was to propose to them a vote of thanks (Hear). He would take this opportunity of declaring his hearty approbation of the terms of the address, as well as those used by the gentlemen who had spoken upon it. Indeed, if he had any thing in the way of complaint to

---

[1] Report in *The Times,* 1 Jan. 1821. Ricardo's speech was reprinted in *A Selection of Speeches Delivered at Several County Meetings in the Years 1820 & 1821,* London, Ridgway, 1822, pp. 47–8.

On this meeting, see VIII, 330.
[2] On the third reading of the Bill of Pains and Penalties, 10 Nov. 1820, both Lord Sherborne and Lord Ducie had voted in favour of the Queen.

urge or cavil with, it was, that the address had not gone as far as it ought to have gone; for it appeared to him that many of the evils of which they complained were to be traced to the present constitution of the House of Commons (Applause). If that house fairly and fully represented as it ought the people at large, the country would not now have to deplore such an accumulation of wrongs (Applause). It would have been quite impossible for ministers to have pursued a career so diametrically opposite to the general opinion of the country; nor would a House of Commons, representing the general voice of the community, have suffered such a departure from the public wishes and interests. Entertaining, as he unequivocally did, such an opinion, he must say that he should have still more approved of the address, if it promptly and plainly recommended that no delay should be lost in making the House of Commons what it ought to be, and what its name imported it should be, namely, a representative of the public voice—an organ acting in sympathy with the tone of popular feeling, and constitutionally embodying and expressing the voice of the country at large in a full and unquestionable manner (Great applause). The hon. gentleman concluded by proposing a vote of thanks to Lords Sherborne and Ducie.

'The motion was unanimously agreed to and followed by three cheers.'

VII

MEETING AT HEREFORD IN HONOUR
OF JOSEPH HUME[1]

7 December 1821

A meeting in honour of Joseph Hume, M.P. was held at
Hereford on 7 December 1821, to present him with 'a superb
silver tankard' and 'a hogshead of prime Hereford cider', in
recognition of his efforts in Parliament to lessen taxation and
reduce corruption. Mr. E. B. Clive presided.

7 Dec. 1821

Addressing the meeting, Mr. HUME urged the people to resume
their ancient right of control over their representatives in
Parliament—the only remedy for the existing abuses in public
expenditure. He later complimented Mr. Ricardo and other
members 'for the zealous assistance they had rendered him in
Parliament', and regretted that Mr. Ricardo had been so unjustly
misrepresented as a friend of the fundholder and an enemy of
the landowner.

The PRESIDENT spoke next and concluded by proposing 'the
health of one of the first political economists of this or any other
age, Mr. Ricardo, who I am happy to say is a considerable
freeholder amongst us.'[2]

Mr. RICARDO said, he felt highly gratified by the manner
in which the mention of his name had been received by the
respectable company before him, and begged to return his

---

[1] Report in the *Scotsman*, 22 Dec.
1821. A similar report of the
speech is contained in a pamphlet
entitled *The Proceedings in Herefordshire connected with the visit
of Joseph Hume, Esq. M.P....*,
Hereford and London, 1822. On
the meeting cp. also Ricardo's
letters of 11 Dec. 1821 to Trower
and of 3 Jan. 1822 to McCulloch,
below, IX, 121 and 141, n. 1.
[2] In the letter of invitation, dated
Hereford, 10 Nov. 1821, John
Allen, Junr., writing on behalf of

the Committee, addressed Ricardo
as 'a Herefordshire Free-holder,
and one of the very few Members,
who on every occasion supported
Mr. Hume's exertions in the
House'. 'The Committee' he
concluded 'hope that a gentleman
who has purchased estates in the
County, and whose parliamentary
conduct has been long well-known
and respected, will honour the
occasion by his presence.' (MS in
R.P.)

grateful thanks for the honour which had been conferred on him. With respect to the misapprehension of an opinion he had given, alluded to by his Honourable Friend Mr. Hume, he should endeavour in very few words to remove it, as he did not wish to occupy the attention of the company by any thing personal to himself. Thinking, as he did, that the national debt was a most oppressive burden on the industry of the country, he had, in his place in Parliament, expressed his opinion that it would be a measure of wisdom to submit once for all to a great sacrifice in order to remove it, and for that purpose recommended a general and fair contribution of a portion of every man's property;[1] not, as had been said, of the property of the landowner only, but of that of the merchant, the manufacturer, and the fundholder. He should have been ashamed of himself if any thing so unfair could ever enter his mind as that of exonerating the fundholder from the payment of his quota of so equitable a tax. On this subject he should say no more, as he fully agreed with his Hon. Friend, Mr. Price,[2] that as this day was set apart for the purpose of acknowledging the services of Mr. Hume, questions wholly extraneous should be avoided. Of Mr. Hume's services to the public, he entertained as high an opinion as any gentleman present; and as he had seen much of his persevering exertions, he could perhaps speak of them with more accuracy than many others. Mr. Hume's exertions in Parliament had been unremitting as they all knew; but he had duties to attend also in different committees, and few could have a just idea of the number of documents which he had had to consult. When he considered the variety of accounts which came under his notice, and the voluminous reports which he had read, he believed he might say, that in persevering exertions, Mr. Hume had never been surpassed

[1] See above, p. 34.   [2] Vice-President of the meeting.

by any former or present member of Parliament. It was a pleasure to him (Mr. Ricardo) to reflect, that he had voted on all occasions in favour of economy; and while he had a seat in the House of Commons, he would continue to give his Hon. Friend his best support in opposing every wasteful expenditure of the public money. He concurred fully with the Hon. Chairman and with Mr. Hume, that a reform in the representation was of vital importance to the interests of the country.—Without it good government might truly be said to be impossible. To obtain a reform, then, every exertion should be made; but he recommended to those who heard him to consider well what constituted a real and efficient reform of the Parliament; for much error might and did prevail on this important question. The subject might be considered under three views—First, the extension of the elective franchise; secondly, the frequency of elections; and, thirdly, the mode of election. With respect to the first of these, the extension of the elective franchise, he did not consider it the most important object of the three he had mentioned, yet no reform could be an adequate one which did not greatly extend the elective franchise—for he should be contented if it went so far as householder suffrage. Upon the second point, frequency of elections, he should say that without it there would be no check in the hands of the electors against the corruption of the members. If elections were not frequent, we should not very materially improve our system, and if they were, it would be but reasonable to allow each member to act as he thought proper, notwith-standing the known sentiments of his constituents—those constituents would have the power to displace him at the following election. With respect to the third point, the mode of election, he thought that of the greatest importance on a question of real reform. To secure a real representation of the people in Parliament, there must be secrecy of suffrage, or as it was commonly called election by ballot. It was nothing but mockery and delusion to pretend to give the right of voting to a man, if you prevented him from exercising it without control. Let the kind offices and superior talents of those above him in station have their due effect in influencing his will—this was a just and legitimate influence, but do not subject his will to the will of another. If you do it, it is not his vote you obtain, but the vote of another man, and it would be better and more honourable to give it to that man in the first instance. He (Mr. R.) had thought much on this subject: he had attentively considered all the objections which were brought against voting by ballot, but he could see no weight in them. He hoped whenever the important subject of reform came under the consideration of the gentlemen present, they would not fail to pay due attention to this vital security for good government.

'Mr. R. concluded amid loud cheers.'

VIII

WESTMINSTER REFORM DINNER[1]

23 *May* 1822

23 May 1822   'The Independent Electors of Westminster held their 15th anniversary dinner at the Crown and Anchor Tavern, in commemoration of the patriotic struggle, which terminated in the election of Sir Francis Burdett as their representative in Parliament.' Sir Francis BURDETT was in the chair, and, after several other toasts, he proposed the health of 'Mr. C. H. Hutchinson,[2] Mr. Ricardo, and the reformers of Ireland.' After a speech of Mr. Hutchinson,

[1] Report in *The Times,* 24 May 1822.   [2] Christopher Hely-Hutchinson, M.P. for Cork.

Mr. RICARDO, in returning thanks, declared that there was   not in the room a more real friend to the cause of reform than he was. He was a friend, not to a sham reform, but a real one, which would give to the people a majority, and more than a majority, in the House of Commons. This desirable and most necessary end might still, he thought, be attained in the House of Commons; not, indeed, by any efforts of the members within doors, but by the exertions of the people without—exertions which would compel attention, and which must be obeyed. He fully agreed with the noble lord (Nugent) that it was a silly question to ask the reformer to put his finger on the page of history which he deemed his model. His plain answer would always be, that the people had a right to demand the best government they could obtain in their own times, and that if their ancestors had refrained from asking it, it was no reason why their posterity should.

IX

GENERAL COURT OF THE EAST INDIA COMPANY[1]

12 *June* 1822

A Special General Court of Proprietors of the East India   Company was held 'to consider a Bill pending in Parliament, for consolidating the several Laws relating to the Private Trade with the East-Indies; and also to consider the propriety of concurring in the repeal of the law by which ships under the burden of 350 tons are at present precluded from engaging in such trade from the United Kingdom.' Mr. C. FORBES, who opened the debate, said that the East-India interest was not as powerfully

[1] Report in *The Asiatic Journal and Monthly Register for British India and its Dependencies,* August 1822, vol. XIV, pp. 152–3.

represented in Parliament as the West-India interest; he thought it would be good policy if all the Directors were provided with seats in the House of Commons.

Mr. RICARDO regretted the absence of the gentlemen who usually spoke from that part of the Court, and more particularly of Mr. Hume, who was obliged to attend a Committee of the House of Commons, and could not, in consequence, take a part in the discussion; he hoped, however, that the Court would favour him with their attention while he made a few observations. The Hon. Proprietor who had just spoken[1] had very properly observed, that, in the House of Commons, the interest of the public only should be looked to; that the Members of that House ought not to be swayed by a partiality for the East or the West-India interest. He admitted that it ought to be so; but that man must be blind, who would say, that the House of Commons, as now constituted, performed its duty in that immaculate manner which the Hon. Proprietor described.

Mr. LOWNDES rose to order.

Mr. RICARDO assured the Court he would not say another word on the subject. An Hon. Proprietor (Mr. Robertson) seemed to be adverse to opening a free-trade with all European states. If that were the question before the Court, he would willingly meet him on the subject. But the question was not, whether France or Spain should be allowed to enter into the India trade; it was one which entirely concerned English interests. The Gentleman who opened the debate, said he asked only for justice and equality; he wished to be placed on the same footing as the West-India merchant; he did not seek for a monopoly. In those views he (Mr Ricardo) entirely concurred; and, if he wanted to prove their truth and policy, he would refer to the speech of the Hon.

[1] Mr. S. Dixon.

Proprietor (Mr. Robertson); for he had shewn that, by taking off restrictions, the trade to the Brazils and to the free-states of South America had increased in a wonderful degree; and, in doing so, he had himself pronounced the warmest eulogium on unrestricted trade. He thought no country could trade advantageously, if she placed restrictions on the commodities with which any state, to whom she was commercially related, could furnish her. It was in vain for the Company to think of sending their goods to India, unless they could take what India was enabled to afford in return. (Hear, hear!) This position was so clear and self-evident, that he wondered any man could doubt it. If all restrictions were removed from the commerce of the country, and it was left to pursue that course which its own active principle would strike out, it would, most assuredly increase in an almost infinite degree. He had no hostility to the West-India interest; on the contrary, he participated in the feelings of regret which their sufferings excited; and if he could assist them, without doing so at the expense of others, he would not be found tardy in affording relief: but he would not support them at the expense of other interests. The buying their sugar at an advanced price was not the only disadvantage which the country suffered from the system. For his own part, he would give to them the difference in price between the East-India and the West-India sugar, as a gratuity, rather than suffer this unjust privilege should be granted to the West-India interest. (Hear, hear!) An Hon. Gentleman (Mr. Carruthers) had protested against the charge that had been levelled at his Majesty's Ministers, who were said to entertain the intention of giving to one class of persons an unjust advantage over another. That Hon. Gent. seemed to have a very high opinion of his Majesty's Government. Perhaps he also thought that they meant well. But

12 June 1822   Gentlemen must shut their eyes, if they did not perceive, that Ministers were not unfrequently obliged to favour particular interests. The power some bodies possessed, the clamour they raised, the interest they commanded in the House of Commons, frequently compelled Ministers to adopt a course which they did not think a proper one. They had an instance of this in the last week. A bill, altering the navigation laws, was passing through the House, and Ministers wanted to carry a clause relative to the importation of thrown silk; but, with all their efforts, they were unable to succeed. In that case Ministers could not carry a point, which appeared to him to be correct. He wished to see a House of Commons free from party, where the interest of the public would alone be considered, in which a deaf ear would be turned to all partial application. (Hear, hear!)

X

GENERAL COURT OF THE EAST
INDIA COMPANY[1]

19 March 1823

19 March 1823   After the quarterly meeting the General Court of Proprietors resolved itself into a Special Court, at the request of nine Proprietors (including Ricardo), 'to take into consideration the present state of the East-India sugar trade'. Mr. C. FORBES moved:

'That it appears to this Court, that since the repeal by the act of last session of Parliament, of the restrictions formerly imposed on the West-India trade, no pretension exists for any exclusive protection to the sugars of the West-Indian colonies against those of British India.

'That as the present unequal duties on the sugars of the East and West-Indies terminate in March 1824, this Court do earnestly recommend to the immediate attention of the Court of Directors

[1] Report in *The Asiatic Journal   India and its Dependencies,* April *and Monthly Register for British*   1823, vol. xv, pp. 370–2.

the necessity of using their strenuous efforts with his Majesty's 19 March 1823 ministers, to obtain an equalization of the said duties.'

Mr. FORBES said that Mr. Whitmore intended to bring this subject under the consideration of Parliament after the recess.[1]

Mr. A. ROBERTSON, opposing the motion, raised again the question of shipping which had been debated the previous year.[2]

Mr. D. RICARDO said, he could not follow the Hon. Gent. in his observations with respect to ships of small tonnage; at the same time he thought it was a question of very great importance. The Hon. Gent. had entered into a great number of arguments, in order to dissuade the Court from agreeing to the resolution now under discussion. If he had heard the Hon. Gent. in any other place, or if he had been ignorant of his sentiments, he should indeed have conceived that the Hon. Gent. was addressing an assembly of West-India planters, for he (Mr. Ricardo) should use precisely such arguments as the Hon. Gent. had done, in order to overturn their claims. (A laugh!) The Hon. Gent. had stated truly, that when there was a surplus of sugar in this country, prices must be higher on the continent than here, to induce the merchant to export it; but he would ask the Hon. Gent. was that any reason why an unsound principle should be contended for? He would ask of the Hon. Gent., and of those whose cause he espoused, 'Are you afraid to give equal rights and an equal protection to all classes of His Majesty's subjects?' (Hear!) The Hon. Gent. had also stated, very correctly, that the mere enumeration of exports and imports would not give a true idea of the commerce which one particular country carried on with another. They might export to a country, but it did not follow that that country should pay in a direct manner: because the exporting country might wish to receive the proceeds in commodities which

[1] See the debate in the House of Commons on 22 May 1823, above, p. 297 ff.

[2] See above, p. 475.

were the growth of another state. The Hon. Gent. said, this was a mere question between the agents of different interests: he (Mr. Ricardo) thought otherwise. He viewed it in the light in which it was regarded by the Hon. Director before him (Mr. Bebb), and he could view it in no other. He considered it to be a question in which the public were the great parties concerned; (Hear!) for he should not have appeared in that Court, he should not have interfered, or raised his voice on this question, but in behalf of the public. (Hear!) It might be very true, that the price of sugar was so low as not to encourage its cultivation; it might be very true that it did not fetch a remunerating price: but were not arts resorted to for the purpose of raising the price? It was acknowledged that there were. And was not a hope held out in some publication, that, by diminishing the supply, the planter might get firm hold of the home-market, keep it without a surplus, and then raise the price as he pleased? Now, he would ask, had the people of England no interest in all this? Had they no interest in procuring their sugar from other countries, and preventing the continuance of this most odious monopoly? They were called on, as the ground for their decision, to compare the exports and imports with reference to the East and West-Indies: but that mode did not satisfy his understanding. He asked, what was the object of this measure? It was to procure sugar at a cheaper rate; and, if it were made manifest to him that, by adopting it, they would make sugar cheaper, he would throw open the trade, although they exported millions of manufactures to the country which at present monopolized it. He thought the Hon. Gent. had encumbered the subject with many things which did not belong to it. He took a large view of the question, with reference to the greater likelihood of retaining our East-India or our West-India possessions. If they

entered into these subjects, as connected with the question
before them, they would be totally unfit to decide on it, so
extremely difficult were they of solution; and he must say,
that, for his own part, if he could not give a sound opinion
on this particular question, without well understanding the
subjects which the Hon. Gent. had brought forward, he
would not attempt to give an opinion at all; but, if he thought
that the East-Indies or the West-Indies would be severed
from this country in a month, it would not alter the vote that
he would give: for, would it not still be to the interest of
India to send her sugars to this country if she were placed
under the Government of any other power? Certainly it
would; and, therefore, the parties immediately concerned
had little to do with this point. (Hear!) He again asserted,
that the public interest was concerned. He would go farther
than either of the contending parties were inclined to go. He
thought no exclusive protection should be granted to either
the East or the West-Indies, and that we should be free to
import our sugar from any quarter whatsoever. No possible
injury could arise from this. The Hon. Gent. also alluded to
another subject, but in a manner which he (Mr. Ricardo) was
sorry to hear. He professed his love for freedom of trade, as
the principle under the influence of which commerce was
sure to prosper; but then he made so many qualifications
that he quite lost sight of his original proposition. (A laugh!)
He would protect the monopoly of the landed interests, he
would protect the monopoly of the tea-trade; and several
others, all of them, he believed, just as objectionable as the
very monopoly they were discussing. With respect to the
shipping-interest, no argument appeared to him to be so
weak as that adduced by them. They asserted that, by the
adoption of this measure, the shipping of the country would
be greatly reduced. But could they get sugar from the East-

Indies without shipping? and was not the voyage much longer? Every view he could take of this subject proved to him that those interested in shipping, would be particularly benefited by the proposed equalization. There were some other points to which he meant to call the attention of the Court, particularly with respect to cotton. The Hon. Gent. had instanced the cotton-trade, and argued that by the aid of machinery, by importing cotton from America, and by exporting the manufactured goods to India, great injury was inflicted on the manufacturing class in that country. Undoubtedly some injury was done to that class; but one would think the Hon. Gent. would have turned his attention to the accompanying good. He would ask the Hon. Gent. in what commodities those exports were paid for? Those who exported must have got a return in something else they had not before had. If we send cotton goods to India, they must be paid for. Our cotton goods were purchased with other manufactures; new branches of trade were thus struck out, and both countries were ultimately benefited. The one country was employed in making machinery and working it, and the other in fabricating those manufactures by which our cottons were paid for. Instead of pointing out in what line capital should be employed, he thought it would have been as well if the Hon. Gent. had left that point to be settled by the individual. (Hear!) It was undoubtedly very kind of the Hon. Gent. to lecture those who might be inclined to embark their capital in the East-India sugar-trade; (A laugh!) it was very considerate of him to warn them of their danger; and he thanked the Hon. Gent. for his admonition. (A laugh!) But he could not think, at this time of day, when they had advanced so far in commercial knowledge, that the Hon. Gent. was perfectly competent to decide on the manner in which capital should be laid out (Hear!)

Indeed, he seemed anxious to apply the customs of the East to the commerce of Europe, and to keep the same system going on, from father to son, without variation, to all eternity. (Hear!) An Hon. Gent. (Mr. Tucker) had alluded to the subject of slaves, and declared that he was proud to be an Englishman, more particularly in consequence of what had occurred in the last few months. In truth, he had reason to be proud of it. No man could possibly value this country more than he did. It had signalized itself gloriously a thousand times. But he confessed that he really was inclined to blush with shame, to hide his face, when West-India slavery was mentioned. (Hear!) It was a stain on the otherwise pure character of the country, which he ardently desired to see wiped away. (Hear!) The question of slavery was one of infinite importance. It well deserved the consideration of the country. He meant to cast no imputation on the planters; it was the infamous custom, the shocking system, against which he directed his reprobation; for, surely it was impossible that any man could, for a moment, reflect on the treatment and punishment of slaves without shuddering. (Hear!) It was this country that had to answer for the continuance of that abominable system. On this day, he believed, a petition would be presented to Parliament by a most benevolent individual (Mr. Wilberforce) in favour of that unfortunate race of men, who were subjected to the horrors of slavery. He hoped the application would produce its just effect, and that this grievous stain would be removed from the national character. (Hear!)

Mr. ROBERTSON explained that 'he had not attempted to direct individuals how they were to dispose of their capital'.

Mr. RICARDO said, when he spoke of the Hon. Gent.'s offering his advice as to the disposition of capital, he did not mean it in any invidious sense.

XI

WESTMINSTER REFORM DINNER[1]

23 *May* 1823

23 May 1823   'The Anniversary Dinner of the Electors of Westminster, in
commemoration of the establishment of their Independence in the
Election of Sir F. Burdett, took place at the Crown and Anchor
Tavern. At five o'clock upwards of 400 persons sat down to a
very substantial dinner.' Mr. J. C. Hobhouse took the chair, in
the absence of Sir F. Burdett who was prevented from attending
by illness.

The first toast proposed was, 'The People, the only source of
legitimate power' (applause).

The next was 'The King, and may he always recollect his
declaration, that he holds the Crown in trust and for the benefit
of the people' (with three times cheers).

Mr. RICARDO next rose and said, a toast had been put into
his hands, which he should give with the greatest pleasure—
'The only remedy for the national grievances, a full, fair,
free, and equal Representation of the People in the Commons'
House of Parliament.' To him it appeared that such a
representation of the people was absolutely necessary, as a
check and security against misgovernment. It was absolutely
necessary that we should have a House of Commons which
should represent the people fully and efficiently, instead of
representing only a small portion of the people of England.
Great difference of opinion existed and might very fairly
exist as to the extent to which the Elective Franchise should
be carried. A numerous class of persons in this country
thought that it should be extended to the whole of the people;
others thought it would be sufficiently extensive if given only
to householders. Between these two opinions there was
much debateable ground; he did not think this a point of such

[1] Report in the *Morning Chronicle*, 24 May 1823.

essential importance, as some appeared to consider it, and in his opinion there would be sufficient security for good government if the Elective Franchise was extended no farther than to those who paid direct taxes, or who were fairly called householders. What he considered a point of much greater importance was, that to whatever classes the elective franchise might be given, the privilege should be fairly exercised by those classes (applause). They ought not to be in any degree influenced by those who were superior to them in rank or fortune. He did not deny to the higher classes the fair influence arising from talents, property and good offices, but he did deny to them the privilege of dictating to Electors in the exercise of the elective franchise. He did think it of the utmost importance that the elective franchise should be exercised in such a manner as to give the most complete security, that the votes given should be the real votes of the people. It was said by Mr. Fox in the House of Commons, that he should be a friend to Universal suffrage if he knew any mode by which the real votes of the people could be effectually obtained under such a system, but he objected to Universal Suffrage because he was satisfied that it would in reality give a greater power to the Aristocracy than it at present possessed. In that opinion of Mr. Fox, he (Mr. R.) should entirely concur, if he did not think that there was an easy and practicable mode of securing to the people the free choice of their Representatives. The mode he alluded to was that of secret suffrage, or what was commonly called voting by ballot (applause). By the establishment of such a system he was fully persuaded, that we should have a House of Commons which would fairly express the opinions of the people; and that no measures would originate in such a House of Commons which had not the good of the people for their object. It was to him a subject of congratulation that so small a change as this would secure to the people of this country all the blessings of good government. We were not in the situation of other countries, which in order to obtain those blessings were compelled to go through all the horrors of a revolution. We were so happily situated that nothing but a rational and practicable Reform was wanting to put us in possession of all the blessings we could desire. He knew, it was objected to them, that if they had such a House of Commons as this the Crown and the Aristocracy could no longer exist. He believed no such thing; he believed the people of this country were attached to their institutions. Let them have no motive for changing those institutions, and that attachment would remain. Englishmen were not naturally fond of change; they were not a fickle people; on the contrary, they rather endured abuses too long (applause). There was another security for good government, which he should have been sorry to have forgotten on this occasion. Our Parliaments should be frequently chosen (applause). Without frequent Parliaments there was no security for liberty. It could not be denied that we possessed in this country a good deal of practical liberty, though it was not administered in the way which would contribute most effectively to the happiness of the people. While a free press, and the privilege of meeting to discuss their grievances remained, even shackled as those privileges now were, this country could never be said to be entirely without liberty. The perseverance of the Electors of Westminster had set a great example to the rest of the country, and he trusted the time was not far distant when their firm, consistent, and persevering efforts in the cause of Reform would be crowned with success. The Honourable Gentleman concluded by giving 'A full, fair and free Representation of the People in the Commons' House of Parliament.'

TWO PAPERS ON
PARLIAMENTARY REFORM

NOTE ON TWO PAPERS ON
PARLIAMENTARY REFORM

THESE two papers were published posthumously by McCulloch in the *Scotsman* newspaper.

The *Observations on Parliamentary Reform* appeared in the issue of 24 April 1824, together with an editorial article which opened: 'We shall be excused, we trust, for taking some pride, in being able to state, that our leading article of to-day is from the pen of the late Mr RICARDO; and when we have made this announcement, it is almost unnecessary to add, that, from what is due to the memory of the author, as well as to the public, the Essay has been printed *verbatim,* and without the alteration of a word or syllable, from the manuscript.'

McCulloch reprinted it, under the same title, in his edition of Ricardo's *Works,* 1846, with the following note: 'The manuscript of the following Essay on Parliamentary Reform was given by Mr Ricardo, a short time before his death, to Mr McCulloch. The latter, not thinking it right that so important a paper should be withheld from the public, printed it in the *Scotsman* of the 24th of April 1824.'

The *Defence of the Plan of Voting by Ballot* appeared in the *Scotsman* of 17 July 1824, which introduced it with the following paragraph: 'The following Report of one of Mr RICARDO's speeches in Parliament—most probably the one he delivered on the 24th April, 1823, in the debate on Lord JOHN RUSSELL's motion—written in his own hand, was found among his manuscripts subsequently to his death. His friends have kindly communicated it to us, and we now publish it verbatim from the manuscript, without alteration of any kind whatever. Mr RICARDO was always a decided supporter of the system of election by ballot; and he has here stated, with that brevity, clearness, and comprehensiveness of view peculiar to himself, the grounds on which he approved of that system. We will not presume to say that Mr RICARDO has entirely obviated all the objections that have been urged against the ballot; but every one will readily allow that his defence of it is most able and ingenious, and that he has said almost all that can possibly be said in its behalf.'

McCulloch reprinted this paper, with the note, in his edition of Ricardo's *Works,* under the title 'Speech on the Plan of Voting by Ballot'.

Professor Cannan, referring to McCulloch's supposition that this was a report of Ricardo's speech on 24 April 1823 in the debate on Lord John Russell's motion, says: 'That McCulloch had not taken the most ordinary pains to verify a haphazard conjecture by referring to Hansard is shown by his use of the words "most probably"; that he had not taken the trouble to read the speech which he was reprinting is shown by the fact that it talks of "the Bill", and is particularly addressed to criticism of two "clauses" in the Bill.[1] If Hansard is to be trusted, it was never delivered.'[2]

Not only was the speech never delivered, but it appears that it was not written for delivery, having been almost certainly composed *before* Ricardo entered Parliament. The latest date for its composition is fixed by its allusion to the law 'against the exportation of the coin' as being 'on our statute-book'.[3] The law was repealed early in July 1819, and its existence could hardly have been used as an argument by Ricardo after 26 May 1819 when Peel's Resolutions for the Resumption of Cash Payments, which recommended the repeal, were adopted by the House of Commons. Now, between February 1819, when Ricardo took his seat in Parliament, and this date, the question of Reform did not come before the House in any shape.

In 1818, however, when Ricardo was negotiating for a seat in Parliament, the question of Parliamentary Reform was a constant subject of discussion with his friends. In May he had daily walks with Mill in Kensington Gardens, and he wrote to Malthus 'we could make a very tolerable reformer of you in six walks if your prejudices be not too strongly fixed.'[4] Trower, when on a visit to

---

[1] Below, pp. 508–10.
[2] 'Ricardo in Parliament', *Economic Journal,* June 1894, p. 251, reprinted in Cannan's *The Economic Outlook,* 1912, p. 91.
[3] Below, p. 511–12.
[4] Letter of 25 May 1818, below, VII, 263.

London, joined in some of these walks[1] and after his return to the country continued the discussion with Ricardo by letter. In August Mill went on a visit to Ricardo at Gatcomb and in September they were both in London for a fortnight, always continuing their discussions.[2]

A comparison of the Ricardo-Trower correspondence in the summer of 1818 with the *Observations on Parliamentary Reform* and the *Defence of the Plan of Voting by Ballot* points to the two papers having been also written in 1818. This is confirmed by a comparison with his later speeches on Reform, which he actually delivered in Parliament on 18 April 1821 and 24 April 1823;[3] in these speeches he put forward proposals identical with those of the *Observations* and the *Defence,* but he omitted certain arguments which were relevant to the political situation of 1818 but would have been uncalled for in 1821 and 1823. Thus the argument in favour of the ballot in the letter to Trower of 27 June 1818 that 'we should get rid of the disgusting spectacle of the lowest blackguards in every town assembling about the Hustings, and insulting in the grossest, and most cruel manner, those respectable candidates against whom their antipathies are excited',[4] which is echoed in the *Defence of the Ballot,*[5] but not mentioned in the later speeches, was occasioned by the behaviour of the mob at the Westminster election in June 1818. Also, both in his letters to Trower of 1818 and in the *Observations* Ricardo finds it necessary to defend his proposals for Reform against the charge that, 'by extending the franchise, you open the door to anarchy, for the bulk of the people are interested, or think they are so, in the equal division of property, and they would choose only such demagogues as held up the hope to them that such division should take place'[6]—a danger which is not referred to in the speeches of 1821 and 1823. The fears entertained in the disturbed years 1818 and 1819 by 'those who have property to lose',[7] had by that time largely disappeared.[8]

---

[1] Letter from Trower, 7 June 1818, below, VII, 268, and to Trower, 27 June 1818, *ib.* 275.
[2] Below, VII, 285, 298–9.
[3] Above, pp. 112 and 283.
[4] Below, VII, 272–3.

[5] Below, p. 504–5.
[6] *Observations,* below, p. 499; and cp. to Trower, 27 June and 20 Dec. 1818, below, VII, 273 and 369–70.
[7] Below, p. 501.
[8] As evidence of how fully the

If the supposition that the two papers were written in 1818 is accepted, they may be identified as two of the 'Discourses' which Ricardo wrote at the instance of Mill as an exercise in speech-making before entering Parliament. In a letter of 23 September 1818, written from Bagshot and occasioned by the successful conclusion of the negotiations for Ricardo's seat, Mill urges him to familiarise his mind with the things which must go to the composition of 'good government'. 'Then' he writes 'there will be no fear about the language in which your thoughts will spontaneously clothe themselves. Let those discourses, therefore, which we have so often talked about, be written without delay.'[1] He then gives detailed instructions on the method of composition, and adds: 'When the writing is done, you should *talk* over the subject to yourself. I mean not *harangue,* but as you would talk about it in conversation at your own table; talk audibly, however, walking about in your room.' The discourses were to be sent to Mill, who would be 'the representative of an audience, of a public'.[2] By 26 October Mill had heard from Ricardo that he was about to begin writing,[3] and by 18 November, having returned to London, he had received and read two discourses.[4] A third discourse was written shortly after, according to a letter from Mill of 4 December, but does not appear to have been sent to Mill.[5]

The fact that the *Defence of the Ballot* is in the form of a parliamentary speech suggests that Ricardo wrote it for a

ruling classes had recovered their self-confidence by 1823, a passage from a speech of Robinson, then Chancellor of the Exchequer, describing 'the condition of those great masses of our population which are congregated in the manufacturing districts', may be quoted: 'What was the state of that population three or four years ago, when they laboured under the severe pressure of acknowledged distress, and what is its actual condition? Where is the disquietude, the tumult, the sedition, the outrage of that period? Vanished. What have we in their place? Peace, order, content and happiness.' (Speech on the Financial Situation of the Country, 21 Feb. 1823; *Hansard,* N.S., VIII, 201.)

[1] Below, VII, 301.
[2] *ib.* 302.
[3] *ib.* 317.
[4] *ib.* 329. Mill promised 'a more detailed criticism', but no such criticism is extant. The tenour of the other letters leaves little doubt that reform was the subject of the discourses.
[5] *ib.* 349–50, 358, 364.

fictitious debate on a Bill for the Reform of Parliament in which he imagined himself to be taking part,[1] attributing to previous speakers the objections which were then current.[2]

Since the above has been in proof, the original MS of the two papers has been found with the Mill-Ricardo papers. It consists of a quire written over 38 pages in Ricardo's hand, containing four items:

1. 'Extract of a letter from Hutches Trower to D. Ricardo dated 18 Oct.ʳ 1818.'
2. 'The answer to the above (dated 2ᵈ Nov.ʳ 1818).'
3. Defence of the Plan of Voting by Ballot.
4. Observations on Parliamentary Reform (3 and 4 have no titles in the MS).

This combination confirms the conjecture that the papers were written in 1818.

Besides, from Ricardo's letter to Mill of 8 November 1818, we learn that of the 'two discourses' mentioned by Mill on 18 November one was a copy of the letter to Trower of 2 November and the other 'a subsequent paper which I have just written'. The latter we may suppose, from the sequence in the MS, to be the *Defence*. The *Observations* would then be the third discourse of which Ricardo thought so ill that, after announcing in his letter to Mill of 23 November 1818 that he was sending another of his 'wise discourses', he added in the postscript: 'On looking over the papers which I was going to send you, I am so discontented

---

[1] He may have had before him the report of the debate in the House of Commons on 2 June 1818, on the Resolutions for the Reform of Parliament which had been drafted by Bentham and introduced by Sir Francis Burdett. See *Hansard*, XXXVIII, 1118–1185 and cp. Bentham's *Works*, ed. by Bowring, vol. x, p. 491 ff.

[2] Thus cp. the passage in the *Defence of the Ballot* that 'One Hon. Gentleman has observed, that he is prepossessed in favour of open voting, without being able to give any reason why he prefers it' (below, p. 512) with the allusion to the opponents of the ballot in a letter to Trower of 18 Sept. 1818: 'I have never heard any solid reasons for their objections:—they are all to be resolved to an antipathy, for which they can give no account' (below, VII, 299).

with it that I cannot send it.' In the end, however, he sent it: 'yesterday I dispatched to you the paper on reform ... of which I was ashamed at the moment that I was about to enclose it.' (Letter to Mill, 28 December 1818.)

The text printed in the *Scotsman* contains occasional changes in wording which, though slight, are not likely to have been introduced by the printer: this suggests that the two papers were printed from copies corrected by Ricardo or possibly by Mill or McCulloch. Therefore the text below adheres to that of the *Scotsman*, except for the correction of a few misprints.

OBSERVATIONS ON PARLIAMENTARY
REFORM[1]

By the late Mr. Ricardo

A monarch, or any other ruler, wishes to have no other
check on his actions but his own will, and would, if he could,
reign despotically, uncontrolled by any other power. In
every country of the world some check, more or less strong,
exists on the will of the Sovereign, even in those Governments
which are supposed to be the most despotic. In Turkey, and
at Algiers, the people or the army rise up in insurrection, and
frequently depose and strangle one tyrant, and elevate another
in his place, who is checked in his career by a dread of the
same species of violence.

The only difference, in this point, between the Governments of countries which are called free and those which are
called arbitrary, is in the organization of this check, and in
the facility and efficacy with which it is brought to bear upon
the will of the Sovereign. In England the Monarch's authority
is checked by the fear of resistance, and the power of organiz-
ing and calling forth this resistance is said to be in the aristocracy and the people, through the medium of the two
Houses of Parliament.

It is undoubtedly true that the Monarch would not long
venture to oppose the opinion decidedly expressed by the
House of Commons, and therefore he may be said to be
checked and controlled by those who appoint the House of
Commons. All great questions are decided in the House of
Commons; the House of Lords seldom gives any opposition
to important measures to which the other House has given

[1] *Scotsman,* 24 April 1824.

its sanction. Nor, when the constitution of that House is considered, is such opposition necessary, for the House of Commons is not appointed by the people, but by the Peers and the wealthy aristocracy of the country. The really efficient power of Government is, then, in the hands of the wealthy aristocracy, subject, indeed, to an irregular influence which I shall presently explain. What is the consequence of this?— A compromise between the aristocracy and the monarchy; and all the power and influence which Government gives are divided between them. The Monarch has the appointment to all places of trust and profit—to the Ministry—to the army and navy—to the courts of law; he has also the power of appointing to many other lucrative situations, such as ambassadors, heads and subordinates of public offices, &c. &c. Notwithstanding this great power, his measures can be controlled by the House of Commons, and, therefore, it is of importance to Government to get a majority in that House.

This is easily obtained by giving a portion of these lucrative places to those who have the choice of the majority of the House of Commons; accordingly, it is well known that no means are so effectual for obtaining situations of trust and profit from the Crown as the possession of Parliamentary influence; and, as the appetite for lucrative places is insatiable, both in Ministers and their followers, and the oligarchy and their's, places are often created for the men, and others are frequently continued after they have become unnecessary, for the advantage solely of these favoured individuals. If, then, there were no other check on both these bodies, England would not have to boast of a better Government than what exists in those countries in which it is called despotic. But, happily, there is another check, and that a tolerably efficient one, which is with the people, and would not, without a violent struggle, be wrested from them. The check on this Government, which operates on behalf of the people, is the good sense and information of the people themselves, operating through the means of a free press, which controls not only the Sovereign and his Ministers, but the Aristocracy, and the House of Commons, which is under its influence. This is the great safeguard of our liberties. Every transaction of the great functionaries of the state is, by means of the press, conveyed in two days to the extremities of the kingdom, and the alarm is sounded if any measure is adopted, or even proposed, which might in its tendency be hurtful to the community. This check, then, like others that we have been speaking of, resolves itself into the fear which government and the aristocracy have of an insurrection of the people, by which their power might be overturned, and which alone keeps them within the bounds which now appear to arrest them. The press, amongst an enlightened and well-informed people, is a powerful instrument to prevent misrule, because it can quickly organise a formidable opposition to any encroachment on the people's rights, and, in the present state of information, perhaps there would not be found a minister who would be sufficiently daring to attempt to deprive us of it. This power, however, is irregular in its operation. It is not always easy to rouse the people to an active opposition to minor measures, which may be shewn to be detrimental to their interests—neither is it powerful, on ordinary occasions, in getting a repeal of those laws, which, however detrimental, have been long in force, and therefore it is in a certain degree braved. In spite of the thunders of the press men continue to be placed in parliament whose interests are often at direct variance with the interest of the people. The offices of state, and the lucrative situations under government, are not bestowed according to merit; bad laws continue to disgrace our statute-book; and good ones are rejected, because they would interfere with particular interests—wars are entered into for the sake of private advantage, and the nation is borne down with great and unnecessary expenses. Experience proves that the liberty of the press is insufficient to correct or prevent these abuses, and that nothing can be effectual to that purpose but placing the check in a more regular manner in the people, by making the House of Commons really and truly the representatives of the people. Of all the classes in the community the people only are interested in being well-governed; on this point there can be no dispute or mistake. Good government may be contrary to the interests of the aristocracy, or to those of the monarch, as it may prevent them from having the same emoluments, advantage, or power, which they would have if government was not busied about the happiness of the many, but chiefly concerned itself about the happiness of the few, but it can never be prejudicial to the general happiness.

If, then, we could get a House of Commons chosen by the people, excluding all those, whether high or low, who had interests separate and distinct from the general interest, we should have a controlling body whose sole business and duty it would be to obtain good government. It is not denied that, in innumerable instances, the interest of the aristocracy and that of the people will be the same, and therefore many good laws and regulations would be made if the aristocracy were to govern without control. The same may be said of the Monarch, but in many important instances they will also be opposed, and then it is that we shall look in vain for good laws and for good government. A reform in the House of Commons then, the extension of the elective franchise to all those against whom no plausible reason can be urged that they have, or suppose they have, interest contrary to the general interest, is the only measure which will secure liberty and good government on a solid and permanent foundation. This is so self-evident that one is surprised that an argument can be offered against it; but, to do the opponents of this measure justice, they do not advance any direct argument against it; their whole endeavour is to evade it.

A House of Commons such as you contend for, they say, would be a good, but how are you to obtain it? Has not the country flourished in spite of the imperfections you mention, and why would you wish to improve what is already demonstrated to be so good? The House of Commons is not chosen by the people generally, but it is chosen by men who have received a good and liberal education—whose characters are unimpeachable, and who are much better judges of what will conduce to the happiness of the people than they themselves are. By extending the franchise you open the door to anarchy, for the bulk of the people are interested, or think they are so, in the equal division of property, and they would choose only such demagogues as held out the hope to them that such division should take place. To which it may be answered, that although it be true that the country has flourished with a House of Commons constituted as ours has been, it must be shewn that such a constitution of it is favourable to the prosperity of the country, before such an argument can be admitted for its continuance. It is not sufficient to say that we have been successful, and therefore we should go on in the same course. The question to be asked is, notwithstanding our success has there been nothing in our institutions to retard our progress? A merchant may flourish although he is imposed upon by his clerk, but it would be a worthless argument to persuade him to keep this clerk because he had flourished while he was in his employ. Whilst any evil can be removed, or any improvement adopted, we should listen to no suggestions so inconclusive as that we have been doing well. Such an argument is a bar to all progress in human affairs.

Why have we adopted the use of steam engines? It might have been demonstrated that our manufactures had flourished without them, and why not let well enough alone? Nothing is well enough whilst any thing better is within our reach; this is a fallacy which can only be advanced by the ignorant or designing, and can no longer impose on us.

What signifies, too, the unimpeachable characters and the good education of those who choose the members of the House of Commons? Let me know what the state of their interests is, and I will tell you what measures they will recommend.

If this argument were good for any thing, we might get rid of all the checks and restraints of law, as far at least as they regarded a part of the community. Why ask from Ministers an account of the public income and expenditure annually? Are they not men of good character and education?

What need of a House of Commons or of a House of Lords? Are they to restrain the Sovereign? Why should you not place the fullest reliance in his virtue and integrity?

Why fetter the Judges by rules, and burden them with Juries? Is it possible that such enlightened and good men could decide unjustly or corruptly? To keep men good you must as much as possible withdraw from them all temptation to be otherwise. The sanctions of religion, of public opinion, and of law, all proceed on this principle, and that state is most perfect in which all these sanctions concur to make it the interest of all men to be virtuous, which is the same thing as to say, to use their best endeavour to promote the general happiness.

The last point for consideration is the supposed disposition of the people to interfere with the rights of property. So essential does it appear to me, to the cause of good government, that the rights of property should be held sacred, that I would agree to deprive those of the elective franchise against whom it could justly be alleged that they considered it their interest to invade them. But in fact it can be only amongst the most needy in the community that such an opinion can be entertained. The man of a small income must be aware how little his share would be if all the large fortunes in the kingdom were equally divided among the people. He must know that the little he would obtain by such a division could be no adequate compensation for the overturning of a principle which renders the produce of his industry secure. Whatever might be his gains after such a principle had been admitted would be held by a very insecure tenure, and the chance of his making any future gains would be greatly diminished; for the quantity of employment in the country must depend, not only on the quantity of capital, but upon its advantageous distribution, and, above all, on the conviction of each capitalist that he will be allowed to enjoy unmolested the fruits of his capital, his skill, and his enterprise. To take from him this conviction is at once to annihilate half the productive industry of the country, and would be more fatal to the poor labourer than to the rich capitalist himself. This is so self-evident, that men very little advanced beyond the very lowest stations in the country cannot be ignorant of it, and it may be doubted whether any large number even of the lowest would, if they could, promote a division of property. It is the bugbear by which the corrupt always endeavour to rally those who have property to lose around them, and it is from this fear, or pretended fear, that so much jealousy is expressed of entrusting the least share of power to the people. But the objection, when urged against reform, is not an honest one, for, if it be allowed that those who have a sacred regard to the rights of property should have a voice in the choice of representatives, the principle is granted for which reformers contend. They profess to want only good government, and, as a means to such an end, they insist that the power of choosing members of Parliament should be given to those who cannot have an interest contrary to good government. If the objection made against reform were an honest one, the objectors would say how low in the scale of society they thought the rights of property were held sacred, and there they would make their stand. That class, and all above it, they would say, may fairly and advantageously be entrusted with the power which is wished to be given them, but the presumption of mistaken views of interest in all below that class would render it hazardous to entrust a similar power with them—it could not at least be safely done until we had more reason to be satisfied that, in their opinion, the interest of the community and that of themselves were identified on this important subject.

This concession would satisfy the reasonable part of the public. It is not Universal Suffrage as an end, but as a means, of good government that the partisans of that measure ask it for. Give them the good government, or let them be convinced that you are really in earnest in procuring it for them, and they will be satisfied, although you should not advance with the rapid steps that they think would be most advantageously taken. My own opinion is in favour of caution, and therefore I lament that so much is said on the subject of Universal Suffrage. I am convinced that an extension of the suffrage, far short of making it universal, will substantially secure to the people the good government they wish for, and therefore I deprecate the demand for the universality of the elective franchise—at the same time, I feel confident that the effects of the measure which would satisfy me would have so beneficial an effect on the public mind, would be the means of so rapidly increasing the knowledge and intelligence of the public, that, in a limited space of time after this first measure of reform were granted, we might, with the utmost safety, extend the right of voting for members of Parliament to every class of the people.

But it is intolerable, because the House of Commons is not disposed to go the full length of what is perhaps indiscreetly asked of them, that therefore they should refuse to grant any reformation of abuses whatever; that against the plainest conviction they should assert that a House of Commons, constituted as this is, is best calculated to give to the people the advantages of good government; and that they should continue to maintain that the best interests of the people are attended to, when it is demonstrated that they not only are not, but cannot be, whenever they are opposed to the interests of those who are in full possession of power, namely, the King, and the Oligarchy, who are bribed to support his government.

DEFENCE OF THE PLAN OF VOTING
BY BALLOT[1]

By the late Mr. Ricardo

Sir—The general question of a reform in the representation of this House, has been so fully discussed, and so ably supported by many honourable gentlemen that have preceded me in the debate, that I shall not detain the House by offering any observations on it, but shall confine myself to the consideration of that part of the subject, which has been little noticed, but which, in my opinion, is of so much importance, that, without it, no substantial reform can be obtained:— I mean, Sir, the changing the present mode of open election for members of Parliament, and substituting in its room the secret mode, or ballot.

In order to appreciate the advantages which will result from the proposed change, it may not be improper to state, as briefly as possible, to the House, the inconveniences attending the present mode of election; that, having the nature of the evil before them, they may be the better able to judge of the efficacy of the proposed remedy. By some, indeed, it may be thought a vain and useless occupation of the time of the House to recapitulate the evils of our present system, for it may with justice be asked, who amongst us is not acquainted with the bribery, the riots, the intoxication, and the immoralities of every description, which take place on the occasion of every general election? These disgusting facts are unfortunately too notorious, yet it may not be unuseful to submit them to the attention of the House.

The scenes which occur at such times, would disgrace a

[1] *Scotsman*, 17 July 1824.

barbarous people. The reign of the law appears to cease, and impunity to be proclaimed for every species of violence. A rude and brutal populace, the offscourings of our population, surround the hustings, and heap every sort of insult and indignity on the candidate who happens not to enjoy their favour. Dirt, filth, and often stones, are thrown at him—the most unmanly attacks are made upon his person, and it is frequently a task of difficulty to his friends to protect him from the effects of their savage and brutal animosity.

Nor is it the candidate only that is thus exposed to their rage, but every elector is applauded, or hissed, caressed, or furiously attacked, as he may favour or oppose by his vote, the favourite of the mob. Idleness and the neglect of work always follow in the train of an election—they are succeeded by debauchery and intoxication, and for a period the country suffers under all the evils of anarchy. I know that these violences are in almost all cases committed by the lowest of the mob, that they are not to be imputed to the electors themselves, but to the assemblage of the idle and disorderly which every great town affords, but the evil is not less serious on that account, and does not less imperiously call on us for a remedy.

These, however, constitute but one portion, and indeed a very inferior portion, of the evil which attends the present mode of election. Bad as it is, if even at this price we obtained a parliament freely chosen by the people, we should have some consolation, although it would be our duty to endeavour to retain the good, and get rid of what was bad in the system. But this consolation is not afforded us, and in addition to the evil which I have already mentioned, we have the far greater one to guard against, which arises from the influence exercised over the voters at elections. Of what use is it to mark with precision how low in the scale of rank the right of voting for members of parliament shall commence, if you take no steps to secure to the electors the right which you propose to accord to them? It is the most cruel mockery to tell a man he may vote for A or B, when you know that he is so much under the influence of A, or the friends of A, that his voting for B would be attended with destruction to him. He cannot justly be said to have a vote, unless he have the free exercise of it, without prejudice to his fortunes. Is this the case at present? Is it not a delusion to say that every freeholder of 40*s.* a year has a vote for a member of parliament, when in most cases he cannot vote as he pleases, without ruin to himself? It is not he who has the vote, really and substantially, but his landlord; for it is for his benefit and interest, that it is exercised on the present system. Of what advantage would be the reform that is proposed, of extending the elective franchise to all householders, or as others recommend, to all males of twenty-one years of age, if this increased number of electors were to be, as they now are, completely under the influence of the same men, or of men having precisely the same views and interests, as those who play so grand a part in returning members to parliament? The more extended the suffrage, the more influence would be possessed by Peers, and the wealthy aristocracy of the country, and therefore the more certainly should we have a parliament which would be their representatives, and the advocates of their particular interests, and not of the interests of the great mass of the people. In many populous cities, householders are now said to have votes for the representatives of their city; but are not the cases numerous in which they dare not openly exercise the right? Is it to be expected that they will expose themselves to a resentment which will overwhelm them, whether it be from their best customers, the rich consumers, if they are shopkeepers,—the magistrates, if they are publicans,—their

employers, if they are clerks, and in subordinate situations,—
or any other class, who may be supposed to have an influence
over their property? By extending the suffrage, an additional
security is afforded against bribery, because the greater the
number of electors the more difficult will it be to provide
funds for the purpose of directly influencing votes by means
of bribes. But it must not be forgotten that bribery is only
one of the modes, and by no means the most efficacious mode,
by which voters are influenced. Mr. Bentham's sagacity did
not fail to discover that terror was the great instrument of
influence and corruption. Votes are more effectually secured
by the fear of loss than by the hope of gain. Those whose
characters afford security against the offering of bribes, and
who would think themselves disgraced by a practice which
is universally condemned, do not disdain to make use of the
persuasive instrument of fear. In its operation it is silent—
it is not necessary to proclaim to the voter the danger which
he runs of disobliging his landlord, or patron; it is understood
without explanation, and no one who hears me, can doubt of
its powerful effects on every occasion. Although, then, by
extending the suffrage you weaken the corruptive effect of
bribery, you increase that which is produced by alarm and
fear, for in proportion as the fortunes of the voter are more
humble, the more surely will he be under the influence of
those who have the power to sway those fortunes. Happily
a security can be found against this influence, but if it could
not, I should deem that an improvement which should raise
the qualification, and limit the number of voters; for the
chance of finding an independent spirit in electors would be
increased, if the qualification was raised to £100 per annum,
rather than if it continued as it is, or were lowered below
40 shillings. These, then, are the evils against which we have
to provide, and the House will readily perceive that those

which arise from riots, intoxication, and idleness, are of a different description from those which are the consequence of undue influence exercised over the minds, directly or indirectly, of the electors; and accordingly the bill before you offers two distinct remedies. To obviate the first evil, it is proposed to take the votes throughout the country on the same day, and, instead of the elections being for the whole of a county, and held in one single place, that votes be received in several districts at the same time. To obviate the second, it is proposed that the ballot, or the secret mode of election, be substituted for the open mode.

These two propositions are very distinct, and they should not be, as they often are, confounded; for one might be rejected, and the other adopted. Those, for example, who are of opinion that the public and noisy assemblage of the rabble about the hustings is attended with benefits outweighing the evils which have been stated, might reject that clause which proposes to take the votes by districts, but might nevertheless adopt the other which requires that the election should be by ballot. The people might assemble about the hustings as they now do; they might listen, or not listen, to the speeches of the candidates as their humour might dictate; they might shew all the usual marks of their sympathy or disapprobation, and yet the voting might be secret; and, on the contrary, those who are in favour of open voting, might approve of votes being given in districts, although they rejected the ballot.

According to the best judgment which I can form on this important subject, we ought to adopt both these clauses. That respecting time and place of voting will give us sufficient security against the disgusting exhibitions and riotous proceedings which have hitherto attended elections. Through the medium of the press, the candidate may make known his pretensions; through the same channel, objections may be made to his principles, or to his former conduct—the press is open to all, and the candidates would no longer be subjected to an ordeal which is not a test of merit but of endurance. Because a man has the honest ambition of representing a populous city in Parliament, must he make up his mind to endure all the insults which can be heaped upon him by the lowest of the rabble? It is said, that it is fit his claims should be examined into,—that without preparation he should be called upon immediately to explain what has been ambiguous in his former conduct;—what are his principles on the grand questions which are likely to be submitted to him; and, that he should be called upon to speak on any other matters which may be proposed to him. This might be useful if he presented himself before an impartial tribunal, but those who make this objection, are bound to shew that candidates on both sides are fairly listened to, and that even the semblance of justice is extended to them. One of the arguments now offered in favour of the borough system, and it is one of considerable weight, is, that without such boroughs, many men of merit would never be in Parliament—and why? because they are troubled with modesty; and with the feelings of gentlemen, which makes it intolerable to them to submit to the injustice, the insolence, and the insults of the lowest of the rabble. That we may be sure of the services of these men, then, I demand that this clause be adopted. These public meetings, it has been said, are useful in giving a tone to public feeling, and raising the lowest of the community in his own estimation, by making him feel that he has a share in the government of his country. Can he be said to have this share if he is without a vote? Does he show his importance by spitting at the candidate, by throwing dirt and filth in his face? This is not calculated to raise him in his own estimation; and if it be right that he should have a voice in the government of his country, give him that voice, and allow him to exercise it legally on the same terms with the first elector in the land, but do not delude us or him, by giving him the shadow, and calling it the substance of power!

The other clause, namely, that which establishes the ballot, appears to me to offer complete security against those evils which flow from the influence of power. If voting took place by ballot, all the influence now practised on voters would, in a great measure, cease; for, to what purpose would you threaten a man for the vote he should give, or how could you punish him for it when given, if by the regulation you were absolutely precluded from knowing for which candidate he voted? Establish the ballot, and every elector is from that moment in possession of a real and not of an imaginary privilege. Of what use would it be to threaten a publican with the loss of his licence, a farmer with the deprivation of his lease, a tradesman with the loss of your custom, when you can never know how he voted, unless he chose to communicate it to you? The elective franchise, if it should be thought expedient, might be extended. The very extension would secure you from direct bribery, for no fortune would be equal to bribe a nation of electors, and terror would cease to operate, for it would be in vain to endeavour to mark the victims. An honourable gentleman has said, that if the ballot were established it would not prevent candidates and the friends of candidates from endeavouring to get the promise of votes, and then he observes, that if the electors keep their promises, there will be no advantage from the ballot, as they will vote then precisely as they do now; but if they do not keep their promises, they will be guilty of an immoral act, which may justly be charged on this law. It is the latter proposition only which I am called upon to answer, for if the voters give and keep their promises, no objection can be made to the ballot on that account; it may be said to be useless, but cannot be proved to be pernicious. And with respect to the immorality of not keeping promises, the guilt would lie with those who exacted such unlawful promises. To make a promise of a vote which could not be conscientiously given, would be a crime, but it would be a still greater crime to keep it. The promise is unnecessary upon any other supposition than that of its not being right to perform it. What occasion to exact a promise of any man to do that which his own interest will lead him to do? and in giving his vote he is called upon by duty to act in conformity with his own interest. It may be expedient to instruct such a man, to enlighten him on the subject of his real interest, but here our efforts should cease, and we become criminal if we induce him to act contrary to the dictates of his own conscience, and, instead of condemning him for breaking a promise so criminally exacted and given, the most en-lightened morality would teach and require that such promises should be violated. The law does not recommend or encou-rage any species of crime or immorality,—it is enacted with a view to correct an evil which is an insurmountable bar to good government; it requires that every man shall vote according to his conscience, without any deceit or subterfuge; and shall such a law be given up, because the enemies of good government may take advantage of the respect with which men ought to regard their promises, in order to subvert it. If the end we have in view be good, we must not be diverted from our purpose by any partial evil which may attend the means by which we are to attain it. All punishment is an evil, but is justified by the good end which it is to accomplish. It might much more rationally be objected to the excise laws, that they should not have been enacted because they offer temptations to crimes which would not have been committed but for those laws. And what shall we say of the laws against usury, and against the exportation of the coin? The end of these laws is bad—they are binding only on the conscientious, and have opened a wide door to the commission of the crimes of fraud and perjury. With these laws on our statute-book, are we to be discouraged from making one, which has the happiness of the people for its object, because it would be immoral (as it is alleged) to break a promise unlawfully and immorally exacted. But supposing that the breaking of such promises were immoral, would the practice be of long continuance? Would any man persevere in exacting promises, when he found by experience that the promisers did not consider them binding? He would not be tempted to continue an offence with great trouble to himself, as soon as he found that it was unattended with advantage. The immorality, then, to whomsoever it might attach, would soon be at an end; and the law would be efficacious without even this alloy.

One Hon. Gentleman has observed, that he is prepossessed in favour of open voting, without being able to give any reason why he prefers it. To that Hon. Gentleman I might answer, that I have a different prepossession from him, and the instinct of my mind would be just as good, as an argument, as the instinct of his. In fact one mode of voting can be preferred to another only as means to an end, in themselves they are alike indifferent.

To conclude, Sir, the establishment of the ballot would make this House what it ought to be, the real representatives of the electors, and not the representatives of those whose situation gives them a commanding influence over the will of the electors. I am not now considering whether it would be desirable that the elective franchise should be extended, kept on its present footing, or contracted within narrower limits, for on any of these suppositions, the ballot appears to me to be equally expedient. Whoever may be the electors, the representatives should represent them, and their interests, and not those whose interests may, on many occasions, be in direct opposition to theirs.

APPENDICES

DRAFT OF A LETTER TO A NEWSPAPER
ON THE EFFECTS OF PEEL'S BILL

[After the meeting at Hereford in his honour (see above, p. 471), Joseph Hume went to Monmouth where he was admitted a free-man of the borough on 10 December 1821. A brief report of the proceedings was given in *The Times* of 17 December. Ricardo was not present on this occasion, when some of the speakers attacked him for his currency plan to the operation of which they attributed the fall in the prices of agricultural produce.

The following draft letter was intended for an unidentified newspaper which had reported those speeches: there is no evidence of its having been published or even sent.

A similar reply to the same attacks is in Ricardo's letter to McCulloch of 3 January 1822; the latter used it as material for an article in the *Scotsman* (see below, IX, 140, n. 2).

The MS, in Ricardo's handwriting, is in the Mill-Ricardo papers.]

In your account of what passed at the meeting at Monmouth when Mr. Hume was admitted a member of the Corporation of that city it appears that Mr. Moggridge and Mr. Palmer entered pretty fully into the question of the effect which had been produced on the circumstances of farmers by the operation of Mr. Peel's bill passed in 1819 and Mr. Palmer in particular alluded to the opinion on that subject given by Mr. Ricardo at various times—he said that[1]

It appears to me Sir that the effects ascribed by those gentlemen to Mr. Peel's bill by the great rise which has been occasioned in the value of money should rather be ascribed to a great fall in the value of the commodities of which they were speaking viz. Corn, cattle and the other raw produce of the earth. It is at all times exceedingly difficult when two commodities alter considerably in relative value to determine accurately to the alteration in the value of which it is prin-

[1] Blank in MS.

cipally to be ascribed, and the least which those gentlemen could have done would have been to have given their reasons for thinking that since 1819 gold had risen so enormously in value as they contended for. It must be recollected that gold is a commodity as well as corn and cattle, and that its price is equally operated upon by the rise and fall in the value of paper money not regulated by any standard. Mr. Palmer cannot deny that in 1819 when Mr. Peel's bill [was passed][1] a quarter of wheat sold for ___ [2] in paper money, at the same time it sold for £ ___ in gold or for ___ pennyweights in gold. At the present time a quarter of wheat sells for £ ___ in gold or for ___ pennyweights in weight. What is the cause of this difference,—it is owing entirely to the alteration in the value of gold say Mr. Moggridge and Mr. Palmer. I want to know to what cause they ascribe this alteration in the value of gold and on this subject they are silent, they give us no satisfaction whatever. If the question had been asked them at the Meeting when they delivered their opinions they would probably have said it is owing to the contracted quantity of paper currency,—but this would have been far from a satisfactory answer, for they were bound to shew how the contraction of a paper currency acted on the value of gold. Mr. Palmer alluded to the opinions given [by][3] Mr. Ricardo in the following terms—I regret that Mr. Ricardo was not present to answer for himself, but I think it would not be difficult to justify the opinions which were attacked. It will be recollected that Mr. Ricardo wrote a pamphlet to shew that a currency might be regulated by a metallic standard without the use of any other metal as money but silver and copper the latter for payments under a shilling the former[4] for payments under a pound. For this

---

[1] Omitted in MS.
[2] Blank in MS, here and below.
[3] Omitted in MS.
[4] In MS 'latter'.

purpose Mr. Ricardo proposed that the Bank should be obliged to give gold in bullion in exchange for their notes if of a certain amount on the demand of the holder of them. It was with reference to this plan that Mr. Ricardo was examined before the Committee on Bank Affairs and it is probable that seeing there was no necessity for the use of any gold in the circulation and being satisfied that the Bank had a sufficient quantity of that metal to answer all the demands that could be made on them on such a system of currency he answered that   Did Mr. Ricardo mean by this that gold itself could not thereafter vary, and that if it did the currency which was to be[1] regulated by the value of gold would not vary with it? quite the contrary, it is evident from the whole of the reasoning of the pamphlet in question that he considered gold as a variable commodity, as well as corn or any other merchandize, but his argument was, "adopt my system which will render all demand for gold unnecessary, and will therefore probably be unattended with any variation in the value of that metal, and then the whole variation in the value of money will be only equal to the difference between the value of paper and the value of gold or 5 pc^t. You can now buy a quarter of corn with as much gold as is coined into £   for the same quantity of corn you are obliged to give £   in bank notes. Diminish the quantity of bank notes and you will raise them 5 pc. in value and when this is effected you will obtain a quarter of corn for £   in paper as well as in gold—the price of corn in gold will not be altered, its price in paper[2] will fall 5 pc^t." it is for Mr. Palmer to shew what is defective in this reasoning. Mr. Ricardo could not mean to say that no variation should thereafter take place in the value of gold, he must have known full well that the currency of every country regulated by a metallic

---

[1] 'to be' replaces 'on his plan'.   [2] In MS 'gold'.

standard was liable to all the variations of that standard. In
Mr. Ricardo's speeches on Mr. Peel's bill, to which reference
has been made, he said that we should be still liable to have
our currency vary in proportion as the metal varied which
was the standard, but that this was an inconvenience to which
all metallic currencies were exposed—it was one to which
France, Holland, Hamburgh and all those countries whose
currencies were on the most solid system were exposed, and
no case could even be imagined to exempt a currency from
such variations.—It may be said that this is a good defence
for Mr. Ricardo's evidence before the committee, when he
had reason to think that his plan was the one contemplated
respecting the operation of which only he was examined, but
it is not equally good for the opinion which he afterwards
expressed in his speech when he had seen Mr. Peel's bill and
which was essentially different from his proposed plan as it
provided for payments in coin in 1823 and therefore made a
demand for gold obviously necessary and the rise of its value
certain. To this Mr. Ricardo would probably answer that he
saw no such obvious necessity for the demand for gold—
that as he understood the bill no specie would be necessary
till May 1823 four years distant from the time of discussion
and he might confidently reply that if for 3 out of these
4 years his plan had a fair trial it would be found so efficient
for all the objects of the most improved currency that the
legislature would have altered the law and dispensed with
specie payments altogether: In the speech to which allusion
has been made I recollect he advised the Bank to sell gold
instead of buying it so little did he think the quantity actually
in the possession of the Bank inadequate for all the purposes
of bullion payments.

 Mr. Ricardo cannot fairly be held responsible for the
narrow views, and obstinate prejudices of the Bank of

England. He could not contemplate that the Bank would so narrow the circulation of paper as to occasion such a rise in its comparative value to gold and the currencies of other countries as to make the influx of gold into this unexampled in amount. He could not foresee that they would immediately provide themselves with so large a[1] quantity of gold coin as to make it incumbent on them to apply to the legislature to permit them to withdraw all their small notes and fill the circulation with gold coin even so early as the middle of 1821—this is what Mr. Ricardo could not anticipate—he relied on there being no demand for gold and the Bank by their injudicious measures occasioned a demand for many millions. He supposed that the reverting from a currency regulated by no standard, to one regulated by a fixed one, the greatest care would be taken to make the transition as little burthensome as possible, but the fact is that if the object had been to make the alteration from the one system to the other as distressing to the country as possible no measures could have been taken by the Bank of England so well calculated to produce that effect as those which they actually adopted.

In saying this it must not be supposed that I agree with Mr. Moggridge and Mr. Palmer that any thing like the effect which they compute has been produced on the value of the currency by reverting to specie payments. I am of opinion with Mr. Ricardo that if the Bank had followed the obvious course of policy which they ought to have pursued this great measure might have been accomplished with no other alteration in the value of money but 5 pc^t, but by the course which they did adopt and the demand which they in consequence occasioned for gold bullion they have raised the value of that metal about 5 pc^t more and consequently that the whole alteration in the value of the currency since 1819 has been

---

[1] 'so large a' replaces 'a sufficient'.

about 10 pc^t. My reason for thinking that the demand for gold has caused a rise of 5 pc. in that metal is nearly the same as that expressed by Mr. Tooke in his evidence before the Agricultural committee. This rise in the value of gold it must always be remembered is not confined to this country, it is common to all, and if the standard of all were gold and not silver, the money of all would have varied 5 pc^t. What cannot be too often insisted on is that that paper money has only increased in value 5 pc. more than gold—it could not have increased more because it is now on a par with gold and in 1819 and for 4 years before 1819 had not been depressed more than 5 pc. below gold. When Mr. Palmer says therefore that money has altered 50 pc^t in value in consequence of Mr. Peel's bill he must mean that Paper money has risen 50 pc^t and gold bullion 45 pc^t. If this be true all commodities in this country as well as in every other ought to have varied 45 pc. as compared with gold—Does he or any other man believe this to be the fact? Are the people of France, Germany, Italy, Spain, Holland and Hamburgh obliged to give nearly double the quantities of commodities for the purchase of a given weight of gold. Can the Stock holder with the same money dividend procure double the quantity of all the commodities he desires—it is notoriously otherwise and how men with such good understandings as Mr. Moggridge and Mr. Palmer can be made the dupes of such an absurd theory I am at a loss to conceive.

That raw produce is frightfully depressed no one can deny but that this depression is either wholly or in any very great part occasioned by the rise in the value of money is not made out by any plausible arguments. Corn and raw produce are not exempted from a fall of value more than other commodities and if it be true that they have fallen 50 pc^t 40 of that 50 pc^t fall is entirely owing to causes which have operated on their value. Such variations are by no means uncommon. In 1792—wheat was at 39/- in 1800—134/- 1804 52/- 1808 81/- 1812 140/- 1814 67/- 1816—53/- 1817—109/- and it cannot be pretended that these variations were occasioned by the altered value in money. That some part of these variations may be imputed to variations in the value of money is not disputed, but while money varied 10 pc. corn varied 100 pc. and why may not the same have occurred now. Those who deny this are bound to give some reason for their opinion— hitherto they have given none.

II

NOTES ON WESTERN'S 'SECOND ADDRESS
TO THE LANDOWNERS', 1822

AMONGST the pamphlets from Ricardo's library which are in the Goldsmiths' Library of the University of London, there is a copy of the *Second Address to the Landowners of the United Empire,* by C. C. Western, Esq., M.P., second edition, London, Ridgway, 1822, which is annotated by Ricardo.[1] The pamphlet was first published late in 1822, when Ricardo was on his continental tour;[2] by the end of the year, when Ricardo returned to England, a second edition had appeared; and his notes must have been written after his return.[3]

The pamphlet contains a violent attack against Peel's Act of 1819 and against the supporters of the resumption of cash payments. It was referred to by Ricardo in a speech on Western's motion respecting the resumption of cash payments, on 11 June 1823 (above, p. 317 ff.), when he replied to Western's accusations.

Ricardo's notes are written on the margins of the pamphlet and have been partly cut off by the binder. They are here printed in italics.

Ricardo's first comment is occasioned by Western's discussion of the 'inconsiderate and hasty course' which led to the resumption of cash payments in 1819, as proposed by Peel's Committee. 'Of the probable consequences of such a course upon the general prosperity of the country,' writes Western, 'the Committees of the Lords and Commons, incredible as it may appear, not only made *no* adequate enquiry, but seemed purposely to turn their backs upon information tendered, and prophetic warnings given by persons who possessed the fairest claims to attention.' (p. 5.)

---

[1] Bound with other pamphlets in vol. VI of the Ricardo Collection of Tracts. The notes are here reproduced by kind permission of the Goldsmiths' Librarian.
[2] Ricardo left London on 12 July 1822; the first edition of the pamphlet was advertised in the *Morning Chronicle* of 9 Nov. 1822.
[3] On 23 Nov. 1822 Ricardo had written from Paris that he expected to be 'the object of much personal attack' from the country gentlemen. See below, X, 349.

Ricardo notes: '*This Committee recommended a recurrence* [*to*][1] *Cash payments after a period of 4 years. When* [*they*] *did so gold was* £4.2.—*p^r oz. Mr. Western sup*[*por*]*ted a measure which was to make us recur to Cash* [*payments in a single day*] *altho' gold was then* £4.15.—*p*[*^{r} oz.*]'.[2]

Western then discusses the effects upon the agricultural situation of the measures respecting the currency: 'Peel's Bill, I say, is the SOLE cause of our EXCESSIVE and unparalleled distress. [Ricardo underlines 'SOLE' and notes: '*Take notice sole cause!*'] It is not that abundant harvests may not lower the price of corn occasionally to some degree of temporary injury to the growers; but no human being ever heard before of their being RUINED by the blessing of Providence on their labours.... It is not a *ruinous* abundance of corn, but a destructive famine of money that is the bane of the country' (pp. 6–7). Ricardo notes: '*See Mr. Western speech* 1 *March* 1816, *in which he shews the effects of abundance on price.*'[3]

Western's remedy is the revision of Peel's Bill of 1819 and the lowering of the standard, in order to obtain a more abundant currency. The effect would be an advanced money price of commodities, but, he asks, what mischief therefrom? 'The mortgagee would prefer paying higher for his wheat, and his mutton, &c. with the continuance of an interest of five per cent. for his money. The fundholder would enjoy in security, and upon a *good title*, what he possessed, instead of risking it by a robbery of the public [Ricardo notes: '[*R*]*obbery!*'], which can be retained only by force, and not by right. The labourer would again perceive that his labour, which is *his* property, had *some* value [Ricardo twice underlines '*some*' and notes: '[*H*]*as it no* [*v*]*alue now?*']; he would soon find an eager demand for it in the market; and wages, like all other commodities for which there is an increasing demand, would experience a consequent advance.' (p. 24.) Ricardo notes: '[*W*]*hy should an* [*al*]*teration in* [*the*] *value of* [*mo*]*ney cause* [*an*] *increased* [*de*]*mand for* [*la*]*bour?*'

---

[1] Cut off by the binder here and below.
[2] On Western's attitude in 1811 see above, p. 316.

[3] See the quotation from Western's speech of 7 (not 1) March 1816, above, p. 318–19.

Western quotes Hume in his support: 'Give us a *sufficient* currency, and we should be in the situation which Mr. Hume in his
Essay upon Money, written nearly 100 years ago, describes a
country in which money began to flow more abundantly. "Every
thing," he says, "takes a new face—labour and industry gain life—
the merchant becomes more enterprising—the manufacturer more
diligent and skilful—and the farmer follows the plough with more
alacrity and attention." ... We are in the situation in which Mr.
Hume, contrasting his former picture, shews us, of a country in
which the quantity of money is DECREASING. "The workman,"
he says, "has not the same employment from the manufacturer
and merchant—the farmer cannot sell his corn and cattle—the
poverty, beggary, and sloth *that* MUST ENSUE, *are easily* FORE-
SEEN."' (pp. 24–5.) Ricardo notes: '*An erroneous view of Mr.
Hume*'.

On Western's incidental remark, that 'A further increased quantity of currency has *recently* taken place by the advance of about
two millions to the Government by the Bank, to make the payments to the 5 per cent. creditors' (p. 26), Ricardo notes:
'[*I d*]*eny* [*t*]*his*.'

Western then considers the question whether the people at
large would be sufferers from the rise in prices consequent upon
the suggested abundance of money. He admits that when high
prices are the consequence of scarcity, they must be 'considered
amongst the most severe inflictions to which a people are subject' (p. 31). But, '*High* price from *abundance* of *money* is purely
nominal; as if shillings were rained down from heaven, it would
very soon require a great number of them to purchase a loaf of
bread, and the price would be high; or if sixpences were proclaimed to be shillings, we should *nominally* pay as many shillings
as we do now sixpences. But from *high* price *so* caused, or rather
low value of money, no evil follows, no alteration of course takes
place in the relative proportion of food, to the number of mouths
there are to consume it. The bulk of the people *must* have an increased quantity of money, before the sellers can obtain the
higher price, the demand of the opulent classes being too trifling,
hardly indeed varying at all. I have often wished that some of
those persons, who keep up the fallacy respecting a high MONEY

price, would tell me why the people should not be able to obtain as ample a share of the larger quantity of money as of the smaller; this is the point, which if truth were their object, they would see they were bound to make out, and for their own credit, I earnestly invite them for once, at least, fairly and calmly to make the attempt.' (p. 31.) Ricardo notes: '*I do not dispute the principle here laid down but I ask in my turn what injury the people w[ould] suffer if the quantity of money was reduced o[ne] half or three fourths. It is entirely a question.*'[1]

Western continues: 'Now when *debts* and *taxes* are considered, the *advantage* of a high *money* price becomes as apparent as the destructive consequences of the *lower* measure of value are now.... The farmer with 40s. for his quarter of wheat, and the labourer with his 8s. per week, must feel the excessively *increased* difficulty of paying the *same* taxes as they did when the wheat produced 80s., and the labour 16s. The former are indeed sinking under it, and their labourers participate, as of necessity they must, in the distress of their employers. The renewed burnings in many parts of England, with the resolutions of societies of farmers, published in the newspapers, against the use of thrashing machines, are sufficient proofs that the agricultural labourers are reduced, in those districts at least, to a state of acute misery.' (pp. 31–2.) Ricardo notes: '*very sophistical. When wheat is at 40/- the labourer will not receive the same money wages as when it is at 80/-. If the real value of the farmer's taxation as a grower be increased he can [pass on] that increase to the consumer.*'

Western gives an illustration to show that the effect of a rise in the value of money on debtors is out of proportion to the effect of a fall upon creditors: 'suppose a man with an income of two hundred per annum, arising from the efforts of industry in the production of ANY species of commodities, and that a portion of his capital is borrowed, the interest of which amounts to one hundred per annum—*raise* the value of money one half [Ricardo underlines the last seven words and notes: '*Do you not mean, "double the value of money?"*'], his commodities can only return half their money price, that is to say, one hundred pounds per annum, and this industrious man is obviously left *wholly destitute;*

---

[1] The remainder of the note is cut off by the binder.

but this is not all—the creditor receiving only, it is true, the same nominal sum, nevertheless obtains that which enables him to possess himself of twice the quantity of the industrious man's commodities; in truth he seizes the whole property of his debtor: now *lower* the value of money and let us see what follows; the industrious man pays the debt with half the quantity of his commodities, their MONEY value being doubled, and his creditor retaining the same nominal sum, can only command *half* of them; this is *horrid injustice:* but the man is not left *destitute;* he retains *half* his income; there is exactly the difference between the *half* and the *whole'* (p. 34). Ricardo notes: '*Because the degree of variation is less. In one case you raise the value of* £1- *to* £2- *in the other you lower the value of* £1- *to* 10/-'[1]

Western proceeds: 'As to calculating the effects of raising or lowering the value of money, without reference to debtors and creditors, it would be absurd; because we know the vast extent of public and private debts, and because all our national establishments, civil and military, are charges upon national industry, and as such, operate as debts; the Monarch and the private soldier, the First Lord of the Treasury, and the lowest Clerk in office, are alike in the predicament of *creditors;* they suffered by lowering the value of money, but were not ruined [Ricardo notes: '*fallaci*[*ous*]']; their suffering was acknowledged and alleviated, if not removed, but they are now, in conjunction with public and private creditors, absorbing the entire fruits of the industry of the country' (p. 35).

There are no comments on Western's text after p. 35, but Ricardo underlines certain passages (as reproduced below) which are obviously directed against himself. It is to these charges that he replied in his speech of 11 June 1823 (above, p. 317 ff.).

'The more I reflect upon the state of this country, its immense public debt and taxes, its unrivalled complication of private debts and engagements, the more I am astonished that the idea should ever have suggested itself to the mind of any Statesmen, to *raise* the value of the money in which they were created; the measure certainly owes its origin, in chief, to men who were gainers or expectant gainers by it; namely, Ministers receiving salaries from

---

[1] The remainder of the note is cut off by the binder.

the public, others who wish to be Ministers, and some great monied proprietors were called in, who were supposed to be specially qualified to advise upon such a subject. Difficult, however, as it is to account for such an extraordinary proceeding, I do not entertain a suspicion of any selfish motives on the part of the Ministers or their rivals; and I try to believe the same of the great monied men; but when I see public creditors and mortgagees swallowing up the rents of the landowners, the profits of the tenant, and the general fruits of industry, it requires the fullest effort of charity to believe they did not intend it; if we allow them to be honest, they must all of them be content to be regarded by us sufferers, as extremely ignorant of the subject they not only pretended fully to understand, but exclusively to be the only competent judges of. They told us at first that Peel's Bill would only produce a difference of three or four per cent. in the money price of commodities; they have now nearly admitted its operation to the extent of fifteen or twenty, which of itself must be allowed to be proof sufficient of ignorance at all events: but the actual amount of degradation is in fact much nearer fifty per cent. than twenty.' (pp. 36–7.)

'Some of you have estates which were in cultivation centuries ago, and which now yield NOTHING: to preserve them in cultivation at all, without any rent, is in various instances actually a burthen. [Ricardo writes three exclamation marks on the margin.] … Why will you not INVESTIGATE the question? why give up the exercise of your own understanding? why surrender up common sense to the *parade* of science? Believe me, the economists and bullionists are not gifted with *more* sense than other people, though they have more pedantry; their *confidence* and pretensions are imposing certainly, and I do believe have imposed upon some of our more ingenuous Statesmen; but the mist in which they have involved the subject is disappearing, and the dreadful consequences brought upon us by their advice are fully exposed to view; the practical illustration before our eyes of the terrible mistake the Government has been led into, can hardly longer be denied.' (pp. 39–41.)

'No. 5 [of the tables in the Appendix] shews the amount of *undue gain* of the public creditors, by the alteration of the currency through Peel's Bill, and which is a distinct breach of faith on the part of the Government towards the people of this country, and a *palpable robbery.* It really appears to me, that our Statesmen, on either side the House, evince by their conduct, a want of any just comprehension of *faith* towards the public, who *pay* taxes. I should have thought their first care, at all events the first care of the House of Commons, should have been, that the public should *not* pay MORE *than they borrowed.* It is hardly denied by any body, that, at *this time,* the public *are* compelled to pay *substantially,* to the extent of twenty or twenty-five per cent. more than they borrowed, and not one word of complaint is uttered by those guardians of the public purse. It is only for the creditors, and all who *receive* taxes, that they appear solicitous; and for the preservation of sacred faith towards whom, we hear so much *canting* declamation.... If these observations find their way to the public, I shall of course undergo the censure of those arrogant pretenders to exclusive good faith; but it is high time to speak out, or we shall be inevitably crushed.' (pp. 44–5.)

Western reprints in an Appendix a 'Letter upon the Cause of the Distress in Ireland', to the editor of the *Dublin Morning Post,* signed 'A Native of Connaught' and dated 'Killcongoll, July 15, 1822.'; on this letter Ricardo comments: *'According to this letter, the ruin of the poor tenant is caused by the increased value paid to some of the persons who have an interest in the land. If he retain less of the produce they get more—this will not account for scarcity in the country, nor for the high price of potatoes. What I contend for is that there is no anomaly in a glut of wheat from abundance, and a starving population, when that population lives exclusively on the potatoe.'*

INDEX OF PERSONS
IN VOLUME V